SOVIET
INFLUENCE IN
EASTERN
EUROPE

SOVIET INFLUENCE IN EASTERN EUROPE

POLITICAL AUTONOMY AND THE WARSAW PACT

CHRISTOPHER D. JONES

Studies of Influence in International Relations
Alvin Z. Rubinstein, General Editor

PRAEGER

PRAEGER SPECIAL STUDIES • PRAEGER SCIENTIFIC

Library of Congress Cataloging in Publication Data

Jones, Christopher D.
  Soviet influence in Eastern Europe.

  (Studies of influence in international relations)
  Bibliography: p.
  Includes index.
  1. Soviet Union--Foreign relations--Europe, Eastern.
2. Europe, Eastern--Foreign relations--Soviet Union.
I. Title. II. Series.
JX1555.Z7E784   327′.0947   81-5848
ISBN 0-03-049076-6   AACR2
ISBN 0-03-049081-2 (pbk.)

Published in 1981 by Praeger Publishers
CBS Educational and Professional Publishing
A Division of CBS, Inc.
521 Fifth Avenue, New York, New York 10175 U.S.A.
© 1981 by Praeger Publishers
123456789 145 987654321
Printed in the United States of America

To my parents

Preface

The National Council for Soviet and East European Research supported most of the work that went into the writing of this study. A grant from the American Council of Learned Societies made it possible for me to begin the research that led to this work. I used a portion of a fellowship from the Ford Foundation to revise the final text. I am very grateful to each of these institutions for its assistance.

Throughout the course of research and writing the Harvard Russian Research Center provided office facilities and moral support. I am particularly indebted to its directors, Adam Ulam and Abram Bergson, and to its administrative staff, Mary Towle, Rose DeBenedetto, Mary Christopher and Helen Constantine.

My parents, my wife, Helena, and my children, Gwendolen and Nicholas, provided equally necessary support for the writing of this book.

I would like to thank several people for their valuable advice and criticism: Susan Jo Gardos, Timothy Colton, Dale Herspring, Priscilla MacMillan, Morris Janowitz, Robert Bathurst, Jane Sharp, Derek Leebaert and Boris Rumer.

Editor's Preface

Moscow's imperial system in Eastern Europe ultimately rests on the military power of the Soviet Union. This truism, though dramatically demonstrated in East Berlin in June 1953, in Hungary in October–November 1956, and in Czechoslovakia in August 1968, is more often than not overshadowed by the absorption of Western analysts with the putatively cohesive forces of ideology, party, and economics.

In the West, the assumption that an officially shared commitment to a common ideology was the cement binding the Soviet bloc together and was the key to the USSR's influence in Eastern Europe held sway well into the 1960s. In the case of Yugoslavia, for example, there was a tendency for quite a while to underestimate the extent to which Marshal Tito's pertinacity was rooted in his determination to rule without the Kremlin's interference and to accept at face value Soviet criticisms of the Yugoslavs as "revisionists" and ideological deviationists who were threatening the unity of the socialist camp through their anti-Marxist heresies. However, the Sino-Soviet rift of the 1960s and 1970s, culminating in Beijing's (Peking) formal abrogation in 1980 of the treaty of alliance concluded in 1950, made unmistakably clear that the era of unity fashioned by adherence to a common ideology had passed, if indeed it had ever existed or been the real adhesive in the bond. Ideology may not be dead, but it is assuredly not a sufficient condition for community building.

Then there was the attention devoted to the unifying role of the Communist party. Politically, the network of compliant Communist parties imposed by the Red Army in Joseph Stalin's time was intended to assure Moscow of friendly regimes in Eastern Europe. Soviet rule was to be institutionalized by supporting and strengthening political elites who lacked a popular base of genuine loyalty in their own countries and who therefore acceded to the Kremlin's wishes as the price for retaining power and position. The assumption that these elites would, out of their inherent weakness, be reliable instruments for safeguarding Soviet imperial rule in the region was similarly shown to be of limited value.

With the ebb of Stalinism, nationalism flourished, and indigenous Communist elites acquired legitimacy at home and with this a growing measure of self-confidence and assertiveness. The Czechoslovak crisis in 1968 brought home to Moscow the hazards of national communism.

Increasingly, party elites sought to arrogate to themselves greater and greater measures of internal autonomy and independence from Moscow, usually to the detriment of bloc integration. As long as their new political structures and social systems had been weak, they had willingly accommodated to Moscow's imperial rule. In the 1950s the East European party elites, each for a somewhat different combination of reasons, had been content with the maintenance of a Soviet protectorate over them, but by the 1960s the mood and situation had altered, and the Soviet procuracy had become a liability to the exercise of power by indigenous party bosses. Concomitantly, the mounting internal difficulties in the Soviet Union prompted the Soviet oligarchs to explore ways to decentralize and normalize relations between the Soviet Union and the countries of Eastern Europe. The formula adopted by Nikita Khrushchev was greater voluntarism in the realm of economic integration through a revitalized Comecon (Council for Mutual Economic Assistance). What Khrushchev pioneered, Leonid Brezhnev and Aleksei Kosygin continued.

The attempt to make Comecon perform political-ideological, as well as economic, functions faltered on the refusal of member states to undertake far-ranging structural changes in patterns of production and economic interaction. In their quest for a multilateral regional organization that would institutionalize Soviet influence and yet permit reforms in Eastern Europe, Soviet leaders had to internationalize the USSR's relationship with Eastern Europe, moving from bilateralism to multilateralism, at least in terms of the regulations and procedures governing Comecon. They were compelled to move from coercive politics to consensual politics, and Comecon increasingly relied on consensus-building procedures. But the East Europeans have been slow to come around; their residual suspicions of Moscow and fear of losing the autonomy they acquired in the aftermath of de-Stalinization transcend their economic dependence on the USSR as a supplier of energy and as a market for East European goods that are not readily salable in the West.

In recent years, Moscow has intensified the pressure inside Comecon for more joint projects such as another natural gas pipeline and cooperation in machine building, agriculture, and electric power generation. Moscow has high hopes for Comecon and sees it as a useful, potentially important vehicle for serving Soviet purposes in Eastern Europe, but knows that for the preservation of Soviet influence a more forceful and powerful instrument is needed.

This study by Dr. Christopher Jones provides a comprehensive and systematic assessment of the role that Soviet military policy in the Warsaw Pact plays in the maintaining of the USSR's influence in Eastern Europe. The multilateral military Treaty of Friendship, Mutual Assistance and

Cooperation, signed in Warsaw on May 14, 1955 by the governments of the Soviet Union, Poland, Czechoslovakia, the German Democratic Republic, Hungary, Romania, Bulgaria and Albania, and known as the Warsaw Pact, is the military sinew that holds the imperial tissue together. As Dr. Jones shows, the Soviet Union's influence permeates the network of interlocking and overlapping structures that makes the Warsaw Pact primus inter pares among the regional and multilateral institutional forms intended to safeguard the Soviet position in Eastern Europe.

In his richly textured and impressively researched study, Dr. Jones makes two points that go to the heart of his argument about the methods and limits of Soviet influence in Eastern Europe: first, in Bulgaria, Hungary, East Germany, Poland, and Czechoslovakia, Moscow uses the Warsaw Pact to reinforce Soviet influence by preventing *national* armed forces of the Pact countries "from adopting military policies that would give these *national* armies the capabilities of defending *national* territory by *national* means" (italics added); and second, the national Communist leaderships of Romania, Yugoslavia, and Albania, however, have been able to retain independent national control of their Communist Party organizations and effectively deter threatened Soviet military interventions "by demonstrating a capability for prolonged resistance to a Soviet occupation" through the formation of military units able to mount a "territorial defense." The implications of his argument are enormous, contributing new insights for our evaluation of the nature of the Soviet-East European influence relationship, the extent to which differentiation within the bloc is politically significant, the political as opposed to the military purposes of the Warsaw Pact, and of the confidence with which Moscow can assume political reliability on the part of the armed forces of the various Warsaw Pact countries.

The analysis of the political-military aspects of the Warsaw Pact is based on an exhaustive combing of the relevant Soviet and Eastern European literature, and the documentation of the key propositions is formidable. No study has as carefully examined the institutional forms and procedures whereby Moscow binds Pact members to the Soviet Union and hampers their potential for effective resistance to its pre-eminent authority, or has so convincingly demonstrated that the Warsaw Pact is the most important organization for perpetuating Soviet influence in Eastern Europe.

Dr. Jones breaks new ground in the ongoing effort to fathom the nature of the Soviet-East European influence relationship. Specialists on military and military-political affairs, in particular, will find invaluable the detailed information on the operations of the Warsaw Pact's military exercises and the administrative structure through which Moscow controls

political and military elites. All students of Soviet-East European relationships will have to consider the author's data and arguments in any
assessment of the USSR's capacity to prevent anti-Moscow Communist
party factions from coming to power. This significant work comes at a
timely moment and it is a most welcome addition to the Praeger series of
STUDIES OF INFLUENCE IN INTERNATIONAL RELATIONS.

Alvin Z. Rubinstein

CONTENTS

Chapter One
Soviet Hegemony in East Europe

This study argues that Soviet influence in East Europe depends on Soviet control over appointments to the upper echelons of the East European party leaderships and on the preservation of a Soviet capability for military intervention to prevent either the capture of the local party hierarchies by Communists with domestic bases of support or the destruction of the party control system by local anti-Communist forces. Moscow and its proteges in the East European parties together prevent the defense ministries of the loyal East European states from adopting military strategies which would greatly limit the Soviet capability for intervention against either a rebellious faction of an East European party or against local anti-Communist forces.

Romania, a member of the Warsaw Treaty Organization (WTO), Albania, a former member, and Yugoslavia, the first Communist state to stand outside the Soviet bloc, have adopted military strategies designed to deter Soviet intervention by mobilizing their nations for prolonged resistance to a Soviet occupation. These strategies provide the military bases for the political independence of these three states. The Soviets use the agencies and programs of the WTO to prevent the national armed forces of Bulgaria, Hungary, East Germany, Poland and Czechoslovakia from adopting military policies that would give these national armies the capabilities of defending national territory by national means.

The first and second chapters of this study argue that the Soviets have sought control over the leaderships of the East European parties as both the means and ends of Soviet policy toward East Europe. These chapters also argue that Soviet control over the party hierarchies of the region insures that the loyal East European states will pursue military, economic, and cultural policies which contribute to their integration into a larger international system in which each national Communist party is

Portions of this chapter appeared earlier in the following article by the author, "Soviet Hegemony in East Europe: Political Autonomy and Military Intervention," *World Politics* 29 (January 1977).

dependent on the Soviets to stay in power. The policies promoting integration seek to pre-empt the possibility that a rebellious domestic faction of an East European party can cultivate enough domestic support to overthrow the ruling Muscovite faction of the party and lead its nation out of the system of overlapping Soviet controls in East Europe.

The third chapter of this study argues that the leaders of independent East European Communist regimes have deterred Soviet military interventions by demonstrating a capability for prolonged resistance to a Soviet occupation. Western analysts generally call a strategy of national resistance to military occupation a strategy of "territorial defense." The Yugoslavs call their strategy "General People's Defense." The Romanians call theirs "War of the Entire People." For the Soviets, such a strategy, by whatever name, defends neither the territory nor the people of an East European state but the rebel leaders of its Communist party. In the event of the internal collapse of a Communist government, a national capability for a war of territorial defense could also be used to defend the successor regime. Pro-Soviet Communist regimes in East Europe deliberately reject strategies of territorial defense. These regimes fear that national defense systems based on such strategies will shield their domestic opponents, both inside and outside the party, from threat of Soviet military intervention in support of the local Muscovites.

Chapter Three also argues that the strategies adopted by the Communist regimes in Romania, Yugoslavia and Albania do not seek military victory over a Soviet expeditionary force but political stalemate between the resistance movement and the occupation regime in the struggle for political authority over the civilian population. If the defenders achieve a political stalemate they expect to bring about the withdrawal of the occupation forces through the interaction of two factors: (1) international support for an East European state waging a war of national liberation against the Soviet army, and (2) a breakdown of political cohesion among Soviet soldiers and civilians during the course of a protracted military occupation of an East European socialist state.

The fourth chapter argues that the system of joint WTO military exercises introduced by Marshal Grechko (1) pre-empts the development of national capabilities for territorial defense by drilling the WTO armies for an offensive coalition war using nuclear weapons; (2) enhances the Soviet capability for rapid occupation of an East European state by Soviet forces and symbolic detachments of East European armies; (3) prepares Soviet and East European troops for the political strains of an occupation. The East European soldiers and non-Russian Soviet military personnel who render fraternal assistance in a WTO intervention in East Europe serve to camouflage as much as possible the Russian core of the intervention force.

The fifth chapter argues that the military-administrative agencies of the WTO detach the components of East European defense systems from the exclusive control of national defense ministries, with the exception of the Romanian defense ministry. Chapter Five also argues that the loyal East European members of the WTO accept the authority of three other de facto agencies of the alliance: (1) an agency which synchronizes military doctrines; (2) an agency which coordinates the interaction of the WTO political administrations; (3) an agency which facilitates a coordinated program of officer education.

The sixth chapter argues that the loyal WTO states accept Soviet doctrine as the doctrine which defines the organization and missions of each national defense system within the alliance. The military-technical components of Soviet doctrine require the integration of the East European forces into a coalition assigned offensive actions using nuclear weapons. The military-technical components of Soviet doctrine are based on the military-political components. The military-political axioms of Soviet doctrine and of the loyal WTO members call for the collective defense of the "gains of socialism" by a socialist military coalition against a coalition of "imperialists." These axioms also require the collective defense of socialism in each country against "internal reaction." These axioms specifically reject the conceptions of unidentified socialist states which define the mission of a socialist army as the defense of national sovereignty by national armed forces.

The seventh chapter argues that an integrated system of WTO political administrations enforces external adherence to the military-political axioms of the WTO and rejection of the military-political axioms of the Romanians and Yugoslavs. This system also enables the Soviet Main Political Administration to monitor the political reliability of East European personnel. Chapter Seven, in addition, argues that the links of the WTO political administrations facilitate a Soviet effort to integrate the multinational personnel of the WTO with the multinational personnel of the Soviet armed forces.

Chapter Eight argues that an integrated officer education system in the WTO instructs East European officers in the military-political and military-technical applications of Soviet doctrine. This chapter also argues that East European officers cannot reach the top military commands of East Europe without receiving degrees from certain Soviet military academies, in particular the Voroshilov General Staff Academy. The Soviet and East European alumni of these academies constitute a greater socialist officer corps whose members preside over various national detachments of the WTO, accept the missions defined by Soviet doctrine, and execute orders issued by the Soviet commanders of the central WTO agencies.

The ninth chapter suggests that the WTO is the core of a broader Soviet military alliance system which is based in part on many of the Soviet control devices used in the WTO. The Soviet military alliance system seeks to mobilize the multinational personnel of the alliance system for pursuit of Soviet objectives in various regions; to deny national defense ministries exclusive control of their own military forces; and to legitimize the use of Soviet and other socialist armed forces to supress internal threats to "the gains of socialism" in each of the countries of the Soviet alliance system.

Policy and Personnel in the Communist Parties of East Europe

After the Bolshevik revolution, Communist parties were formed in every country of East Europe. In order to join Lenin's international organization of Communist parties, the Communist International (Comintern), a national Communist party had to accept the Comintern's 21 conditions of membership. These conditions required the strict subordination of party members to the party leadership. During the 1920s the East European Communist parties accepted an additional but unwritten condition for membership in the Comintern: subordination of the national party as a whole to the leadership of the Communist Party of the Soviet Union (CPSU). By the 1930s the leaders of the Soviet party appointed and purged the leaders of the East European parties and decided the basic outlines of their policies. Stalin's control over the East European parties was so great that he could order the dissolution of the Polish Communist Party in order to improve Soviet relations with Hitler. The ties of the East European parties to Moscow often reduced the constituencies of these parties because the local Communists appeared to have abandoned national interests for the sake of Soviet interests and also because the domestic policies advocated by Stalin were often inappropriate for the political conditions of East Europe.

From Stalin's perspective, control over the East European parties may have been one of the prerequisites for maintaining control over the Soviet party. An independent East Communist party probably would have inspired factions in other East European parties to seek independence for their parties. This process, once begun, might have inspired factions within the Soviet party to reconsider the proper relationships of national Communist parties to each other, including the mutual relationships of the national party organizations of the Soviet republics.

At the end of World War II Soviet armies installed Communist parties in power in Poland, Czechoslovakia, Romania, Hungary and Bulgaria with the assistance of symbolic military detachments of Poles, Czechs, Slovaks and Romanians and with the assistance of anti-Nazi resistance movements in Hungary and Bulgaria. In Yugoslavia and Albania, Communist parties had come to power by organizing movements of national resistance against the occupation of their countries by German and Italian armies. The bases for the independence of the Yugoslav and Albanian parties were the same as that of the Chinese party: the achievement of political power largely by their own military forces. Despite their different military routes to political power, all the leaders of the East European parties, including Tito, had originally been Stalin's appointees, with the possible exception of the Albanian leaders, who appear to have owed their appointments to Tito. In the period from 1945 to 1948 the parties installed by the Soviet army and the parties that had come to power on their own adopted domestic policies addressed to specific features of each country. Some of these parties won popular support by carrying out extensive land reforms and nationalizations of industry.

After coming to power by their own military forces, the Yugoslav Communists no longer regarded obedience to the leaders of the Soviet party as their primary duty. They viewed their task as that of constructing a socialist society in Yugoslav. As members of a ruling party the leaders of the Yugoslav state were no longer willing to cede control over matters of personnel and policy to Moscow. The bickering between Stalin and Tito over the role of Soviet advisers in the military, economic, cultural and political hierarchies of the new Yugoslav state revealed that the Leninist principle of centralism and the Stalinist model of industrial development concentrated political power in an East Europen state in the hands of the leaders of the local East European party. In 1947 and 1948 Stalin attempted to wrest control over the Yugoslav party back from Tito. There appear to have been several interrelated reasons for Stalin to act against Tito: (1) the possibility that the leaders of other East European parties might attempt to follow Tito's example; (2) the possibility that one or more independent East European parties would revive the possibility of factionalism within the Soviet party on the questions of the relationship of national Communist parties to each other, including the question of the mutual relationships of the national parties of the union republics of the USSR; (3) the possibility that a successful rebellion by Tito might demonstrate that if a Communist party wanted to rule as an independent party, it would have to come to power by its own military means, without Soviet military assistance; (4) the possibility that the

Communist parties that came to power on their own and asserted their independence of the Soviet party might stimulate desires for independence of the part of the Communist parties brought to power by the Soviet army.

After failing to overthrow Tito, Stalin launched a campaign to prevent the East European parties still dependent on the Soviet army from consolidating sufficient power to achieve autonomy. He ordered a purge of the East European parties, especially of the "home" Communists who had spent the war years in their own countries. Stalin reserved the leading positions in the East European parties for the "Muscovites"— the Communists who had spent the war years in the USSR and were largely dependent on Stalin for their positions in the national parties. Stalin justified these purges by asserting that Titoist agents had infiltrated the East European parties as part of an imperialist plot to begin a new world war.

Stalin demanded that the East European party leaders imitate Soviet domestic policies: forced collectivization, even at the price of drastically reduced agricultural production; rapid development of heavy industry, even at the price of poor investment of industrial resources; and police terror, even at the price of the demoralization of society. By insisting that his policies be adopted throughout the Soviet bloc Stalin established clear criteria by which to evaluate the loyalty of the East European party leaders. These policies had the effect of so alienating the peoples of East Europe from their political leaders that the ruling party in each country became even more dependent on the Soviet army to stay in power. Within the East European parties, Stalin's policies also had the effect of making the Muscovite factions even more dependent on Moscow, since they lacked any genuine domestic bases of their own.

In a 1949 essay on relations among socialist states, Milovan Djilas, the leading theorist of the rebellious Communist Party of Yugoslavia, claimed that Stalin's policy toward the East European Communists was that of "formation of clandestine factions within the various parties for the purpose of exercising control over their line and over individual forums and individual leaders."[1] Khrushchev later corroborated what Djilas had written. In his secret speech to the CPSU Twentieth Congress, Khrushchev declared that Stalin had demonstrated "suspicion and haughtiness" not only to Soviet party members but to "whole parties and nations."[2]

Wladyslaw Gomulka also complained that Stalin had tyrannized over the leaders of the East European Communist parties. Using Khrushchev's euphemism for Stalin's dictatorship, "the cult of personality," the Polish leader declared:

The cult of personality is a certain system which prevailed in the Soviet Union and which was grafted probably to all Communist parties. . . .

The essence of this system consisted in the fact that an individual hierarchic ladder of cults was created. Each such cult comprised a given area in which it functioned.

In the bloc of socialist states it was Stalin who stood at the top of this hierarchic ladder. All those who stood on lower rungs of the ladder bowed their heads before him.

Those who bowed their heads were not only the other leaders of the Communist Party of the Soviet Union and the leaders of the Soviet Union, but also the leaders of the Communist and workers' parties of the socialist camp.

The latter, that is, the first secretaries of the central committees of the parties of the various countries who sat on the rungs of the ladder of the cult of personality, in turn donned the robes of infallibility and wisdom.

But their cult radiated only on the territory of the countries where they stood at the top of the national cult ladder. This cult could be called only a reflected brilliance, a borrowed light. It shone as the moon does. . . .

Under the system of the cult of personality, the party as a whole could act independently only within the framework of subordination to the chief cult.

If someone attempted to transcend these limits, he was threatened with excommunication by his comrades. If the matter concerned a whole party, it was excommunicated by the remaining Communist parties.[3]

Gomulka made these remarks to the session of the Polish Central Committee that elected him first secretary over the strenuous objections of Khrushchev, who had threatened the day before to use military force to prevent Gomulka's accession to power.

In an essay written in December 1955, shortly after his expulsion from the Hungarian Communist Party, Imre Nagy declared that Stalin and his Hungarian lieutenant, Matyas Rakosi, had "exterminated" party members who had opposed the establishment of a Stalinist dictatorship in Hungary and the subordination of Hungarian interests to Stalin's hegemony.[4] When Nagy became premier of the Hungarian government as a result of the revolution that broke out in October 1956, the Soviet government obliquely acknowledged the truth of what Nagy had written. In an effort to quell anti-Soviet sentiment in Hungary, the USSR issued a declaration on October 30, 1956, in which the Soviet government admitted that in the history of relations among socialist states there had been "violations and errors which demeaned the principle of equality in relations among socialist states."[5] The government of the People's Republic of China immediately expressed full agreement with the Soviet declaration. According to the Chinese, there had indeed been "mistakes... misunderstandings and estrangement between certain socialist countries." The Chinese government specifically mentioned Soviet relations with Yugoslavia, Poland and Hungary.[6]

The New Course

Stalin had succeeded in pre-empting the autonomy of the East European parties that had been installed by the Soviet army, but his success came at the cost of forcing these parties to face the prospect of popular anti-Communist uprisings. Following Stalin's death in 1953, violent demonstrations broke out among workers in East Germany and Czechoslovakia. After the violence of 1953, Georgi Malenkov and Khrushchev, Stalin's successors, tried to stabilize the explosive situations that Stalin had bequeathed to them in East Europe. To invest the East European regimes with a modicum of legitimacy, they ordered the leaders of the fraternal parties to adopt a "New Course." The New Course required the East European Communist leaders to adapt their domestic policies to fit local conditions, to satisfy as much as possible the popular demands for consumer goods, and to appear as sovereign as possible.

The purpose of the New Course was not to eliminate Soviet hegemony over East Europe but to camouflage it. Stalin's successors were no less willing to part with control over the East European parties than Stalin had been. In 1955, Khrushchev resumed relations with Yugoslavia in the hope that rapprochement with Tito would aid the East European parties in their quest for legitimacy. If the Soviets could claim that the Yugoslavs voluntarily maintained cordial relations with the USSR, then the other parties in the region could also claim that cooperation with the Soviet Union was in fact a demonstration of national independence. In 1955 and 1956, Tito and Khrushchev signed statements that endorsed the right of every socialist state to determine its own methods of socialist development. At the Twentieth Party Congress in 1956, Khrushchev made it part of the Soviet canon that each socialist country would pursue its own road to socialism.

To the extent that Khrushchev succeeded in removing the danger of popular anti-Communist uprisings in East Europe, he succeeded in bringing back the specter that had haunted Stalin: the possibility that an East European party would win enough domestic support to become master in its own domain, even if the party had not come to power by its own efforts. In ordering the fraternal parties to adjust their domestic policies to fit local conditions, Khrushchev was ordering them to tread a fine line between dependence and autonomy.

Nationalism and Internationalism in East Europe

Since the mid 1950s the Soviets have defined the dependence of East European parties on the Soviet Union as loyalty to Marxism-Leninism, to proletarian internationalism and to the unity of the socialist camp. The Soviets have defined the autonomy of East European parties as ideological deviations either to the right or to the left combined with nationalism.

After the Twentieth Congress of the CPSU, internal power struggles developed in the Polish and Hungarian parties between the Muscovite factions associated with Stalin and loose coalitions of reformers who took Khrushchev at his word and began to seek popular support for extensive domestic reforms and to criticize the local leaders who had been associated with Stalin. The Soviets came out in favor of the idea of reform but against the reformers not linked to Moscow. A July 1956 editorial in *Pravda* addressed to the intraparty power struggles in Hungary and Poland qualified Khrushchev's proclamation of separate roads to socialism by asserting that though the national roads to socialism were separate, the goal was the same. *Pravda* declared that "the necessary consideration of national peculiarities" would not lead to the "estrangement" of socialist countries but would contribute to their "solidarity." No one, said *Pravda,* would succeed in destroying the "unity of the socialist camp."[7]

After the upheavals in Poland and Hungary, it no longer served Soviet purposes to endorse Tito's conception of the relationship between the Soviet party and the parties of East Europe. In November 1957, the leaders of the East European parties and the ruling Asian parties met in Moscow to sign a declaration that condemned Yugoslavia for its ideological deviations and named the USSR as the leader of the socialist camp. The 1957 Moscow Declaration warned of the dangers inherent in both the earlier formulas for maintaining Soviet hegemony over East Europe: "Disregard of national peculiarities by a proletarian party inevitably leads to its divorce from reality, from the masses, and is bound to prejudice the cause of socialism. . . . and, conversely, exaggeration of the role of these peculiarities . . . is just as harmful to the socialist cause."[8]

The only solution that the 1957 Declaration could offer for this dilemma was to urge the fraternal parties to combat both tendencies "simultaneously."[9] The international meetings of Communist parties organized by the Soviets in 1960, 1969, and 1976 each endorsed the inherently unstable formula of the 1957 Declaration for maintaining Soviet control over the East European parties, as have the Soviet party congresses which met after 1957. The 1960 Declaration of ruling Communist parties directly cited the text of the 1957 statement and added its own elaboration:

> Disregard of national peculiarities by the proletarian party could lead to the latter's detachment from life and from masses and harm the cause of socialism. . . . Manifestations of nationalism and national narrow-mindedness do not disappear automatically with the establishment of a socialist system. Strengthening of fraternal relations and friendship among the socialist countries requires a Marxist-Leninist internationalist policy on the part of the Communist and Workers' parties; education of all the working people in the spirit of internationalism and patriotism, and a resolute struggle to overcome the survivals of bourgeois nationalism and chauvinism.[10]

The 1961 CPSU Congress passed a resolution reaffirming the principles of the 1960 Declaration.[11] In his address to the 1966 Congress of the CPSU, Leonid Brezhnev specifically endorsed the propositions of the leader he had overthrown concerning the proper norms governing relations among Communist states. Brezhnev declared:

> Experience shows that deviations from the Marxist-Leninist line either to the right or left become doubly dangerous when they are combined with nationalism, great-power chauvinism and hegemonic ambition. Communists cannot help drawing the proper conclusions from this.
>
> In the opinion of the Central Committee of the CPSU, there is good common Marxist-Leninist ground for closing Communist ranks, namely, the general line worked out by the 1957 and 1960 meetings of the fraternal parties.
>
> Developments since then have put it to the most exacting test and it has withstood that test. Today there is every reason for saying that loyalty to this line is a dependable guarantee of the unity of new successes in the revolutionary movement.[12]

In 1971, Brezhnev told the delegates to the Twenty-Fourth Party Congress that success in the construction of socialism in the countries of the socialist confederation depended on the "correct combination of the general and the national particular."[13] In 1976, the Soviet general secretary told the Twenty-Fifth Congress that within the socialist confederation "the process of a gradual drawing together of socialist countries is now quite definitely operating as an objective law." Brezhnev added,

"Of course, much depends on the policy of the ruling parties and their ability to safeguard unity, combat isolation and national exclusiveness, honor their common international tasks, and act jointly in performing them."[14]

At the international meetings of Communist parties in 1969 and 1976 the leaders of the loyal East European parties had endorsed Brezhnev's conception of the correct combination of the national and the general in the policies of their parties. Gustav Husak, who in April 1969 had succeeded Alexander Dubcek as first secretary of the Czechoslovak party, explained to the June 1969 meeting of world Communist parties that for a party to carry out its specific national tasks it had to act jointly with the other parties:

> . . . the sovereignty of a Communist party and socialist country consists in the right to determine, according to national conditions, the forms and methods of socialist development and also the obligation to bear full responsibility for this before one's own people.
>
> However, guaranteeing the sovereignty of each party and socialist country at the same time requires them to defend and protect the power of the working class and all the revolutionary gains of the socialist order.
>
> In this sense, the class content of the sovereignty of a socialist state is directly linked to its international responsibility to the confederation of socialist countries and the international Communist and revolutionary movement.[15]

At the 1976 meeting of East European and West European Communist parties in East Berlin, Todor Zhivkov, first secretary of the Bulgarian party, explained how his party combined the national and the general in its policies:

> For us Bulgarian Communists, our relationship with the Soviet Union and its Communist Party remains, as they were sixty years ago, the most reliable criterion—the touchstone—of loyalty to the Communist ideal.
>
> Internationalism means a dialectical unity between the responsibility of every party to the working class and people of its own country and its duty and responsibility for the destiny of our common Communist cause.
>
> Proletarian internationalism does not mean any derogation of the principles of the independence and equality of individual socialist countries or of national detachments of the Communist and workers' movement.
>
> But the equality of the Communist parties is expressed not only in their equal and sovereign rights but also in the equality of their internationalist commitments.[16]

East Europe and the Socialist Confederation

The correct combination of the national and the general in the policies of the loyal East European Communist parties facilitates the integration of their nations into a polity, which the Soviets identify as the socialist confederation *(sotsialisticheskoe sodruzhestvo).* The socialist confederation has three distinct but interrelated sets of members: the inner members of the confederation, consisting of the 15 union republics of the USSR; the outer members of the confederation, consisting of East Germany, Poland, Czechoslovakia, Hungary and Bulgaria, Mongolia and Afghanistan; the overseas members of the confederation, consisting of Cuba, Vietnam and probably Ethiopia, Angola, Mozambique and South Yemen as well.

In statements addressed to the East Europeans, the Soviets frequently and specifically discuss the political, military, economic and cultural mechanisms which have integrated union republics into the USSR as the prototypes for the political, military, economic and cultural mechanisms which are to integrate the East European states into the socialist confederation. In attempting to integrate the inner and outer members of the confederation, the Soviets have deliberately chosen to link the cohesion of the socialist confederation to the cohesion of the Union of Soviet Socialist Republics. The Soviets acknowledge that the successful integration of the socialist confederation will require many decades, just as the integration of the constituent republics of the USSR has required many decades. It remains to be seen whether the Soviets can succeed in overcoming the formidable obstacles to the integration of East European states into the confederation, but there is no doubt that the Soviets are committed to trying. As Brezhnev remarked to the CPSU's 25th Congress, whose audience included not only Soviet delegates but representatives from the fraternal parties as well:

> If you please, there is not a session of the Politburo which has not considered various questions connected with the development of cooperation with the fraternal countries, with the strengthening of their unity, and with the consolidation of our common international positions.[17]

The Soviets do not expect the policy of integration of national states into the socialist confederation to win popular support in East Europe. As in the Soviet Union, the mechanisms of integration are those of linking the national-territorial bureaucracies and national-territorial elites into one interdependent system. In East Europe, and perhaps in the Soviet Union as well, the leaders of the CPSU expect that the privileged local elites will be more closely bound to Moscow if they lack the legitimacy necessary to govern without support from the center.

The central institution in the socialist confederation is not the Soviet state but the Communist Party of the Soviet Union. The CPSU relies upon the "internationalist" Communist parties to execute the policies which draw socialist nations into the socialist confederation. In a speech to the meeting of East European and West European Communist parties in East Berlin in 1976, Brezhnev noted:

> The deep organic and constantly growing ties of friendship between party and state agencies, between enterprise collectives, scientific institutions and public organizations, between millions upon millions of citizens, enable us to talk about a fundamentally new phenomenon —a genuine fraternal alliance of peoples united by common convictions and aims. The confederation of Marxist-Leninist parties is its firm foundation and its cementing force.[18]

The East European parties closely linked to the Soviet party carry out policies that require the party, military, economic and cultural bureaucracies of their nations to forge links to their Soviet counterparts. The ties of these bureaucracies to the Soviet Union in turn reinforce Soviet control over the East European parties.

The Soviets maintain party-state ties through regular bilateral and multilateral meetings of party and state officials to coordinate policies. The agencies and joint activities of the Warsaw Pact systematically link the Soviet Defense Ministry to the defense ministries of East Europe. The council for Mutual Economic Assistance (CMEA) engages in extensive joint planning, joint investment and joint production activities that aim at the creation of an interdependent set of economic bureaucracies. Cultural-scientific ties develop on the basis of annual Soviet-East European plans of exchange and of joint research. Within each of the four principal bureaucracies, the party, military, economic and cultural hierarchies, certain Soviet mid-career institutes serve as gateways to the top positions in these hierarchies: the Academy of Social Sciences of the Soviet Central Committee (formerly the CPSU Higher Party School); the Voroshilov General Staff Academy of the Soviet Defense Ministry; the Academy of the National Economy of the USSR; and the analogous institutes under the Soviet Academy of Sciences and the Soviet Ministry of Higher Education. Service in the bilateral and multilateral agencies of the socialist confederation, such as the United Command of the Warsaw Pact and the central agencies of CMEA, also appear to serve as gateways to the elite posts of the socialist bureaucracies.

For the Soviets the complexity of integration is due to the great historical, cultural, religious and sociological differences among the nationalities of the Soviet Union and East Europe and in some cases the deep mutual antagonisms of certain nationalities. But for the Soviets, the only alternative to integration of Communist regimes into the socialist confederation is disintegration into separate national states. The national Communist parties which accept the goal of integrating their nations into the socialist confederation recognize the need in practice to pursue different domestic policies in each of the national-territorial units of the socialist confederation, both within the USSR and in East Europe. For the CPSU, the problem in East Europe remains that of ensuring that the national policies of the national parties do not lead either to nationl autonomy or to popular rebellion. The problem of national autonomy is particularly acute in East Europe because three Communist states— Romania, Yugoslavia, and Albania—advocate the supremacy of national sovereignty over obligations to the socialist confederation. The Communist regimes in each of these three states base their legitimacy mainly on nationalist support for their stands as independent Communist regimes. The Soviets find the examples of the Romanian, Yugoslav and Albanian parties to be contagions capable of infecting the other Communist parties of the region and perhaps even the Communist parties of the western republics of the Soviet Union with a desire for national autonomy.

Stalin's heirs have continued to rely on control over the central committees and politburos of East Europe as the means of preserving Soviet hegemony over East Europe. The principal threat to Soviet control over the party leaderships of the region has come from "domestic" factions of the local parties which have sought to wrest control over the party, military, economic, and cultural bureaucracies from the local "Muscovites." The other threat to Soviet hegemony has been the possibility of anti-communist uprisings like those in East Germany in 1953 and in Hungary in 1956. The Soviets and the Muscovite factions of the East European parties have allied with each other against their common East European opponents both inside and outside the local parties. The greatest challenge to Soviet domination of an East European state has come from the alliance of the domestic faction of an East European party with local anti-Soviet forces outside the party.

The Pursuit of Autonomy by East European Communists

An East European party leader may seek autonomy for the party for several reasons. A Leninist party tends to concentrate power in the hands of the party leader to such a degree that at some point the leader may secure personal control over the political, military, economic, and cultural bureaucracies of a given country. The leader of an East European party may foster this tendency in order to seek power for its own sake; out of fear of being replaced one day by Soviet fiat; or perhaps by discovering that the only way particular policies can be implemented is by first establishing political independence. Whatever the reasons for seeking independence from the Soviet Union, the leader must seek it by acquiring control over personnel appointments to the party leadership. There have been two ways in which East European Communist leaders have wrested the power of appointment from the Soviets.

One way is for a party leader originally installed by Moscow to travel so far down an alternate road to socialism that the country eventually leaves the socialist confederation. By gradually winning popular support for domestic policies and by gradually acquiring foreign allies, especially within the Communist bloc, the party leader can consolidate control over the central committee and politburo. Thus when an open challenge to Moscow's authority is finally made, the local Muscovites are put in the position of being traitors to the East European party.

This process has been so gradual that it has been extremely difficult for Moscow to halt it before it has passed the point of no return. The party leader originally appointed by the Soviets, who subsequently decides to seek autonomy, can make a public show of solidarity with Moscow on many issues and make it awkward for Moscow to intervene in opposition. If the Soviets decide to force the issue, they will be reduced to denouncing "hypocritical" protestations of loyalty from a Tito or a Hoxha or a Gheorghiu-Dej. The Soviets will find it difficult to reconstitute a Muscovite faction because the rebel leader of the East European party will be able to strike at this faction as soon as it begins to organize. Tito took this road to autonomy during the course of leading the Communist resistance to the Nazi occupation of Yugoslavia. When the Soviets attempted in 1948 to organize a new Muscovite faction around Andrija Hebrang and Sretan Zujovic, Tito expelled them from the party, jailed them and their alleged supporters, and threatened similar reprisals against any prospective pro-Soviet elements. Enver Hoxha pursued a similar course in Albania. He had obtained a considerable degree of control over his party while organizing, under Yugoslav auspices, the Albanian resistance to the Italian occupation. He appears to have become dependent on the Soviet Union after 1948 because he feared that Yugoslavia would annex Albania and because he needed economic aid for his small and backward country. But when the Soviets demanded that Hoxha break off relations with Beijing, Hoxha purged the pro-Soviet elements of his party and fully established his independence of Moscow. In Romania,

Gheorghiu-Dej successfully pursued autonomy by assuring the Soviets of his loyalty, purging his domestic opponents, and gradually severing the links between the Romanian political, military, economic and cultural bureaucracies and those of the Soviet Union.

A high-ranking member of the Czechoslovak party writes that Antonin Novotny may have tried to establish his autonomy of Moscow in the mid-1960s. This former party official asserts that Novotny feared that the overthrow of Khrushchev in 1964 would result in Moscow's shift of its support from the Novotny faction of the Czechoslovak Communist party to a faction led by three other prominent party members. According to this official, Novotny took measures to prevent the rival faction from establishing close links with Moscow. He also began to court the Czechoslovak intelligentsia, to make overtures to the Chinese, Yugoslavs and Romanians, to prepare to resist Soviet economic pressure and to revise Czechoslovak military doctrine.[19] If Novotny did indeed try to embark on the road to autonomy, he found that in the process he unleashed forces in the Czechoslovak party which eventually turned on him and made him even more dependent on Moscow.

The second way in which Moscow can lose control over the central committee and politburo of an East European party is through an intraparty battle between Muscovites and reformers in which the reformers triumph. The battle is joined when the ruling Muscovite faction, by neglect or incompetence, drives its country into a general economic, social and political crisis. This crisis may result in industrial strikes and public demonstrations against the regime. In response to the crisis, a reform faction begins to coalesce within the party around a program of correcting mismanagement, eliminating corruption, satisfying popular demands for improved living standards and perhaps even championing the democratic socialist ideals enshrined in the party's official ideology. The reformers seek support from the general public, from economic technocrats, and from the humanist and scientific intelligentsia.

During the early 1950s in Hungary and Poland, and during the early 1960s in Czechoslovakia, the extreme centralization of the economy practiced by the ruling Muscovites led to general economic stagnation. The reformers in these countries called for the decentralization of management and the replacement of the party *apparatchiki* by technical specialists. To carry out economic decentralization in these countries, the reformers advocated a corresponding decentralization of the state bureaucracy. The Communist reformers in Hungary and Czechoslovakia also wanted to give greater freedom to scientists and to intellectuals in the hope of revitalizing their societies.

The Communist reformers in East Europe do not intend to have their parties surrender power. They have sought to make each national party more worthy of its power. Many of these reformers come to realize that the Soviets have provided a kind of insurance for whatever risks they run in carrying out a program of decentralization of power. The threat of Soviet military intervention against anti-Communist movements has enabled them to appear as the lesser of evils before domestic critics who might otherwise be tempted to raise the demand for an end to the Communist monopoly on power.

The reformers find that their opponents in the party, military, economic and cultural bureaucracies resist reform because they view reform as a threat to their tenure in office. Those who refuse to accept the program of the reformers find themselves even more closely bound to Moscow as the protector of their positions. In time, the reformers realize that to remove their domestic opponents from the party leadership the reformers must do battle with Moscow for control of the party. The reformers also discover that they must emphasize those reforms that have the political effect of reducing the power of the Muscovites. The most effective weapons of the reformers are public revelations of the mistakes, illegal actions and hypocrisies of the Muscovites. These revelations give the intraparty feud the quality of a moral battle between truth and falsehood. In this struggle, control over the information media becomes crucial.

In his efforts to oust the Muscovites from control of the Hungarian party, Imre Nagy circulated an essay in which he accused the party's first secretary, Matyas Rakosi, of forcing people to relinquish their convictions and their morals. According to Nagy, the renunciation of morality in Hungary "has assumed mass proportions here and must be considered virtually a disease of our society."[20]

In the midst of the battle that erupted in the Polish party between Muscovites and reformers after the Twentieth Congress of the CPSU, the poet Adam Wasyk wrote, in his "Poem for Adults":

> The dreamer Fourier beautifully prophesied
> That the sea would flow with lemonade,
> And does it not flow?
>
> They drink sea water
> And cry—
> Lemonade!
>
> They return quietly home
> To vomit
> To vomit.[21]

During the Central Committee plenum that elected Wladyslaw Gomulka first secretary of the Polish party, Gomulka warned his audience, "There is no escaping from the truth. If you cover it up, it will rise as an awful specter, alarming, and madly raging."[22]

According to the Czech economist Radoslav Selucky, the entire social fabric of Czechoslovakia had begun to disintegrate during the 1960s as the public gradually became aware of the corruption and incompetence of the Novotny regime. According to Selucky, the problem in Czechoslovakia was that "the players observe one set of rules, the umpire, another."[23] In a lecture delivered in the spring of 1968, Ivan Svitak, a Czech philosopher, declared:

> The totalitarian dictatorship in which we have lived for the past twenty years has, by nature, several national peculiarities. The first great advantage of the regime was especially the fact that it was headed by full-blooded Czechs, who combined their Austrian tradition of joviality with the sluttish incompetence of concierges.
>
> To define in more specific detail this quality of the Czech leaders would require a team of brilliant men developing in depth C. Northcote Parkinson's law of the inevitable growth of inefficiency.
>
> The Czechoslovak dictatorship has been totalitarian in the measure of the chaos it created; to attribute to it the term "dictatorship" is a rather comic paradox.
>
> Apart from the several assassinations it did carry out, the government, despite its absolute power, has been as helpless as a baby with a slide rule. The occasional fits of democratization, periodically installed and withdrawn, never brought about any basic changes, and the foundations of this regime were undermined again and again by its aggressive stupidity.
>
> The spontaneously spouting geyser of this stupidity, tirelessly gushing forth for twenty years in the official press and the tolerated cultural publications, and in the speeches of the politicians and of youth leaders, has not been able, nevertheless, to undermine the foundations of the socialist system.
>
> The common-sense of good-natured Slovaks, Moravians, and to an extent, also Czechs, has always corrected the worst excesses and reduced them to a tolerable level.
>
> Thus our history of the last twenty years may be likened to a phase of marking time; sometimes we would raise our feet as if marching, sometimes as if running—yet we did not move from the spot.
>
> Under such circumstances, one might ask one's companions what the purposes of the "march" might be.
>
> It is like the question that a mischievous girl I know used to ask the soldiers confined to the barracks. When she asked them over the fence whether they liked the service, and they answered "No," she would ask them why they did not leave. To voice this kind of question is now the duty of everyone.[24]

In late 1978, a loose coalition of reformers within the Polish United Workers' Party issued a document entitled, "Report on the State of the Republic and on the Ways of its Revitalization" in which they observed:

The regime established at the end of the war has not been able to the present day to elaborate operational rules of political life which are accepted by society as a whole.

Those in power systematically refuse any consultation, any dialogue, any negotiation.

On the contrary, they govern while generating relationships of inequality and dependence and exacerbating them.

Their conception of politics excludes all spontaneous initiatives of the citizens and causes every mechanism of the system's self-regulation to disappear.

The atomization of society thus governed is confirmed by sociological research. Poles today have only two points of reference: they identify with the nation and with . . . the family.

Between these two collective entities there are no intermediate social relations.

The place of social institutions (political and professional organizations, labor unions, etc.) are swallowed up in the designation of a single impersonal pronoun: THEM.[25]

In reply to the intraparty debates in Hungary and Poland, a *Pravda* editorial of July 1956 complained of "hopeless, confused individuals within the ranks of the workers' movement who are capable of losing their way among three pine trees. . . ."[26] Brezhnev reminded the delegates attending the Polish party congress that convened after the invasion of Czechoslovakia that Communist parties invariably had certain members who could not keep their bearings during times of stress. The Soviet leader told his Polish audience:

Yes, difficulties have occurred in the development of socialist countries. They occur now and they will occur in the future; every stage has its difficulties. . . .

When petit-bourgeois leaders encounter difficulties, they go into hysterics and begin to doubt everything without exception.

The emergence of difficulties makes the revisionists ready to cancel out all existing achievements, repudiate everything that has been gained and surrender all their positions of principle.

Real Communists confidently continue forward, finding the best solutions for the problems that have arisen and defending the gains of socialism.[27]

In Czechoslovakia, Poland and Hungary there have been three different outcomes in the battles for control of the local party waged by the Soviets and the domestic factions of the East European parties. In Czechoslovakia, the Soviets were able to defeat the reformers in the party only after eight months of military occupation. Not until April 1969 did a pro-Soviet faction of the Czechoslovak party manage to wrest control from the reformers and initiate a general purge of anti-Soviet party members. In Poland in 1956, the reformers defeated the Muscovites, but their leader failed to retain enough popular support to maintain the autonomy he had won and eventually his party reverted to open dependence on the Soviets. According to the "memoirs" attributed to Gomulka, in 1970 when workers demonstrated against his regime, Gomulka appealed to the Soviets for military assistance. In the account presented in Gomulka's "memoirs," Brezhnev told Gomulka that the economic crisis had to be settled by "political means": Gomulka's resignation.[28]

In Hungary in 1956 the Communist party disintegrated during the course of the intraparty battle. As the two factions struggled for power, a popular insurrection broke out and almost swept away both factions of the party. In the middle of the uprising, Moscow agreed to the installation of Imre Nagy, the leader of the reform faction, in the hope that he would be able to quell the rebellion. But when Nagy formed a multiparty coalition in which the Communists were a minority, and when rebel officers of the Hungarian army began to prepare for armed defense of Nagy's multiparty coalition government, Khrushchev sent the Soviet army into Hungary to suppress both Nagy's government and the popular insurrection.

Pursuit of autonomy either by a reformer or by a party leader originally installed by Moscow has clearly been a risky venture: the Communist leader seeking autonomy has had to give up one source of support for the party while simultaneously acquiring others. During this process an East European Communist leader aspiring to autonomy may find that there is not enough support within the party necessary to retain control of the central committee and politburo and that the party as a whole does not have enough popular support to stay in power without Soviet military support. If an East European Communist is to successfully challenge Soviet control over the party three tasks must be carried out, whether the leader is a first secretary originally named by Moscow or a reformer who seeks to wrest control of the party from the Muscovites:

(1) The party must be purged of Muscovites and potential Muscovites. In order to preclude the appearance of any fifth column within the party, the leader's personal control must be established over the politburo, central committee and its secretariats. Sooner or later a party congress must be convened that will recognize the leader as the incarnation of the Communist movement in the given country—as Tito, Hoxha and Ceausescu have done. Such public acclaim will make the leader's removal difficult.

A Communist leader seeking autonomy from the USSR should link up the fate of other prominent figures in the party with the leader's own, making it clear that in the event of Soviet military intervention, they will all stand or fall together. The leader has to insist on the unity of the party ranks, doing well to repeat Mehmet Shehu's warning to the prospective Muscovites in the Albanian party. Shehu told the delegates to the Albanian party congress in 1961, "For those who stand in the way of party unity, a spit in the face, a sock in the jaw, and if necessary, a bullet in the head. . . ."[29]

(2) The party leader has to find diplomatic allies in the Communist camp, in the West, and in the Third World. China can offer both economic and military aid to resist Soviet pressure. Yugoslavia and Romania are always prepared to participate in paeans to the principles of sovereignty, noninterference in internal affairs and respect for territorial integrity. The West, particularly the United States, may offer economic and even military assistance. The Third World countries courted by the USSR may be able to exercise some restraint on Soviet actions.

(3) The regime has to win broad public support. There are two sources of this support. One is a domestic program for the development of a socialist society. If the party is to preserve its cohesion its members will have to believe—or at least profess to believe—that the party has a genuine commitment to socialist ideals. If the party leader is to win the cooperation of those segments of the population whose energies are required for economic development, genuine popular enthusiasm must be evoked for "the socialist transformation of Yugoslavia," "the Polish road to socialism" or Czechoslovakia's "socialism with a human face." Not only party members but large numbers of ordinary citizens will have to believe that it is worth supporting their domestic order—or at least the future domestic order promised by the party leader.

The second source of potential popular support is nationalism, a sentiment that in East Europe often takes a specifically anti-Soviet and anti-Russian form. Appealing to anti-Soviet nationalism for popular support is an extremely complex matter. Many party members, particularly those who joined the party before 1945, have found anti-Soviet nationalism repugnant. They may be reluctant to take up the cause of "national Communism" because they sincerely believe in the ideals of fraternal cooperation with the USSR and of unity within the Communist movement. In 1948, many of the Yugoslav leaders under attack by Stalin found it very difficult to break with the Communist Party of the Soviet Union. In 1968, most of the leading reformers of the Czechoslovak party could not accept the idea of opposing Czechoslovak nationalism to the claims of Soviet hegemony.

Cultivation of nationalism is a risky undertaking for an East European Communist for another reason. Anti-Soviet and anti-Russian nationalism may take an anti-Communist form directed not only at the Soviet leaders, but at the local Communist leaders as well. Nagy faced this problem during the Hungarian uprising. But seeking support as a nationalist is essential, for nationalism can provide an East European Communist leader with broader and deeper popular support than will his socialist program. All of the East European Communists who have achieved autonomy of the USSR have taken stands as both socialists and nationalists.

In their conflicts with the domestic factions of East European parties over control of local party hierarchies, the Soviets have always tried to prevent the rebel Communists from identifying themselves as the defenders of national sovereignty. The Soviets have argued that the issues in question are those of various ideological deviations, alleged threats to the socialist order, and excesses of nationalism. Such Soviet arguments deliberately attempt to shift the debate away from the attempt of the Soviets to obtain control over the party leadership and away from the possibility that rebellious East European Communists will appeal for nationalist support to gain control of their party.

Chapter Two
Communist Parties in Conflict

The evidence for the argument of the previous chapter that the principal means of Soviet influence over East Europe is control over appointments to the party leaderships of the region comes into view only when the domestic factions of the East European parties challenge the Soviets for control of the local party hierarchies, as the Yugoslavs did in 1948, the Poles and Hungarians in 1956, the Albanians and Romanians in the early 1960s and the Czechs and Slovaks in 1968. In their struggles with the rebellious factions of East European parties the Soviets have described their opponents as (1) ideological heretics guilty of either right-wing or left-wing deviations that threaten the leading role of the party, and (2) as nationalists and chauvinists intent on withdrawing their nations from the socialist confederation and joining the imperialist camp. The Soviets have described the Muscovite factions of the East European parties as the healthy forces in the party and as the honest Communists faithful to Marxism-Leninism, proletarian internationalism and friendship with the Soviet Union.

In examining these conflicts between the Soviets and the leaders of the domestic factions of East European parties, Western observers have usually regarded as genuine the Soviet expressions of dismay over the political, military, economic or cultural policies of a Communist rebel and have not seen in these Soviet protests Moscow's attempt to control personnel appointments to the highest party bodies in East Europe. Western analysts have generally argued that the Soviets have been concerned only with keeping the political, military, economic or cultural policies of the East European parties within certain limits rather than with controlling appointments to the party leadership.

The evidence in this chapter argues that even if the Soviets have been primarily concerned with the ideological or other issues which they have

Portions of this chapter appeared earlier in the following articles by the author, "Soviet Hegemony in East Europe: Political Autonomy and Military Intervention," *World Politics* 29 (January, 1977) and "Autonomy and Intervention: The CPSU and the Struggle for the Czechoslovak Communist Party, 1968," *Orbis,* 19 (Summer 1975).

raised in their conflicts with East European parties in 1948, 1956, the early 1960s and in 1968, the Soviets have acted on the assumption that the only reliable method for assuring the adoption of "correct" policies in constantly changing circumstances has been to remove the recalcitrant domestic faction of an East European party and replace it with a pro-Soviet faction. In East Europe control over personnel appointments to the highest party bodies has been both the means and end of Soviet policy. In dealing with the Communist parties of East Europe the Soviets have found that to cede control over personnel is to cede control over policy.

The Soviet-Yugoslav Crisis of 1948

During the spring of 1948 the Soviets accused the leadership of the Yugoslav Communist Party (YCP) of several failings: hostility to Soviet military and economic advisors; favoritism to rich peasants and the urban bourgeoisie; adoption of an overly ambitious industrialization program; premature plans to collectivize agriculture; merging the YCP into the People's Front, a union of political, economic, and cultural organizations; manifestations of bourgeois nationalism; plans to align Yugoslavia with the West; and failure to attend a meeting with the other members of the Communist Information Bureau (Cominform).[1]

Two Central Committee members, Andrija Hebrang and Sretan Zujovic, supported the accusations made by the Soviets in the spring of 1948. They evidently found some support in the Yugoslav party for their stand. The chief of the Yugoslav General Staff, General Arso Jovanovic, may have joined them in the spring; later in the summer he was killed while allegedly trying to cross the border.

Like Brezhnev in 1968, Stalin kept pressing for an international meeting of the fraternal parties at which the Soviets and their allies could appeal in person to the members of the Yugoslav Central Committee. Unlike Dubcek, Tito refused to attend any such meeting. On March 25, the Yugoslav Central Committee announced that the YCP would hold a party congress on July 21. The only reason given by the Central Committee for holding a congress was to elect a new Central Committee[2]—that is, to unify the party around Tito and purge the Muscovites. Stalin's response was to summon the other members of the Cominform to Romania where they issued a declaration on June 28, the eve of the elections to the Yugoslav Party Congress. The parties of the USSR, Bulgaria, Hungary, East Germany, Poland, Czechoslovakia, France, and Italy expelled the Yugoslav party from their organization. In a note to the

Yugoslav government in 1949 the Soviet government explicitly declared that the Cominform resolution of June 28, 1948, was directed both to the delegates of the party congress as well as to the Central Committee to whom it was officially addressed.[3]

After specifically attacking Tito and three of his colleagues, Edward Kardelj, Milovan Djilas, and Alexander Rankovic, and after itemizing the various ideological transgressions of the rebel Communist leaders, the Cominform declaration expressed confidence that

> ...inside the Communist Party there are sufficient healthy elements, loyal to Marxism-Leninism, to the internationalist traditions of the Yugoslav Communist Party. . . .
>
> Their task is to compel their present leaders to recognize their mistakes openly and honestly and to rectify them. . . .
>
> Should the present leaders of the Yugoslav Communist Party prove incapable of doing this, their job is to replace them and to advance a new internationalist leadership of the party.[4]

When *Borba,* the Yugoslav party newspaper, published the resolution of the Cominform it also published the draft program of the party congress and announced that Hebrang and Zujovic had been expelled from the party. The publication of both of these items testified to Tito's victory in securing control of the party congress. Two days after the Yugoslav congress opened, *Pravda,* the Soviet party newspaper, claimed that many of the delegates elected to the congress had been opposed to the "nationalist, anti-Soviet platform of the leading big-shots." Unfortunately, according to *Pravda,* Tito had imprisoned all the pro-Soviet delegates.[5]

While the congress met, the Soviets organized YCP members outside Yugoslavia to denounce Tito and to call upon the congress to elect a new internationalist leadership. Yugoslav diplomats stationed in Washington and in New York at the United Nations issued a statement supporting the Cominform resolution and calling upon their fellow party members to take a stand against Tito.[6] In Moscow, army officers studying in Soviet military academies sent an open letter to the party congress in which they urged the delegates ". . . to choose a new leadership of the YCP capable of leading our party on to the correct Leninist-Stalinist path. . . ."[7]

Pravda complained that at the congress Tito openly threatened the Communists' true proletarian internationalism.[8] *Pravda* was correct. In his speech to the congress, Tito warned against "anti-party elements who raised their heads at the call of the Cominform." He appealed to the delegates, ". . . comrades, let us be merciless to all deviations in our party. . . ."[9] Tito specifically drew the attention of the delegates to the fact that the party had purged Hebrang and Zujovic and declared that the same fate awaited any other "unsound, irresolute and hostile elements."[10] Tito also told the delegates that although the Cominform resolution on the surface appeared to be an attack only on the leadership of the Yugoslav party, it was in fact an attack on the "unity" of the party as a whole and the "unity" of the country as a whole.[11]

After the Yugoslav Party Congress, the Soviet Central Committee issued a declaration in which the Soviets objected to Tito's tactic of portraying the Cominform resolution as a "campaign" against the Yugoslav party and the Yugoslav nation. The Soviet Central Committee declared, "The 'campaign' is being conducted not against the peoples of Yugoslavia and the Yugoslav Communist Party as a whole but against the nationalist group of Tito."[12] The Soviet Ministry of Foreign Affairs rejected as unfounded the protests of the Yugoslav Foreign Ministry that the Cominform resolution had called for the overthrow of the Yugoslav government. In one of its diplomatic notes, the Soviet ministry cited the text of the Cominform declaration and then pointed out to the Yugoslavs:

> There is, as you see, no mention of the overthrow and even less of the forcible overthrow of the state order in Yugoslavia.
>
> The resolution simply says that the Communists in Yugoslavia should compel the existing leadership. . . .to change the course of its policy, or, if they are unable to do so, to change the leadership of the YCP, to elect a new leadership.[13]

The Soviet-Polish Crisis of 1956

The events of the "Polish October" of 1956 testify to the continuation of Stalin's policy of maintaining control over an East European party by controlling appointments to the party leadership. During 1956 Stalin's heirs openly—and unsuccessfully—tried to prevent the leader of the domestic faction of the Polish party from gaining control of the party as a whole.

After the excommunication of Tito, Stalin subjected the Polish Workers' party to a purge of the "home" Communists who had led an underground resistance movement during the war. One of these "home" Communists, Wladyslaw Gomulka, had demonstrated some mild support for Tito in 1948, had opposed rapid collectivization of Polish agriculture and had suggested that Poland follow its own path to socialism rather than mechanically copy Soviet practices. Gomulka went to prison for having committed a "rightist-nationalist deviation." According to a Western historian, Adam Bromke, the Communist regime made Gomulka a popular hero by attacking him for his alleged nationalism.[14]

The Polish Communists, led by Boleslaw Bierut, subordinated themselves to Stalin and tried to copy in Poland the Soviet model of political, economic, and social development. Bierut appointed Konstantin Rokossovsky, a Soviet general of Polish descent, as Poland's minister of defense and as a member of the Polish Politburo. Khrushchev's criticism of Stalin at the Twentieth Congress of the CPSU required the Polish Communists to examine the party's past mistakes and the question of its domestic legitimacy. The man most likely to resist a thorough investigation of the past, Boleslaw Bierut, died in Moscow shortly after Khrushchev delivered his "secret speech." Khrushchev came to Warsaw for the Central Committee plenum of March 20 to witness the election of Bierut's successor, Edward Ochab. But Ochab, having been elected with Soviet approval, began to side with the reformers in the party against the Moscovites, much as Dubcek did in 1968. In an act without precedent for a Communist leader, Ochab eventually decided to give up his position as first secretary to the man who emerged as the leader of the reformers, Wladyslaw Gomulka.

The reformers sought a partial decollectivization of agriculture, a truce with the Catholic Church and more cultural freedom for intellectuals. In pursuit of these goals, which the Muscovite faction opposed, the reformers also came to stand for an assertion of Poland's autonomy against the patrons of the Polish Muscovites. The reformers expected that the Polish population, if given a choice between the Muscovites and the domestic faction of the party, would support the domestic faction. The other reformers in the Polish Politburo in addition to Ochab were premier Josef Cyrankiewicz, and, after their election in July, Edward Gierek and Adam Rapacki. The reformers won support from the liberal Communist journalists, in particular, Jerszy Morawski, editor of the party daily *Tribuna Ludu,* and from influential economists like Oscar Lange, a member of the Central Committee.

The Muscovites, collectively known as the "Natolin" faction (after the Warsaw suburb where most of them lived), saw reform and de-Stalinization as threats to their positions. According to one observer, most Communist bureaucrats sided with the Natolin faction because they saw their own jobs threatened by "democratization."[15] The de-Stalinization program initiated by Khrushchev forced two Politburo members associated with Stalin, Jacob Berman and Stanislaw Radkiewicz, to give up their seats in May. In early October, Hilary Minc, who had been in charge of economic development, lost his Politburo seat. This left four members of the Natolin faction on the party's highest body: Marshal Rokossovsky, Zenon Nowak, Franciszek Mazur, and Franciszek Joswiak-Witold. The reformers also held four seats: those of Ochab,

Cyrankiewica, Gierek, and Rapacki. The deciding votes in the Politburo in early October 1956 were held by Roman Nowak, Alexander Zawadski, and Roman Zambrowski.

The catalyst of the struggle for control of the Polish Politburo was the Poznan uprising of June 28, 1956. In Poznan, a protest by industrial workers over economic grievances turned into a battle between demonstrators and the police. The reformers in the party said that the Poznan uprising indicated that the party had to make a radical shift in its policies in order to secure popular acceptance of the regime. The reformers argued that the protest in Poznan—but not the violence—was entirely justified. They went on to argue that the appropriate response of the party was to purge the Natolin faction.

The Natolin faction did not agree that the protesters had legitimate grievances against the party. The conservatives claimed that the uprising had been the work of imperialist provocateurs who wanted to disrupt an international trade fair being held in Poznan. The implication of the Natolin interpretation of the events in Poznan was that Poland did not need more liberal policies but a strengthening of the party's dictatorship. The Soviets publicly supported the arguments of the Natolin faction. *Pravda* blamed the Poznan uprising on "imperialist provocateurs."[16] During the July Central Committee Plenum, at which the reformers and the Natolin faction fought over the interpretation of the events in Poznan, Nikolai Bulganin, the Soviet premier, and Marshal Zhukov, the Soviet defense minister, visited Poland and gave their open support to the Natolin faction. In a speech delivered on Poland's national holiday, Bulganin blamed the Poznan uprising on "international reaction."[17]

Neither faction of the party was able to prevail at the July Central Committee plenum. The resolution adopted by the plenum simultaneously espoused the positions of both sides: "It is a fact that demagogues and hostile rabble-rousing elements succeeded in exploiting the particular dissatisfaction of the workers... caused by procrastination in dealing with their serious grievances and justified demands. . . . . ."[18] The resolution noted that the 20th CPSU Congress had generated "an immensely animated, fertile and on the whole correct discussion in our party" and added that the press had criticized justly the "distortions of the past." But the resolution also maintained that in this discussion there have been "clear symptoms of one-sidedness."[19]

During the late summer, the struggle between the two party factions centered on the question of Gomulka's reinstatement as a party member. The Natolin faction was willing to issue him a party card as long as he was denied an important party post. The reformers, led by Ochab, wanted to make Gomulka the first secretary of the party. On

August 4 the party reinstated Gomulka. On October 15, the reformers called for a Central Committee plenum to be held on October 19. They planned to have the plenum elect Gomulka as first secretary and to expel from the Politburo Marshal Rokossovsky,the symbol of Soviet hegemony in Poland. Khrushchev decided to attend the plenum of October 19.

When Khrushchev arrived at the Warsaw airport on the morning of October 19 with Molotov, Mikoyan, Kaganovich and several high-ranking Soviet generals, he was greeted by the leaders of the party's reform faction, who had brought Gomulka with them to the airport. According to several accounts, when Khrushchev saw Gomulka he demanded to know who the unfamiliar figure was and what he was doing with the Polish leaders. Ochab replied that the man was Gomulka and that the Poles intended to make him first secretary of the party. Khrushchev is alleged to have turned to his colleagues and said, "We shed our blood for this country and they're trying to sell it out to the Americans and the Zionists."[20]

According to a transcript of the plenum of the Polish Committee, Alexander Zawadski, the head of state, explained to the Central Committee members the reasons for the visit of the Soviet delegation to Warsaw:

> The Russian visitors were . . . interested in our proposals for the composition of the leadership which will emerge from the Eighth Plenum.
>
> They pointed out that the proposed membership was known everywhere, but in spite of our ties we had not informed our Soviet comrades of our plans."[21]

Zawadski did not say that the Soviets complained that they had been unable to find out the composition of the proposed new leadership. According to Zawadski, the Soviets had objected to the fact that they had not been consulted.

The Soviet-Hungarian Crisis of 1956

During the period from Stalin's death to the Soviet military intervention of November 4, 1956, Stalin's successors frequently demonstrated that they had not surrendered the traditional Soviet right to appoint and dismiss the leaders of the party and state hierarchies of Hungary.

By the time of Stalin's death the rule of Matyas Rakosi in Hungary had produced a severe economic crisis. Stalin's successors recommended a "New Course" for Hungary and the other People's Democracies, a reform program that called for de-emphasizing heavy industry in order to improve living conditions and pre-empt violent demonstrations of popular discontent of the sort that had erupted in East Germany and Czechoslovakia in the spring of 1953. Malenkov and Khrushchev personally harangued Rakosi for the results produced by his loyal execution of Soviet policies. In June 1953, the Soviet leaders appointed Imre Nagy as prime minister to carry out the Hungarian version of the New Course. Rakosi retained his position as first secretary and did all he could to sabotage Nagy's reform program. When Khrushchev ousted Malenkov in late February 1955, Rakosi took advantage of the fall of the Soviet premier to dismiss the Hungarian prime minister in the late spring. In November of 1955, Rakosi expelled Nagy from the party.

The removal of Nagy from power did not mean the removal of the economic and social crisis festering in Hungary. Nagy's brief pursuit of the New Course had generated an intraparty opposition to Rakosi over the questions decollectivization of agriculture, restoration of small-scale private business, and greater freedom for artists and intellectuals. The support for these reform proposals came from the economic bureaucracy and the Communist intellectuals. The reformers wanted to preserve the political monopoly of the Hungarian Workers' Party because they believed that they could make their party worthy of its power. This program was the Hungarian counterpart of the programs of the Polish reformers in 1956 and the Czechoslovak "progressives" in 1968. Nagy became the unofficial leader of the loose coalition of Hungarian reformers by virtue of his guidance of the New Course, his personal integrity and his prestige as the theoretician of a Hungarian path to socialism.

Nagy had established himself as a theoretician in a series of treatises written in 1955 and 1956, after his expulsion from the party. In his writings, Nagy urged that Hungarian-Soviet relations be conducted according to the principles endorsed by the 1955 Bandung Conference of nonaligned nations: national independence, sovereignty, equality, noninterference in internal affairs, and self-determination. He also wanted to apply to Hungary the principle endorsed by the 1955 Soviet-Yugoslav declaration: each socialist country is free to determine its own methods of socialist development. To assure Hungary's independence, Nagy recommended that Hungary avoid membership in any "power bloc" and, like Yugoslavia, pursue a policy of "active coexistence" with states having different social systems. According to Nagy, the main obstacle within the party to the pursuit of such a foreign policy was the "dogmatist" faction, which he predicted would denounce this course as nationalistic, chauvinistic and contrary to proletarian internationalism.[22] A Soviet commentator has described Nagy's essays of 1955 and 1956 as "nationalistic" and "anti-Soviet" and directed at separating Hungary from the socialist camp.[23]

In dismissing Nagy, Rakosi seemed to have triumphed over his intraparty opposition. But after the Twentieth Congress of the CPSU, Khrushchev forced Rakosi to rehabilitate Lazlo Rajk and other victims of the Hungarian purges that had been carried out under Rakosi's auspices. The public revelations of the illegalities of the Hungarian purges revived the intraparty opposition to Rakosi. According to a Western historican, Paul Kecskemeti, Rakosi was no longer able to intimidate his opponents within the party, because the police, whom Rakosi had publicly blamed for the purges, refused to engage in further arrests of party members.[24] Rakosi tried to call a halt to the de-Stalinization process in the late spring of 1955 by trying to ban the discussion clubs which the reformers had created as forums in which to air their grievances against Rakosi. In June, Rakosi had his Central Committee condemn the most influential of the discussion clubs, the Petofi Circle of Budapest, which included many of the party's leading reformers. The Central Committee resolution used the standard terminology employed by a Muscovite faction under attack by a reformist faction: it complained of "anti-party" attacks on "honest Communists." The resolution specifically objected to "open opposition against the party . . . by a certain group which has formed around Imre Nagy." It denounced those who were trying to "drive a wedge" between the Central Committee and the party membership[25]—that is, to win the support of the lower echelons of the party for the Nagy faction. According to another Western historian, Paul Zinner, on the eve of the July Central Committee plenum Rakosi planned to arrest about 500 party members opposed to him.[26]

But shortly before the opening of the plenum, Khrushchev dispatched Anastas Mikoyan to Budapest to prevent Rakosi from reversing the de-Stalinization process initiated by Khrushchev.[27] Rakosi announced to the Central Committee plenum that he had decided to retire for reasons of health. According to Ferenc Vali, a Hungarian official who later fled to the West, Mikoyan personally recommended the election of Erno Gero as Rakosi's successor.[28] Gero committed himself in principle to more liberal policies. The July plenum of the Central Committee promised improved living conditions, and the Hungarian parliament promised amnesty for certain political prisoners, legal and penal reforms, parliamentary elections by district rather than by national list, greater autonomy for local authorities, and fewer compulsory deductions from workers' pay.

But the Communist reformers were not satisfied with the replacement of Rakosi by Gero. They continued to press for the installation of Imre Nagy. On October 13, the reformers in the party succeeded in having

Nagy reinstated as a party member. On October 17, the leadership of the Hungarian writers' union called for the appointment of Nagy to a government post and for the expulsion of Rakosi from the party. The writers' union also criticized a number of Gero's policies, although they did not mention Gero by name.[29]

On October 23, Gero's government banned a march planned by university students in Budapest. When the student leaders decided to go ahead with their march despite the official prohibition, Gero lifted the ban and by nightfall tens of thousands of Hungarians joined the student demonstration. The students demanded the appointment of Imre Nagy as prime minister, the removal of Rakosi's associates, the withdrawal of Soviet troops from Hungary, the release of political prisoners, elections with the participation of several parties, elections within the Communist party by secret ballot and a series of economic and cultural reforms.[30]

In a radio address that night, Gero defended Hungary's ties with the Soviet Union; condemned "those who strive to spread the poison of chauvinism amoung our youth"; denounced those Communists who violated party discipline (i.e., supported Nagy); and called for the suppression of attempts to create "disorder, nationalist well-poisoning and provocation."[31] The question facing the Hungarian people, Gero said, is whether they want "socialist democracy or bourgeois democracy."[32] This was precisely the question the reformers in the Polish party had avoided placing before their citizens. The Polish reformers argued that the only political choice for the Poles was the choice between the domestic and Muscovite factions of the party. Gero's statements and actions gave his compatriots a choice between a Communist regime dominated by Moscow and an anti-Communist uprising.

Later that night the Hungarian police fired on a crowd that had gathered outside the main radio broadcast building. The crowd fought back and a general insurrection broke out in the Hungarian capital. When Gero discovered that his own police and soldiers refused to take any further actions against the rebels, he called in or permitted others to call in the Soviet troops stationed outside Budapest. The result was that the Hungarian party and the Soviet army jointly declared war on the Hungarian people and forced them to choose between surrender and resistance. So many Hungarians chose to resist that within 48 hours a massive explosion of popular hatred demolished the Communist apparatus in every part of Hungary. As the party apparatus collapsed, workers' councils sprang up in factories and new organs of self-government appeared in towns, cities and sometimes entire provinces.[33] In late October, rebels in the northwestern provinces had established an autonomous government of "Trandanubia" in the city of Gyor; on November 1, rebels in several eastern provinces formed the "Hungarian National Council" in the city of Miskolc. In the last days of October, Josef Dudas, one of the Budapest rebels, was attempting to establish a government in the capital itself.

In the early hours of October 24, Gero appointed Nagy as prime minister. That afternoon the Soviet plenipotentiaries, Anastas Mikoyan and Mikhail Suslov, arrived in Budapest. The next day Gero left for retirement in the Soviet Union and Janos Kadar succeeded to the post of first secretary of the Hungarian party. While about 20,000 Soviet troops under Major General Grebennik fought the rebels in Budapest and Nagy made radio appeals to the rebels to cease fighting, Mikoyan and Suslov pondered over the question of just what government the Soviet soldiers were fighting to protect. By the time the two Soviet dignitaries climbed into a tank on October 26 to make the hazardous journey from central Budapest to the city's airport, they and their colleagues in Moscow had evidently decided to empower Nagy to form an autonomous Communist government. Shortly after the departure of Mikoyan and Suslov the Hungarian Central Committee issued a statement saying that Nagy had taken over the leadership not only of the government but of the party as well—despite the fact that Kadar had just been appointed first secretary the day before.

A Soviet academic specialist on Hungary suggests that the Soviets were willing to accede to Nagy's formation of an autonomous Communist government because they preferred such a regime to the alternative of military intervention. In his analysis of the events of 1956, P.P. Bezushko declares that ever since Nagy assumed office in 1953 he had been guilty of "bourgeois nationalism," "revisionism," "anti-Sovietism," and "connivance with the imperialists." Bezushko specifically accuses Nagy of advocating "national Communism" before he took office on October 24, 1956. In the midst of this polemic Bezushko explains why the Soviet government endorsed the appointment of an advocate of "national Communism" as head of the Hungarian government during the most critical days of the Hungarian uprising: ". . . the impression was formed that the new head of the government, I. Nagy, was ready to take decisive measures for the liquidation of the counterrevolutionary putsch."[34] Unfortunately, adds Bezushko, ". . . this was not the case."

The Soviet-Albanian Crisis of 1961

There is clear evidence from Albanian and Soviet sources that during 1960 and 1961 Khrushchev tried to overthrow the leaders of the Albanian party and replace them with a pro-Soviet faction. The battle between Khrushchev and Hoxha for control of the Albanian party took place during a barrage of ideological disputes concerning the nature of Stalinism, the likelihood of a world war, the nature of imperialism, and the proper norms governing relations among Marxist-Leninist parties.

It is not clear at precisely what point the domestic faction of the Albanian Party of Labor (APL) headed by Enver Hoxha and Mehmet Shehu had consolidated its grip over the party. During the resistance struggle of the APL against the Italian occupation, the Albanian party had accepted the guidance, if not control, of the Yugoslav resistance movement. Following the Soviet-Yugoslav split of 1948, Hoxha purged a group of party rivals headed by Koci Xoxe. Hoxha accused the members of the Xoxe group of being Titoist agents. If purging the Xoxe group and breaking ties to Yugoslavia left Hoxha dependent on Stalin's support in the period after 1948, by 1956 Hoxha had sufficiently consolidated his grip on the party to resist Khrushchev's efforts to replace East European party leaders with officials of Khrushchev's own choosing. According to William Griffith, after the Soviet-Yugoslav rapprochement of 1956 and after Khrushchev's denunciation of Stalin in 1956, "a significant minority" in the Albanian party tried to overthrow Hoxha with Soviet support. Hoxha purged the intraparty opposition that developed in 1955 and 1956 and allegedly executed Liri Gega, one of its leaders.[35]

In 1960, Khrushchev tried to force Hoxha to give up Albania's close ties with the Chinese party. Several Western analysts have argued that Khrushchev also tried to replace Hoxha with two pro-Soviet Albanian Communists, Liri Belishova and Koco Tashko.[36] A 1962 article in the Albanian newspaper *Zeri i Popullit* claimed that during 1960 the Soviet embassy in Tirana had tried to recruit party members and army officers for a coup against Hoxha.[37] In 1961, the leaders of the Soviet and Albanian parties conducted a public struggle over the control of the APL. In his speech of October 17, 1961, to the Twenty-Second Congress of the CPSU, Khrushchev told the delegates, "We are pained to see that rank-and-file Albanian Communists and the whole Albanian people...are obliged to pay for the mistaken line of the Albanian leaders."[38] Four days later the Albanian Central Committee issued a declaration which condemned "the most vicious slanders against the Albanian Party of Labor...by certain members of the Soviet leadership."[39] The declaration of the APL Central Committee added that "differences...have long existed between the leaderships of the CPSU and the APL,''[40] but did not specify just how long or precisely what the differences were.

Khrushchev replied to the Albanian declaration by returning to the rostrum of the Twenty-Second Congress on October 27. In this speech he itemized some of the stages of the Soviet-Albanian conflict. He claimed that the Albanian leaders had refused several Soviet requests for bilateral meetings of the party leaderships in August and November of 1960.[41] Other Soviet sources later revealed that the Soviets had requested bilateral conferences with the Albanians in March of 1960 and February of 1961.[42] In their conflicts with the Yugoslavs in 1948, the Poles in 1956, and the Czechoslovaks in 1968, the Soviets often sought bilateral meetings to appeal over the heads of party leaders to potential Soviet supporters. In his speech of October 27, 1961, Khrushchev argued that the reason the Albanian leaders differed with him on the nature of Stalinism is that they feared that revelation of the crimes they had committed with Stalin's backing would result in their removal from power. Khrushchev explained:

> . . . the resolute condemnation of the Stalin cult and its harmful consequences is not to the liking of the Albanian leaders. They are displeased that we should have resolutely denounced the arbitrary rule, the abuse of power from which many innocent people suffered. . . .
>
> After all, to put an end to the cult of the individual would in effect mean that Shehu, Hoxha and others would have to give up their key positions in the party and government.[43]

Khrushchev then told the delegates to the CPSU Congress that Hoxha and Shehu were purging the pro-Soviet members of the APL:

> For a long time now there has existed in the Albanian Party of Labor an abnormal situation in which any person objectionable to the leadership is liable to meet with cruel persecution.
>
> Today people of integrity incur punishment in Albania just for daring to come out for Soviet-Albanian friendship. . .
>
> Comrades Liri Belishova and Koco Tashko, prominent figures in the Albanian Party of Labor, were not only expelled from the party's Central Committee but are now being called enemies of the party and the people.
>
> And all this merely because Liri Belishova and Koco Tashko had the courage honestly and openly to voice their disagreement with the policy of the Albanian leaders and take a stand for Albanian solidarity with the Soviet Union. . .
>
> People who today advocate friendship with the Soviet Union, with the CPSU, are regarded by the Albanian leaders as enemies.[44]

In his speech to the Soviet party congress, Mikhail Suslov echoed Khrushchev's objections to the consolidation of power by the Hoxha-Shehu leadership: "Today," declared Suslov, the party secretary in charge of ideological relations with other Communist parties, "matters have reached a point in Albania where people who advocate preservation of friendship with the Soviet Union . . . are dismissed from their posts and subjected to repressions."[45]

About two weeks after Khrushchev's speech of October 27, Hoxha delivered an address in which he emphatically rejected the right of the Soviet party congress to pass judgment on other parties. In this speech, which commemorated the twentieth anniversary of the APL, Hoxha argued, ". . . however important the congress of a party may be, however large and authoritative the party of a country may be, the decisions of its congresses are binding only on its members." The Albanian leader went on to declare:

> The First Secretary of the Central Committee of the Communist Party of the Soviet Union and Chairman of the Council of Ministers of the Soviet Union . . . openly issued from the rostrum of the Twenty-Second Congress an appeal for a counterrevolutionary coup to overthrow the leadership of the Albanian Party of Labor and to liquidate the party, something which he refrains from doing even in the case of the governments of capital countries because he considers it interference in their internal affairs.[46]

The Soviet-Romanian Dispute of the Early 1960s

In the course of breaking free of Soviet control, the leaders of the Romanian party publicly called attention to the link between control over personnel in an East European Communist Party and control over the policies of an East European state. In the early 1960s the Soviets and Romanians engaged in a series of policy debates over Romania's insistence on remaining neutral in the Sino-Soviet split and over Romania's relationship to the Council for Mutual Economic Assistance. In April 1964, the Central Committee of the Romanian Workers' Party issued a statement which summarized the Romanian views on all these questions. The collation of Romanian policies by Gheorghe Gheorghiu-Dej, the party leader, constituted a public declaration of Romanian independence from the Soviet Union. The Romanian statement openly accused the Soviets of past interference in matters of policy and personnel in the Romanian party and openly stated that the Romanians anticipated future Soviet attempts to regain these prerogatives. According to the Romanians, during the existence of the Comintern (1919–43) the Soviets had practiced "wrong methods" in their relations with other Communist parties. The 1964 Romanian statement declared:

> Interference in the domestic affairs of the Communist parties went as far as the removal and replacement of leading party cadres and even of entire Central Committees, as far as the imposing from without of leaders, the suppression of distinguished leading cadres of various parties....
>
> In that period our party also underwent hard trials. Interference in its internal affairs was most detrimental to the party line, to its cadre policy and organization work and to the party's ties with the masses.

The Romanian statement went on to note that during the existence of the Cominform (1947–55) there were similar cases of Soviet interference in the affairs of the fraternal parties. The statement noted that during the existence of the Cominform "in some socialist countries there were numerous cases of expulsions from the party, arrests, trials and suppression of many leading party and state cadres." The 1964 statement of the Romanians noted that the Twentieth Congress of the CPSU had condemned such interference in the affairs of other parties as one of the negative aspects of the "cult of the individual." However, the Romanians warned: ". . . under present circumstances, when sharp divergencies prevail in the Communist movement . . . the danger of the recurrence of the methods and practices generated by the cult of the individual seems possible."

The Romanian declaration went on to make observations clearly applicable to Soviet-Albanian relations and probably to Soviet-Romanian relations as well:

> There does not and cannot exist a "parent" party and a "son" party, or "superior" parties and "subordinate" parties....
>
> We consider as unjust the practice in party documents, in the press, over the radio, at meetings of international organizations and so forth of using offensive assessments, accusations and epithets against fraternal parties and their leadership . . . of expounding in an unfriendly and distorted manner within the ranks of the party or among the mass of the people the stand of other parties, of condemning at congresses or in the resolution of a party the point of view or positions adopted by other Communist parties.
>
> No party is allowed to go over the heads of the party leaders of one country or another and even less to launch appeals for the removal or change of the leadership of a party.[47]

Historians of postwar Romania have noted that the Romanian Communists were highly dependent on Moscow during the late 1940s and early 1950s.[48] But by the early 1960s the leader of the Romanian party, Gheorghe Gheorghiu-Dej, appears to have established the bases for the autonomy of his regime. According to Jacques Levesque's account, Gheorghiu-Dej found that by copying the tactics of the leaders of the CPSU he could simultaneously consolidate his control over the Romanian party and his party's control over the country.[49] In the best Stalinist tradition, Gheorghiu-Dej gradually purged his opponents from the upper echelons of the party. A "home" Communist who had spent the war years in Romania, Gheorghui-Dej was able to win Stalin's approval for the purge of the party's "Muscovites," most of whom happened to be Jewish. According to Stephen Fisher-Galati's analysis, Gheorghiu-Dej further secured his control over the party in the period immediately following Stalin's death when he purged his major rival and then conducted a major purge of pro-Soviet party members in 1957.[50]

In Levesque's analysis, Gheorghiu-Dej drew the conclusions from the Polish and Hungarian crises of 1956 that the people of East Europe were not antisocialist but anti-Russian. According to Levesque, the Romanian leader also drew the conclusion that his people would support a Communist regime if it steadily raised living standards and took a stand for Romanian independence against the claims of Soviet hegemony.[51] In the view of another Western observer, David Floyd, by the early 1960s Gheorghiu-Dej had freed himself of his dependence on Moscow by simultaneously fostering rapid economic development and anti-Russian nationalism.[52] In Floyd's analysis, Khrushchev's attempt to subordinate the Romanian economy to the dictates of the Council for Mutual Economic Assistance (CMEA) was not just a debate over economic development in Romania, but a Soviet attempt to acquire control over Romania's economic and political bureaucracies.[53] Khrushchev had wanted Romania to become a producer of agricultural products and industrial raw materials for the other CMEA nations, rather than to develop a self-sufficient national industrial base of its own. Development along these lines would have left Bucharest dependent on the Soviet bloc for most of its industrial commodities. It also would have placed the Romanian economy under the control of the CMEA planning bodies.

The 1964 statement of the Romanian Central Committee specifically noted that the Romanians could not accept the political consequences of the subordination of the Romanian economic bureaucracies to the central agencies of the CMEA:

> The idea of a single planning body for all CMEA countries has the most serious economic and political implications. The planned management of the national economy is one of the fundamental, essential and inalienable attributes of the sovereignty of the socialist state. . . .

The state plan is one and indivisible; no parts of sections can be separated from it in order to be transferred outside the state.

The management of the national economy as a whole is not possible if the questions of managing some branches or enterprises are taken away from the competence of the party and government of the respective country and transferred to extrastate bodies.[54]

Both Fischer-Galati and Levesque have concluded that the efforts of the Romanians to avoid taking sides in the Sino-Soviet dispute and to act as an occasional mediator in this conflict were not efforts to seek genuine reconciliation between the two quarreling Communist parties, but efforts to consolidate the independence of the Romanian party.[55] The 1964 declaration issued by the Romanian Central Committee ostensibly claimed that the Central Committee felt "... great concern that the present divergencies and ever-sharper public controversy within the international Communist and working-class movement have repercussions in the field of relations among the countries of the socialist camp...."[56] But the 1964 Romanian statement quickly seized on the divergencies and public controversies in the international Communist movement to argue that the Soviets should not attempt to force the Romanian regime to abandon its pursuit of autonomy: "It is possible for differences of view to appear among the socialist countries in relation to certain problems, but whenever such is the case they should be analyzed and tackled in a comradely, way in a spirit of mutual understanding, without resorting to measures of a discriminatory character."[57]

The absence of evidence of direct Soviet attempts to overthrow the leadership of the Romanian party in the early 1960s does not necessarily indicate that the Romanian-Soviet arguments over Bucharest's economic and diplomatic policies had no relation to a Soviet-Romanian struggle over control of the Romanian party. The 1964 statement of the Romanian Central Committee made it clear that the Romanian leadership viewed its economic and diplomatic disputes with Moscow as part of the overall question of the independence of the Romanian regime. The 1964 declaration had specifically noted that a prerequisite for Romanian sovereignty was Romanian control over the Romanian party. The events of 1968 offer confirmation of the forebodings of the Romanian Central Committee that, just as Stalin had engaged in "the removal and replacement of leading party cadres and even of entire Central Committees," the current Soviet leadership was just as capable of attempting such acts: "... under the present circumstances, when sharp divergencies prevail in the Communist movement ... the danger of the recurrence of the methods and practices generated by the cult of the individual seems possible."[58]

The Soviet-Czechoslovak Crisis of 1968

The Soviets justified their military intervention in Czechoslovakia in August 1968, by claiming that the Communist Party of Czechoslovakia had given up its leading role and lost control of political developments in the country. The consensus among most Western analysts is that the Soviets resorted to military intervention either because they feared a repetition of the Hungarian events of 1956, or because they feared that Prague's liberal heresies might endanger the stability of Communist regimes in the neighboring states of the region, including the USSR.[59]

But the Soviet statements of 1968, together with those subsequently published by the pro-Soviet Czechoslovak regime of Gustav Husak and later Soviet analyses of the events of 1968, suggest a different explanation for the intervention: the Soviets acted to prevent the takeover in 1968 of the Czechoslovak Communist party by a loose coalition of party members who called themselves "progressives." By mid-July of 1968, the progressives had won a large majority among the delegates elected to the extraordinary party congress scheduled for early September. At the congress, the progressives planned to take over complete control of the party's Central Committee and Presidium. During the second half of July, the Soviets made strenuous efforts to prevent the convocation of the party congress. In August, the Soviets intervened to prevent the congress from meeting and to place the pro-Soviet conservative faction in control of the party. Moscow could count on the loyalty of the conservatives because they owed their power to the presence of Soviet troops. The working definition of a conservative in 1968 was someone who in the last analysis was dependent on Soviet support for a given position in the party. Members of the party gravitated toward this position partly out of opportunism and partly out of conviction. Many members of the conservative faction often could not survive the revelations about their past activities that the progressives made public. Often they could not meet the progressives' criteria of professional skills and public popularity.

The Czech conservatives came almost exclusively from the party and state *apparat*. Party officials in Slovakia tended toward the conservative camp, although there were some progressives in the Slovak party. For many Slovak Communists, such as Gustav Husak, the most opportune line to take was that of supporting Slovak aspirations for greater autonomy within the Czechoslovak Socialist Republic through federalization of the republic. They may have believed that the issue of Slovak nationalism would enable them to promote their own careers without risking the uncertainties of the quasi-public debates the Czech Communists engaged in. For the conservatives in the Slovak party, Moscow may have been not so much a patron as an ally in the pursuit of Slovak objectives.

The progressives often possessed some professional qualifications besides their experience in the party. They wanted to decentralize the economy, the government and even the party. Their program had its roots in the democratic traditions of Bohemia and Moravia. The progressives hoped to gain control of the party by mobilizing public support to help them purge the conservatives. The main weapon of the progressives was the press, which was made up largely of journalists who carried party cards. The press enabled the progressives to identify each other and to develop their program. It destroyed the careers of many members of the conservative faction by exposing damaging information about their previous activities, by discussing openly the economic and social crises brought on by the regime's mismanagement of affairs, and by revealing past instances of Soviet interference in the Czechoslovak republic and Czechoslovak party.

The progressives knew that by opening intraparty politics to public inspection they risked giving up the party's political monopoly, but they were willing to run this risk in order to purge the conservatives and enact the reforms they thought necessary. The ultimate objective of the progressives in the first eight months of 1968 was to take over the Central Committee of the Czechoslovak Communist Party (CSCP). They planned to elect a new Central Committee at the Extraordinary Fourteenth Party Congress scheduled for September 9. After the purge of the Novotny faction in the early spring by a coalition of the future progressive and conservative factions, neither wing in the party controlled a stable majority in the party's Presidium or Central Committee. During the late spring and the summer of 1968, the two factions fought for the allegiance of the 1.7 million members of the CSCP. As the progressives began to purge their opponents and to establish a popular domestic base, the Soviets came to the aid of party members who gradually banded together in the "conservative" faction. In their struggle to regain control over the leadership of the Czechoslovak party, the Soviets employed a number of code words to camouflage their intervention in Czechoslovak politics:

"Revisionists," "rightists," "rightist-opportunists" referred to the progressives.

"Anti-socialist forces" referred to the nonparty supporters of the progressives.

"Counterrevolution," "threats to the foundations of socialism," "threats to the leading role of the party" were euphemisms for the seizure of the party leadership by the progressives.

"Nationalism" referred to the desire of the progressives for autonomy from Soviet control.

"The leading role of the party" meant the leading role of the leaders backed by the Soviets.

"Marxist-Leninist forces," "honest Communists," "healthy forces," "Communists loyal to proletarian internationalism" referred to the conservatives.

The postinvasion regime of Gustav Husak used this lexicon in its official history of the events of 1968, entitled *The Lessons of Crisis Development.* The Soviets republished this history along with other documents of the Husak era on the events of 1968 in a volume entitled *The Truth Shall Prevail.* In the introduction to this volume, the Soviet editor offered his analysis of the events of 1968:

> Part of the party leadership went over to a position of rightist opportunism and nationalism.
> The rightist-revisionist forces turned out to be in a majority of the leadership of the Communist Party of Czechoslovakia. They succeeded for a time in paralyzing the leading role of the Czechoslovak Communist Party in society.[60]

If the Soviets intervened in Czechoslovakia because they detected a political contagion in the Prague Spring, the contagion was not liberalism but autonomy. For the Czechs to have exported their reforms to other parties of the Soviet bloc they would have had to find Communists who believed that the domestic situations in their countries were similar enough to those in Bohemia and Moravia to warrant the adoption of policies designed for the Czech lands. But apart from small enclaves of intellectuals, no other population in the Soviet bloc in 1968 shared the Czech tradition of liberal political values. Not even Slovakia provided fertile soil for the flora of the Prague Spring. The only one of Prague's reforms that won broad support among Slovak Communists was the policy of greater autonomy for the Slovak Communist Party.

The progressive faction of the CSCP was hardly the only group of East European Communists infected with a desire for political autonomy. The parties in Yugoslavia, Albania, and Romania had developed chronic cases of autonomy. But each of these parties, and the progressive faction of the Czechoslovak Communist Party as well, have proven immune to the specific ideological deviations of the other autonomous parties. The ideological symptom which has alarmed the Soviets in each of these parties was the adaptation of ideology to the specific conditions of each country in order that the local party could secure the domestic and foreign support necessary to become independent of the Soviet party. The political significance of the Czech heresies in 1968 was that they promised to provide the progressives in the Czechoslovak party with the domestic and foreign support to break free of Soviet control.

From January to March

The historians of the Husak regime have accused Antonin Novotny of creating the "rightist-opportunist bloc,"[61] an assessment that is probably not far from the truth. Novotny's stranglehold on promotion within party ranks and his neglect of the country's economic and social problems generated opposition within the party. This opposition consisted of purge victims of the 1950s, let out of confinement because of Khrushchev's direct intervention in the affairs of the CSCP; members who joined the party in the 1950s and were denied access to higher party and state posts; economists and technocrats appalled at the economic stagnation Czechoslovakia was experiencing during the 1960s under Novotny's rule; artists and intellectuals desirous of more freedom for creative work; and Slovak Communists exacerbated by Novotny's extreme centralism.

At the September 1967 Central Committee (CC) plenum Alexander Dubcek, the party secretary in Slovakia, complained of Novotny's haughty attitude toward Slovakia. At the December CC plenum, the economist Ota Sik condemned Novotny's economic policies. At the January 1968 CC plenum Josef Smrkovsky, then Minister of Forestry, demanded that Novotny give up his post as first secretary.

According to Zdenek Hejzlar, the director of Czechoslovak radio before the invasion, at the January 1968 plenum Drahomir Kolder, Alois Indra, and Lubomir Strougal joined the anti-Novotny coalition. These three later emerged as leaders of the party's conservative faction. They apparently had concluded that Novotny had to be removed before the system experienced a complete breakdown. Jiri Hendrych, another member of the future conservative faction, may have reached the same conclusion, for he, too, turned against Novotny in January. According to Hejzlar, Hendrych's defection tipped the balance against Novotny.[62]

At the CC session of January 4, Novotny reluctantly agreed to give up his position as first secretary. Novotny and his opponents then struggled over selection of a successor. When Oldrich Cernik was nominated as a compromise candidate, he declined and instead proposed that Alexander Dubcek become first secretary. Novotny gave his support to the nomination of Dubcek.[63]

It seems likely that Novotny, still president of the Republic, hoped that he could retain much of his power if Dubcek served as first secretary. The Slovak leader had a reputation as a weak administrator, had no political base in the Czech *apparat* and had no program for the country as a whole. Dubcek was acceptable to the anti-Novotny opposition because he had initiated the criticism of Novotny at the September 1967 CC plenum. But according to a *Rude Pravo* article of July 1970, the progressive wing of the anti-Novotny opposition at first received him "coldly and with restraint." The same article implied that Dubcek may have owed his new position partly to Soviet support: "The fact that Dubcek had spent his youth in the Soviet Union played a role: this established the hope that he would act in accordance with the internationalist traditions of our party. . . ."[64] There is one report that Brezhnev immediately tried to have Dubcek acknowledge Soviet suzerainty over the CSCP: Hejzlar claims that Brezhnev asked Dubcek soon after his election to make no more cadre changes without first consulting Moscow.[65] Dubcek went to Moscow on January 29 for consultations. Brezhnev returned the visit on February 22, the twentieth anniversary of the Communist coup in Czechoslovakia. According to Hejzlar, during this visit Brezhnev tried to bolster the position of the Novotny faction.[66]

If Brezhnev tried to restrict Dubcek's freedom for maneuver, Dubcek did not respond favorably. *Rude Pravo* later objected to "the indifference of Dubcek to the liquidation of party cadres and to the disintegration of the party."[67] He probably was indifferent to the purges conducted by the progressives because these purges removed officials hostile to Dubcek. By permitting the progressives to purge their opponents, he was able gradually to acquire the support of the progressives.

William Shawcross noted in his biography of Dubcek that in 1963 the Slovak leader had consolidated his position as the new first secretary of Slovakia by giving greater freedom to Slovak reformers, who obligingly criticized the Novotny faction in Slovakia and stimulated the development of reformist and nationalist sentiments. His tolerance of these reformers won him support within the Slovak party as the champion of Slovak aspirations for greater national autonomy.[68] According to Drahomir Kolder, one of the leading conservatives, Dubcek tried the same tactic to consolidate his position as first secretary of the CSCP. Kolder later declared that after January 1968, "Dubcek based himself on his experience in Slovakia, where the intensity of development after the April 1963 plenum [after the exposure of the Czechoslovak purge trials] was greater than in the Czech lands and did not 'slip out of hand.' "[69]

Until the late spring of 1968, Dubcek did not seem to know what goal he was maneuvering toward. Perhaps he entertained the hope that if he simply dealt with problems as they came up, everything would work out as well as it had in Slovakia. An indication of his lack of a strategic sense was the fact that he permitted his successor as first secretary of the Slovak party, Vasil Bilak, to make Slovakia a stronghold for the conservatives. The progressives took full advantage of Dubcek's indecision in the first months of 1968. They campaigned for the support of the regional organizations of the party, whose members were generally uninformed about the nature of the power struggle at the top of the party hierarchy. The progressives concentrated their energies on the removal of Novotny and his entourage from power.

In late February and early March the progressives succeeded in virtually abolishing press censorship. In the press, in the March 9–18 district party conferences, and in the National Assembly they made sharp attacks on Novotny and the officials close to him. On March 22 the National Assembly forced Novotny into resigning under the threat of a vote of no confidence. A series of high officials resigned along with him.[70]

Brezhnev responded immediately to the liquidation of the pro-Soviet faction of the CSCP. The next day the Soviet leader summoned to Dresden, East Germany, three of the leaders of the emerging conservative faction, Vasil Bilak, Drahomir Kolder, and Josef Lenart, and two leaders of the emerging progressive faction, Alexander Dubcek and Oldrich Cernik. Representatives from the parties of Bulgaria, Hungary, East Germany, and Poland also attended the meeting in Dresden. The accounts of the Dresden meeting published by the Husak regime indicated that Brezhnev was alarmed because the progressives had taken control of major cadre decisions and were establishing the bases for the autonomy of the CSCP. Bilak later explained:

> The allies were disturbed by the fact that things were getting out of the control of the CSCP when, for example, it allowed the President of the Republic to be recalled without preliminary discussion of such an important step by the party Central Committee.
>
> This was—at least in its form—a violation of the fundamental principles of cadre policy.[71]

At the Dresden meeting Brezhnev may have tried to construct a platform for Bilak, Kolder, and Lenart to take back to the conservative faction in Prague. According to Bilak, Brezhnev drafted the original communique for the Dresden meeting. In the code words of 1968, it complained that the progressives were purging the Soviet faction of the CSCP in order to gain control of their party and to establish its autonomy. Bilak quoted Brezhnev's draft as saying:

> Concern was expressed over the recent activization of antisocialist elements which are trying to distort the spirit of the latest plena of the CSCP Central Committee in order to undermine the political and economic foundations of socialism in Czechoslovakia and the leading role of the CSCP and in order to weaken the relations of the Czechoslovak Socialist Republic with the socialist countries.[72]

But the Dresden meeting did not adopt Brezhnev's draft communique. Dubcek requested that the meeting adopt a milder communique which did not implicitly condemn the first secretary of the CSCP. The conservatives later claimed that Dubcek promised at this meeting (and at subsequent meetings) to take the measures Brezhnev deemed necessary but always failed to carry them out. They also claimed that he failed to inform the party about the views expressed by Czechoslovakia's allies. According to Alois Indra, a conservative CC secretary, Dubcek came back from Dresden and had "the effrontery to talk about economic problems having been discussed there."[73]

The April Plenum and the Action Program

April was a cruel month for the conservatives and their Soviet patrons. The progressives continued their purge of all those who would not subscribe to their policies. In early April, they took over many of the top positions in the party and state hierarchies. At the Central Committee plenum, lasting from March 29 to April 5, Novotny and five of his allies lost their seats on the party Presidium and most of their other political posts.[74] The new 11-member Presidium, which sat until the Soviet invasion, had five members who usually voted for the policies of the progressives: Dubcek, Cernik, Josef Smrkovsky, Frantisek Kriegel, and Josef Spacek. There were only three sure conservative votes, those of Vasil Bilak, Drahomir Kolder, and Oldrich Svestka. Three centrists held the balance of power on the Presidium: Jan Piller, Frantisek Barbirek, and Emil Rigo.

The progressives also took over three important government posts. Cernik became chairman of the Council of Ministers, Smrkovsky became chairman of the National Assembly, and Kriegel became chairman of the National Front.[75] The post of president went to the aging military hero, Ludvik Svoboda, who had confined the Czechoslovak army to its barracks during the coup of 1948. During 1968, the elderly Svoboda did not take an active role in day-to-day political affairs. Novotny's supporters retained their seats in the Central Committee, for according to the party statutes only a party congress could elect a new CC. But at the April plenum the progressives began agitating for the convocation of an extraordinary party congress to meet in 1968. The progressives hoped to use the congress to purge Novotny's supporters from the Central Committee and elect a new CC dominated by the progressives.[76]

The April Plenum also adopted the "Action Program," an ambiguous document which contained many proposals the conservatives also supported, such as the federalization of the republic to satisfy Slovak demands for greater autonomy. The progressives, however, achieved a virtual monopoly on the interpretation of the Action Program. The progressives wanted to give the citizens of Czechoslovakia higher living standards and the right to express their own opinions in their workplaces, social organizations and representative bodies. The progressives hoped to achieve these objectives by entrusting the management of economic, social and political organizations to professional experts. The progressives wanted the party to retain its leading role in society, but promised that the party would earn this role by virtue of its enlightened policies. The "democratic socialism" of the progressives did not mean that the public would have the right of political participation but only the right of political exhortation.

The task before Brezhnev in April was to form a pro-Soviet ruling faction out of the remnants of the Novotny group and out of the party members apprehensive about the assault of the progressives on their jobs. On April 10, the Soviet general secretary convened a CPSU Central Committee plenum which placed "special emphasis on the Dresden meeting"; affirmed the readiness of the Soviet party to take all necessary measures for the "political, economic, and defensive consolidation of the socialist confederation"; warned against anti-Communist attempts to weaken the "unity of the socialist camp"; and called for a campaign against "bourgeois ideology."[77] *Pravda* gave its readers a hint about the current manifestations of bourgeois ideology when it reported that "democratization" was a slogan used by "anti-socialist elements" who had attended the April plenum of the Czechoslovak Communist Party. According to *Pravda,* the anti-socialist elements had used the democratization slogan to undermine the leading role of the party, attack party organs and discredit cadres in the party and government.[78]

The struggle between the progressive and conservative factions continued during the regional party conferences that took place in late April and early May. New first secretaries were elected in ten of the eleven regions.[79] Josef Spacek, the progressive Presidium member and the CC secretary for ideological affairs, retained his position as head of the South Moravian party organization and began a purge that transformed his region into a bastion of the progressives.[80] The most important victory for the progressives in the party conferences of April–May 1968 was the election of Bohomil Simon as first secretary of the Prague City Party Committee, which enjoyed the status of a regional party organization. The Prague party committee included many of Czechoslovakia's leading journalists, academics, artists, and intellectuals. Under Simon's leadership the Prague City Party Committee became what *The Lessons of Crisis Development* called "the second center" of the party, a rival to the Central Committee it was determined to purge. Simon's committee called for the convocation of an extraordinary party congress to elect a new CC and also demanded the abolition of the People's Militia, a paramilitary party organization that had carried out the coup of 1948 and was controlled by the conservatives in 1968. In mid-May the Prague City Party Committee made an unsuccessful attempt to circumvent the existing Central Committee, proposing that the party elect a separate Central Committee for the Czech lands on the model of the separate Central Committee of the Slovak party.[81]

The May Plenum and the '2000 Words Manifesto'

In May Brezhnev mobilized the resources of the Soviet party to provide the conservative faction of the CSCP with the support necessary to gain control of the Czechoslovak party. He summoned Dubcek, Cernik, Smrkovsky, and Bilak to Moscow on May 4. Bilak later reported that the Soviet leader told his guests that the situation in Czechoslovakia had deteriorated since the Dresden meeting and that the Soviets feared "the growth of counterrevolutionary forces."[82] The official communique of the meeting of May 4 noted that both fraternal parties wanted to expand contacts "at all levels" and to develop their relations on the basis of "proletarian internationalism."[83]

Brezhnev's measures appear to have produced the results desired by the Soviets. At the CSCP Presidium meeting of May 7 and 8, a majority —which according to Bilak, included even Smrkovsky—agreed that there was a rightist danger in Czechoslovakia and that the Presidium would take measures against "rightist-opportunists" and "anti-socialist elements."[84] The Presidium voted to share its conclusions with officials of the lower party organs. On May 12 and 13, when secretaries of the regional and district party organizations met in Prague, *Pravda* reported that the participants in the discussion had spoken about "attempts to abuse the process of democratization."[85] A reporter from *Literarni Listy,* a paper sympathetic to the progressives, wrote that the meeting was held in secret and that the resolution adopted by the meeting had criticized "anti-socialist forces."

Immediately after this meeting delegations of high-level Soviet military and political figures descended upon Czechoslovakia.[86] Either before or on May 25, Bilak and his fellow Presidium member Frantisek Barbirek went to the Ukrainian border of the Czechoslovak Socialist Republic (CSSR) to meet with P. Ye. Shelest, first secretary of the Ukrainian CP and a member of the CPSU Politburo, and V.V. Shcherbitskii, head of the Ukrainian Council of Ministers and a candidate member of the CPSU Politburo.[87] Alois Indra, a conservative CC secretary, claims that later in the day of May 25 Bilak met with Dubcek, Cernik, and other party leaders to propose that the Presidium recommend to the Central Committee that the party convene an extraordinary congress in the late summer of 1968.[88]

Bilak may have had Soviet support for his proposal to convene an extraordinary party congress.[89] Indra later reported that the progressives at the Presidium meeting of May 27 were perplexed when the conservatives on the Presidium proposed the convocation of a party congress. The Presidium voted to recommend the proposal to the Central Committee plenum scheduled for May 29. Apparently, the conservatives hoped that with strong Soviet backing they could turn the progressives' ploy against them and convene a congress at which the conservatives would obtain control of the new Central Committee and oust the progressives from the leadership of the party. As *The Lessons of Crisis Development* explained, "...the change in the attitude toward the question of convening an extraordinary party congress...was based on the intention of the Marxist-Leninist forces to take the initiative into their own hands by speeding the convocation of the congress."[90]

The CC plenum opened on May 29. The next day Soviet airborne troops landed at the Prague airport and Soviet troops crossed the East German border into Bohemia. Startled Czechoslovak citizens called the newspapers to find out if the country had been invaded. The newspapers called the Ministry of Defense. Eventually the new defense minister, Martin Dzur, informed the press that Warsaw Pact maneuvers had just begun. A spokesman for the ministry added that even the participants in the May 30 exercises had not been informed until the last moment so that the exercises would be "as close as possible to reality."[91] At least one of the Soviet officers on maneuvers took time off to address a group of Czechoslovak party members. According to *Literarni Listy,* he told them that if "anti-socialist forces" threatened the country, the "honest Communists" had only to call and they would have at their disposal "the entire Soviet army."[92]

The May CC plenum voted to convene an extraordinary party congress on September 9 and also voted to fight against a "rightist" threat to socialism in Czechoslovakia.[93] The plenum provided for the election of delegates to the party congress at district party conferences in late June and regional party conferences in early July. But by agreeing to the convocation of an extraordinary party congress the conservatives unintentionally enabled the progressives to seize control of the party. A *Pravda* editorial of July 19 admitted that the idea of convening a special party congress had proven to be a political blunder: "The facts have shown that the offensive proclaimed by the May plenum of the CSCP Central Committee against the rightist, antisocialist forces was not backed up either ideologically, politically or organizationally. It simply did not take place."[94]

What *Pravda* complained about was the victory of the progressives in the election of delegates to the party congress. According to *The Lessons of Crisis Development,* "In the period of preparation for the Fourteenth Extraordinary Congress of the party, a period characterized by an atmosphere of hysteria, intimidation and terror, a decisive battle for the party took place between the Marxist-Leninist forces and the rightists."[95] During the campaign for the election of delegates to the party congress, party members had to choose between the progressive and conservative factions of the CSCP. According to one party member, only 40–60 percent of the party's members participated in the elections, but most of them supported the progressives.[96]

When Brezhnev tried to intervene on behalf of the conservatives by inviting Dubcek to Moscow for consultations, Dubcek put off the Soviet leader by promising to meet with him when he traveled to the USSR for his vacation in the second half of June. But by mid-June Dubcek reported to Brezhnev that the CSCP Presidium had ruled that none of its members could leave the country.[97] The Soviets did bring Smrkovsky to Moscow as the head of a parliamentary delegation. High-level CSSR–USSR economic talks also took place in the Soviet capital in mid-June. On June 20, the week of the first round of elections to the party congress, Soviet troops began Warsaw Pact maneuvers on Czechoslovak soil.

The progressives may have made a commitment at the May CC plenum to refrain from public electioneering. Apparently they did not openly try to bring public pressure to bear on the elections to the party congress. But their nonparty supporters did, perhaps because they were alarmed by the political impact of the Soviet troop maneuvers taking place in the CSSR. On June 27 *Literarni Listy* and several other papers published the "2000 Words Manifesto," two days before the first round of election of delegates to the Fourteenth Congress. The writer Ludvik Vaculik drafted the manifesto and a number of prominent nonparty Czechoslovak figures signed it. The manifesto made a scathing indictment of the period since 1948, called for public discussion of political affairs, and demanded the removal of discredited local officials by popular demonstrations. But the "2000 Words" did not challenge the political monopoly of the Communist Party. It proposed that the public pursue its objectives by supporting the progressive wing of the CSCP:

> Above all, we will oppose the view. . . that it is possible to conduct some sort of democratic revival without the Communists or possibly against them. . . .
>
> The Communists have well-structured organizations and we should support the progressive wing within them. They have experienced officials and last, but not least, they also have their hands on the decisive levers and buttons.
>
> . . . the CSCP is preparing for a Congress which will. . . elect a new Central Committee. Let us demand that it be better than the current one. . . .
>
> . . . if the Communist Party now says that in the future it wants to base its leading position on the citizens' confidence and not on force, let us believe it as long as we can believe in the people whom it is sending to the district and regional conferences.[98]

To the five progressives in the Presidium (Kriegel, Spacek, Smrkovsky, Dubcek, and Cernik) publication of the "2000 Words" was the most unnerving event yet in their risky strategy of relying on forces outside the party to help them purge the conservatives. The manifesto's threat of permanent public participation in party affairs prompted Smrkovsky to label the document "counterrevolutionary."[99] On June 27, the Presidium passed a resolution condemning the manifesto. Cernik proposed that telegrams be sent to the district party conferences to inform them of the Presidium's view of the manifesto. Indra, in his capacity as a CC secretary, was to draft and send the message.

But within a few hours of passing the resolution which condemned the manifesto, the progressives on the Presidium realized that condemnation of the "2000 Words" would damage their chances at the district conferences.[100] Cernik reversed his position and instructed Indra not to send the telegram because it could only "dramatize the situation."[101] Dubcek and other progressives on the Presidium refrained from public comment on the manifesto.

Pravda waited until the elections at the district party conferences had been completed before commenting on the "2000 Words." *Pravda* then concluded that the "2000 Words Manifesto" was "an overt attack" on the socialist state, the leading role of the CPCS and Czechoslovakia's alliance with the Soviet Union.[102] Later documents indicate that the Soviets and the conservatives of the CSCP regarded the manifesto as a successful attempt to influence the outcome of the election of delegates to the party congress in favor of the progressives. *Rude Pravo* of July 16, 1970, wrote: "The '2000 Words' was addressed to the extraordinary district conferences of the party. . . in a series of cases the criterion for the election or non-election of candidates as delegates of the district conferences was whether they agreed with the '2000 Words' or disagreed."[103]

The Lessons of Crisis Development complained that "nearly half the district conferences in the Czech regions supported the '2000 Words.' "[104] Another commentary of the Husak era declared that the purpose of the manifesto was "to thwart the implementation of the May plenum, and to influence unilaterally, from an expressly right-wing opportunist standpoint, the discussion at the district conferences and also to slant the preparations for the congress in this direction."[105] It concluded that the "2000 Words" enabled the "bearers of right-wing opportunism to seize the party leadership."[106]

In the final round of elections at the regional party conferences in early July, the progressives won a clear victory. Neither Kolder nor Indra had been able to win election as delegates to the party congress. *The Lessons of Crisis Development* lamented that among those elected as delegates to the party congress there were ". . . many rightist-opportunist, nationalist and wavering members of the party. . . .Thus the rightist forces established the conditions for their seizure of power at the congress."[107] According to a CSCP Central Committee survey, by early August only 30 percent of the current members of the Central Committee had been nominated for election to the new Central Committee and of this 30 percent "none of those who represent the conservative wing in the leadership have been nominated."[108]

At its regional conference on July 6 and 7, 1968, the Prague City Party Committee not only elected a slate of progressive delegates to the Fourteenth Congress but began functioning as a rival Central Committee of the CSCP. Alarmed by the presence of Soviet troops in Czechoslovakia, the Prague City Party Committee arrogated to itself a right reserved to the Central Committee—that of convening a party congress. By a vote of 287–165, the Prague City Party decided to go into permanent session until the congress convened. The permanent session was instructed to convene the congress immediately if circumstances required.[109] The Prague City Party Committee justified its violation of the principles of democratic centralism by arguing that "the majority of the members of the [current] Central Committee. . . are not able to guarantee that in internal and external questions they will adhere to a position which would agree with the views of the Communists of the city party organization."[110] The Prague City Party Committee later circulated a pamphlet containing its views, a list of those candidates it endorsed for election to the new Central Committee and a blacklist of those it did not want elected.[111]

The Warsaw Letter and the Bratislava Declaration

In late June and early July Brezhnev repeatedly asked Dubcek for a meeting between the leaderships of the two parties. At such a meeting, Brezhnev probably hoped to draw Rigo, Barbirek and Piller over to the three conservatives on the CSCP Presidium, Kolder, Bilak, and Svestka. If the Soviet leader could succeed in this effort, the conservatives would then convene a CC plenum to remove the progressives from the Presidium, postpone the party congress and perhaps even declare the elections to the congress invalid. After failing to persuade the CSCP Presidium to attend a bilateral meeting, Brezhnev assembled his East European allies in Warsaw on July 14 to help him camouflage the Soviet pressure on Czechoslovakia. The five fraternal parties wrote the "Warsaw Letter" which they addressed to the Central Committee of the CSCP. After noting that the Presidium of the Czechoslovak party had failed to respond to Brezhnev's requests for a bilateral meeting, the five parties told the members of the Czechoslovak Central Committee:

> The forces of reaction. . .abusing the slogan of 'democratization' unleashed a campaign against the CSCP and its honest and devoted cadres, with the clear intention of liquidating the party's leading role, undermining the socialist system and pitting Czechoslovakia against other socialist countries. . . .
>
> We know that there are forces in Czechoslovakia that are capable of upholding the socialist system and dealing defeat to the anti-socialist elements. . . .
>
> The tasks today are to give these healthy forces a clear perspective, rally them to action and mobilize them against the forces of counter-revolution. . . .[112]

From Moscow's perspective, the healthy forces should not be discouraged by a mere electoral defeat. As the *Pravda* editorial of July 19 observed, "Needless to say, the forces of socialism in the CSSR, objectively measured, are far greater than those now striking at the revolutionary gains of the Czechoslovak people."[113]

On July 17, Brezhnev convened a plenum of the CPSU CC. It appears that the meeting considered, and perhaps even approved, a military intervention if Brezhnev and his colleagues concluded that only military intervention could bring the conservatives in the Czechoslovak party to power. Under banner headlines, *Pravda* reported that the plenum unanimously endorsed the conclusion of the Warsaw meeting about the "necessity for a decisive struggle for the cause of socialism in Czechoslovakia."[114]

To the disappointment of the Warsaw Five, the Central Committee of the CSCP did not answer the letter. The Presidium did, on July 17. In a 1969 interview Kolder claimed to have a document which had been submitted to the CSCP Presidium meeting of July 17. According to Kolder, this document declared that the Warsaw Letter "basically is demanding the calling of a plenum of the CC of the CSCP." The document also declared, ". . . it cannot be excluded that the present membership of a plenum of the CSCP CC and the situation which has arisen could combine to bring about the election of a new Presidium and new organs of the CPCS CC, which would approve the contents and analyses of the situation contained in the [Warsaw] letter."[115]

The document which Kolder cited proposed that since delegates to the Fourteenth Congress had already been elected, the best response to the Warsaw Letter was to convene the Congress immediately. According to Kolder, the conservatives gained enough support in the Presidium to reject the proposal to convene the Congress immediately, but the progressives secured the votes necessary to write a reply to the Warsaw Letter.[116]

The Presidium's reply to the Warsaw Letter declared that the party was determined to convene a congress that would elect "a new Central Committee that has the full authority and confidence of the people and the entire party." It further declared that "all pressure directed at forcing the party. . . to settle basic questions of its policy elsewhere and at a time other than at the Fourteenth Congress is the principal danger to the successful consolidation of the leading role of the party."[117]

When the Czechoslovak Central Committee met on July 19 to approve the missive written by the Presidium in reply to the Warsaw Letter, the progressives brought in journalists to attend the plenum. Bilak later complained that some members of the Central Committee did not dare speak openly for fear that the media would accuse them of being traitors.[118] At the CC plenum, Dubcek warned, "In the current complex situation we cannot even dismiss the possibility that . . . conservative, sectarian forces might try to abuse the letter of the five parties to cause a rupture in the party. . . ."[119]

On the same day that the plenum endorsed the letter written by the Presidium, Brezhnev requested another meeting with the CSCP leadership. The Soviet general secretary apparently hoped to make another effort—which the July plenum of the CPSU CC had probably endorsed—to help the conservatives take power in the party by normal voting procedures. Dubcek accepted the invitation, but insisted that the meeting take place on Czechoslovak soil. He seemed confident that the progressives were capable of retaining their hold over the Presidium.

Before the meeting scheduled in the Czechoslovak town of Cierna on Tisou on July 29, Kriegel and Smrkovsky met frequently with groups around the country to rally nationalist support for the progressives. A mass petition campaign gathered over a million signatures endorsing the Dubcek leadership. On the night of July 28, Dubcek accepted the petition on a television program and warned his colleagues "not to break ranks" at the talks the next day with the Soviets.[120]

All but two of the members of the CPSU Politburo attended the Cierna meeting, plus two candidate members of the Soviet Politburo and two secretaries of the Soviet Central Committee.[121] The Czechoslovak delegation consisted of the 11 Presidium members and five others. Three of these five were closely identified with the conservatives—Josef Lenart and Antonin Kapek, both candidate members of the Presidium and Milos Jakes, chairman of the Central Control and Revision Committee of the Central Committee. The other two were Ludvik Svoboda, president of the Republic, and Bohomil Simon, head of the Prague City Party Committee. But the Soviets were not able to break the progressives' hold on this ad hoc collection of Czechoslovak leaders and achieve what they had sought in the Warsaw Letter: the convening of a CC plenum that would vote out the progressive members of the Presidium and postpone the Fourteenth Congress.

When it became clear to Brezhnev that he could not rally a conservative majority in the Czechoslovak delegation, the Soviet leader adopted a "conciliatory mood," according to Pavel Tigrid's account of the meeting[122] and agreed to withdraw the Soviet troops still present in Czechoslovakia. Dubcek agreed to a proposal of Brezhnev's to meet in early August with representatives of the other fraternal parties to sign a joint declaration. The leaders of the Communist parties of the Soviet Union, Czechoslovakia, Poland, East Germany, Hungary and Bulgaria met on August 3 in Bratislava, the capital of Slovakia. The Bratislava statement argued that all the socialist countries had aided the socialist development of each individual socialist state and that it was "the common international duty of all socialist countries to support, strengthen and defend these gains . . ."[123] After the intervention, the Soviets invoked the Bratislava Declaration as the legal and ideological basis for the military intervention of the five parties.[124]

Fraternal Assistance

As he had promised at Cierna, Brezhnev withdrew his troops. Tito and Ceausescu each made state visits to Prague, where they received enthusiastic welcomes. The Soviet press ceased its polemics against the progressives in the Czechoslovak party. Organizations deemed offensive to the Soviets—K-231, a club of former political prisoners, KAN, the club of nonparty political activists, and the Social Democratic party (included in the government as part of the settlement of 1948)—voluntarily suspended their activities. The general impression in Czechoslovakia was that the crisis had passed. Yet on August 6, when the CPSU Politburo approved the Bratislava Declaration[125] it probably also agreed to go ahead with the military intervention that had probably been approved in principle at the July plenum of the Soviet Central Committee.

On August 17, the CPSU Politburo drafted a letter to the CSCP Presidium in a last effort to draw Piller, Rigo and Barbirek over to the conservatives in that body so that the Presidium would officially welcome the invaders and then postpone the Fourteenth Party Congress. This letter noted that the Prague City Party Committee had been sitting in permanent session and complained, "The right-wing forces are attempting . . . to form a second CC out of the Prague Committee . . . they are actively trying to influence the results of the Fourteenth Party Congress."[126]

While the Czechoslovak Presidium held its scheduled weekly session during the afternoon and evening of August 20, the Soviets launched their invasion. At 11:40 the members of the Presidium learned that the armies of the USSR, East Germany, Poland, Hungary and Bulgaria had entered Czechoslovakia. After a stormy shouting match, the Presidium voted to condemn the invasion. Rigo joined the three conservatives— Kolder, Bilak, and Svestka—in voting against the resolution. By five o'clock the next morning the Soviet had seized Dubcek, Cernik, Smrkovsky, Kriegel and Spacek and taken them out of the country.

The Vysocany Congress

The permanent session of the Prague City Party Committee did just what it was established to do: it convened the Fourteenth Extraordinary Congress of the CSCP. The Congress met in the Prague working class district of Vysocany on August 22, with 1,192 of its 1,543 delegates in attendance.[127] Only five of the 292 Slovak delegates attended. The Congress elected a new Central Committee of 144 members, the great majority of whom were identified with the progressive faction. The Vysocany Central Committee then elected Alexander Dubcek first secretary and appointed an engineer, Venek Silhan, to serve as acting first secretary in Dubcek's absence. The Congress demanded the immediate withdrawal of the Warsaw Pact forces and began to organize systematic passive resistance to the occupation.[128] According to the accounts of the Vysocany Congress published later by the Husak regime, the Congress acted in violation of party statutes and was therefore invalid.[129] *Pravda* denounced the Vysocany Congress immediately:

> Yesterday the clandestine assemblage was held. The facts bear witness to it illegal character. It was convened over the heads of the CSCP Central Committee. No one checked the credentials of the participants. . . .
>
> The main reason all this was undertaken was the attempt to seize the party leadership. The underground radio stations broadcast the lists of those elected to its Central Committee and Presidium.
>
> These lists eloquently attest to evidence of an anti-party plot, the aim of which was to remove from the party leadership the best loyal sons of the CSCP and to replace them with adventurers ready to go to any lengths.[130]

The Czechoslovak party now had two rival Central Committees. In Moscow the Soviets assembled an ad hoc delegation of the Czechoslovak leadership including the progressive members of the Presidium seized by Soviet troops on August 21. The Soviets brought to Moscow 15 additional party leaders, most of them members of the conservative faction.[131] About midnight on August 26, the Czechoslovak delegation signed a document that became known as the Moscow Protocol. Only one member of the Czechoslovak delegation, Frantisek Kriegel, refused to sign.

The Moscow Protocol declared the Fourteenth Party Congress invalid, prohibited the dismissal of pro-Soviet party members from their posts and required the purge of party members unacceptable to Moscow. After affirming the Bratislava Declaration in Point One of the Protocol, the Protocol declared in Point Two:

> . . . the so-called Fourteenth Congress of the CSCP, opened August 22, 1968 without the agreement of the Central Committee, violated party statutes.
>
> Without the participation of the members of the Presidium, secretaries of the CC, secretaries of the Slovak party CC, most of the delegates from the army and many other organizations, it is invalid.[132]

Point Three of the Moscow Protocol required that the Central Committee of the CSCP hold a plenum at which it would "discharge from their posts those individuals whose further activities would not conform to the needs of consolidating the leading role of the working class and the Communist party."[133] Point Four demanded strict control over the press and required that "essential personnel changes will be carried out in the leadership of the press and radio and television stations." Another point of the Protocol required a halt to the process of purging the members of the pro-Soviet conservative faction from their posts: "The representatives of the CSCP announced that they would not tolerate that the party workers and officials who struggled for the consolidation of socialist positions against antisocialist forces and for friendly relations with the USSR be dismissed from their posts or suffer reprisals."[134]

Conclusion

The evidence presented here suggests that the Soviets sent their troops into Czechoslovakia in 1968 not because they feared that the Czechoslovak party had lost power, but because they feared that the progressive faction of the CSCP was about to capture power. Moscow's real objection to the policies of the Prague Spring was that they promised to give the progressives the popular political base from which they could take over the party and establish the autonomy of the Czechslovak party from Soviet control. Even if the Soviets were in fact concerned about other issues, they sought to install a pro-Soviet faction in control of the party leadership as the only possible means for achieving their objectives. The examinations of the Soviet conflicts with the Communist parties of Yugoslavia, Poland, Hungary, Albania and Romania presented in this chapter reached a similar conclusion: whatever the ideological or other protestations raised by the Soviets about the policies of East European Communists, Moscow has sought control over the East European party leaderships as the only reliable means for achieving Soviet objectives.

When he contemplated the occupation of his country by half a million Soviet soldiers, Jiri Pelikan, the director of Czechoslovak television before the invasion, concluded:

> Whenever the Soviet leaders lose complete control of the upper echelons of any Communist party they will seek to replace them by a takeover inside the party with the help of elements loyal to them within the central committee—elements often under some obligation to the Soviets and corrupted by them.
>
> ...If they fail, they will not hesitate to embark on a military policing action.[135]

But military intervention was not the Soviet response to the takeover of East European Communist parties by domestic factions in Yugoslavia in 1948, Poland in 1956, and Albania and Romania during the early 1960s. It may be true, as most Western analysts have concluded, that the Soviets did not consider the ideological deviations committed by the Yugoslavs,

Poles, Albanians and Romanians sufficiently heretical to require military intervention. But there is evidence, presented in the following chapter, that suggests a different explanation: Dubcek failed to deter Soviet military intervention because he did not follow the examples of the East European Communist heretics who had prepared to summon their armies and peoples to the armed defense of national sovereignty.

Chapter Three
The Dynamics of Soviet Military Intervention in East Europe

The Soviets have dealt in different ways with the rebellious leaders of domestic factions of East European Communist parties. During the period from 1948–1953 Tito faced both verbal assaults and overt threats of military intervention against Yugoslavia. In October 1956, Gomulka faced both political and military threats from the Soviets. Khrushchev launched a sharp polemical attack on the leaders of the Albanian party in 1961, but did not threaten any military action. When the Romanians broke out of the Soviet orbit in the early 1960s, the Soviets refrained from taking even verbal reprisals. Yet in 1968, the Soviets carried out a full-scale military intervention in Czechoslovakia that ultimately resulted in the removal of the leaders of the Czechoslovak party.

Western observers have usually concluded that in these conflicts with East European Communist regimes the Soviets resorted to military intervention only when certain ideological or strategic issues were at stake. In their view, East European Communists who avoided challenging the Soviets in these particular areas have been able to break free of Soviet control and be subjected only to a greater or lesser degree of ideological criticism.

The chapter presents a different view. It argues that in the open conflicts between the Soviet leaders and the rebel Communist leaders of Yugoslavia from 1948 to 1953, of Poland in October 1956, of Albania in 1961, and of Czechoslovakia in 1968, and in the barely-camouflaged conflict between the Soviet and Romanian parties in the early 1960s, what determined whether the Soviets resorted to military intervention was whether the rebel leader had demonstrated to Moscow that he had acquired the capability of leading the nation in a war of resistance against

---

Portions of this chapter appeared earlier in the following articles by the author, "Just Wars and Limited Wars: Restraints on the Use of the Soviet Armed Forces," *World Politics* 28 (October 1975); and "Soviet Hegemony in East Europe: Political Autonomy and Military Intervention," *World Politics* 29 (January 1977).

a Soviet military occupation. In the West, the strategy of national resistance against a military occupation is generally known as a strategy of "territorial defense." The Yugoslavs call their version of such a strategy "General People's Defense"; the Romanians call their version "War of the Entire People." For the Soviets, an East European strategy of resistance to military occupation defends neither the territory nor the people of an East European state, but the rebellious leaders of its Communist party. The Soviets have reluctantly demonstrated that a capability of national resistance by whatever name is an effective deterrent against Soviet military intervention.

In 1956 in Hungary, Khrushchev did not intervene against a rebellious faction of the Hungarian Communist party. He sent his troops to put down a popular anti-Communist uprising directed against all elements of the Hungarian party leadership committed to preserving a one-party dictatorship. Imre Nagy, a leader of the reform faction within the Hungarian Communist party, had taken it upon himself to assume leadership of the popular effort to restore a multiparty system. The precipitants of the Soviet intervention appear to have been not only Nagy's defection to the rebels but the attempt of rebel officers in the Hungarian party to prepare for armed defense of the coalition regime that had emerged under Nagy's leadership.

By 1968, the Soviets had drawn the armies of the Warsaw Treaty Organization (WTO), including the Czechoslovak People's Army, into an interlocking network of joint programs that denied the loyal East European armies of the WTO national capabilities for conducting wars of territorial defense. In the spring of 1968, several high-ranking political officers of the Czechoslovak armed forces circulated a memorandum which pointed out the political consequences of the subordination of Czechoslovak military doctrine to the missions of the WTO. This memorandum proposed doctrinal revisions which would give Czechoslovakia an independent military capability. Within six weeks of the drafting of the memorandum, Soviet troops entered Czechoslovakia on WTO maneuvers and began drilling for military intervention. The absence of a Czechoslovak capability for national resistance was the critical prerequisite for the Soviet intervention of August 21, 1968.

The leaders of domestic factions of East European parties have mobilized their nations for military resistance to a Soviet occupation by shifting their debates with Moscow from arguments over ideology to arguments over the right of East European nations to national sovereignty. A dispute over ideology is a conflict between two Communist parties. A dispute over the right to national sovereignty becomes a conflict between an East European nation and the multinational Soviet state.

The leaders of domestic factions of East European Communist parties have been able to find much broader and deeper support on the issue of resistance to the Russian imperialism of the Soviet state than they have on the fine points of their ideological differences with Moscow. By raising the issue of national sovereignty, Tito, Gomulka, Hoxha, Gheorghiu-Dej, and Ceausescu have presented the Soviets with the necessity of leading their multinational army into battle against an East European nation in order to obtain control over its Communist party. To prevent East European Communist leaders from seeking support as anti-Russian nationalists, the Soviets have insisted that there are no conflicts between the "internationalist" interests of the "socialist confederation" and the national interests of an East European state, provided that these interests are "correctly understood."[1]

In their disputes with the leaders of the domestic factions of the Yugoslav party from 1948 to 1953, the Polish party in 1956, the Albanian party in 1961, and the Czechoslovak party in 1968 the Soviets have made virtually the same criticism of each party: the local East European party has come under the control of an antiparty clique guilty of a right or left ideological deviation, nationalism and anti-Sovietism. The "anti-socialist forces" who have seized control of the local party are threatening the "gains of socialism" in their country and are "objectively" conspiring with the imperialists to wrest the country from the socialist confederation. The Soviets often find proof of the duplicity of the East European revisionists in their "hypocritical" expressions of loyalty to the world Communist movement, to the Soviet Union, to the Warsaw Pact and to the Council for Mutual Economic Assistance.

In each case of conflict between the leaders of the Soviet party and the rebel leaders of an East European party the Soviets have recommended the same solution: the "true Marxist-Leninists, loyal to proletarian internationalism" are to rally the working class to oust the revisionist, chauvinist, anti-Soviet clique. The "healthy forces" in the local party consist of "honest Communists," that is, party members loyal to the Soviet Union out of ideological conviction, political opportunism or a combination of these motives. Whatever their reasons for siding with Moscow, the "healthy forces" are dependent on Soviet support. But the Soviets are equally dependent on the "healthy forces." The Soviets require a fifth column within an East European party if they are to remove the rebel leaders by military intervention.

To deter the Soviets from intervention, the rebel leaders of East European Communist parties have had to demonstrate four capabilities to Moscow: (1) that of mobilizing regular and paramilitary forces for prolonged resistance to a Soviet military occupation; (2) that of maintaining the continuity of political leadership underground or in exile; (3) that of branding any prospective collaborators as traitors to the cause of national sovereignty; and (4) that of mobilizing international support for a war of national liberation against the Soviet army.

Soviet military theorists are extremely sensitive to the question of whether a war appears to Soviet soldiers as a just one in defense of their socialist homeland or an "unjust" war of imperialist expansion. They warn that the war aim determines the "moral-political factor"—the extent to which soldiers and civilians on both sides support the war efforts of their governments. They emphasize that the strongest military effort comes from an army that believes it is fighting in defense of its country's sovereignty. Soviet military doctrine declares that a multi-national army (such as the Soviet army), is potentially unreliable when committed to offensive wars. According to the Soviets, multinational armies are most likely to be reliable in defensive wars. Soviet military theorists also caution that war has a "reverse effect" on politics: if an army fighting an "unjust" war encounters difficulties on the battlefield, army morale may plummet and domestic opposition to the war may develop. In addition, domestic tensions that existed before the war broke out may become severely exacerbated. As a result of the "reverse effect," a government may face threats to the morale of its troops, the stability of its homefront, and possibly even to the legitimacy of the regime itself.[2]

By drawing battlelines over the right of an East European nation to national sovereignty Tito, Gomulka, Hoxha and the two Romanian leaders, Gheorghiu-Dej and Ceausescu, have made the political risks of military intervention too high for the Soviets. To offset Soviet military superiority the leaders of the domestic factions of East European parties have not needed geographical terrain suited for guerrilla warfare, but political terrain suited for preventing the Soviet army from installing pro-Soviet factions of their parties. By threatening to put up prolonged resistance to a Soviet military occupation, the rebel Communists of East Europe have confronted the Soviets with the necessity of military action against East European soldiers, civilians and party members. For the Soviets to use the destructive power of their army against a domestic faction of an East European Communist party is to apply a scorched-earth policy to the ground on which the East European political allies of the Soviets must stand. After foregoing military interventions against dissident East European Communist regimes, the Soviets have bided their time in the hope that a rebel leader like Gomulka may lose his domestic base of support and again accept the Soviet Union as the principal support of his regime. The Soviets have also sought to remove the military basis for political autonomy by drawing the national armed forces of

East Europe into a network of Soviet controls within the Warsaw Treaty Organization.

The evidence to support the argument that the leader of the domestic faction of an East European Communist party can achieve political independence of the Soviet Union only by demonstrating a national capability for prolonged resistance to a Soviet military intervention comes from the following cases: (1) the military-political dynamics of the Soviet-Yugoslav conflict of 1948–53; (2) the military-political dynamics of the Soviet-Polish crisis of October 1956; (3) the military-political dynamics of the Soviet intervention in Hungary in 1956; (4) the formulation of the doctrine of "General People's Defense" by the Yugoslavs in the late 1950s and early 1960s; (5) the adoption of a virtually identical military doctrine by the Romanians in the early 1960s; (6) the revival of a doctrine of territorial defense by Albania in 1961–62, a doctrine based on Albania's war of national liberation against the Italians during World War II; (7) the fragmentary evidence which suggests that Poland attempted to adopt a doctrine of territorial defense in the period immediately after Gomulka's accession to power; and (8) the clear evidence that in 1968 several high-ranking political officers of the Czechoslovak People's Army called for the formulation of an independent Czechoslovak military doctrine to serve as the military basis for Prague's pursuit of independent domestic policies.

The Military-Political Dynamics of the Soviet-Yugoslav Dispute, 1948–53

After the 1948 resolution of the Communist Information Bureau failed to provoke a split within the Yugoslav party, the Soviets made preparations both for the creation of a rival Yugoslav Communist party and for a military intervention to install the rival party in power. At the same time, Tito prepared for the conduct of a war of national liberation like that waged by his partisan forces against the Nazis.

In April of 1949, the Soviets began to report public denunciations of Tito by Yugoslav emigres living in the USSR. Tito's government protested to Moscow about Soviet support for the individuals whom the Yugoslav Foreign Ministry described as "traitors to their socialist homeland."[3] The Soviet government replied that the Yugoslav emigres in Moscow who were issuing public condemnations of Tito were not traitors, but rather "revolutionary exiles . . . true socialists and democrats, faithful sons of Yugoslavia."[4] In November of 1949, Stalin launched a campaign on behalf of the faithful sons of Yugoslavia who had taken up residence in Moscow. He called the members of the Communist Information Bureau

(Cominform) to Hungary where they adopted three resolutions. The first called for heightened vigilance to Western plans for aggression. The second called for a purge of the bourgeois nationalists and Titoist agents who, according to the resolution, had infiltrated the Communist parties of East Europe. The third resolution, "Yugoslavia in the Power of Murderers and Spies," claimed that Tito had fully revealed himself as a tool of the Anglo-American imperialists. The 1949 resolution of the Cominform declared that the Communist Party of Yugoslavia had "forfeited the right to be called a Communist party" and called for the creation of a "true" Yugoslav Communist party. The resolution urged Yugoslav Communists to bring about "a regeneration of the revolutionary, genuine Communist Party of Yugoslavia, loyal to Marxism-Leninism and the principles of proletarian internationalism. . . ."[5]

Within five days of the Cominform appeal, the revolutionary Yugoslav Communists in Moscow published the first issue of their own newspaper, *For a Socialist Yugoslavia*. Within a few weeks revolutionary Yugoslav exiles in Warsaw, Prague, Bucharest and Sofia were publishing similar newspapers.[6] These newspapers were unanimous in their calls for the replacement of Tito by "honest Communists, faithful to the principles of proletarian internationalism." They were also unanimous in their condemnation of Tito's policy of inciting "chauvinist hysteria" in Yugoslavia.[7]

Two days after the appearance of *For a Socialist Yugoslavia,* the Soviet newspaper *Pravda* published an editorial which called for the creation of a new Yugoslav Communist party and predicted that the true Yugoslav Communists would soon establish such a party.[8] The journal of the Cominform made the same prediction and promised that Communists of all countries would extend their full support to the true Yugoslav Communist party.[9] The prospective leader of the new Yugoslav party may have been a General Popivoda, who, in the spring of 1950, was unanimously elected to the governing board of the All-World Congress of the Supporters of Peace. General Popivoda served as the representative of a country identified as "struggling Yugoslavia."[10]

The preparations for the formation of a Yugoslav Communist party in exile coincided with a flurry of incidents on Yugoslavia's borders and with a build-up of Soviet forces in south-eastern Europe. The Yugoslav *White Book* claims that 110 border provocations took place in 1949.[11] Vladimir Dedijer, a leading Yugoslav spokesman and Tito's official biographer, wrote that during 1950 there were 937 military incidents on Yugoslavia's borders with Bulgaria and Hungary and that between 1950 and 1952 there were over 5,000 such incidents. According to Dedijer, the Yugoslav intelligence services had concluded that the Soviets had undertaken preparations for an invasion of Yugoslavia in the autumn of 1949 and the autumn of 1950.[12] Dedijer also wrote that the consensus among the Yugoslav leaders was that the Soviet military threats were attempts to mobilize a fifth column within Yugoslavia.[13]

In late August 1951 Tito told the New York *Herald-Tribune* that the Soviet military build-up on Yugoslavia's borders was "a war of nerves."[14] Tito also told the *Herald-Tribune* that Stalin would not dare to attack Yugoslavia if the West demonstrated that it would support Tito's efforts to resist. He added that if Stalin attacked NATO, Tito would send his armies into battle to help save the West.[15] He left it to Western leaders to reciprocate his offer of military assistance against a Soviet attack.

Tito's army, which numbered 33 divisions in 1949, had successfully organized a war of national liberation after the Nazis had occupied Yugoslavia in the summer of 1941. Yugoslav officers prepared in 1948 and 1949 to conduct a similar war of national liberation against the Soviet army. Colonel General Savo Drljevic later wrote that in the period after the Cominform resolution of 1948,

> By force of circumstances we were compelled quickly to revert to and rely upon our own experience of a national liberation war and the partisan method of warfare. . . .
>
> In a manner of speaking, the young generation of revolutionaries was still under arms and we were prepared to go on from the point we had reached in May, 1945.
>
> In our plans for armed resistance, partisan units . . . were given a place next to the operational army; the necessary preparations were carried out and a number of other measures were taken which contributed to the elaboration of the principles on which the economy would be adjusted to suit wartime conditions [and] on which the evacuation of people and property would be organized in the event of war. . . .
>
> We did all this in a very short time despite the fact that we had no ready-made plans of national defense nor a clearly-defined war doctrine.[16]

Another Yugoslav officer later quoted Tito the effect that the Yugoslav leader had based his military policy in the period after 1948 on plans to wage a war of national liberation like the one he had led from 1941 to 1945.[17] In 1953, Tito had told the Yugoslav army newspaper that the experience of the Yugoslav partisans in fighting the Nazis had demonstrated that a "small nation with a well-trained army. . . bent on defense and not on conquest . . . can resist even the strongest enemy."[18] In 1946, Tito had summed up the experience of his partisan army in fighting the Nazis. This experience demonstrated, according to Tito, that a numerically smaller army supported by a population motivated by nationalism could eventually defeat a larger occupation force. Tito added, in rebuttal to Western explanations of his victory against the Nazis,

> Many people abroad, even certain left-wingers who are friendly to our country, have explained (and still persist in doing so) not only the heroic People's Liberation struggle but also the revolutionary transformation . . . [of Yugoslavia] as being the result of certain fortuitous circumstances, certain coincidences and so on.
>
> The nation-wide people's uprising and the victorious outcome of the People's Liberation struggle are senselessly attributed to such factors as the high mountains, the forests, the national inequalities that existed in pre-war Yugoslavia, and even a certain fatalistic attitude toward life and death, typical of primitive peoples, which our people are supposed to have.
>
> All these reasons are, of course, inaccurate, senseless and humiliating. Such arguments are an offense to our people for they aim to portray the uprising in Yugoslavia as an act of unconscious spontaneity, as a desperate step bordering on adventure and suicide, and not as the result of the profound social consciousness and complete awareness of the people of Yugoslavia of the full difficulty of that struggle and the sacrifices they would have to make in it.
>
> Furthermore, such arguments either forget or deliberately overlook the boundless hatred felt by the peoples of Yugoslavia toward the fascist occupiers who invaded the country and enslaved it; they ignore the traditional love of our people for liberty and independence for which our ancestors have shed blood and made sacrifices for centuries, giving up what they held dearest when the need arose.
>
> They forget or even underestimate the most important factor which not only made the uprising possible but assured its success; that is the organized character and proper guidance of the insurrection for which the Communist Party of Yugoslavia deserves the credit.
>
> Its members selflessly remained with the people in the most agonizing days in their history, they were the first to take arms in hand and go into combat, to offer heroic examples of loyalty to the people.
>
> Yugoslavia does not consist of mountains and forests alone. The uprising flared up throughout the whole country, in the plains of Srem as well as in the hills of Bosnia and elsewhere. Our people did not go to war and die because they hated life but because they loved life and loved freedom.[19]

Vladimir Dedijer wrote that after Stalin's death Belgrade learned that Moscow had made a decision in principle to invade Yugoslavia. But, according to Dedijer, there were differences among the Soviet leaders about the military and political difficulties that were likely to arise if the Yugoslavs managed to bog down the Soviet army in a stalemate; Dedijer claims that Nikolai Bulganin, who served as the Soviet defense minister during Stalin's last years, later told the Yugoslavs that he had personally warned Stalin "not to strike at a hornets' nest."[20] In his "secret speech" to the Soviet party congress of 1956, Khrushchev hinted that Yugoslav plans to offer military resistance had deterred the Soviet occupation of Yugoslavia. In his denunciation of Stalin, Khrushchev said that in the spring of 1948 Stalin had told Khrushchev that he would shake his little finger and Tito would fall. "But this did not happen." Khrushchev then declared:

> No matter how much or how little Stalin shook not only his little finger but everything else he could shake, Tito did not fall.
> Why?
> The reason was that, in this case of disagreement with the Yugoslav comrades, Tito had behind him a state and a people who had gone through a severe school of fighting for liberty and independence and a people which gave support to its leaders.[21]

The Military-Political Dynamics of the Polish-Soviet Crisis of October 1956

Most Western accounts of the Polish-Soviet crisis of October 1956 are in agreement that the threat of armed resistance deterred the Soviets from executing a military intervention aimed at the restoration of the pro-Soviet Natolin faction of the Polish United Workers Party. According to several of these accounts, on the night of October 18, 1956, the Natolin faction planned to arrest Wladyslaw Gomulka and 700 of his supporters. The Gomulka faction of the party expected to elect Gomulka first secretary at a Central Committee plenum scheduled for October 19.[22] On the night of October 18, Konstantin Rokossovsky, a Soviet marshal who had assumed Polish citizenship and become Poland's defense minister, ordered the Polish army to coordinate troop movements with the Soviet forces which had left their bases in southern Poland and East Germany.

But Gomulka's supporters outmaneuvered the members of the Natolin faction and their Soviet patrons. General Komar, an ally of Gomulka, had taken over the security police in late August. He deployed his forces for resistance both to Soviet troops and to the Polish troops loyal to Rokossovsky. Stefan Staszewski, the head of the Warsaw party organization, distributed weapons to groups of students and industrial workers and alerted the intended victims of the purge.[23] According to the "memoirs" attributed to Gomulka:

> Komar sensed in time what the Natolinians were up to and immediately put the state security committee on full alert.
>
> He then contacted the military behind Rokossovsky's back and secured the army's support.
>
> Now, holding all the trumps, he sent his man to the Natolinians to declare: "If you want to take action, go ahead. We are prepared." And they couldn't do a thing.[24]

Khrushchev and the rest of his uninvited Soviet delegation arrived in Warsaw on the morning of October 19 to discuss the proposed changes in the Polish leadership. According to Konrad Syrop, at the meeting in the Belvedere Palace Khrushchev declared that what the reformers in the Polish party called democratization was in fact anarchy.[25] A *Pravda* article with a dateline of October 19 reported that the Polish press was rife with "anti-Soviet pronouncements," "open calls for the restoration of capitalism," and "a broad campaign against the very bases of the people's democratic order." The participants in this "anti-socialist campaign" were "revisionists and capitulationists." According to *Pravda*'s special correspondent in Warsaw, these anti-Soviet and antisocialist actions were being conducted under the pretext of removing the consequences of the cult of personality and of restoring Leninist norms to party life.[26]

According to Western accounts of the Belvedere meeting, Edward Ochab, the party first secretary who wanted to pass his position on to Gomulka, argued that the Polish party could retain the legitimacy necessary to govern only if Gomulka became first secretary, if Marshal Rokossovsky gave up his seat on the Polish party Politburo and his post as defense minister, and if the Central Committee adopted a reform program aimed at raising living standards. Ochab warned that there would be more worker uprisings like that in Poznan in June 1956 if the party did not accept the personnel and policy changes demanded by the party's reform faction.[27] The Western accounts of the meeting in the Belvedere Palace report that Gomulka demanded that Khrushchev halt the movement of Soviet troops toward Warsaw. Gomulka warned the Soviet leader that unless Soviet troops ceased their movements, he would make a radio broadcast about the actions of Soviet military forces.[28] Gomulka's ally, General Komar, attended the Belvedere meeting and continuously received reports on the military preparations being carried out by his officers.[29] Komar's activities at the meeting must have called the attention of the Soviet delegation to the fact that Khrushchev and his colleagues were in virtual custody of General Komar's troops.

According to a Western correspondent, at the end of an afternoon of stormy debate, Khrushchev became suddenly conciliatory. He told the

Poles that he had not come to threaten them but to offer economic aid.[30] Several observers concluded that Khrushchev had backed down from his attempt to deny Gomulka the post of first secretary because Khrushchev came to the realization that large numbers of armed Poles were prepared to fight Soviet troops in order to secure Gomulka's accession to power. Konrad Syrop, a British journalist, reports that Marshal Rokossovsky told Khrushchev that the Polish troops under his command were not reliable and that the party committee in Warsaw was getting ready for military action. Syrop adds:

> It all added up to the conclusion that the only way to impose Soviet will on the Poles was by throwing Russian troops into action.
>
> The outcome would not be in doubt; but before the Poles could be subdued the Russians would have to fight a bloody war and this Khrushchev and his colleagues were not prepared to do at that moment.
>
> They decided to play a waiting game.[31]

Flora Lewis, at the time The New York *Times* correspondent in Warsaw, came to the same conclusion.[32] A Western historian, Richard Hiscocks, suggests that another factor restraining Khrushchev from taking military action was the fear that armed conflict would spread to other East European Communist states.[33] Another Western historian, Adam Bromke, concluded that on October 19 Poland was "on the verge of a bloodbath." He wrote that Gomulka had presented Khrushchev with the choice of going to war against the Polish nation or accepting a Communist regime bent on autonomy in domestic affairs but willing to coordinate its foreign policy with that of the USSR.[34] In his history of Soviet foreign policy, Adam Ulam concluded that on October 19 Khrushchev faced the prospect of another Russo-Polish war. According to Ulam, the problem raised by such a war was not that Poland could successfully resist, but that 25 million Poles could make the war last long enough to create uncertain repercussions in the West, in China and "even within the USSR."[35]

As Syrop noted in his study of the Polish October, Khrushchev may have backed down from the threat of military intervention on October 19 in the hope that the Natolin faction might yet outmaneuver Gomulka at the Central Committee plenum rescheduled for October 20. Khrushchev and his colleagues left Warsaw shortly before the plenum began. In his speech to the Central Committee, Gomulka made a declaration of Polish sovereignty that identified him as the leading champion of Polish nationalism. Gomulka declared that in the past Polish-Soviet relations had not been conducted on the basis of equality. He promised that in the future Poland would be fully sovereign.[36] Gomulka also presented a bitter critique of the economic and social policies of the previous leadership of Boleslaw Bierut and declared that the Poznan workers had been fully justified in their economic protests. He called for the disbanding of most of the collective farms and thorough reform of industrial policies.[37]

During the Central Committee plenum of October 20, the Polish troops under General Komar, the Polish troops under Rokossovsky, and the Soviet forces in Poland continued to maneuver for position, evidently in anticipation of armed conflict. The members of the Gomulka faction at the Central Committee plenum demanded that Rokossovsky explain the actions of the Soviet troops in Poland. But the Defense Minister refused to give clear answers.[38] At the same time, thousands of public meetings took place in Warsaw and other cities. Most of these meetings adopted resolutions in support of the Gomulka faction and sent their resolutions to the plenum. The members of the Natolin faction objected that these resolutions were attempts to influence the decisions taken by the Central Committee on the election of a new first secretary. Edward Ochab, Gomulka's principal supporter, spoke in favor of "...the declarations by students and workers and the statements made by many people and the resolutions taken at many meetings in Poland, which want to defend the Central Committee against the army allegedly threatening it or against the Soviet army."[39]

Syrop concluded that the military maneuvers which took place during the course of the plenum strengthened Gomulka's position because he emerged as the symbol of Polish sovereignty and made the members of the Natolin faction appear as "traitors."[40] In its session of October 21, the Central Committee elected Gomulka as first secretary and ousted Rokossovsky from the Polish Politburo. The Central Committee elected a nine-member Politburo dominated by Gomulka's allies. On October 23, Gomulka appointed General Marion Spychalski as the head of the army's political administration and deputy commander of the armed forces. This appointment may have provided Gomulka with a device for contesting Rokossovsky's command over the Polish armed forces. Later in the day on October 23, Khrushchev telephoned Gomulka from Moscow to inform the new Polish first secretary that the Soviet troops on maneuvers in Poland would return to their bases in Silesia and East Germany.[41] Two weeks later Rokossovsky resigned as defense minister and returned to the USSR. Spychalski then became Gomulka's defense minister.

Khrushchev did not reveal whether he accepted Gomulka's accession to power because the alternative appeared to be armed struggle against Polish regular and volunteer forces or because, as Zbigniew Brzezinski has argued, Gomulka persuaded Khrushchev of his fundamental orthodoxy.[42] If the events of October 18–23, 1956, do not prove that a rebel Communist leader can deter Soviet intervention by mobilizing his nation for armed resistance, the Polish October at least suggests that the Soviets are more likely to accept protestations of ideological orthodoxy if the party leader under criticism has threatened to lead his nation in military resistance to a Soviet occupation.

The Military-Political Dynamics of the Soviet Intervention in Hungary

The Soviet military intervention in Hungary in 1956 was not aimed at overthrowing the leaders of an East European Communist party. In Hungary, the Soviets did not send their troops into battle against a united Communist party defended by the nation's regular armed forces and civilian volunteers. The Soviets sent their soldiers to fight a bitter but very brief campaign against isolated groups of anti-Communist rebels.

After the mass uprising of October 23 had demolished the entire apparatus of Communist power under Enro Gero, the Soviets authorized what had previously been anathema: an autonomous Communist government under Imre Nagy, the leader of the reform faction of the party. Nagy became prime minister on October 24. It is possible that the Soviets hoped that the Hungarian rebels would accept the Nagy government as their own and spare the Soviets the necessity of suppressing the Hungarian revolution with Soviet soldiers. It is also possible that the Soviets hoped that appointing Nagy to rule would give the Soviet army the time necessary to mobilize for a full-scale intervention.

By October 30, when the Soviets formally proclaimed their willingness to accept an autonomous Communist government under Nagy, Nagy had evidently concluded that his compatriots would not accept any Communist government, even an autonomous one. He probably saw two choices: aligning himself with the Soviets to crush the rebels or aligning himself with the rebels to resist the Soviets. He chose to join the rebels and formed a coalition government dominated by non-Communists. Before rebel officers of the Hungarian army could organize the military defense of Nagy's government, the Soviet army crushed the rebellion and installed a new Communist party in power. The Soviet army did not attack the Hungarian Communists—it rescued them.

Moscow and Nagy

Shortly after the departure on October 26 of the Soviet emissaries, Anastas Mikoyan and Mikhail Suslov, the Hungarian Central Committee

(CC) issued a statement declaring that Nagy had taken over leadership of the party as well as of the government. The CC statement offered the Hungarians a program very similar to that Gomulka had devised for Poland. The Central Committee called for an affirmation of Hungary's sovereignty, pledged a new relationship of equality with the USSR and promised that Soviet troops would be withdrawn as soon as the fighting ceased—that is, as soon as the rebels accorded the Nagy regime de facto recognition. The CC acknowledged that the Hungarian party had been guilty not only of "mistakes" but actually of "crimes." It promised to correct all mistakes and crimes and to carry out extensive social and economic reforms.[43]

In its coverage of a radio address by Nagy on the following day, *Pravda* noted that the Hungarian prime minister had declared that he would incorporate into his government the workers' councils that had sprung up in Hungarian factories and the new organs of self-government which had appeared in many cities and provinces. *Pravda* also noted that Nagy had offered amnesty to all those who stopped fighting.[44] In his analysis of the situation in Budapest on October 27, *Pravda*'s correspondent wrote that the people's democratic order in Hungary had survived its ordeal and had emerged with renewed vitality. He expressed confidence in the capability of the Nagy government "to fulfill its responsibilities."[45]

On October 28, Nagy appointed a new cabinet. It included four non-Communists but in fact was still a one-party regime.[46] On the same day the Central Committee of the Hungarian Workers' Party named a new six-member presidium to lead the party. Janos Kadar served as chairman of the presidium; he and two other members, Antol Apro and Ferenc Munnich, later made the appeal of November 4 for Soviet military intervention. It is likely that the appointment of Kadar as chairman of the party presidium was an effort to restrict Nagy's power within the new regime.

In his radio address of October 28, Nagy promised to seek a withdrawal of Soviet troops, to put Soviet-Hungarian relations on a basis of equality, and to carry out social and economic reforms. His promises contained the two essential policies of an autonomous East European Communist regime: an assertion of sovereignty against the claims of the USSR and a promise of domestic policies adjusted to the special needs of the nation. Enacting this program depended on the willingness of the Hungarian rebels to lay down their arms and accept Nagy's government.

In its coverage of the formation of Nagy's government of October 28, *Pravda* demonstrated its special flair for reporting what the Soviet leaders wanted to happen. According to *Pravda,* the Hungarian workers had accepted Nagy's new government "with satisfaction." In the view of the CPSU newspaper, Budapest was returning to normal.[47] According to The New York *Times* correspondent in Hungary, the Hungarian rebels were split on the question of whether to cease fighting the Soviet troops in Budapest and accept Nagy's government of October 28.[48] The *Times* also reported that the rebels were virtually unanimous in their demand that Soviet troops leave Hungary.[49] For Nagy to win popular support for his government of October 28, Nagy had to prove that he was a nationalist determined to achieve autonomy of the USSR. But the main force behind his government was the main force behind all previous Communist governments in Hungary: the Soviet army. Soviet military support for Nagy's government of October 28 only undercut Nagy's claim to head a genuinely independent Hungarian Communist regime. As the Soviet government admitted in a declaration issued on October 30, the continued presence of Soviet troops in Hungary ". . . could serve as an excuse for the further aggravation of the situation. . . ."[50] On October 28, at Nagy's request, the Soviets began to withdraw their troops from Budapest in order to bolster Nagy's claim to be the champion of Hungarian sovereignty.

But while Soviet troops departed from Budapest in the period from October 28 to 30, other Soviet units entered Hungary from the USSR. The Soviet forces that had withdrawn from Budapest formed a ring around the city.[51] In Moscow, Marshal Zhukov, the Soviet Defense Minister, told foreign correspondents that Soviet troops would not leave Hungary.[52] Although the Soviets had evidently agreed to remove Soviet troops from Budapest in order to enhance the legitimacy of Nagy's government of October 28, the Soviets were not prepared to forfeit their capability for immediate military intervention should the Nagy regime fail to re-establish the power of the Hungarian Workers' Party. On October 30, the Soviet leaders offered the Hungarian rebels a substitute for a withdrawal of Soviet forces from Hungary: a declaration that the Soviets would negotiate with the Nagy government at some future date over the complete withdrawal of Soviet forces from Hungary.

Mikoyan and Suslov had returned to Budapest on October 30 to present Nagy with this declaration which the Soviets evidently hoped would certify to the Hungarian rebels that the Nagy government was a fully independent government. In addition to pledging a negotiated withdrawal of Soviet troops, the declaration voiced support for the "just demands" of the Hungarian workers for improved living conditions and for the elimination of "bureaucratic distortions." The USSR further pledged to conduct relations with all socialist states on the basis of "complete equality, of respect for territorial integrity, state independence and sovereignty and non-interference in one another's internal affairs."[53]

Mikoyan and Suslov found that the enticements of their declaration were wasted not only on the Hungarian rebels but on Nagy as well. By October 30, Nagy had given up any hopes of being able to maintain an autonomous Communist government in Hungary. One reason was that it was impossible to reorganize the shattered fragments of the Communist party into a unified organization. Ferenc Vali, a Hungarian official who fled after the revolution, distinguishes among four deeply divided factions of the Budapest Communists during the chaotic last days of October: (1) the Rakosi-Gero Stalinists; (2) the centrists around Kadar; (3) the "national Communists" around Nagy; and (4) the reformist Communists around Geza Losonczy who were in favor of restoring a multiparty democracy.[54]

The most important reason for the failure of Nagy's government of October 28 to emerge as an autonomous Communist regime is that it could not win nationalist support as the champion of Hungarian sovereignty. Nagy's government of October 24 had relied on Soviet troops to suppress the Hungarian rebels. Nagy's government of October 28 had tried to win over the rebels by obtaining Soviet pledges to respect Hungary's sovereignty and to negotiate an eventual withdrawal of Soviet forces from Hungary. By the time Mikoyan and Suslov had returned to Budapest with a new charter of Soviet-Hungarian relations, Nagy had evidently concluded that he had only two choices: to align himself with the Soviet army and agree to the suppression of the rebels or to align himself with the rebels and agree to the restoration of the multiparty system. In a radio address of October 30 Nagy proclaimed that his government "abolishes the one-party system and places the country's government on the basis of democratic cooperation among the coalition parties reborn in 1945."[55] Nagy also announced the formation of a new cabinet in which the Communist held only three of seven posts. On November 3, Nagy formed another cabinet in which the Communists held only four of thirteen ministries. As prime minister and foreign minister, Nagy held two of the Communists' four posts.[56]

Moscow and Kadar

The Soviets may have endorsed Nagy's government of October 28 merely to give the Soviet army more time to mobilize for a full-scale intervention. But it appears more likely that the Soviets endorsed the government of October 28 because they hoped it would preserve Communist rule in Hungary, even if the new regime became independent of the USSR. The coalition government that Nagy established on October 30, after announcing the restoration of the multiparty system, was a genuine coalition in which the Communists were likely to become the weakest partner. Nagy's decision to give up his attempt to form an autonomous Communist regime left the Soviets with the choice of crushing Nagy's government of October 30 or permitting the rest of the Soviet bloc to witness the transformation of a Communist state into a democratic one.

Ferenc Vali argues that Nagy's decision of November 1 to withdraw from the Warsaw Pact and to declare Hungary a neutral state did not provoke the Soviet military intervention of November 4. He argues that after October 30 the primary issue for the Soviets was not that of Hungary's membership in the Soviet alliance system but that of the collapse of the Communist power in Hungary. Vali writes that once Nagy had abandoned the one-party system, Hungary's formal adherence to the Pact was of no value at all to Moscow. He argues that a non-Communist Hungary would in fact have proven an extremely unwelcome member of the Warsaw Treaty Organization (WTO). In rejecting the argument that Nagy's withdrawal from the Warsaw Pact prompted the Soviet intervention of November 4, Vali suggests just the opposite: the imminent threat of Soviet intervention against Nagy's multiparty system prompted Nagy to withdraw from the WTO. Vali maintains that Nagy had concluded that the Soviets had begun to prepare for a military intervention shortly after he announced the restoration of the multiparty system. Vali argues that Nagy withdrew from the WTO and proclaimed Hungary a neutral state in order to generate international pressure against a military intervention by the Soviets.[57]

The United Nations report on Hungary offers evidence to support Vali's contention that Nagy withdrew from the Warsaw Pact in a desperate effort to deter Khrushchev from intervening. According to the UN report, virtually all the forces that went into action on November 4, some 75,00 to 200,000 soldiers and 1,600 to 4,000 tanks, had been placed in Hungary by November 2.[58] On November 1, Nagy protested to the Soviet government several times concerning Soviet troop movements into Hungary before his cabinet voted to withdraw from the Warsaw Pact.[59]

Before the Soviets could execute a military intervention against Nagy's multiparty coalition government of October 30, the Soviets first had to conjure up a "new" Communist party that would request fraternal military assistance and be prepared to restore a one-party dictatorship. In the evening of November 1, Janos Kadar broadcast a radio message to the Hungarian people: "In these momentous hours the Communists who fought against the despotism of Rakosi have decided, in accordance with the wishes of many true patriots and socialists, to form a new party."[60]

Kadar called his new party the Hungarian Socialist Workers Party. He named Nagy as one of the members of the party, but was ambiguous about whether or not the new party supported the multiparty democracy Nagy had just proclaimed. Kadar did not comment on Nagy's withdrawal from the WTO, which Nagy had announced two hours earlier. Kadar issued several warnings in his speech about the threat of counterrevolution in Hungary and told his compatriots that unless they crushed this counterrevolution immediately, their country could become a battlefield.[61] Kadar made no effort to clear up the ambiguity concerning his party's attitude toward the multiparty system. Immediately after his radio address, he disappeared from Budapest.

Kadar clarified matters on November 4. In a radio address made from the town of Uzhgorod in the USSR, he proclaimed the formation of the Revolutionary Worker-Peasant Government of Hungary. Kadar declared that his government had been formed on November 1, the same day he founded the new Communist party. Kadar appealed to the Hungarian populace to assist his government in crushing the counterrevolution.[62] Before he spoke, the Soviet army had gone into action against the Hungarian rebels.

The Soviets did not intervene against a national Communist government, as Zbigniew Brzezinski has argued.[63] Soviet troops intervened to restore a Communist regime that had been destroyed by a revolutionary upheaval. The formula used by both the Soviet government and the Kadar government following the intervention was that "the government of Imre Nagy. . . cleared the path for the reactionary forces, disintegrated and ceased its existence."[64] The Soviets and Kadar were referring to Nagy's government of October 28, not his government of October 30 or his government of November 3. According to Kadar, Nagy had proceeded from factionalist activity within the Hungarian party to the establishment of "legal possibilities for the activity of counterrevolutionary organizations and political parties." In Kadar's view, Nagy was guilty of "unprincipled treachery," "traitorous surrender of the power of the working class," and "open alliance with the bourgeoisie and the imperialists."[65] In other words, Nagy had agreed to the surrender of the Communist political monopoly in Hungary. According to the *Pravda* editorial of November 4: "The question posed is: will Hungary proceed further along the path of socialist development or will the forces of reaction take the summit?"[66] In *Pravda*'s view, the question was whether a non-Communist government would assume control of what had been a Communist country.

Military Intervention

The Soviet intervention appears to have been directed not only against the consolidation of domestic and foreign support by the Nagy governments of October 30 and November 3, but also against the mobilization of the Hungarian armed forces to defend Nagy's regime. On October 30, General Bela Kiraly and other anti-Soviet officers in the Hungarian armed forces formed the "Revolutionary Committee of the Armed Forces," a body that attempted to unite the army, the police, and the armed rebels under one command. Kiraly later claimed that if the Committee had had more time, it would eventually have wrested control of the regular armed forces from the pro-Soviet commanders in the Hungarian officer corps. According to Kiraly's account, pro-Soviet officers, led by General Janza, the Minister of Defense from October 30 to November 3, ordered most Hungarian units to stay away from the major cities and towns. After Kiraly had become commander of the Hungarian troops in Budapest on October 30, Janza split the city into two separate military zones in order to prevent Kiraly from obtaining full control over the Hungarian forces still in the capital. On November 1, a group of high-ranking Hungarian officers returned to Hungary from their studies in Moscow and immediately set about obstructing the efforts of the military rebels to take over Hungary's army of 200,000 soldiers.[67] This force was roughly equal in size to the Soviet force that went into action on November 4.

The immediate precipitant of the intervention of November 4 may have been Nagy's replacement of General Janza as defense minister with Colonel Pal Maletar on November 3. Maletar had defected with his unit to the rebels shortly after the Budapest uprising of October 23. On November 3, Maletar and his aides agreed to meet at 10 p.m. with the Soviet military commanders in Hungary to discuss the details of a Soviet plan for withdrawing Soviet troops from Hungary. According to Vali, at this meeting General Serov, head of the Soviet KGB, supervised the seizure of Maletar and his staff. When Soviet troops went into action a few hours later, the only countermeasure Nagy could take was to issue a radio appeal to Maletar and his staff to return to their headquarters in the defense ministry.[68]

Soviet troops quickly reoccupied Budapest and the other major cities of Hungary. The Hungarian army did not go into action. Resistance from small, isolated groups of rebels lasted for about ten days.[69] As Soviet troops entered Budapest, Nagy and 17 of his associates took refuge in the Yugoslav embassy. After 22 days, they accepted a safe conduct pass from Kadar. The Soviets then seized Nagy and held him prisoner in Romania. A Soviet firing squad executed him on June 16, 1958.

The Soviet military intervention in Hungary was not directed against a ruling autonomous Communist party. The Soviet intervention struck down a non-Communist government and pre-empted the possibility that rebel officers would organize the armed defense of this government.

The Yugoslav Doctrine of General People's Defense

After the Soviet intervention in Hungary, the Yugoslav Defense Ministry began to develop a doctrine of "General People's Defense" aimed at deterring a Soviet intervention to install a pro-Soviet Communist regime in Yugoslavia and at providing a military basis for the pursuit of a diplomatic policy of nonalignment. The Yugoslav doctrine, formulated in the late 1950s and early 1960s, has served as a model doctrine for any East European Communist state seeking to secure its political autonomy of the Soviet Union and to pursue an independent foreign policy.

One Yugoslav officer dates the origins of the current conception of General People's Defense to 1957.[70] Another Yugoslav officer sees the charter of the current doctrine in the 1958 program of the League of Communists of Yugoslavia. This program declared that the Yugoslavs "can successfully defend their liberty only through the organization of nationwide resistance."[71] During the early 1960s, the Yugoslav defense system relied on four components: the regular forces of the Yugoslav Peoples Army (YPA), partisan units, territorial militia forces, and a small civil defense corps. The Yugoslavs also sought to develop a national armament industry capable of supplying most of Yugoslavia's war materiel.[72] After the Soviet intervention in Czechoslovakia, the Yugoslavs carried out a major program of modernization of their defense system. The National Defense Law of 1969 and the Yugoslav party program of 1969 provided the charters for this program.[73]

The 1969 reforms organized the armed forces of Yugoslavia into two main components: the 260,000 elite forces of the Yugoslav Peoples Army plus reserves and the 1,000,000 members of the Territorial Defense Forces (TDF).[74] The 1969 reforms also provided for a separate system of youth training formations and civil defense units. The TDF are organized at the larger factories, in urban and rural communes (municipalities) and at the level of the federal republics within Yugoslavia. Permanent staffs at the communal and republican levels supervise the training of the TDF, whose members drill for about 100 hours a year under the command of reserve officers of the YPA.[75]

Belgrade's doctrine of General People's Defense is based on the assumption that there is virtually no chance of a nuclear attack on Yugoslavia.

Major General Dusan Dozet argues that nuclear strikes would prove of little value against the dispersed forces of the Yugoslav defense system.[76] Yugoslav doctrine is also based on the assumption that none of its neighbors is likely to launch an attack on Yugoslavia except as part of an attack by either NATO or the Warsaw Pact. Colonel General Savo Drljevic writes that of Yugoslavia's neighbors, only Bulgaria would even consider an attack on Yugoslav territory (no doubt, on the Macedonian republic of Yugoslavia) and that Bulgaria would undertake such an action only as part of a general European war. In such circumstances, according to Drljevic, neither European military alliance would commit its major forces to Yugoslavia. And even in the event of a general European war, writes Drljevic, "there is only the slightest of possibilities, if any at all, of this kind of local aggression actually taking place."[77] In his view, the only real possibility of attack against Yugoslavia is ". . . an aggression by one or the other bloc as a whole, i.e., an aggression involving the main power, too."[78] In Drljevic's view, the objective of such an attack would not be to secure Yugoslavia as a base for further military operations but to replace the existing government with a collaborationist regime.[79] The 1963 Yugoslav Constitution attempts to deny the aggressor the legal basis for installation of a collaborationist regime. Article 254 reads:

> No one shall have the right to sign or acknowledge the capitulation or occupation of the country on behalf of the Socialist Federal Republic of Yugoslavia.
>
> Any such act is unconstitutional and punishable.[80]

Yugoslav military analysts write that the probable enemy would carry out blitzkrieg assaults on major political, economic, and communications centers and attempt to seal off the borders of the country.[81] According to Ross Johnson, an American analyst, in their 1971 maneuvers, the Yugoslav armed forces practiced defense against a large force of mechanized infantry, tanks and airborne troops coming from the Hungarian border which simulated the seizure of Zagreb and other key points in Croatia. Johnson also notes that the Yugoslavs have also conducted exercises to defend the Adriatic coast against naval and airborne landings.[82]

According to Yugoslav military planners, the regular army faces its supreme test during the first few hours of the intervention: that of delaying the occupation of the country's major cities long enough to permit the mobilization of the Territorial Defense Forces. Once the TDF have been mobilized, they are to engage in a prolonged resistance struggle coordinated with the regular army units, which will operate from the central mountain regions of Yugoslavia. The Yugoslavs have developed a highly-flexible command structure which permits the assignment of both YPA and TDF forces to commands at the national, republic, and communal levels. The TDF are responsible for a wide range of missions: combat in conjunction with units of the YPA; independent combat actions; terrorist reprisals against the occupation forces; signal, reconnaissance, and intelligence missions; and protection of civilians and industrial installations. To the extent feasible, the members of the TDF are expected to conduct their normal economic functions when not committed to military actions.[83]

According to Ross Johnson, the Yugoslavs expect the occupation forces to number about two million soldiers.[84] Yugoslav officers claim that their strategy of General People's Defense will be able to mobilize three to four million people in the YPA and TDF and that these forces will be able to wear down any likely enemy force over an extended period of time. They write that their own experience of 1941–45 and the experience of other armies which have waged wars of national liberation have demonstrated that a well-organized resistance movement based on nationalist appeals to the entire population can deny an aggressor effective use of his superior conventional forces. This strategy requires eliminating the differences between civilians and soldiers and between front and rear areas.[85] It requires that the resistance forces constantly attack the occupation forces and prevent the aggressor from going on the offensive. The Yugoslavs claim that in these circumstances the enemy will be unable to concentrate firepower on the regular army and will be forced to disperse their troops among a hostile population trained to execute guerrilla actions.[86]

The first objective of General People's Defense is not victory but deterrence. Colonel General Ljubicic claims that "the readiness to resist determinedly is the most important obstacle to anyone's plans of conquest."[87] Colonel Gabelic adds:

> It is safe to say that a potential aggressor, no matter what his intentions, would not easily decide to infringe upon the freedom and independence of a country if he knew that such a country would put up a tenacious resistance and involve him in a long and exhausting war and also inevitably involve him in a staggering burden of international complications.[88]

The Yugoslavs also use their strategy of General People's Defense to provide a military basis for a nonaligned foreign policy. Major General Dozet argues that no state can hope to pursue an independent foreign policy without an independent capability for national defense. He writes:

> The small and medium-sized countries are the lasting objects of intensive pressures, intervention and aggression, this applying equally to the non-aligned and bloc-aligned countries.

> They are not in a position to achieve security in a bloc mechanism or under its protection.
>
> Security can be achieved only by their relying on their own forces and fighting for international relations on the principles of independence, sovereignty, equality and non-interference in the affairs of other countries.[89]

Yugoslav officers argue that because the strategy of General People's Defense precludes the development of Yugoslav offensive capabilities this strategy makes Yugoslavia a potential ally rather than potential adversary of each of its neighbors. Colonel General Lekic pushes this argument to its logical limit by arguing that "a world organized into a system of General People's Defense would strengthen the dam against militarism and decrease the danger of invasion and military pressure."[90]

The area of the world to which the Yugoslav defense ministry has been most anxious to export its conception of General People's Defense is the world immediately adjacent to Yugoslavia's borders, particularly its northern and eastern borders. Yugoslav discourses on General People's Defense are more or less open critiques of the military-political mechanisms of the Warsaw Treaty Organization. Colonel Gabelic argues that the small and medium-sized members of NATO and the WTO forfeit the possibility of organizing defense systems based on the concepts of General People's Defense. He maintains that each alliance requires its members to prepare for a coalition war fought by elite regular formations equipped with highly complex and extremely expensive weaponry. The military-technical requirements of each alliance make the national defense ministries of the smaller states dependent on the defense ministry of the dominant member of the alliance for doctrine, technology, and command facilities. He writes:

> The crux of the matter is that a bloc military mechanism comprises national units of unequal power. This inequality is all the more pronounced for the fact that those forces basically begin and end with the operational army and do not extend into the system of nationwide defense.
>
> Under such conditions, the logic of military power pursues its own laws, reflected, axiomatically, in the fact that, given the existing political relations, the stronger dominates and imposes on the others his solutions, his command, his doctrines, etc.
>
> Beyond doubt, the aforementioned logic explains why Norway, Romania and France—countries belonging to blocs but pursuing independent or rather more independent policies—have chosen to develop defensive systems on a broad popular basis.[91]

In the early 1960s, two of the Warsaw Pact states on Yugoslavia's borders, Albania and Romania, began to refine their own systems of territorial defense. Albania remained a loyal member of the Warsaw Pact until 1961 and was a formal member until 1968. The Albanian defense system developed out of the Albanian experience in organizing a war of national liberation against the Italians during World War II. The Albanian system also appears to have developed in part because of the absence of effective Soviet measures to draw the Albanian armed forces into WTO before Marshal Grechko introduced such measures in 1961–62.

As Colonel Gabelic observed, Romania developed a system of territorial defense to support its independent position within the WTO. The available evidence suggests that the Romanians have consciously imported the major concepts of General People's Defense for the purpose of deterring a Soviet intervention aimed at the installation of a pro-Soviet faction of the Romanian Communist Party.

The Romanian Doctrine of War of the Entire People

In 1968, the leader of the Romanian Communist Party demonstrated that his defense ministry had acquired the capability to mobilize for a war of territorial defense. The day after the Soviet invasion of Czechoslovakia President Ceausescu convened a mass meeting in Bucharest at which he declared:

> It has been said that in Czechoslovakia there was a danger of counterrevolution.
>
> Perhaps tomorrow they will say that our meeting has mirrored counterrevolutionary tendencies. . . .
>
> If so, we answer to all that the Romanian people will not permit anyone to violate the territory of our fatherland . . . be ready, comrades, at any moment to defend our Socialist Fatherland, Romania.[92]

Ceausescu then mobilized the components of his territorial defense system: the 520,000 troops of his regular armed forces, including active reserves, and the 700,000 members of the Patriotic Guard, a force closely resembling the Territorial Defense Forces of Yugoslavia.[93]

It is not clear at what point before 1968 Romania had acquired a territorial defense capability sufficiently developed for Ceausescu to mobilize it as a demonstration of Romania's intention to resist a Soviet intervention. Romanian military historians claim that their defense system has its medieval origins in the campaigns of Romanian Prince Vlad the Impaler against the Ottoman Turks and its twentieth-century origins in the territorial defense plans of the pre-World War II Romanian General Staff.[94]

The available evidence suggests that Gheorghe Gheorghiu-Dej, Ceausescu's predecessor, made a decision sometime between 1959 and 1964 to begin deployment of a territorial defense system. The precondition for the development of this defense posture was Khrushchev's decision to withdraw Soviet troops from Romania in 1958. In his study of Gheorghiu-Dej's achievement of independence from the Soviet Union, Stephen Fischer-Galati argues that the Romanian leader used Chinese support to persuade Khrushchev to withdraw his military forces. According to Fischer-Galati, the Romanians supported their arguments by embracing the Chinese views that each socialist state should rely on its own forces for the defense of national territory and on the Soviet nuclear arsenal to deter the West from using atomic weapons against the non-nuclear socialist states.[95]

In his analysis of the Soviet troop withdrawal from Romania, Jacques Levesque does not find conclusive evidence of Chinese influence on the Soviet decision. Levesque suggests that Gheorghiu-Dej probably persuaded Khrushchev that Soviet troop withdrawals in southeastern Europe would invest the local Communist regimes with greater domestic legitimacy and help defuse the popular resentments that had exploded in Hungary. In support of this argument, Levesque notes that in 1958 Khrushchev also withdrew one Soviet division from Hungary.[96] In informal conversations,[97] some Romanian officials have said that Gheorghiu-Dej based his arguments for the Soviet troop withdrawal on the terms of the 1955 Austrian State Treaty.

Later chapters of this study document the disengagement during the early 1960s of the Romanian armed forces from certain Warsaw Pact control mechanisms which collectively bind the armed forces of the East European states to the Soviet defense ministry. In 1960 or 1961, the Romanians ceased sending officers to study in Soviet military academies. In these academies, other East European officers pursued curricula designed to prepare them for the command of national troops in joint Warsaw Pact missions. The curriculum of officer education in Romania appears to have focused exclusively on the defense of national territory by national means.[98] In 1962 and 1963 the Romanians permitted the conduct of joint WTO maneuvers on Romanian territory, but as of 1964 the Romanians no longer allowed such exercises. The Romanians also refused to send any but token forces to WTO exercises outside Romania.[99] This policy made it more difficult for Soviet forces to train for the occupation of Romania and also freed the Romanian command from having to subordinate national strategy to joint WTO missions. In 1964, the Romanians replaced their Main Political Administration with a system of party committees in the military which closely resembled the system of party committees in the Yugoslav armed forces. This decision appears to have severed the links between the Soviet Main Political Administration and the Romanian army and to have prevented the synchronization of political indoctrination in the Romanian military with political indoctrination in the armed forces of the other WTO states.[100]

In 1964, the Romanian Central Committee also issued its statement on the world Communist movement, a statement that constituted a declaration of Romanian independence from the Soviet Union. In one section of this declaration the Romanians proclaimed an objective that has since become a permanent feature of Romanian foreign policy: the call for incremental steps leading to the simultaneous abolition of both NATO and the WTO. The 1964 declaration of the Central Committee stated: "We stand for the abolition of all military blocs and, as a transitional measure in this direction, we declare ourselves in favor of a non-aggression pact between the Warsaw Treaty Organization and the North Atlantic Treaty Organization."[101] The Romanian declaration also called for the conclusion of a peace treaty with Germany and for the designation of the Balkans as a nuclear-free zone.[102] These proposals testified to a Romanian desire to establish the military-political basis for a non-aligned foreign policy and an independent national defense system.

Like the Yugoslavs, the Romanians responded to the Soviet intervention in Czechoslovakia by modernizing their territorial defense system. The charter of the current Romanian system of "War of the Entire People" is the 1972 Defense Law.[103] Romanian military writing specifically cites the Yugoslav experience in World War II and the current Yugoslav system as a demonstration of the practical possibility for a medium-sized Balkan state to wage a war of national liberation against the army of a much larger state.[104] The Romanians have published more detailed information on the Romanian system of "War of the Entire People" than the Yugoslavs have on their system of "General People's Defense." The Romanian leaders may have concluded that foreign scepticism about the combat qualities of pre-Communist Romanian armies, and perhaps domestic scepticism as well, requires public evidence of the thoroughness of Romanian preparations for a war of national liberation. In any case, the publication of information on the components of the Romanian defense system is compatible with the Romanian objective of deterring a potential aggressor.

Romanian military writers all but openly identify the political objective of the probable enemy as the installation of a pro-Soviet faction of the Romanian Communist Party. In an article on the organization of resistance to the occupation of Romania, Colonel Gheorghe Stanculescu declares that the practical objective of the Romanian strategy of "War of the Entire People" is "to prevent the aggressor from establishing a new administration on the occupied territory and from forming a puppet government with whose help it legalizes the aggression and seeks to justify the character of the war unleashed by pretending it is an action 'in support' of a so-called 'legal government.' "[105]

The Romanian Defense Law of 1972, like the Yugoslav Constitution of 1963, seeks to remove the legal basis for collaboration between Romanian citizens and an occupation force. Article 1 of the 1972 law declares:

> It is forbidden to accept or recognize any action of any foreign state or any situation regardless of its nature, including the general capitulation or occupation of the national territory, which in times of peace or war, would infringe upon the national sovereignty, independence and territorial integrity of the Socialist Republic of Romania. . . .
>
> Any such act of acceptance or recognition is null and void as being contrary to the state regime and the supreme interests of the socialist state.[106]

Romanian military analysts argue that an aggressor seeking to install a puppet regime would probably not resort to the use of nuclear weapons, because the use of such weapons would not contribute to the attainment of the political objective of the war and might risk the escalation of the conflict into a general war.[107] Like the Yugoslavs, the Romanians expect their probable enemy to carry out a massive attack employing ground forces, airborne troops and naval forces. The Romanians expect the enemy forces to seize the country's principal administrative, economic, and communications centers, to cut off naval access to the outside world via the Black Sea and the Danube River, to seal off Romania's land borders, and to attack the Carpathian mountain strongholds of Romania's operational army.[108] The primary objective of the regular military forces of Romania during the enemy attack is to slow the enemy advance sufficiently to permit mobilization of the Patriotic Guards so that the war will enter a second stage of nationwide resistance to the occupation. According to Colonel Cernat, the objective of the resistance effort is "prevention of the aggressor's attempt to set up a puppet regime."[109] Cernat writes that pursuit of this objective has four elements:

> 1. Prevention of attempts "to colonize with foreign populations." Cernat may be referring to Moldavians from the Moldavian Soviet Socialist Republic and to Hungarians, who might be sent to the predominantly Hungarian region of Transylvania. The Soviets regard the Moldavians as a distinct nationality, which happens to use Romanian as its native language. The Romanians regard Moldavians as Romanians living in the lost province of Soviet Moldavia.

2. Defense of the population against repressive measures by the occupation regime.

3. Prevention of attempts by the aggressor to mobilize the national labor force to serve the occupation regime and prevention of attempts by the aggressor to deport skilled laborers and other personnel to foreign countries in order to deny their services to the resistance movement.

4. Protection of economic facilities from destruction by the occupation forces.[110]

According to calculations by the Romanian defense ministry, the history of past wars suggests that to occupy Romania an aggressor would have to deploy 700,000 troops (on the basis of three soldiers per square kilometer) to 1,000,000 troops (on the basis of five soldiers per 100 inhabitants). Colonel Cerant claims that an occupation force ranging between 700,000 and 1,000,000 soldiers "is difficult to maintain over a long period even for big powers."[111] Colonel Grozea adds that recent military history has demonstrated that a modern industrial state can muster only six to twelve percent of its population for military service as regular cadre personnel. A state relying on paramilitary personnel to conduct a war of territorial defense can, according to Grozea, mobilize 23–32 percent of the entire population for military service in one form or another. In Romania, mobilization of 23–32 percent of the population would produce regular and paramilitary forces numbering between 4,680,000 and 6,245,000. Colonel Grozea concludes, ". . . despite the difference in technical equipment that might exist between them and the aggressive army, such a number of defenders would be a powerful force, capable of successfully defending this country."[112]

According to Romanian doctrine, the resistance movement against the occupation will take place through both armed and unarmed actions. The unarmed actions, conducted mainly in the urban centers, will consist of (1) "disobedience" to the occupation authorities, including those collaborating with the enemy; (2) "protests"—organized public actions directed against specific measures introduced by the occupation authorities; (3) "demonstrations" in favor of certain objectives such as the release of prisoners by the occupation authorities; (4) "strikes" to prevent the use of national economic facilities by the occupation regime; and (5) "sabotage" of the economic and administrative facilities required by the occupation regime.[113]

The goal of the armed resistance is to force the occupier to disperse its forces so widely that it loses effective use of its superiority in regular armed forces. The Romanians hope to force the dispersal of enemy troops by engaging in constant offensive actions against the enemy such as (1) "ambush" of smaller enemy units; (2) "incursions" against command and control centers; (3) "raids" against economic and transport facilities; (4) "harassment"—that is, terrorism directed against rank-and-file enemy soldiers for the purpose of undermining their morale.[114]

The Romanians expect that dispersal of enemy forces outside the major urban occupation zones will divide the rest of the country into small occupation zones and small "free zones" controlled by the resistance movement.[115] If the Romanian military and paramilitary forces can succeed in forcing the enemy to disperse its forces, the struggle will, according to Romanian theorists, shift from a military conflict in which the enemy enjoys superiority to a political conflict in which the defenders will enjoy superiority. Colonel Stanculescu explains:

> Territorial dispersion is based on the identification of the forces and actions of the resistance movement with the mass of the civilian population.
>
> This identification . . . has a powerful moral effect on the enemy, makes him feel insecure and restless, and undermines the basis of his propaganda and his ideological and psychological influence.
>
> Seeing that every citizen is a potential fighter for national independence and sovereignty, sensing the manifest and continuous hostility of the population, suffering losses at the strokes of the armed resistance forces, the enemy troops will intuit, at least in part, the frailty of the political and military goals of the invasion and the unjustness of the cause they actually represent.[116]

Colonel Cernat writes that if the Romanians succeed in achieving a stalemate in their struggle with the enemy for political control of the country, they may be able to negotiate the withdrawal of enemy forces.[117] If the political stalemate does not lead to a negotiated troop withdrawal, Cernat sees the possibility of the initiation of a third stage of the war in which the Romanians will launch offensive actions aimed at forcing the retreat of enemy troops from Romanian territory.[118] Cernat and his colleagues believe that either the negotiated withdrawal or the forced withdrawal of enemy troops will be the result of the interaction of three factors: (1) the achievement of a political stalemate between the occupation regime and the Romanian resistance movement; (2) international diplomatic support for the Romanian resistance movement; (3) internal political upheavals among the soldiers and civilians of the enemy. Colonel Grozea predicts the following developments:

> When the duration of the war is longer than the aggressor expected, a situation is created whose consequences are unfavorable to him.

The gradual reduction in the intensity of his blows, the lower rhythm of his actions and the delays caused by the large-scale participation of the masses of the people in the defensive struggle thwart the intentions of the aggressor to present the world with a "fait accompli."

In the present international circumstances . . . any aggression produces external and even internal consequences which are a disadvantage for the aggressor.

The demands for the observance of international law and order can no longer be ignored by any state, and every violation of this demand has its impact on overall inter-state relations, leading to political attitudes and actions condemning aggressions. . . .

Any aggression which becomes a lengthy armed conflict might also create internal complications for the enemy, in the form of upheavals in the ranks of his own armies and population.[119]

Components of the Romanian Defense System

In arguing the practicality of their military doctrine Romanian officers emphasize that mere enunciation of the principles of guerrilla warfare is not enough to conduct a successful campaign. Colonel Cernat cautions that "an enemy who is superior in numbers cannot be defeated in battle by intellect alone."[120] Colonel Arsintescu notes that many wars of national liberation have been lost because the defenders lacked the necessary training, equipment, and logistical support.[121]

Romanian military theorists claim that their country has the economic base, command structures, trained forces, and logistical network to sustain a "War of the Entire People." The State Planning Committee maintains an on-going program to plan for military production during the first year of a war of national liberation.[122] The seriousness of the Romanian planning effort may be indicated by the 1976 appointment of Ion Ionitse, the former defense minister, as the minister in charge of the national armament industry.[123] The Romanians claim that they have developed the industrial infrastructure to manufacture the small arms necessary for conducting a war of territorial defense.[124] According to Alex Alexiev, an analyst for the RAND Corporation, since the mid 1960s the Romanians have been steadily increasing the proportion of national income devoted to military spending.[125] Alexiev notes that the Romanians and Yugoslavs jointly manufacture a jet interceptor outfitted with British engines. He also notes that the Romanians have purchased French helicopters and Chinese naval vessels suitable for use on the Danube.[126] In departing from their policy of self-sufficiency in armament production, the Romanians may have decided that the difficulties of procuring spare parts during wartime are offset by the diplomatic advantages of having Yugoslav, French, and Chinese suppliers. Romania also uses some Soviet weapons, including tanks, artillery pieces and small rockets.[127] It may be that the Romanians do not expect to be cut off from their Soviet suppliers during a war: Romanian doctrine calls for training military personnel to use weapons captured from the enemy.[128]

The Romanians have entrusted the conduct of a "War of the Entire People" to the State Defense Council. Its chairman is Nicolae Ceausescu in his capacities as supreme commander of the Armed Forces, president of the Republic, and first secretary of the Central Committee. The other members of the Defense Council are the minister of defense, the chief of staff of the Patriotic Guards, the secretary of the Higher Political Council of the Armed Forces, the minister of the interior, the chairman of the State Planning Commission and the minister of foreign affairs. The State Defense Council has control over all military, paramilitary, political, and economic bureaucracies. Under the Defense Council are corresponding defense councils at the county, city and town levels. The city of Bucharest has four subcouncils under its main defense council. Each of the regional councils consists of the regional commander of the regular armed forces, the chief of staff of the regional Patriotic Guard, and the heads of local party, government and economic agencies. The chairman of each local defense council is the head of the corresponding party organization.[129]

According to Romanian doctrine, the regular and paramilitary forces of the country can be assigned either to the national, county, or municipal defense councils, depending on the necessities of military action. The importance of the defense councils may be indicated by the appointment in 1976 of Lieutenant General Dinca as first secretary of the Bucharest party committee and head of the Bucharest People's Council, the city government.[130] As head of the party and government agencies in Bucharest, Dinca is ex officio chairman of the Bucharest Defense Council. Prior to his appointment of 1976, Dinca had served as the Chairman of the Higher Political Council of the Armed Forces, the highest party agency in the military. Dinca's deputy in the Bucharest party and government organizations is the former chief of the Romanian General Staff, Colonel General Ion Gheorghe.[131]

The principal military components of the national defense system are the regular armed forces and the Patriotic Guards. The armed forces consist of the ground forces, the air force, the air defense force and the navy. The ground forces have 145,000 peacetime personnel and 300,000 reserves.[132] The main element of the ground forces is the infantry, which is outfitted with light-weight antitank weapons and mechanized transport equipment. The infantry is trained to be a highly mobile force capable of fighting in every region of the country, either in independent small units or in combined operations with other formations.[133] The mission of infantry units is to surprise and attack enemy forces "superior in numbers and equipment."[134] The antitank troops and the artillery troops of the ground forces appear to share the mission of destroying enemy tanks.[135] The engineering troops have the missions of demolition and camouflage.[136] A special branch of the infantry, the mountain corps, has the separate mission of "firm maintenance of natural strongholds in the mountainous regions." According to Romanian doctrine, these regions must be held "at all costs."[137] The Carpathian mountains, which make up about 30 percent of the area of Romania, serve as the base for the regular armed forces assigned to take constant offensive actions against the occupation troops.[138]

The small air defense force and air force are both assigned missions of interdicting enemy air power, although the air force has a separate reconnaissance and transport mission as well.[139] The Romanians have assigned their navy two missions: that of mining the coastal areas of the Black Sea and that of keeping the Danube open for river convoys,[140] which could have only one possible destination: Yugoslavia. Romanian doctrine requires that all military personnel, whatever their specialty, be trained to carry out highly mobile infantry actions.[141]

An additional mission of the regular armed forces is to provide military training to the rest of the population, either through service directly in the armed forces or through service in paramilitary organizations trained by regular officers and reserve officers.[142] The most important of paramilitary organizations is the Patriotic Guard, which in peacetime numbers about 700,000.[143] The Patriotic Guards consist of men aged 21-60 and women aged 21-55, who volunteer for service. Detachments of Patriotic Guards are formed at the larger state factories and public enterprises. Each village, town, and city also raises its own formations of Patriotic Guards. The Patriotic Guards have full-time staffs at each of their administrative levels. The members of the Guard are trained for actions in platoons, companies, and battalions to use the following weapons: submachine guns, mortars, demolition devices, antitank weapons, antiaircraft weapons, and flame throwers. Detachments of the Patriotic Guards are also trained for signal, reconnaissance, transport, and medical missions. The members of the Patriotic Guard are expected to perform their normal economic functions to the extent possible during wartime, but are also to be available for combat in regions outside their own locality.[144]

The Youth Defense Training Formations consist of youths aged 16-20 who drill under the command of noncommissioned reserve officers for service either in the Patriotic Guards or the regular armed forces. In the event of war, the Youth Formations are to function as auxiliaries to the Patriotic Guard. Additional paramilitary formations include the air-defense units, fire-fighting units, and medical units.[145] The units of the ministry of the interior have been assigned the special mission of assassinating collaborators and enemy commanders. The 20,000 troops of the interior ministry are also responsible for providing security for the personnel of the defense councils and for enforcing the directives of the defense councils.[146]

The unanswered question about any national plan for territorial defense is whether the population as a whole will be willing to make the colossal sacrifices necessary to fight a war of national liberation. Colonel Stanculescu acknowledges that "the role of morale is the major problem of the resistance movement."[147] The Romanians plan to find the source of morale in nationalism—a nationalism that has an implicitly anti-Russian focus. The Romanians seek to cultivate nationalism through the entire ideological and educational apparatus of the state and in particular through patriotic indoctrination in the Youth Defense Training Formations, the Patriotic Guard, and the regular armed forces.[148] The texts for patriotic education include carefully selected histories of Romanian military traditions.[149] Romanian military theorists believe that the morale of their compatriots will be inversely related to the morale of the enemy soldiers. They expect that if the Romanian people demonstrate their determination to resist at any cost, enemy morale will deteriorate over the course of a long war. Colonel Arsintescu claims:

> The mass of the people cannot be mobilized for participation with all its forces in an unjust war of aggression and occupation against other peoples.
>
> As a rule, they do not accept for a long time the privation and sacrifices demanded by a war whose aims are alien or opposed to their own interests and do not willingly make the efforts implicit in an armed clash.[150]

Other East European Strategies of Territorial Defense: Albania, Poland and Czechoslovakia

Albania, a Communist state that remained a formal member of the Warsaw Pact until 1968, openly embraced a doctrine of territorial defense in the early 1960s. This doctrine was a revival of the military concepts the Albanian leaders had developed while waging a war of national liberation against the Italians during World War II. The history of the Soviet

Albanian dispute may offer some additional support for the argument that deployment of a territorial defense system is a military prerequisite for an East European state seeking political autonomy from the Soviet Union.

In his study of the Soviet-Albanian conflict, William Griffith offers three reasons why Hoxha escaped a Soviet military intervention: (1) the geographic isolation of Albania from the Soviet Union ". . .which makes impossible intervention by the Red Army as in Hungary"; (2) support by China; and (3) ". . . the unity of the Albanian Communist leadership and . . . the inability of Moscow to infiltrate, factionalize and create a pro-- Soviet majority in it."[151] The available evidence indicates that the Albanian leaders consciously added to these deterrents a national defense system for fighting a war of national liberation. At the very least, Albania's defense system is politically appropriate for a tiny country seeking to pursue a fully-independent foreign policy. If the Albanian case is too exotic to confirm the argument that an East European party leader seeking independence from the Soviet Union must be prepared to conduct a war of territorial defense against the Soviet army, the Albanian case at least does not contradict the argument.

In some ways, Albania has the best claim of any East European state to have demonstrated the practicality of a strategy of territorial defense against a larger and better-equipped occupation army. Hoxha's is the only East European Communist regime that did not require the actual presence of Soviet troops to secure the final liberation of its country from foreign occupation. In the period from 1948 to 1960 the Albanian defense ministry turned to the Soviet Union for weapons and for advanced training of Albanian officers,[152] but the Albanians appear to have been mainly interested in Soviet doctrine on mountain warfare.[153]

Following the break with the Soviets, the Albanian leader, Mehmet Shehu reaffirmed the contemporary relevance of the experience of the Albanian national liberation war as the basis for the organization of national defense.[154] After 1962, the Albanians substituted Chinese weaponry for Soviet weaponry in their arsenals.[155] In his study of Albania, Peter Prifti notes that after the Soviet intervention in Czechoslovakia, Hoxha formally withdrew from the Warsaw Pact, increased defense spending considerably, and obtained additional military aid from the Chinese.[156] Prifti suggests that one reason for the purge of Defense Minister Bequir Ballaku and other officers in 1974 may have been the possibility that they had wished to place greater emphasis on preparation for a conventional war rather than for a war of territorial defense. Prifti cautions, however, that Ballaku may have been engaged in a complex power struggle against Hoxha which involved debates over a wide range of military and political policies.[157] In 1961, Hoxha indicated that he viewed the capability of his army for a war of territorial defense as one of the factors aiding him in his efforts to resist Khrushchev's efforts to over-throw him. A few days after Khrushchev had called for Hoxha's removal in October 1961, the Albanian leader publically declared, "Our glorious armed forces are in full form and are prepared militarily to defend the Albanian People's Republic successfully and give a worthy rebuff to any enemy rash enough to violate the sacred frontiers of our beloved socialist fatherland."[158] The Albanian press later complained that just prior to the break of 1961, the Soviet embassy in Tirana had tried to organize against Hoxha "the army cadres and other cadres who had studied in the Soviet Union. . . ."[159] As part of Albania's declaration of independence, the Albanians ceased sending officers to study in the Soviet Union, expelled Soviet military advisers from Tirana, and ordered the Soviets to abandon their naval base in the Albanian port of Vlore.[160]

At the very least, the revival of a strategy of territorial defense after 1961 cut off channels of Soviet influence over the Albanian armed forces and provided a symbolic support for Albania's declaration of independ-ence from the Soviet Union. At most, Hoxha may have relied on his capability for waging a war of national liberation as one of several inter-related factors that deterred intervention by the Soviet Union.

A "Polish Front" Within the Warsaw Pact?

There is some evidence which suggests that after Gomulka's assertion of independence against the Soviet Union in October 1956, certain offi-cers in the Polish armed forces began to consider the adoption of a terri-torial defense system. A former Polish intelligence officer, who emigrated to the West, has written that in the late 1950s General Zygmunt Dusynski headed a group of high-ranking Polish officers who attempted to draw up plans for establishing within the Warsaw Pact "a separate, compact, well-defined 'Polish Front' intended as an exclusive theater of operations for the Polish armed forces. . . ." According to this account, Dusynski's plans called for the formulation of a specifically Polish military doctrine, a Polish national defense system and an independent Polish armament industry.[161]

During 1957 and 1958, Gomulka's foreign minister, Adam Rapacki, advanced a series of proposals which might have established the military-political basis for a "Polish Front" manned exclusively by Polish soldiers. The Rapacki Plan of 1957 called for the creation of a nuclear-free zone in Central Europe. In 1958, Rapacki also proposed limited withdrawals of foreign troops from the two Germanies and Poland.[162] The adoption of

Rapacki's proposals might have resulted in the disengagement of Polish troops from any Soviet plans for the conduct of nuclear war by the allied armies of the Warsaw Treaty Organization. Rapacki's proposals might also have enabled the Polish defense ministry to define its mission as solely that of the defense of Polish territory. According to Hansjakob Shehle, the Soviets were not in favor of the Rapacki Plan.[163] But the United States and West Germany did not respond favorably to the Rapacki proposals and never explored the possibility of Soviet-Polish differences on the questions of a nuclear-free zone in Central Europe. A later chapter in this study argues that the Warsaw Pact exercises initiated by Marshal Grechko in 1961–62 permanently drew Poland into WTO plans for the conduct of joint offensive actions using nuclear weapons. The same chapter also suggests that the system of joint WTO exercises removed the military basis for Poland's political autonomy.

There is clear evidence that several high-ranking political officers of the Czechoslovak People's Army in 1968 attempted to formulate the military-political concepts on which to base an independent Czechoslovak military doctrine. The proposals for a new doctrine came from the Klement Gottwald Military-Political Academy in Prague. A Czech commentator who wrote after the removal of Alexander Dubcek from power identified the Gottwald Academy as "the principal base for the working out of a new military policy of the party and state."[164]

The Gottwald Memorandum

Shortly after the Czechoslovak Central Committee had adopted its "Action Program" in mid-April 1968, Colonel Vojtech Mencl, the rector of the Gottwald Academy, Lieutenant Colonel Borivoj Svarc, a department head at the Academy, and several faculty members wrote a critique of Czechoslovakia's national defense system. In a signed document, they complained of the "twenty-year long distorted development of our army." These officers wrote that Czechoslovakia's military strategy in 1968 was "devoid of rational criteria."[165] According to a Czechoslovak officer who analyzed this document for the pro-Soviet regime of Gustav Husak, Colonel Mencl's memorandum tried to prove that Czechoslovak military policy was "dictated by outside interests, the interests and requirements of the Warsaw alliance. So these policies were supposed to be dictated by the interests of the Soviet Union."[166]

By the end of April, the officers of the Gottwald Academy had produced a 100-page document entitled "On the Action Program of the Czechoslovak Peoples' Army." This document proposed five possible military strategies for Czechoslovakia:

1. [acting] within the framework of the Warsaw Pact, but with imminent prospects of its bilateral or unilateral abolition;

2. Safeguarding the security of the state within the framework of its territory or of neutral policies.

3. Initiating proposals for disarmament measures;

4. The creation of conditions that will ensure security in Europe by means of a European regional collective security organization.

5. Contingent planning for self-defense relying on own means.[167]

In early May, the Gottwald Academy drafted a shorter, ten-page document that reduced the five options to three. This document, which became known as the "Gottwald Memorandum" identified the three as:

1. The coalition principle (the alliance with the Soviet Union and the other states of the Warsaw Pact on which our defense system is currently based) is subject to development and it is necessary to reconsider its validity in the coming 10 to 15 years;

2. It is possible to think about coordinated defense in Central Europe without the military potential of the USSR (some kind of military analog to the political Little Entente "in socialist form" or some kind of collective security organization without a class determination;

3. The possibility of neutralizing one's territory or pursuing a policy of neutrality relying on one's own means of defense.[168]

The third option identified by the Gottwald Memorandum, that of proclaiming Czechoslovakia's neutrality and of relying on "one's own means of defense," is the military-political basis of Yugoslavia's defense system. The second option suggested a collective security organization made up of two possible sets of allies: (1) a group of Communist and non-Communist central European states; and (2) a group of states constituting "a military analog to the Little Entente 'in a socialist form.'" The members of the Little Entente, a military alliance of the 1930s, were Czechoslovakia, Romania, and Yugoslavia. The Gottwald Memorandum, in its first option, specifically called for reconsideration of the validity of Czechoslovakia's continued membership in the Warsaw Treaty Organization. One of the commentators of the postinvasion Husak era was probably correct in concluding that the Gottwald Memorandum advocated Czechoslovakia's de facto withdrawal from participation in the WTO.[169]

Colonel Mencl sent copies of the Gottwald Memorandum to the first secretary of the party, the president of the republic, the chairman of the council of ministers, the foreign minister and other high-ranking officials.[170] Within a week of the drafting of the Memorandum, Marshal

Iakubovskii, the Soviet commander of the Warsaw Pact, was in Prague to request assurances of Czechoslovakia's loyalty to the WTO. Within six weeks, Soviet troops were in Czechoslovakia on maneuvers. These exercises, which involved WTO troops in Czechoslovakia, Hungary, Poland, and the USSR, took place under the direct command of Marshal Iakubovskii.[171] On July 2, shortly after the completion of the June WTO maneuvers in Czechoslovakia and shortly before the final round of the election of delegates to the Extraordinary Fourteenth Congress of the Czechoslovak party, *Lidova Armada,* the Czechoslovak army newspaper, published the complete text of the Gottwald Memorandum. According to one of the postinvasion critics of the Memorandum, the publication of this document in *Lidova Armada* constituted a declaration of "the program of the rightists in the army." This critic added, "The rightists intended to force this program through the Fourteenth Congress of the party."[172]

In mid July, Lieutenant General Vaclav Prchlik, who had been promoted in June from his post as chief of the Czechoslovak Main Political Administration to head of the Central Committee department in charge of the military and security agencies of the state, publicly advocated the reformulation of Czechoslovakia's military doctrine. According to a commentator of the Husak era, Prchlik relied on aides who came from the Gottwald Academy.[173] On July 15, Lieutenant General Prchlik held a press conference at which he presented a critique of Czechoslovakia's military and security policies very similar to the critique made by the Gottwald Memorandum.[174] Prchlik went on to outline in detail the "necessary conditions for working out a Czechoslovak military doctrine."[175]

Prchlik proposed that the forthcoming Party Congress adopt a resolution requiring the revision of Czechoslovakia's military doctrine. He also proposed that the specific details of the new doctrine be worked out by the new Central Committee to be elected at the Party Congress and by the new National Assembly to be elected in late 1968. He further proposed that these two bodies establish a State Defense Council to supervise the implementation of the new doctrine.[176] He may have had in mind a body similar to Romania's State Defense Council not only in name but in purpose.

Prchlik also made proposals for the improvement of the command structure of the Warsaw Pact: "strengthening the role of the Political Consultative Committee," giving each member state "genuine equality" in the alliance, and creating "clear guarantees . . . preventing fractionalist activities . . . which . . . would lead in the last analysis to violating the basic items of the Pact, particularly the items concerning the state sovereignty of members."[177] At no point, in either his prepared remarks or in his answers to questions, did Prchlik suggest that his plans for the reformulation of Czechoslovak military doctrine would depend on organizational changes within the Warsaw Treaty Organization. As *Krasnaia Zvezda,* the Soviet army newspaper later charged, Prchlik discussed the possibility of organizational changes within the WTO in order to adopt a false pose of loyalty to the Warsaw Pact.[178] Dubcek responded to Soviet criticisms of General Prchlik's proposals by abolishing the Central Committee department which Prchlik headed, but he reinstated Prchlik as chief of the Czechoslovak Main Political Administration. There is no evidence, however, that Dubcek ever gave serious consideration to the proposals of the Gottwald Memorandum or of General Prchlik's press conference. On the night of the Warsaw Pact intervention, he ordered Czechoslovakia's troops to remain in their barracks.[179]

The authors of the Gottwald Memorandum had suggested that one possible military strategy for Czechoslovakia was to proclaim neutrality and rely "on one's own means of defense." The question remains unanswered as to whether the leaders of Czechoslovakia could ever have summoned the mass heroism necessary to conduct a war of territorial defense. Despite a long cultural tradition, the Czech and Slovak peoples have no precedent of joint armed defense of their territory. The Versailles Treaty had created their country in 1919 out of the wreckage of the Hapsburg empire. Thomas Masaryk, the nation's first president, left his successors with a heritage of cautious maneuver among Czechoslovakia's more powerful neighbors, rather than a tradition of armed defense of national sovereignty. When Hitler threatened to annex the western portions of Czechoslovakia, the leaders of the state chose to let foreign governments decide the fate of their country. Perhaps historical tradition has inclined Czechs and Slovaks to accept the advice of one of Prague's best-known writers: "In the struggle between yourself and the world," counseled Franz Kafka, "place your bets on the world."

Yet, during 1968 and 1969 several Czechs and Slovaks came to the conclusion that Czechoslovakia could not pursue independent political policies without first being willing to make the military sacrifices necessary to defend the sovereignty of the state. The journalist Ludvik Vaculik stated in the "Two Thousand Words Manifesto" of June 27, 1968, that if "foreign forces" tried to interfere in Czechoslovakia's internal developments, "we can assure our government that we will back it—with weapons if necessary—as long as it does what we give it the mandate to do."[180] In an address to a U.S. audience soon after the Soviet intervention, Ivan Svitak, in 1968 a professor of philosophy at the Charles University in Prague, argued that Dubcek's most critical mistake had been his failure to prepare for armed resistance against the Soviets. According to Svitak, "There was absolutely no way of preventing the Soviet intervention except by accepting the risk of war, of open conflict." He added:

> If the Communists had prepared the country for the possibility of armed conflict, they might have prevented the intervention, because the Soviet leadership would have had to deal with a much more complicated military-political problem than the occupation itself presented. . . . .
>
> If Finland could defend itself, if Romania and Yugoslavia are ready to fight for their national independence, there is no reason to doubt that the policy which ruled out armed struggle against the aggressor was fatally wrong.[181]

Although the leaders of the Czechoslovak Communist Party failed to explore the possibility of mobilizing the population for the enormous sacrifices required by armed resistance, Jan Palach, a twenty-year-old university student, did demonstrate the possibility of such a mobilization. On the afternoon of January 16, 1969, Palach carried a sign protesting the Soviet occupation to Prague's main square. After placing himself between the National Museum of Bohemia and the statue of St. Wencelas, the martyr king of Bohemia, Palach poured an inflammable liquid over his body and then burned himself to death.

The news of Palach's self-immolation provoked anti-Soviet demonstrations across Bohemia, Moravia and Slovakia. In Prague, about 800,000 people, a figure almost equal to the city's entire population, marched in Palach's funeral procession. The government and the occupation authorities kept police and soldiers off the streets in order to avoid a confrontation with Palach's mourners.[182] In 1969, Vladimir Dedijer, the Yugoslav Communist leader, began writing a book to explain how Tito had avoided Dubcek's fate. Dedijer dedicated his book to the memory of Jan Palach.[183]

Willingness to resist a Soviet occupation was not confined to journalists, philosophers and students. For several weeks after the invasion, the lower-level party and state bodies and the information media carried on systematic and sustained passive resistance to the occupation forces even within the major urban centers. In a study of Czechoslovakia's spontaneous passive resistance to the Soviet occupation, Adam Roberts, a British analyst of territorial defense systems, reached the conclusion that "such resistance has never previously occurred on such a scale in a militarily-occupied country."[184] According to the "memoirs" attributed to Wladyslaw Gomulka, the Soviets hesitated over the decision to invade Czechoslovakia because of the possibility of armed resistance. Gomulka is reputed to have written:

Although small, the possibility of armed resistance on the part of Czechoslovakia did exist, and the Soviet Union would have lost a lot of face in the event of a confrontation.

This kind of risk had to be taken into consideration. So it was necessary to examine all the arguments against intervention and there was no unity of views in the Soviet leadership on the final result of this calculation.

I must tell you frankly that, until the very last moment, the scales tipped first in one, then in the other direction.[185]

In 1956, Gomulka had deterred Soviet intervention by mobilizing his nation for armed resistance. The "progressive" faction of the Czechoslovak party might have been able to duplicate Gomulka's maneuver if Dubcek and his colleagues had raised the issue of national sovereignty when Brezhnev lectured them on their ideological transgressions. When Tito had been subjected to similar strictures from Stalin, he had told his colleagues, "We must not allow ourselves to be drawn into a discussion of theoretical questions, but rather should cross swords on the matter of relations between states. The Russians want only to deal with the Yugoslav Communist Party and not the entire nation."[186]

Dubcek failed to cross swords on the issue of national sovereignty for two reasons. One was that Dubcek, like many other leaders of the progressive faction, had genuine feelings of loyalty to the Soviet Union, just as many of the Yugoslav leaders did in 1948. Dubcek had spent his youth in the USSR and during the middle of his career had returned to the USSR for a university degree that was soon followed by his appointment as first secretary of the party organization in Slovakia. Dubcek was incapable of contemplating an open political break with the USSR, much less of ordering his troops into battle against the army that had liberated his country from the Nazis. The second reason was that Brezhnev, unlike Stalin and Khrushchev, did not criticize the leaders of the rebellious faction by name but concentrated instead on making rambling ideological discourses in support of the "conservative" faction of the Czechoslovak party. The Soviet leader appears consciously to have avoided forcing Dubcek into a situation in which the Czechoslovak leader had to choose between abject surrender or military resistance. Because he refused to address the political issue of national sovereignty, Dubcek forfeited the possibility of mobilizing his nation for the armed defense of the leadership of the Czechoslovak Communist Party.

The Soviet Intervention in Czechoslovakia

The primary military objective of the Soviet intervention was to seize the rebel leaders of the Czechoslovak Communist Party. About 4:00 in the afternoon of August 20, 1968, Viliam Salgovic, deputy minister of the Czechoslovak Ministry of the Interior, convened a meeting of carefully selected members of the state security forces. He told them that in seven hours the armies of the Soviet Union, Bulgaria, East Germany, Hungary, and Poland were going to invade Czechoslovakia. He then gave the members of the security forces the assignments they were to carry out after the invasion began: they were to assist Soviet forces in seizing the leaders of the Czechoslovak Communist Party.

About 8:30 p.m., an unscheduled plane from Moscow landed at the airport in Ruzyne, just outside Prague. An hour later, another unscheduled Soviet plane landed. Around 11 p.m., the armies of the five invaders crossed the borders of the Czechoslovak Socialist Republic in the north, south, east and west. Shortly after midnight, two Soviet troop planes landed at Ruzyne; several dozen Soviet soldiers jumped out of the planes and seized the airport terminal. Soon other Soviet planes began landing at one-minute intervals. The planes carried soldiers, armored cars, and tanks. Within two hours, a Soviet expeditionary force began to march into Prague. Around 3 a.m. on August 21, Soviet parachutists surrounded the building of the Presidium of the Czechoslovak Council of Ministers. They broke into the office of Oldrich Cernik, chairman of the Presidium and a member of the Presidium of the Czechoslovak Communist Party. The Soviet soldiers lined all the persons present in Cernik's office up against the wall and led Cernik away at bayonet point.[187]

About 5 a.m., a procession of Soviet tanks and armored cars drove up the right bank of the Vltava river in Prague and surrounded the headquarters of the Czechoslovak Communist Party. Four members of the party Presidium, Alexander Dubcek, first secretary of the Central Committee, Josef Smrkovsky, chairman of the National Assembly, Frantisek Kriegel, chairman of the National Front, and Josef Spacek, head of the party organization in south Moravia, watched the approach of the Soviet forces from Dubcek's office. The Soviets brought with them six members of the Czechoslovak security forces. Each of them carried a Czechoslovak flag. Soviet soldiers rushed the building and broke into Dubcek's office. The Czechoslovak security forces tried to enter the building, but the Soviets ordered them to stand in a corner of the courtyard. The Czechs then began to sing their national anthem. Soviet soldiers fired a warning volley into the air, except for a soldier who took aim at one of the Czechs and killed him.

The four Presidium members witnessed the incident from Dubcek's window. Smrkovsky immediately picked up a telephone and called Stepan Chervonenko, the Soviet ambassador to Prague. Smrkovsky shouted over the phone, "This has happened and you, Comrade Ambassador, carry the chief responsibility for the bloodshed!"[188] Before Chervonenko could reply, a Soviet soldier rushed over to Smrkovsky and smashed the telephone to bits. A few seconds later Dubcek picked up another telephone to try to call Cernik; a second Soviet soldier then ripped the phone from the wall.

About 8 a.m., one of the surviving members of the Czechoslovak security detachment informed Dubcek, Smrkovsky, Kriegel and Spacek that in two hours they would be placed before a revolutionary tribunal headed by Comrade Alois Indra, a member of the Czechoslovak Central Committee. Smrkovsky demanded, "What revolutionary tribunal and what Comrade Indra is to head it!" Dubcek pulled Smrkovsky's sleeve and said, "It's no good, Josef, be quiet, let it be."[189] Six hours later, the Soviets took the four Presidium members to the Ruzyne airport. They put Dubcek in a separate plane and put Smrkovsky, Kriegel, and Spacek into another plane and few them to Legnica, Poland. At the airport in Legnica, a Soviet colonel turned to the chairman of the Czechoslovak National Assembly and said, "Comrade Smrkovsky, you have to take things as they are, that's fate. You've got to expect this sort of thing in politics."[190]

The political objective of the Soviet intervention was to install a pro-Soviet faction in control of the Czechoslovak Communist Party. According to *Pravda,* the fraternal armies had responded to a call from a group of party and state leaders who had requested military assistance. *Pravda* printed an appeal made by this group:

> Aware of a lofty responsibility to our people, filled with a sense of real patriotism and international socialist solidarity and aware of our international obligations, we have taken on ourselves the initiative of rallying all patriotic forces in the name of our socialist future and our homeland.
>
> The danger of a fratricidal struggle . . . has confronted us with the necessity of making the historic decision to appeal to the Soviet Union and the other fraternal socialist countries for assistance.[191]

But the pro-Soviet conservative faction of the Czechoslovak party found that it had lost in political legitimacy whatever it gained in military support. The overwhelming majority of party members and ordinary citizens branded pro-Soviet party members as traitors and collaborators. The Soviets found that although their soldiers had seized all their military objectives, they were not able to install in power a group of Communists with the legitimacy necessary to govern. The entry of about half a million Soviet troops, perhaps 50,000 soldiers from Poland, 20,000 from East Germany, 20,000 from Hungary and 10,000 from Bulgaria[192] actually strengthened the political base of the progressives and destroyed the base of the conservatives.

The middle and lower levels of party and government organizations, acting independently but unanimously, organized a mass movement of passive resistance. The press, radio and even television continued to operate from underground, condemning the occupiers and their Czechoslovak clients. The media broadcast the names of Soviet sympathizers, who later complained of being subjected to "moral terrorism." Interior minister Josef Pavel, aided by the media and local police, harassed the Czechoslovak security forces working with the occupation troops.[193] The middle and lower echelons of the Czechoslovak Communist Party so effectively directed the mass movement of passive resistance that within five days they forced the Soviets to release the party leaders they had taken into custody and restore them to power. Brezhnev had to acknowledge that the only Communist regime that could govern after the intervention was a regime including the progressives. All the military actions he had taken against the progressives only strengthened their political hold on the country.

One report says that Alois Indra stepped forward on August 21, 1968, to form a new government. He and Stepan Chervonenko, the Soviet ambassador to Prague, tried to have President Ludvik Svoboda appoint Indra the head of the government, but Svoboda refused to talk to them.[194] Later that afternoon, the Soviets convened a meeting of about 50 conservative members of the Czechoslovak Central Committee, but this group could not agree on any program nor could a smaller group of pro-Soviet Czechoslovak Communists the following day.[195] Brezhnev then accepted Svoboda's request for direct negotiations between the Soviet leader and the president of Czechoslovakia. Brezhnev brought a group of pro-Soviet party members to Moscow to join the negotiations but he also brought the five progressives on the Presidium whom Soviet forces had seized in the morning of August 21.[196] After three days of intense negotiations, the Czechoslovak delegation signed a document that became known as the Moscow Protocol.

The Moscow Protocol demanded that the Czechoslovak Central Committee "discharge from their posts those individuals whose further activities would not conform to the needs of consolidating the leading role of the working class and the Communist Party." Strict controls were to be placed on the progressives' main weapon, the press. There was to be no persecution of those Communists "who stood for friendly relations with the USSR."[197] According to one Czechoslovak party member, the Soviets also insisted that Moscow approve all subsequent personnel changes in the Czechoslovak party.[198]

It required eight months until April 1969, for a group of Communists backed by Moscow to take control of the party from the progressives. Gustav Husak, a highly-skilled politician, outmaneuvered the progressives in intraparty politics during the postinvasion period to forge a new pro-Soviet faction in the Presidium and Central Committee. After April 1969, he then carried out a general purge of the progressives.

Conclusion

In their conflict with the Soviet Union over control of the Czechoslovak Communist Party in 1968, Dubcek and the other leaders of the progressive faction failed to deter military intervention because they failed to demonstrate a capability of summoning their nation to armed defense of its sovereignty. Tito, Gomulka, Hoxha, Gheorghiu-Dej, and Ceausescu had been able to deter Soviet interventions by mobilizing regular and paramilitary forces for prolonged resistance to the installation of a pro-Soviet faction of the local Communist party. The Yugoslavs and Romanians have institutionalized such mobilizations by adopting strategies of territorial defense. The primary objective of the Yugoslav and Romanian strategies is deterrence. If deterrence fails, these strategies aim not at military victory, but political stalemate between the resistance movement and the occupation regime. Yugoslav and Romanian military planners seek the following:

1. to deny an aggressor any collaborators, military or civilian, by branding potential collaborators as traitors, even before the outbreak of war, and by eliminating opportunities for the Soviets to recruit collaborators in the national armed forces;

2. to use patriotic appeals to mobilize the entire national population for waging a prolonged war of national liberation; these strategies also expect that military actions of the invading army will actually intensify the popular determination to resist;

3. to generate international sympathy and eventually international logistical support for a struggle of national liberation against the Soviet army;

4. to provoke a crisis of morale among Soviet soldiers over the course of a long war in which Soviet personnel will conclude that they have been sent to suppress a nation intent on defending its sovereignty. The territorial defense strategies of Yugoslavia and Romania

seek to intensify the moral-political strains on Soviet soldiers by forcing them to fight in small units in actions in which the Soviets will lose the psychological and military advantages of their superior numbers and directly experience the hostility of the local population.

Chapter Four
The Joint Exercises of the Warsaw Pact

By the mid 1960s, both Albania and Romania had adopted strategies of territorial defense. Even if these two members of the Warsaw Treaty Organization (WTO) had not sought to use their capabilities for waging wars of national liberation to deter a Soviet intervention, Albania and Romania had at least made their national armed forces unavailable to the Soviets for exerting military pressure against NATO.

This chapter argues that the system of joint WTO exercises introduced by Marshal A. A. Grechko in 1961 sought to prevent Romania from deploying a territorial defense system and to prevent other WTO defense ministries from copying the Albanian and Romanian examples of disengaging their armed forces from Soviet control mechanisms. Even if the only objective of the joint exercises introduced by Marshal Grechko was to prepare the armies of the WTO for nuclear war with NATO, the command mechanisms and operational characteristics of these exercises had the following consequences: (1) the denial of territorial defense capabilities to the East European armed forces which agreed to participate in the system of joint exercises; (2) the enhancement of the capabilities of the Soviet forces stationed in East Europe and the western military districts of the USSR for rapid, massive interventions in East Europe; (3) the preparation of detachments of East European soldiers for symbolic participation in Soviet interventions.

Marshal Grechko and Multinational Military Forces

Before his appointment in July 1960 as commander-in-chief of the United Armed Forces of the Warsaw Treaty Organization, Alexei Alexandrovich Grechko had acquired broad experience in the command

---

Portions of this chapter appeared earlier in the following article by the author, "The Warsaw Pact: Military Exercises & Military Interventions," *Armed Forces and Society* 7 (Fall, 1980).

of multinational military forces both within the Soviet army and in the Communist military coalitions which liberated East Europe from the Nazis.

Grechko commanded three different armies in the battles of 1941–43 for the Caucasus[1] when the Nazis threatened to cut off the Soviets from their principal oil supplies, which were located in the southern portion of the Caucasus. To defend the Caucasus, the Soviets mobilized soldiers from the national republics and autonomous republics of the region. According to V. A. Muradian, a Soviet historian, during the first ten months of the war (July 1941 to April 1942), the Red Army called up "more than 600,000 Azerbaidjani, Armenians and Georgians."[2] Most of the native military personnel recruited in the Caucasus appear to have served during 1941 and 1942 in national-territorial divisions made up mainly of one particular nationality or in multinational divisions made up mainly of Caucasus nationalities. The Soviets appear to have mobilized such detachments out of necessity rather than preference, for the Soviet army had officially disbanded its national-territorial detachments in 1938.[3]

Another Soviet historian, A. P. Artem'ev, writes that during 1941 and 1942 the Soviets raised 29 rifle divisions in the Caucasus, of which 15 were national-territorial divisions and 14 were multinational divisions.[4] According to Muradian, during the war as a whole, 19 national-territorial rifle divisions were recruited from the three Caucasus republics of Georgia, Armenia, and Azerbaidjan.[5] A Soviet Georgian historian, K. Tskitishvili, claims that during the war the Soviets recruited 33 rifle divisions made up mainly of nationalities from the Caucasus. He writes that "at the beginning of the war" the Red Army raised 16 national-territorial rifle divisions from the Caucasus: eight Georgian divisions, five Armenian divisions, and three Azerbaidjani divisions. Tskitishvili lists 17 multinational rifle divisions and two marine brigades made up primarily of Georgians, Armenians, and Azerbaidjani. According to his figures, these three nationalities made up 60–70 percent of nine of the 17 multi-national divisions drawn from the Caucasus; 50–60 percent of four of these divisions; and "up to 40 percent" of four divisions.[6] These figures allow for the possibility that one portion of the nonnative personnel who served in the national-territorial and multinational divisions of the Caucasus may have been a Russian contingent which served in the upper echelons of the officer corps.

Soviet sources also suggest that the non-Slavs mobilized from the Caucasus for service either in the national-territorial divisions or the multinational divisions were concentrated during 1941 and 1942 almost entirely on the Caucasus front and the Stalingrad front to the northeast of the Caucasus.[7] According to Muradian, in the summer of 1942 the non-Russian contingent on the Caucasus front constituted 42 percent of all Soviet military personnel assigned to this theater.[8] He did not, however, identify the national components of the non-Russian contingent, which could have also included Ukrainians and Belorussians. It is unlikely that Grechko, one of the principal Soviet generals on the Caucasus front during this period, could have avoided experience, direct or indirect, in commanding the non-Russian detachments which fought in the battle for the Caucasus.

In his study of the participation of non-Russian soldiers in the Great Fatherland War, Artem'ev notes that once the Soviets had driven the Nazis out of the Caucasus, there was a very sharp drop in the proportion of Caucasus soldiers serving in the divisions which had originally been raised in their fatherlands.[9] Artem'ev offers the following explanation for the decline during 1943 and 1944 of the proportion of soldiers of Caucasus nationalities in the divisions originally formed in the Caucasus:

> To the degree that these divisions went further and further from their republics, it became more complex to reinforce their personnel in the required time with representatives of the corresponding nationalities.
>
> And furthermore, there was not the same kind of necessity, as in the initial period of the war, since the soldiers of non-Russian nationality had by 1943 received good military tempering and experience, and many of them had mastered the Russian language and received a good internationalist training.
>
> This in no small degree facilitated their blending with the soldiers of all other nationalities.[10]

Grechko acquired further experience in commanding multinational military forces when he served as the commander of the army group that liberated southern Poland and the central and eastern regions of Czechoslovakia. Fighting alongside Grechko's Soviet troops were national detachments of Poles, Czechs, and Slovaks whom the Soviets had organized on Soviet soil. According to a Soviet study, by the middle of July 1944, the Polish forces organized by the Soviets numbered 57,355. Of these personnel, 85 percent were Poles. A contingent of Russians, Belorussians, and Ukrainians made up 10 percent; the other five percent is not identified. Poles made up only 60 percent of the Polish officer corps. The Russian-Belorussian-Ukrainian contingent made up 35 percent. According to this study, the Soviet officers serving in the Polish army held posts as general staff officers, heads of central administrations, commanders of divisions, regiments and special units.[11] In a discussion of the Czechoslovak Corps recruited by the Soviets, this same study notes that as of September 1944, the Corps had 12,000 personnel, among whom were 204 Soviet officers and 419 Soviet noncommissioned officers.[12] In both Poland and Czechoslovakia, the native Communist personnel who had fought in national detachments under Grechko's command played important roles in the postwar political struggles for the control of the national armed forces of Poland and Czechoslovakia.[13]

In 1953, after eight years as the commander of the Kiev Military District, Grechko became the commander-in-chief of the Group of Soviet Forces in Germany (GSFG). While Grechko served in Germany, the East German regime transformed detachments of its national police force into the National People's Army. According to a Soviet study, the GSFG gave extensive fraternal assistance to the East Germans in organizing their army.[14]

In November 1957, Grechko became the commander-in-chief of the Soviet Ground Forces, a post he held until his appointment as commander of the Warsaw Pact in July 1960. During this period the Soviet Defense Ministry dismantled the national "formations" and "units" of the native peoples of the Soviet Baltic republics, the Caucasus republics, the Central Asian republics, and the various autonomous republics within Soviet union republics.[15] Grechko must have had at least some of the responsibility for carrying out this program: Soviet historians indicate that, with the exception of a Latvian air force regiment, all the national "units" and "formations" of the Soviet army since 1918 were either rifle or cavalry detachments ultimately subordinate to the commander of the Ground Forces. In Soviet usage, a military "unit" is usually a regiment. A "formation" is either a brigade, division or corps. Most of the non-Slavic units and formations of the Soviet army were made up of soldiers from the Caucasus, Central Asia, and Siberia.[16]

Placing Soviet military personnel in integrated multinational units and formations (with the possible retention of national sub-units) could not have removed the problems of the military and political training of the non-Slavic nationalities which had previously been assigned to the national-territorial troop units and formations. This policy simply eliminated what had been the battle-tested devices for integrating non-Slavs into the Soviet army. In its article on the national detachments of the Soviet armed forces, the *Soviet Military Encyclopedia* offers two reasons why the Soviets preferred the disadvantages of integrating Soviet nationalities into multinational units and formations to the disadvantages of integrating national units and formations into the armed forces as a whole. The *Encyclopedia* article says that the necessity for national units and formations "fell away" because of the further drawing together of all Soviet nationalities as a result of the sociopolitical, economic and cultural development of the USSR and because of the formation of the world socialist system.[17]

Perhaps by the mid-1950s the non-Slavic recruits of the Soviet army usually knew enough Russian to train in multinational units. The single most important development in the military affairs of the world socialist system in the mid-1950s was the establishment of the Warsaw Pact. If the Soviets had retained national formations and units of the non-Slavic nationalities they would have had to deal with the complexities of integrating these formations and units not only into the Soviet Armed Forces but also into the Warsaw Pact. This problem would have arisen sooner or later in the staffing of the Soviet Force Groups in Europe and of the formations of the western military districts of the USSR.[18]

There is some evidence that Soviet and East European armies began to conduct joint exercises in the late 1950s. According to a Soviet study edited by Marshal I. I. Iakubovskii, the WTO commander from 1967 to 1977, Soviet and East European armies had participated in joint exercises during the late 1950s "primarily on a tactical level."[19] Soviet sources identify at least two such exercises. In August of 1957, while Marshal Grechko was still commander of the GSFG, 11,000 soldiers of the newly-formed National People's Army of the German Democratic Republic and an unspecified number of Soviet personnel conducted a joint exercise which required the interaction of "staffs, formations and units" of both armies.[20] From July 18 to August 19, 1958, the Soviet air force and the Bulgarian ground forces, air force and navy conducted a joint exercise in Bulgaria under the command of Soviet Air Marshal N. S. Skripko.[21]

There is also some evidence that the WTO political administrations had begun conducting joint political actvities in the late 1950s. In an article just prior to the WTO's "Buria" exercise of 1961, Marshal Grechko noted that the soldiers of the Soviet force groups in Germany, Poland, and Hungary had already participated in a wide variety of joint political activities with East European soldiers: evening programs of "combat friendship"; meetings of allied soldiers who had won training competitions; joint visits of WTO personnel to local industrial and agricultural enterprises; meetings of WTO soldiers with veterans of the military and political struggles against the Nazis in East Europe; joint ceremonies marking national holidays; joint concerts and theatrical shows; and joint sports competitions. Grechko added that the party organizations and Military Councils of the Soviet Force Groups regularly discussed "questions of internationalist training."[22]

If the Soviets had not dismantled the national detachments of the Soviet armed forces, it would have been likely that in the course of joint WTO activities, including joint exercises, units of predominantly Russian-Belorussian-Ukrainian composition which used Russian as the sole language of command would have been surrounded by non-Russian speaking units and formations of the East European states and the non-Slavic republics of the USSR. Soviet plans to conduct joint military exercises and joint military-political activities by the units and formations of the WTO may have prompted the Soviet defense ministry to place Soviet soldiers into multinational units and formations in order to pre-empt the development of anti-Russian camaraderie among East European soldiers and the non-Russian soldiers of the Soviet army.[23]

As commander of the Soviet Ground Forces from 1957 to 1960, Marshal Grechko probably had the major responsibility for preparing Soviet forces for participation in joint exercises with the East European armies. Grechko probably owed his appointment as commander in chief of the Warsaw Pact to his exceptional qualifications for resolving the difficulties of placing multinational military personnel under one command. He was particularly well qualified for this task because of his wartime experiences in the Caucasus, Poland, and Czechoslovakia; because of his experience in East Germany in coordinating the interaction of Soviet and East German military forces; and because of his experience in integrating non-Russian Soviet nationalities into multinational units within the Soviet army.

Joint Exercises of the Warsaw Pact

In October-November of 1961, Grechko personally commanded the "Buria" maneuvers, the first large-scale multilateral maneuvers of the Warsaw Pact. These exercises, which stretched from the western military districts of the USSR to East Germany, included the staffs and troops of the ground forces, air forces, airborne troops and navies of the Soviet Union, Poland, East Germany, and Czechoslovakia. The following year Soviet and East European troops conducted multilateral exercises in Romania, Hungary, Czechoslovakia, Poland, and East Germany.

In the WTO exercises of the early 1960s, Marshal Grechko began to drill the armies of the Warsaw Pact for nuclear offense against the West in order to render them incapable of conventional defense against the East. In the joint exercises the WTO Commander in Chief also began to prepare Soviet and East European forces for massive conventional interventions against the member states of the fraternal alliance. The aspects of the system of joint WTO exercises which support these conclusions are: (1) the pattern of the location of the exercises; (2) the pattern of the assignment of command of the exercises; (3) the emphasis on offensive, nuclear, and conventional actions on a continental scale; (4) the creation of multinational staffs for command of the exercises; (5) the assignment of divisions, regiments, and possibly even smaller units to multinational groupings in the exercises; (6) the influence of the joint exercises on the types of training programs conducted by each national army; (7) the influence of the exercises on the careers of East European officers; (8) the nature of the joint political activities conducted during WTO exercises.

This chapter does not deny the potential role of the Warsaw Pact exercises in preparing WTO armies for war with NATO; it argues that preparation for war with NATO is not the primary purpose of the Pact exercises. This chapter does not deny that the Soviet Force Groups in East Europe practice offensive nuclear campaigns against West Europe; it only suggests that the Soviets do not place much confidence in the reliability of their allies in such campaigns. It also suggests that the offensive posture of the Soviet Army facilitates Soviet interventions in East Europe by reinforcing the West's preoccupation with defense. If NATO's armies are convinced that the Soviets are poised for an offensive nuclear war, NATO governments are unlikely to contemplate any military response to Soviet interventions against members of the Warsaw Pact.

Size and Frequency

The system of Warsaw Pact exercises developed by Marshal Grechko involved both bilateral and multilateral maneuvers at the tactical, operational, and strategic levels. According to the translation of the Soviet *Dictionary of Basic Military Terms* by the U.S. Air Force, a tactical exercise can involve a battalion, regiment, division, or corps and may include combined arms actions.[24] Tactical exercises practice tactics, which the Soviet dictionary defines as "the objective laws of combat. . . . Each service and branch has its own tactics."[25]

The Dictionary of Basic Military Terms defines "operational art" as the "theory and practice of preparing and conducting combined and independent operations by major field formations or major formations of the Services."[26] In Soviet usage, a formation is either a brigade, division, or corps. An action at the operational level is "an operational-strategic maneuver," which the Soviet dictionary defines as "an organized movement of large groupings of major field forces of the armed forces within theaters of military operations for the purpose of creating the most advantageous grouping of men and equipment for the completion of assigned missions."[27] *The Dictionary of Basic Military Terms* defines a "strategic maneuver" as an action designed "to secure the rapid and complete destruction of major enemy groupings."[28]

Graham Turbiville, a former U.S. Army intelligence officer, published in a journal of the United States Army a list of 36 major WTO exercises in the period from 1961–77, but carefully disclaimed that his list was complete.[29] This chapter, drawing on Turbiville's list and on Soviet and East European materials, presents a list of 71 major WTO exercises for the period from 1961–79 (See Appendix). This list of 71 is probably short of the true total of the larger tactical, operational, and strategic exercises in the period from 1961–79. But even if the Soviets supplied a complete listing of the larger WTO exercises, such a list might still not give an accurate picture of the activities that take place within the system of joint exercises. Both Soviet and East European sources suggest that the number of lower-level tactical exercises and the number of command-staff joint exercises without participation by troops is much greater than the number of large-scale tactical, operational, and strategic maneuvers involving both troops and staffs.[30]

The Helsinki accords of 1975 required both NATO and the WTO to report only those exercises involving more than 25,000 troops and encouraged the invitation of observers. Whatever the intentions of those who drafted the sections on confidence-building measures, the actual effect of these measures on the Warsaw Pact has been to reduce the size of most tactical and operational-strategic exercises to maneuvers involving less than 25,000 troops. The effect has also been to reduce sharply the publication of all Soviet materials on the system of joint exercises. For all practical purposes, Soviet discussions of the system of joint exercises virtually ceased in 1975. Most of the Soviet discussions of the joint exercises appeared after the appointment of Marshal Iakubovskii as WTO commander in the spring of 1967. Soviet sources reveal that during 1967 the Pact conducted six large-scale exercises; during 1968, seven; during 1969, eleven; during 1970, four; during 1971, six; during 1972, five; during 1973, six; and during 1974, six. But in 1975, the year of the Helsinki agreement, the Soviets reported no joint WTO exercises; in 1976 the Soviets reported two; in 1977, one; in 1978, none; and in 1979, two. If, in fact, the WTO has sharply reduced the number of joint exercises after the signing of the Helsinki accords, then the Warsaw Pact states have virtually ceased the program that until 1975 had been the central focus of the alliance.

Patterns of Location and Command

Marshal Grechko's system of joint exercises made it possible for Soviet troops to re-enter periodically the three countries where they were not stationed in 1961: Czechoslovakia, Romania, and Bulgaria. As a reciprocal gesture, the Soviets invited the armed forces of Czechoslovakia, Romania, and Bulgaria to participate in joint exercises on the territories of other WTO states, including, in at least two cases, multilateral exercises on the territory of the USSR.[31] The different histories of Soviet relations with Czechoslovakia, Bulgaria and Romania after 1961 correspond closely to the different decisions taken by these three East European states on continued participation in WTO exercises.

The regular conduct of WTO exercises in Czechoslovakia enhanced a Soviet capability for rapid and massive occupation of Czechoslovakian soil while simultaneously pre-empting the possibility of the development of a Czechoslovak system of territorial defense. According to Turbiville, Czechoslovakia was the site of joint Czechoslovak-Soviet-Polish maneuvers in September 1962 and the site of joint Czechoslovak-Soviet-East German maneuvers in June 1964. *Krasnaia Zvezda,* the Soviet army newspaper, reported Czechoslovak-Soviet exercises in Czechoslovakia from July 7–15, 1964, which Turbiville does not. In the July 1964 exercises, the Czechoslovak minister of defense, Bohomir Lomsky, commanded staffs and troops from both armies in the presence of V.A. Sudets, the commander in chief of the Soviet Anti-Aircraft Troops and of P.I. Batov, the Chief of the WTO Staff[32], who in 1956 had commanded the Soviet forces which invaded Hungary.

In 1966, General Lomsky commanded Czechoslovak, Soviet, East German, and Hungarian forces in the Vltava exercises in Czechoslovakia. Marshal Grechko attended these maneuvers, which involved more than 20 organs of administration for large formations and special units, including airborne troops. According to *Krasnaia Zvezda,* the materiel used in these exercises could have formed a single column 850 kilometers long,[33] a distance greater than the length of Czechoslovakia from east to west.

When the political crisis of the spring of 1968 threatened to remove from power the pro-Soviet "conservative" faction of the Czechoslovakian Communist Party, the Soviets were able to use the precedent of WTO exercises as a pretext for placing Soviet soldiers on Czechoslovak soil and for preparing the other military forces of the alliance for intervention. In 1968, the only combat the Czechoslovak People's Army prepared for was combat alongside the Soviet army, not against it.[34] During the spring and summer of 1968, the Soviets invaded Czechoslovakia on three separate occasions, although they designated only one as an official intervention. Each of the three sorties into Czechoslovakia was aimed at placing pro-Soviet Communists in control of the Czechoslovak party.

On May 29, 1968, a plenum of the Czechoslovak Central Committee opened. At this session the loose coalition of "progressives" more or less united around Alexander Dubcek, the party's first secretary, proposed a resolution calling for the convocation of an extraordinary party congress two years ahead of schedule in order to elect a new central committee at the congress. The "progressives" expected that they would be able to control the elections that would choose the delegates to the party congress. With Soviet backing, the pro-Soviet "conservatives" surprised the progressives by voting for the resolution, which easily passed.[35] The next day Soviet airborne troops landed at the Prague airport and Soviet troops from the Group of Soviet Forces in Germany crossed into Bohemia. Eventually Defense Minister Martin Dzur informed the press that Warsaw Pact maneuvers had just begun. An official for the ministry later explained that even the participants in the May 30 exercises had not been informed until the last moment so that the exercises would be "as close as possible to reality."[36] At least one of the Soviet officers on maneuvers took time off to address a group of pro-Soviet members of the Czechoslovak party. According to a Czech journal sympathetic to the "progressives," this officer told the meeting that if "anti-socialist forces"threatened their country, "the honest Communists" had only to ask and they would have at their disposal "the entire Soviet Army."[37]

Additional Soviet troops entered Czechoslovakia to conduct a joint exercise held from June 20–30 with Czechoslovak troops while Polish, East German, Hungarian, and additional Soviets troops carried out complementary maneuvers on their national territories. Marshal Iakubovskii, the WTO Commander, directed all these forces in the "Shumava" exercise, which involved more than 30 organs of administration for troop formations and units, including communications and logistics forces and special troops assigned to mark highways and other access routes.[38]

After the "conservatives" in the Czechoslovak party suffered a sharp setback in the contest during late June and early July[39] for the selection of delegates to the Party Congress, the Soviets issued repeated demands that the Czechoslovak Presidium meet with the Soviet leadership.[40] After failing to arrange such a bilateral meeting, Brezhnev assembled his East European allies in Warsaw on July 14. Neither the Romanians nor the Albanians, still members of the Pact, attended this meeting. The five fraternal parties wrote the "Warsaw Letter" addressed to the Central Committee of the Czechoslovak party for the purpose of rallying the "conservatives" in the Central Committee to postpone the Congress and purge the "progressives" on the Presidium.[41] The "Warsaw Letter" declared, "We know that there are forces in Czechoslovakia that are capable of upholding the socialist system and defeating the anti-socialist elements. . . .The tasks today are to give these healthy forces a clear perspective, rally them to action and mobilize them against the forces of counterrevolution. . . .''[42]

From Moscow's perspective, the healthy forces should not be discouraged by a mere electoral defeat in the selection of delegates to the party congress. As the *Pravda* editorial of July 19 observed, ''Needless to say, the forces of socialism in Czechoslovakia, objectively measured, are far greater than those now striking at the revolutionary gains of the Czechoslovak people.''[43] At this time, the Soviet troops which had participated in the ''Shumava'' exercises were still on Czechoslovak soil.

Dubcek finally acceded to the demand of the Warsaw Letter and agreed to meet with the Soviet Politburo on July 29 in the Slovak town of Cierna. Instead of bringing the Czechoslovak Presidium to the meeting, he led an ad-hoc delegation drawn partly from the Presidium and partly from the Czechoslovak Central Committee. But even this delegation would not agree either to changes in the membership of the Presidium or cancellation of the party congress.[44]

On July 24, General S.S. Mariakhin, Commander of the Rear Services of the Soviet Armed Forces, began conducting ''Neman,'' a massive logistical exercise. On July 31, after the Cierna talks ended, *Krasnaia Zvezda* revealed that the ''Neman'' exercise had been expanded to include Polish and East German territory. The ''Neman'' maneuvers ended on August 9 with the establishment of a joint Soviet-Polish-East German headquarters.[45] On August 5, General S.M. Shtemenko was named chief of the WTO Staff. Two days later, Shtemenko began directing an exercise of communications troops in the West Ukraine, Poland, and East Germany.[46] A British analyst reports an exercise of Soviet and Hungarian communications troops took place in Hungary during August 17–20.[47] On the night of August 20–21 the armed forces of the Soviet Union, East Germany, Poland, Hungary, and Bulgaria occupied Czechoslovakia.[48]

According to *Pravda,* the fraternal armies had responded to a request from a group of Czechoslovak party and state leaders for military assistance.[49] A group of pro-Soviet Czechoslovak Communists did in fact prepare to form a new government, but the nationalist reaction in Czechoslovakia against the WTO intervention was so strong that the members of this group decided not to identify themselves publicly.[50] Although the ''progressive'' Communists succeeded in holding in the Vysocany district of Prague an ''underground'' session of the scheduled party congress, the Soviets obtained from Dubcek and the other captured leaders a formal repudiation of the Vysocany Congress and the new Central Committee it had elected.[51]

Warsaw Pact Exercises in Romania

In 1962, the government of Romania, like the government of Czechoslovakia, had agreed to the conduct of joint WTO exercises on its territory. Marshal Grechko attended the October 19, 1962, exercises in Romania, as did defense ministers from several Warsaw Pact states and other high-ranking Sovet and East European military officers. Unidentified forces from Romania, the Soviet Union and Bulgaria participated in the exercises under the command of the Romanian defense minister, General Salajin. Although General Salajin commanded the Romanian, Soviet and Bulgarian forces that participated in this exercise, central WTO agencies did the planning for the maneuvers.[52] Judging by the fact that all the political activities of the exercises (parades, speeches, meetings, etc.) were held in the Romanian port of Constanta[53] it is likely that some naval forces participated in the maneuvers. According to the translations of the classified Soviet journal *Voennaia Mysl'*, made public by the Central Intelligence Agency, General Salajin also commanded an exercise of Romanian, Soviet, and Bulgarian forces sometime during the fall of 1963.[54]

After the 1963 exercises, Romania never again permitted WTO maneuvers on Romanian soil, although it has sent to other WTO exercises personnel whom the Romanians have described as observers and the Soviets have described as participants. The Romanians have also agreed on at least two occasions and perhaps three, to have Soviet officers, sometimes with Bulgarian officers, sit in a map room of the Romanian Defense Ministry and conduct with Romanian officers what both sides have described on two occasions as "command-staff map maneuvers."[55]

It might be possible to understand Romania's refusal to permit continued WTO exercises on Romanian soil if the exercises of 1962 and 1963 were similar to those held in 1964 and 1967 in Bulgaria, the only other WTO state without a Soviet garrison which also had a coast on the Black Sea and extensive mountain and forest areas. *Krasnaia Zvezda* claimed that Soviet, Bulgarian, and Romanian forces participated in the 1964 exercise in Bulgaria, which included naval and airborne landings.[56] A Soviet-Bulgarian study, which claims that Romanian forces joined Soviet and Bulgarian forces in the 1967 Rodopy exercise in Bulgaria, reports that during the Rodopy maneuvers, air forces, naval forces and airborne troops conducted "a defensive battle for the seizure of the sea coast and also for the conduct of actions in mountains and forest areas."[57] If the 1962 and 1963 exercises in Romania also included naval and airborne landings for the defensive seizure of the sea coast, and for actions in the mountain and forest regions so critical to the Romanian strategy of territorial defense, it is possible that the Romanian Defense Ministry concluded that the WTO exercises on Romanian territory were not intended primarily as preparation for battles with NATO.

The Soviet-Bulgarian discussion of the Rodopy exercises revealed a style of operations which, if employed in exercises on Romanian soil, might have pre-empted Romania's ability to determine the capabilities of Romanian forces. According to the Soviet-Bulgarian study:

> For raising the effectiveness of the administration of troops in the [Rodopy] exercises, there were mutual exchanges of groups and representatives among the units and formations of various countries.
>
> This method of work was widely practiced: Bulgarian and Soviet officers [note the omission of any reference to Romanian officers, whose forces were supposed to be participating in the Rodopy exercises] jointly worked out documents or participated in practical measures.
>
> As a result, the operational capabilities of staffs were raised and the possibility was achieved of broadly and openly exchanging opinions on the questions decided.[58]

Warsaw Pact Exercises and the Bulgarian Armed Forces

Unlike the Romanians, the Bulgarians continued to participate in joint exercises with the Soviets. The first such joint exercise in the framework of the Warsaw Pact may have been the maneuvers of July 1958.[59] The sources used to compile Table 1 indicate that in the period from 1961 to 1979 the armed forces of Bulgaria participated in 14 WTO exercises. The pattern of these exercises suggests that they permitted the Soviets to practice the regular restationing of Soviet troops on Bulgarian soil; that they focused the attention of Bulgarian military planners on actions outside Bulgarian territory; and they accustomed Bulgarian officers to taking orders from foreign commanders. In the period from 1961–79, the armed forces of Bulgaria participated in at least four joint ground forces/combined arms exercises held on Bulgarian territory; at least nine exercises conducted completely outside Bulgaria; and one logistics exercise which the Soviets claim was held jointly on Bulgarian and Romanian soil.[60] Of these fourteen exercises, commanders can be identified for twelve. Of these twelve exercises, three had Bulgarian commanders. Of the nine foreign commanders, five were Soviet officers.[61]

WTO Exercises and the Armed Forces of East Germany, Poland, Hungary, and Czechoslovakia

There are common patterns of the location of exercises and assignment of command in the ground forces/combined arms exercises of the armed forces of the German Democratic Republic (GDR), Poland, and Hungary, the three states in which Soviet garrisons were stationed prior to the introduction of the system of joint exercises. These patterns recur in the exercises of the Czechoslovak armed forces after the establishment of the Central Force group in Czechoslovakia.

For each of the national armed forces of the GDR, Poland, and Hungary in the period from 1961–79, about one-third of the ground forces/combined arms exercises in which they particpated were conducted exclusively on their own territory; about one-third were entirely outside the national territory; and about one-third were conducted jointly on home and foreign territory. This pattern of the location of ground forces/combined arms exercises reduces the opportunity for national defense ministries to develop a capability for the conduct of a war in defense of national territory. For each of the national armed forces of the GDR, Poland, and Hungary in the period from 1961–79, at the very most only one-third of the WTO ground forces/combined arms exercises in which they participated took place under the command of an officer of the national armed forces. At least two-thirds of the ground forces/combined arms exercises of any one of these national armed forces took place under the command of a foreign officer, either Soviet or East European. This pattern of the assignment of command reduces the possibility that the officers of a given state will acquire the experience necessary to conduct large-scale combined arms actions in defense of their national territory. This pattern also accustoms national military forces to accept commands from foreign officers.

The armed forces of the GDR participated in at least 27 ground forces/combined arms WTO exercises in the period from 1961–79 and probably many more.[62] Of these 27, 7 took place exclusively on German soil; 9 were held completely outside the GDR; and 11 took place jointly on the territory of East Germany and Poland or Czechoslovakia. Of these 27 exercises, commanders can be identified for 22. Of these 22 exercises, 3 had East German commanders. Of the 19 foreign commanders, 12 were Soviet officers.

The armed forces of Poland participated in at least 25 ground forces/combined arms WTO exercises in the period from 1961–79 and probably more.[63] Of these 25, 7 were conducted entirely in Poland; 7 were held completely outside Poland; and 11 were conducted jointly on the territory of Poland and of the GDR or Czechoslovakia. Of these 25 exercises, commanders can be identified for 21. Of these 21, 6 had Polish commanders. Of the 15 foreign commanders, 10 were Soviet officers.

The same patterns appear in the ground forces/combined arms WTO exercises in which Hungary participated in the period from 1961 to 1979, although Hungary did not fully participate in the system of WTO exercises until 1966. The first WTO exercise in Hungary, the maneuvers of 1962, were probably held in order to invite Romanian troops to Hungary in return for the Romanian invitation to Soviet and Bulgarian troops to participate in the exercises of 1962 in Romania. Another peculiarity of Hungary's participation in the joint exercises is that no large-scale multilateral WTO exercise took place in Hungary until 1979. The gradual induction of Hungary into the system of joint exercises may have been due to the political difficulties of introducing WTO troops into Hungary when memories of the events of 1956 were still recent. In the period from 1961 to 1979, the armed forces of Hungary participated in at least 18 ground forces/combined arms exercises, and probably more.[64] Of these 18, 7 were conducted exclusively in Hungary; 7 were conducted entirely outside Hungary; and 4 took place jointly on Hungarian and Czechoslovak territory. Of these 18 exercises, commanders can be identified for only 10. Of these 10 exercises, 2 had Hungarian commanders. Of the 8 foreign commanders, 5 were Soviet officers.

The pattern of the participation of the Czechoslovak armed forces in WTO ground forces/combined arms exercises prior to 1968 and prior to the establishment of the Central Group of Forces deviates from the GDR, Polish, and Hungarian patterns. Half of the exercises involving the Czechoslovak armed forces took place in Czechoslovakia, which had no Soviet garrison until 1968. For the period from 1961 through 1967, the Czechoslovak armed forces participated in eight WTO ground forces/ combined arms exercises. Of these eight, four took place in Czechoslovakia; two took place entirely outside Czechoslovakia; one took place jointly on Czechoslovak and Hungarian territory; and one took place jointly on Czechoslovak, East German, Polish, and Soviet territory. Of the eight exercises, commanders can be identified for six. Of these six commanders, two were Czechoslovak officers. Of the four foreign commanders, three were Soviet officers.

After the establishment of the Central Force Group, the pattern of exercises coincided with that of the three other states with Soviet garrisons. For the period 1969–79, the armed forces of Czechoslovakia participated in at least 16 ground forces/combined arms WTO exercises and probably more.[65] Of these 16, 5 were conducted exclusively in Czechoslovakia; 4 took place completely outside Czechoslovakia and 7 were conducted jointly on the territory of Czechoslovakia and Hungary or Poland or the GDR. Commanders can be identified for 11 of the 16 exercises. Of these 11 exercises, three had Czechoslovak commanders. Of the eight foreign commanders during this period after the 1968 invasion, only two were Soviet officers.

Joint Exercises of WTO Service Branches

Marshal Iakubovskii's text on the Warsaw Treaty Organization says that joint WTO exercises regularly take place among the Pact anti-aircraft troops, air forces, navies and special troops.[66] Soviet sources reveal very little about such exercises. For the 17 that can be documented, commanders can be identified for 15. Of these 15, 14 were Soviet officers, either the WTO commander in chief, the WTO chief of staff, or the commander of the Soviet Anti-Aircraft Troops, the commander of the Soviet Air Force, the commander of the Soviet Navy or the commander of the Soviet Rear Services. Because Soviet sources occasionally identify the commander of the Soviet Anti-Aircraft Troops as also commander of the WTO Anti-Aircraft Troops,[67] it is possible that the commanders of the other Soviet service branches also serve as *ex officio* commanders of the non-ground forces service branches of the WTO. In any case, the pattern of the assignment of command in WTO service branch exercises suggests that the anti-aircraft troops, air forces, navies and rear services of the loyal Warsaw Pact states do not have an opportunity to practice the support of their sister national service branches in the defense of national territory.

Offense and Nuclear Weapons;
Multinational Staffs; Multinational Formations

Several other aspects of WTO exercises have the effect, intentional or accidental, of denying national armed forces the capability for territorial defense: the emphasis in exercises on the offensive use of nuclear weapons; the use of multinational staffs to direct the exercises; and the assignment of national detachments to multinational formations. WTO and Western sources agree that the larger Warsaw Pact exercises often simulate the use of nuclear weapons in combat.[68] If WTO or Western sources provided more detailed information about the specific kinds of weapons used in Warsaw Pact exercises and the kinds of actions practiced, it might be possible to determine if the WTO exercises trained soldiers only for offensive actions and mainly for nuclear offense. WTO sources usually describe the objective of joint exercises as the destruction of enemy groupings. These sources do not indicate if such actions are "offensive" or "defensive"; they only indicate that the actions are completely successful. Evidence concerning other aspects of WTO exercises suggest that even if Warsaw Pact exercises do practice defensive actions employing conventional weapons, they nontheless rule out the practice of the synchronized defense of national territory by national service branches under national command.

One of these aspects is the organization of staff work for the exercise. Of the 49 WTO exercises from 1961 to 1979 for which commanders can be identified, 21 had East European commanders. But even though East European officers have regularly commanded joint WTO exercises, they do not appear to have obtained the major responsibilities for planning the exercises. Their principal function appears to be that accustoming the armed forces of East Europe to the principle of foreign command, while sparing these armies the humiliation of maneuvering under the command of WTO officers drawn only from the Soviet army. WTO communiques invariably describe the Pact exercises as being conducted "according to the plan of the United Command" or "according to the plan of the United Armed Forces" or "according to the training program of the United Armed Forces" but never according to the plan of a national defense ministry.

The Iakubovskii text on the WTO says that the Staff of the United Armed Forces has the responsibility for the "planning and conduct of joint maneuvers, exercises and military games of diverse scale—from the operational-strategic exercises to troop exercises and to exercises of special troops."[69] (In Soviet usage, "special troops" include engineering, chemical, radio-technical, railway construction, road construction and automotive troops.) A joint Soviet-Polish study echoes the Iakubovskii volume on the role of central WTO agencies in the planning of joint exercises: ". . . troop, naval, command-staff and special troop exercises, joint war games and maneuvers are regularly conducted according to the plan of the United Command of the armed forces of the Warsaw Pact members."[70]

There does not appear to be information available from WTO sources on who serves as the chief of staff for a given exercise. Nor is there any information as to whether exercise staffs are assembled on an ad hoc basis or are drawn from the WTO Staff. The Iakubovskii study of the Warsaw Pact says that the WTO Staff has participated in the conduct of at least five joint exercises and that the WTO Staff is multinational in composition.[71] Whenever *Krasnaia Zvezda* has mentioned the staff of a particular WTO exercise, it points out that the staff is multinational in composition.[72] There is no evidence from WTO sources which indicate that national general staffs are charged with the exclusive preparation or conduct of joint WTO exercises at any level.

The limited information available on the composition of the forces participating in the joint exercises suggests that missions are not assigned exclusively to the armed forces of one state but are always shared by units drawn from the forces of at least two states. This information also suggests that sub-units (companies and battalions) and units (regiments) from several states are often organized into multinational formations (brigades, divisions or corps). Official communiques of the WTO exercises almost always state that the purpose of a particular exercise was to improve the interaction of the allied forces rather than to prepare national armed forces for distinct missions. Other WTO sources often make the same point.[73]

The Iakubovskii text declares that one of the purposes of the joint exercises is "to check capabilities for organizing interaction in coalition formations."[74] This volume also noted in its discussion of the 1969 Oder-Neisse exercises, which it identified as at the time the largest WTO exercise ever held, "In all stages there was extensive interaction and mutual aid among the sub-units and units of the allied armies in carrying out common tasks."[75] During the Oder-Neisse maneuvers, *Krasnaia Zvezda* mentioned a joint action carried out by East German armored forces, Czechoslovak airborne troops and the Polish and Soviet air forces."[76]

A Soviet account of the Brotherhood in Arms exercises of 1970 notes that "the interaction of the friendly armies was carried out not only on the level of troop staffs but also among units, sub-units and even among aircraft and other technical crews."[77] This study further noted a joint action executed by German and Soviet tank companies, a joint battle waged by sub-units of German paratroopers with sub-units of Bulgarian and Czechoslovak tank forces. It also mentioned a joint naval landing conducted by sub-units of Soviet, Polish and German naval infantry supported by sub-units of paratroopers from each country. This account chronicles the concluding phase of the exercise in which the WTO soldiers surrounded and then destroyed the enemy forces. This action was the work of tank forces from the Soviet Union, Poland, Hungary, and East Germany, supported by Bulgarian paratroopers and Czechoslovak troops landed by helicopter.

In a discussion of the Shield 72 exercises in Czechoslovakia, a joint Soviet-Czechoslovak study reported an action in which Hungarian artillery began shelling an enemy position after which unspecified Polish and Czechoslovak forces fought "shoulder to shoulder" while being supported by Soviet mechanized infantry. When the enemy brought up reinforcements, Soviet tank, artillery and air forces went into action and annihilated the enemy.[78] The mutual dependence of WTO armed forces on each other in carrying out joint missions in Warsaw Pact exercises may be characteristic even of low-level joint maneuvers. According to a Czechoslovak officer writing in *Krasnaia Zvezda,* in a small-scale tactical exercise of troops from the Central Force Group and the Czechoslovak army, two Czechoslovak officers declared that they could not have completed their mission "were it not for the aid of Soviet officers."[79]

WTO Exercises and Training Programs

The training programs of the national armies of the Waraw Pact partially determine the capabilities of these armies for specific kinds of wars. Evidence from Soviet sources indicates that central Pact agencies, not national defense ministries, decide upon the types of actions for which East European forces train. Colonel Semin, a Soviet journalist specializing on the Warsaw Pact, notes, "Troop contingents assigned to the United Armed Forces daily carry out combat and political training according to the plans of the national commands, but the working out of the basic questions of the joint actions of these troops is carried out according to the United Command."[80] Soviet sources also indicate that the Soviets acquired control over the training of the East European armies by requiring that the East Europeans orient their training to meeting the requirements of the joint WTO exercises.[81] In 1963, Warsaw Pact officers began meeting annually to review the exercises of the fall and summer and to plan training programs and exercises for the coming year.[83] After the creation of the Military Council of the WTO in 1969, these sessions have been held jointly with sessions of the Military Council. The Iakubovskii volume notes that these joint meetings examine the results of combat and operational training for the preceding year and plan the training and exercise programs for the next year.[83]

The Chairman of the Military Council is the WTO commander in chief; its members are all his Soviet deputies[84] and his East European deputies, including a Romanian officer. The Iakubovskii volume notes that the recommendations of the Military Council have only a "consultative" character, but that "as a rule" WTO members abide by recommendations of the Military Council. This arrangement probably suits the Soviets and the Romanians equally well: the Soviets can avoid Romanian vetoes and the Romanians can ignore the recommendations that as a rule are carried out by the other members of the Pact. The commander of the

WTO does not rely only on the East European members of the Military Council to carry out the recommendations of the Military Council. The commander also relies on a group of senior Soviet officers who serve as the liaison representatives to the armed forces of each member state.[85] According to the Iakubovskii text, one of the functions of these liaison officers is "to give aid to the national commands in the training of troops. . . ."[86]

Evaluations of East European Officers in WTO Exercises

The system of Warsaw Pact exercises affords Soviet officers the opportunity to evaluate the East European officers who participate in the exercises. The Soviets may use such evaluations as one device for ensuring that national defense ministries will promote only those officers who have demonstrated, in the joint exercises, loyalty to the military-political and military-technical concepts on which the Warsaw Pact is based. The opportunity for Soviet officers to evaluate the performance of East European officers arises from the roles of the Warsaw Pact Staff and Warsaw Pact United Command in evaluating the exercises. A 1973 diplomatic convention formally insures Soviet domination of the Staff and other central agencies of the WTO.[87] The opportunity for Soviet evaluation of East European officers also arises from the fact that Soviet officers have directly commanded 28 of the 49 WTO exercises for which commanders can be identified. Of these 28, Marshal Iakobuvskii commanded 12; General S.M. Shtemenko, former Chief of the WTO Staff, commanded 3; the commanders of the Soviet Anti-Aircraft Troops, the Soviet Air Force and the Soviet Navy have together directed a total of 9. The present WTO Commander, Marshal V.G. Kulikov, has been identified as the commander of only one exercise, but Kulikov's low profile is almost certainly the result of the post-Helsinki hiatus in reporting WTO maneuvers.

Soviet sources frequently identify the joint exercises as critical examinations of troops, commanders and staffs. According to the Iakobovskii text, one of the purposes of the first multilateral WTO exercise, the 1961 "Buria" maneuvers under Marshal Grechko, was "checking the preparation of operational staffs to carry out the administration of allied groupings of forces in the complex conditions of a combat situation."[88] Just prior to a WTO exercise of 1970, a *Krasnaia Zvezda* editorial noted, "The personnel of the allied armies have come well-prepared to their autumn examinations (and an exercise is always a rigorous examination.)"[89] After the completion of this particular exercise, the Soviet army newspaper quoted Marshal Iakubovskii as saying ". . . the exercises which have just taken place were a serious examination for the fraternal armies and indicate . . . the skills of commanders and staffs in resolving tasks in complex, swiftly changing circumstances."[90]

A factor which may affect Soviet evaluations of East European officers in joint WTO exercises may be the old-school tie of Eastern Europeans to Soviet military academies. Chapter 8 of this study argues that certain mid-career Soviet military academies have secured a virtual monopoly on the training of senior East European officers for command and staff responsibilities in WTO exercises. One factor affecting promotion to the highest defense ministry posts in East Europe may be receiving favorable evaluations in the joint exercises. Such evaluations may in turn depend on both formal education in the Soviet institutions qualified to train officers for joint exercises and informal connections to other alumni of Soviet academies.

Krasnaia Zvezda's accounts of individual WTO exercises occasionally identify East European officers in the exercises who are graduates of Soviet military academies.[91] *Krasnaia Zvezda* sometimes quotes such officers as saying that their Soviet educations prepared them well for the exercises and that it is very useful in the exercises to have a fluent command of Russian military terminology. These accounts of the interactions of WTO officers in joint exercises also note the friendships of Soviet and East European alumni of Soviet academies. *Krasnaia Zvezda* reported during the 1970 Brotherhood in Arms exercises in East Germany that Lieutenant Colonel Wolfgang Chernig of the East German Army was assigned to work with a group of Soviet officers among whom were graduates of an unidentified Soviet military academy in Leningrad in which Chernig had studied. Chernig told a *Krasnaia Zvezda* correspondent that both he and his wife had warm memories of their years in Leningrad. The correspondent reported that Soviet officers had laughed after Chernig told *Krasnaia Zvezda* about his wife's reaction to the news that her husband had been assigned to work with some fellow graduates of his alma mater. According to the front-page story in *Krasnaia Zvezda,* Frau Chernig had begged her husband, "Take me with you as your driver. I would really like to meet some Russians again."[92]

Political Activities in the Joint Exercises

Judging by accounts in Soviet sources, Warsaw Pact exercises anticipate a conflict in which a series of rapid troop movements and nuclear strikes will alternate with a series of political rallies, friendship meetings, concerts, and visits to sites of historical and cultural interest. Soviet and

East European sources place more emphasis on the military-political aspects of the joint exercises than on the military-technical aspects.[93] Soviet sources began reporting political exercises in the fall of 1962.[94] Since 1962, and perhaps even before 1962, the Soviet force groups in East Europe, the four western military districts of the USSR and the Soviet Black Sea and Baltic Sea Fleets have developed an extensive network of joint political activities directed by the main political administrations of the Warsaw Pact states.[95] The Romanians escaped from this network by abolishing their main political administration in 1964.

Colonel Semin, one of the Soviet military journalists specializing on the Warsaw Pact, presents the following outline of the conduct of political activities in joint exercises. Representatives of the main political administrations of the participating armies form a united operational group. This group organizes meetings among the fraternal troops, meetings of the soldiers with the local population, and programs of "agitation-propaganda" and "cultural enlightenment." This group also supervises a joint press center, a joint multilingual newspaper published during the exercises, joint multilingual radio broadcasts and a joint cinematography group.[96] The film group probably submits entries for the annual Warsaw Pact Film Festival, which began in 1966.[97]

According to Colonel Semin, the main political administration of the officer under whose command the exercise is taking place "as a rule" is responsible for the formation of the united operational group which directs the political activities of a given exercise.[98] According to the Iakubovskii text, the united operational group has its representatives in the staff which directs the exercise and in the political departments of the national forces assigned to the maneuvers.[99] Colonel Semin notes, and Warsaw Pact press agencies confirm, that the highest-ranking party, state and military officials of the host country usually participate in political meetings with the soldiers and in joint meetings of soldiers and civilians in factories, farms, and towns. When the fraternal soldiers meet, they discuss ways of improving combat readiness and military skills. They also proclaim mutual devotion to the principles of proletarian internationalism. In addition to their meetings with the local population, the WTO personnel also visit war memorials and historical exhibits. Colonel Semin writes that "as a rule" political-education activities take place during pauses in military actions. "When the situation permits" the joint operational group organizes joint discussions and seminars on "military-political and theoretical themes," speeches by propagandists, and the exchange of films and stage performances. The meetings of soldiers and civilians often include performances by choral and dance groups and orchestras.[100]

A joint Polish-Soviet study reports that during the Brotherhood in Arms exercises of 1970 in East Germany there were more than 40 meetings of allied military units, more than 200 political rallies involving soldiers and civilians and about 300 cultural programs.[101] Acccording to a Soviet-Czechoslovak volume, during an unidentified joint exercise of the Soviet Central Force Group and the Czechoslovak People's Army there were five meetings of commanders and political officers, six meetings of outstanding enlisted military personnel, four large political rallies and 50 joint excursions.[102] Political activities appear to take place even during low-level tactical exercises. *Krasnaia Zvezda* reported in 1971 that after jointly laying a pontoon bridge across the Danube, Soviet and Hungarian soldiers advanced to a concert given by the orchestra of the staff of the Southern Force Group.[103]

Krasnaia Zvezda gave particularly detailed coverage to the political activities of the 1970 Brotherhood in Arms exercises, perhaps because, as the Soviet army newspaper noted, the fraternal armed forces were simultaneously observing the 15th anniversary of the WTO, the 100th birthday of Lenin, the 21st anniversary of the GDR and the 26th anniversary of the Czechoslovak People's Army.[104] *Krasnaia Zvezda* also reported the visit to a Soviet tank regiment of Erich Mueckenberger, a full member of the East German Politburo. Mueckenberger gave a speech on the contribution of the exercises to the peace and security of the socialist confederation and then presented the regiment with a bust of Karl Marx. After having been reminded of the German origins of Soviet Communism, the officers of the regiment then reminded Mueckenberger of the Soviet origins of German Communism: they ushered him into the regimental room of combat glory where they recounted the history of their regiment, including its participation in the conquest of Germany. A German officer accompanying Mueckenberger replied that in 1945 he had been a child in Swedt, one of the towns captured by this very regiment. *Krasnaia Zvezda* noted that Swedt was now one of the terminals for the Friendship Oil Pipeline from the Soviet Union.[105]

The political activities of the joint exercises attempt to inspire feelings of proletarian internationalism among the multinational personnel of the Soviet armed forces and the multinational personnel of the WTO as a whole. The political activities also attempt to justify the conduct of multinational military maneuvers on the national territories of the members of the Warsaw Pact. Legitimizing multilateral military actions in each country rules out adoption of strategies of territorial defense by the national defense ministries. Political activities which justify the presence of foreign soldiers on national territory also prepare the soldiers and civilians of East Europe for multilateral WTO interventions. During one of the more recent publicized exercises, the "Friendship-79" maneuvers of Soviet and Czechoslovak troops in Czechoslovakia, *Krasnaia Zvezda* reported the visit of a joint delegation of the fraternal armies to local villages and factories. *Krasnaia Zvezda* specifically pointed out the multinational composition of the delegation: it included two Czechs, a Ukrainian, a Georgian, a Dagestani and a Tatar.[106] A *Krasnaia Zvezda* editorial during the Brotherhood in Arms exercises explained the central role of Soviet forces in this multinational alliance:

> Yes, the soldiers of the fraternal armies speak in different languages, but they think in the same way. In this regard they are like brothers in one big family.
>
> Yes, and they understand and recognize that the older brother in this family is the Soviet soldier who defended his Fatherland, who brought freedom to the people of Europe and who in his military victory was always true to the international proletariat and struggled for the happiness of mankind.[107]

There are historical reasons for suggesting that Czechs, Ukrainians, Georgians, Dagestanis, Tatars and the other nationalities of the Warsaw Pact also have other, less fond memories of big brother. The goal of the political activities of the joint exercises is to defend the soldiers of the WTO against such memories. Chapter 7 of this study examines the ideological texts and the organizational techniques used by the political administrations of the Warsaw Pact to stand guard over the collective memory of the personnel of the alliance.

Several Soviet sources testify to the utility of political exercises in preparing WTO soldiers for the moral-political strains likely to occur in an intervention against another member country of the Warsaw Pact. *Krasnaia Zvezda*'s coverage of the events in Czechoslovakia following the intervention of August 20–21, 1968, mentioned friendly meetings of the fraternal soldiers with Czechoslovak civilians in factories, farms, and towns. The Soviet army newspaper also noted the deep concern of Soviet military personnel for the welfare of their comrades-in-arms in the Czechoslovak People's Army—as demonstrated by the Soviet pilot who took it upon himself to fly a seriously-ill Czech soldier directly to Prague for medical treatment unavailable in Slovakia.[108] On his return from invading Czechoslovakia, Lieutenant Christo Radulov of the Bulgarian People's Army and his unit stopped in the Odessa Military District of the USSR to discuss the intervention with the soldiers of the district. At a political meeting he declared, "It was difficult for us in the first days. The counterrevolutionaries and their chorus ranted and raved. It was necessary to have iron nerves in order not to succumb to the provocations.

But for us the example was always the Soviet soldier, who demonstrated obvious self-control and self-mastery."[109] At the same meeting, another Bulgarian officer, Parashkev Palukov, told his audience,

> The joint entry of our troops into Czechoslovakia strengthened our friendship even more. We lived in one big family. And as in every family, we all shared.
>
> Each of us is bringing back a great many addresses from the USSR, Hungary, Poland, the GDR. We are going to write and keep each other informed.
>
> You know, we are more than friends. We are brothers in spirit, brothers in arms. . . ."[110]

For the Bulgarian soldiers who were not able to participate in the invasion of Czechoslovakia, subsequent joint WTO exercises afforded opportunities to meet pen pals from the fraternal armies.

Conclusion: Joint Exercises of the Warsaw Pact

Marshal Grechko and his successors have used the system of multilateral WTO exercises (1) to pre-empt the possibility that East European states would follow the examples of Yugoslavia and Romania in adopting strategies of territorial defense; (2) to enhance Soviet capabilities for rapid, massive interventions in East Europe; and (3) to develop a Soviet capability to mobilize detachments of East European forces for symbolic participation in joint interventions.

The system of joint exercises also reactivated the military-political devices of Soviet control over the East European armies. The upheavals of 1956 had badly damaged these mechanisms. The military-political control devices reactivated by the joint exercises reinforced each other and permitted the Soviets to compete with the national defense ministries of East Europe for control over the personnel assigned to the United Armed Forces of the Warsaw Treaty Organization. The following chapters examine four of these military-political mechanisms:

1. The United Command of the WTO. This collection of central administrative agencies dates back to 1955. After the introduction of multilateral exercises, the Staff of the United Command began to detach the service branches and elite formations of the East European armed forces from the national defense ministries. The Staff (and, after 1969, the Military Council), used the exercises to extend the reach of the United Command over the training programs which determine in part the capabilities of the East European forces assigned to the United Command.

The Staff (and after the mid-1970s, the Technical Committee) also claimed jurisdiction over the weapons development and weapons procurement policies of the member states of the alliance.

2. A WTO agency for military doctrine to serve as a clearinghouse for the formulation of common military-political and military-technical axioms. As the joint exercises began in the early 1960s, Soviet military theoreticians elaborated a comprehensive system of military doctrine which established common alliance norms for the organization of all aspects of the national defense system of a socialist state. Common military-technical axioms require the establishment of parallel agencies and force structures. Common doctrinal propositions define the military capabilities of each state and facilitate the interaction and integration of the armed forces of the alliance. The common military-political axioms justify the mobilization of multinational formations under central command and proscribe the alternative military-political axioms of the Yugoslavs and Romanians.

3. An integrated network of WTO political administrations. This network grew out of the joint political exercises conducted during multilateral maneuvers. The political officers of the WTO coordinate common programs of political indoctrination carried out in the native tongues of the alliance. They also monitor the political reliability of WTO personnel.

4. An integrated system of officer education. The WTO exercises appear to have led to the designation of certain Soviet mid-career academies as the only institutions qualified to train East European officers for high-level command and staff work in the joint exercises. In Soviet and East European undergraduate military colleges and mid-career academies, the common axioms of military doctrine provide a common curriculum. The Soviet and East European alumni of the senior military academies of the USSR constitute a greater socialist officer corps whose members command the various national detachments subordinate to the commander in chief of the Warsaw Pact.

Chapter Five
The Military-Administrative Structure of the Warsaw Pact

During his tenure as commander of the Warsaw Pact, Marshal Grechko conducted Pact affairs through a series of ad hoc meetings of WTO personnel summoned to plan a wide range of joint activities. After 1969, Marshal Iakubovskii transformed these ad hoc devices into formal Pact agencies with specifically defined functions. The military-administrative structure of the WTO, both before and after 1969, sought the same objective: denying East European defense ministries exclusive control over the components of national military forces and maximizing Soviet control over these forces and their officers. Several considerations connected with the events of 1968 appear to have prompted Marshal Iakubovskii to create formal agencies operated by both Soviet and East European officers to preside over the activities initiated by Marshal Grechko. One consideration may have been the complaint of the Czech General Vaclav Prchlik that East European officers served only as liaison personnel who conveyed orders issued by Soviet officers. Another may have been a Soviet preference for using WTO agencies to link the Czechoslovak armed forces to the newly formed Central Group of Soviet Forces in Czechoslovakia. A third consideration may have been a Soviet decision to erect formal legal barriers against the proposals of any future "Gottwald Memorandum."

About a month after the invasion of Czechoslovakia, Marshal Iakubovskii visited Poland "and other states" to discuss questions "concerning the strenthening of the defensive capacity of the member governments of the WTO."[1] In late October 1968, the WTO defense ministers met in Moscow to discuss "questions concerning the strengthening of the Warsaw Pact."[2] By the spring of 1969, the WTO commander in chief had formulated a plan for the reorganization of the military-administrative structure of the Pact. On March 17 in Budapest, he delivered to the Political Consultative Committee of the Pact (PCC) a report on "measures worked out by the [WTO] ministers of defense with the approval of the corresponding governments."[3] After hearing Iakubovskii's report, the PCC unanimously approved the creation of a Committee of Defense

Ministers, a body that required unanimous votes to issue recommendations. The PCC also adopted a revision of the 1955 statute on the United Armed Forces and United Command of the WTO and adopted "other documents having the goal of further perfecting the structure and organs of the defensive organization of the Warsaw Treaty Organization."[4]

The gradual appearance of new Pact agencies after the 1969 meeting of the PCC suggests that the Soviets and Romanians engaged in extended negotiations over the documents designed to perfect the mechanisms of the Warsaw Pact. The first of the new agencies to appear was the Military Council, which announced its existence by meeting for the first time in December 1969. As noted in the preceding chapter, the Romanians were not bound by the "consultative" decisions of the Military Council. In 1975, the Soviet military press revealed the existence of the Technical Committee, without providing any information on its membership or its administrative competence. In 1976, the Pact formally established a Council of Foreign Ministers. The WTO foreign ministers and vice foreign ministers had met frequently on an ad hoc basis during the early and mid-1970s.[5] The Political Consultative Committee remained the highest political agency of the alliance; the Romanians continued to demonstrate their independence in the sessions of this body.[6] During the 1970s, information began to appear in the Soviet press which suggested the functioning of agencies that supervised joint activities which probably took place even before 1969: a Pact directorate for military doctrine and military history; a Pact directorate for the WTO political administrations; and a Pact directorate for officer education in the WTO.

The WTO Convention of 1973

The legal basis for the functioning of the publicly identified agencies of the Pact and the unidentified agencies as well is the "Convention on the Legal Competence, Privileges and Immunities of the Staff and Other Organs of Administration of the United Armed Forces of the Member States of the Warsaw Pact," which the vice foreign ministers of the Pact signed on April 24, 1973. The 1973 Convention indicated that Pact members could legally circumvent the Political Consultative Committee and the Council of Defense Ministers. Marshal Grechko had probably developed informal devices for circumventing the PCC in the early 1960s. These devices were necessary because Albania boycotted all WTO activities, including those of the PCC, from November 1961 until Tirana's formal withdrawal from the Pact in August 1968. They were also necessary because, after 1964, Romania often prevented the PCC from reaching unanimous decisions.[7] In 1968, Marshal Iakubovskii found it convenient to forego sessions of the PCC in order to mobilize five of the eight Pact members for intervention in Czechoslovakia. The 1969 reorganization appears to have formalized the devices for circumventing the Political Consultative Committee.

The preamble to the 1973 Convention notes that "the general tasks and the designation of the Staff and other organs of administration of the United Armed Forces are defined by documents adopted by the member states of the Warsaw Treaty"[8] rather than by the Political Consultative Committee or the Council of Defense Ministers, each of which requires unanimity to issue policy directives. Every article of the 1973 Convention states that the article in question applies to the states that ratify the Convention rather than to all the members of the WTO. Sections 1, 2, and 3 of Article 6 declare that the Convention will go into effect if only three states ratify the Convention and that other states will be bound by the Convention after having ratified it. In other words, the Convention will be in force for three or more WTO members even if one or more WTO members refuses to ratify it. The text reads as follows:

Article 6

1. This Convention is subject to ratification by the states which have signed it in accordance with their constitutional procedures.

2. The ratification instruments will be transmitted to the custody of the Government of the Union of Soviet Socialist Republics, which is designated the depository of this Convention.

3. This Convention will go into force from the day of transmittal for custody of the ratification instruments of three states. In regard to the other states which have signed the Convention, the Convention will go into effect on the day of transmittal for custody of their ratification instruments.[9]

The author of this study has not been able to find any evidence that Romania ratified the Convention. A Romanian vice foreign minister did sign the Convention on April 24, 1973. Inquiries directed to competent officials of the Romanian defense ministry have brought a cryptic reply: if official Romanian publications have not published an announcement of ratification, then ratification has not taken place.[10]

Article 1 of the 1973 Convention provides adequate reason for Romania to refuse ratification. This article established two categories of personnel in the Staff and other organs of administration of the Warsaw Pact. One category consists of personnel from the member states of the WTO. The other category consists of personnel chosen by what the Convention identifies as the government of that country in which the city of Moscow is located.

Article 1

1. The Staff of the United Armed Forces consists of generals, admirals and officers of the member states of the Warsaw Pact, on whom are conferred privileges and immunities in accordance with this Convention for the fulfillment of their service duties.

   On the Staff of the United Armed Forces also work personnel chosen by the government of the place of location of the Staff, part of whom enjoy the privileges and immunities stipulated by this Convention. . . .

2. For the purposes of this Convention the term "Staff of the United Armed Forces" also designates the other organs of administration of the members states of the Warsaw Pact.

3. The place of location of the Staff of the United Armed Forces is the city of Moscow.[11]

Section 1 of Article 1 does qualify somewhat the Soviet right to appoint personnel to the administrative agencies of the WTO:

Article 1

1. . . .

   The category and number of personnel enjoying privileges and immunities is agreed upon by the Staff of the United Armed Forces with the General (or Main) Staffs of the member states of this Convention.

   A roster of these personnel is annually sent by the Staff of the United Armed Forces to the General (or Main) Staffs of the armed forces of the member states of this Convention.[12]

It is not clear from the text of the Convention how the Staff of the United Armed Forces determines the number of personnel enjoying privileges and immunities or for how long a period these personnel will enjoy their status. It is also not clear whether the general staff of a national defense ministry whose government has ratified the Convention has the right to delete names from the roster sent by the WTO Staff. Article 6 of the Convention establishes a procedure for resolving these and any other questions arising from the implementation of the Convention. This procedure by-passes the Political Consultative Committee and the Council of Defense Ministers in favor of state-to-state negotiations among the states that are parties to the Convention:

Article 6

4. Possible contested questions arising from the interpretation and implementation of this Convention will decided by the member states of this Convention by the means of negotiations between the national commands or by diplomatic channels or by any other means of understanding.[13]

The lack of well-defined procedures for resolving disputes through specifically designated agencies suggests that any contested questions will be settled by contests of raw strength. Section 5 of Article 6 establishes the ground rules for such contests:

Article 6

5. This Convention is drawn up in one copy in the Russian language. This Convention will be transmitted to the custody of the Government of the Union of Soviet Socialist Republics which will provide verified copies to all of the other governments which have signed it.[14]

The designation of a Russian-language version as the only legal text of the Convention contrasts with the use of Russian, German, Polish, and Czech-language versions as equally valid texts of the original Warsaw Treaty.[15]

Articles 2, 3 and 4 of the 1974 Convention specify the legal competence, privileges, and immunities conferred upon the personnel of the Staff and other organs of administration of the Warsaw Pact. Article 2 provides that the personnel of these agencies are empowered to conclude agreements, although the article does not specify with whom. The most likely candidates would appear to be corresponding agencies in East European defense ministries. Articles 3 and 4 provide that in concluding and carrying out such agreements the personnel of the Staff and other organs of administration will enjoy full rights of extraterritoriality, diplomatic immunity, and unimpeded access to all national communications facilities. These privileges place the personnel of the Staff and other organs of administration beyond the jurisdiction of national military or civilian officials. The text reads:

Article 3

1. The Staff of the United Armed Forces enjoys on the territory of each state participating in this Convention the legal competence, privileges and immunities stipulated by this Convention.

2. The premises of the Staff, its property, assets and documents, regardless of their location, enjoy immunity from any form of administrative or juridical interference with the exception of cases in which the Staff itself renounces immunity in a specific case. . . .

5. The Staff of the UAF enjoys on the territory of each member state of this Convention no less favorable conditions in regard to priority, tariffs and rates of charge of the postal service, telegraph and telephone communications than those which the national military command or diplomatic representatives enjoy in that country.

Article 4

1. In the performance of their service responsibilities the official personnel of the Staff of the UAF enjoy the following privileges and immunities on the territory of each state participating in this Convention:

a) inviolability of all books and documents; . . .

d) immunity from personnel arrest or confinement and also from the jurisdiction of legal or administrative institutions in regard to all actions which may be taken in their capacity as official personnel; . . .

2. The Chief of Staff of the UAF and his deputies, in addition to the privileges and immunities established in section 1 of this article, enjoy on the territory of all member states of this Convention the privileges and immunities granted in the country in question to diplomatic representatives. The designated personnel receive diplomatic passports.[16]

The five loyal East European Pact members who ratified the 1973 Convention agreed to the existence of a series of sovereign administrative agencies under the direct command of the Soviet officer who serves as the Warsaw Pact commander in chief. These sovereign agencies are not within the purview of national governments, the Political Consultative Committee or the Council of Defense Ministers. The East European states which ratified the 1973 Convention granted the Soviet government the right to appoint personnel to these sovereign agencies and to accord these personnel rights of extraterritoriality on East European soil. In the event of disputes between national governments and the WTO administrative agencies, the Convention has established an arbitration procedure weighted overwhelmingly in favor of the Soviet officer in charge of the WTO administrative agencies.

Administrative Agencies of the WTO

By the time Marshal Kulikov succeeded Marshal Iakubovskii as commander of the Pact in early 1977, the military-administrative structure of the Pact consisted of the Council of Defense Ministers, the Military Council, the commander in chief, the United Command, and several administrative agencies directly under the commander and covered by the 1973 Convention: the WTO Staff, the Technical Committee, the Sports Committee of the Friendly Armies and the unidentified "other organs of administration" mentioned by the 1973 Convention.

The Committee of Defense Ministers (CDM) consists not only of the seven Pact defense ministers but also, according to the *Soviet Military Encyclopedia,* the WTO commander in chief and the WTO chief of staff.[17]

The composition of the CDM enables three Soviet officers to sit on this nine-member body, although it is not known if the WTO commander and chief of staff are full voting members. According to the Iakubovskii text on the WTO, the CDM must reach unanimous decisions in order to issue recommendations.[18] A former member of the CDM, the late chief of the WTO staff, General S.M. Shtemenko, wrote that the CDM functioned as a body of equals. As proof he noted the fact that the chairmanship and place of location of sessions rotated in alphabetical order.[19] From the order of rotation[20] it appears that of the seven WTO alphabets, the CDM uses the Russian one to determine alphabetical order.

The CDM meets once a year for a two-day session. Neither the chairman of a particular session nor the CDM as a body has its own staff. Instead, the CDM relies on the Staff of the WTO as its "working organ."[21] The WTO Staff is also the "administrative organ" of the WTO commander and is under the command of his first deputy, the WTO chief of staff.[22] According to the Iakubovskii text, in its capacity as the working organ of the CDM, the WTO Staff "plays a great role in preparing and carrying out the decisions of the Council of Defense Ministers."[23] According to the communiques issued after its sessions, the CDM has discussed the activities of the WTO administrative agencies, the communications and transport systems of the WTO, the combat readiness of Pact forces, and the organization of WTO national defense systems.[24] The range of concerns addressed by the CDM, the brevity of its sessions, and its dependence on a Staff under the command of two Soviet officers who are also members of the CDM all suggest that the function of the Council of Defense Ministers is to have the East European defense ministers approve policies planned and carried out by the commander in chief of the WTO and the subordinate agencies.

The Military Council (MC) consists of the Pact commander, who serves as a chairman, and all the deputy commanders of the Pact. These include a deputy commander from each East European member (usually the national chief of staff or a deputy national defense minister); the WTO chief of staff; and any other deputy commanders of the WTO.[25] Since its establishment in 1969, the Military Council has annually met in the late fall and sometimes early spring in joint sessions with other high-ranking Pact military personnel. These joint sessions, discussed in the preceding chapter, examine the results of the WTO training and exercise programs of the preceding year and plan the programs for the coming year. Because the recommendations of the MC are only "consultative," the MC can accommodate Romania's refusal to accept its recommendations without disrupting the work of the Military Council. Like the CDM, the MC relies on the WTO Staff to prepare its sessions and carry out its decisions.[26]

The real locus of authority in the WTO administrative structure is in the commander in chief and the administrative agencies directly subordinate to him. Neither the Political Consultative Committee nor the Council of Defense Ministers appears to play a role in the appointment of the Pact commander. A communique issued in 1955 by the foreign ministers who signed the Warsaw Treaty announced the appointment of the first commander, General I.S. Konev. It is not clear exactly what body named Marshal Grechko Pact commander in July of 1960.[27] The Soviet press simply announced as a "decision of the member governments" the appointments of I.I. Iakubovskii in 1967 and V.G. Kulikov in 1977.[28] Both the Iakubovskii text and the *Soviet Military Encyclopedia* declare that the Pact commander is chosen "by decision of the member governments" rather than by the Political Consultative Committee or the Council of Defense Ministers.[29] WTO sources have yet to make clear the relationship of the commander in chief to the PCC or the CDM. The Iakubovskii text says that the commander "periodically reports" to the PCC, CDM, and the member governments of the alliance; the *Soviet Military Encyclopedia* declares that the Pact commander is "guided by decisions of the PCC and member governments."[30] Each of the last three WTO commanders has simultaneously served as a first deputy defense minister of the USSR and a member of the Soviet Central Committee.

The United Command of the WTO consists of the commander; the commander's deputy, the chief of staff; a deputy commander from each of the East European members; and a deputy commander who serves as commander of the anti-aircraft troops of the Warsaw Pact. Until 1969, East European defense ministers were named deputy commanders of the United Command, but after the creation of the Council of Defense Ministers, the East European deputy commanders of the United Command have been either deputy national defense ministers and/or chiefs of national general staffs.[31] According to the U.S. Central Intelligence Agency, the current deputy commander of the United Command who serves as commander of the Pact anti-aircraft troops is Marshal A.I. Koldunov, who also serves as the commander of the Soviet Anti-Aircraft Troops and deputy defense minister of the USSR.[32] According to the *Soviet Military Encyclopedia,* Koldunov's predecessor, Marshal P.F. Batitskii, was named in 1966 to the same posts in the United Command of the WTO and the Ministry of Defense of the USSR.[33] There is no good answer to the question of why the WTO has publicly identified a deputy commander of the United Command for Pact anti-aircraft troops but has not publicly identified deputy commanders for other Pact service branches.

The 1955 documents on the Warsaw Pact specified that deputy commanders of the United Command would be WTO defense ministers and "other military leaders of the member states of the treaty on whom are placed command of the armed forces assigned to the United Armed Forces by each member state of the treaty."[34] This provision may have been the basis for the appointment of Marshal Batitskii in 1966 as a deputy commander of the United Command. In his capacity as a deputy commander, Batitskii presided over at least four joint exercises of WTO anti-aircraft troops.[35]

Several Soviet sources suggest the possible existence of a deputy commander of the United Command for the Pact navies. A joint Polish-Soviet study declares that the Soviet Baltic Fleet and the navies of the GDR and Poland are "united into a single military mechanism."[36] In its discussion of the joint naval exercises of the WTO, the Iakubovskii text notes that joint naval exercises facilitate the "organizational interaction of staffs and fleets."[37] The *Soviet Military Encyclopedia* observes that during the career of Admiral S.G. Gorshkov, commander of the Soviet Navy, the admiral has made "a great contribution . . . to the interaction of the Soviet navy with the navies and other service branches of the member countries of the Warsaw Pact."[38] Admiral Gorshkov has presided over at least one joint WTO naval exercise and the WTO commanders in chief have presided over at least three such exercises.[39]

The WTO has demonstrated its capability to conduct not only anti-aircraft and naval exercises, but also joint air force and rear services exercises[40] and the Iakubovskii text declares that special troops (communications, etc.) also conduct regular joint exercises.[41] It is possible that these capabilities are based on the existence of deputy commanders for Pact navies, air force, rear services and special troops.

In addition to his set of East European deputy commanders, the WTO commander in chief also has a group of liaison representatives to the armed forces of East Europe. The Iakubovskii text explains:

> Representatives of the Commander-in-Chief of the Armed Forces serve in the allied armies with the agreement of the corresponding governments.
>
> Their basic functions consist of giving aid to the national command in the training of troops assigned to the United Armed Forces and also the maintaining of constant and close contacts between the United and national commands.
>
> Being highly qualified generals and officers, having rich experience in the leadership of troops, they are especially useful for the strengthening of military cooperation among the allied armies and in raising the combat readiness of the United Armed Forces."[42]

The U.S. Central Intelligence Agency has published the names of the liaison representatives in 1978 to Bulgaria, East Germany, Poland, Romania, and Czechoslovakia.[43]

The WTO Staff

The "administrative organ" of the commander in chief is the WTO Staff.[44] This organ is without question the most important agency in the WTO. Soviet sources report that the Chief of Staff is chosen by the "mutual agreement" of unspecified selectors rather than by the Political Consultative Committee or the Council of Defense Ministers.[45] This selection process has produced five Soviet officers who have served as chief of the WTO Staff: A.I. Antonov (1955–62); P.I. Batov (1962–65), who served as the commander of the Soviet forces that crushed the Hungarian revolution of 1956; M.I. Kazakov (1965–68); S.M. Shtemenko (1968–1976); and the current chief of staff, A.I. Gribkov. The WTO Staff has a deputy chief from each of the East European members. There are also additional personnel on the WTO Staff who, according to the 1973 Convention, are chosen by the government of the country in which the city of Moscow is located. One of these Soviet officers is Lieutenant General K.K. Pashuk, first deputy chief of the WTO Staff.[46]

As the working organ of both the Committee of Defense Ministers and the Military Council, the WTO Staff has within its purview all the joint activities of the WTO. By far the most important of these is managing the joint programs of troop training and military exercises, which were discussed in the preceding chapter. According to Vice Admiral Studzinski, the Polish deputy chief of the WTO Staff in 1975, the Staff is also responsible for organizing meetings of WTO personnel.[47] The number, frequency, and scope of the meetings organized by the WTO staff is such that these meetings virtually constitute part of the WTO administrative structure. According to the Iakubovskii text, there are regular meetings, both bilateral and multilateral, among corresponding specialists in all branches of the WTO armed forces.[48] This text adds that many of these meetings "have the objective resolving separate questions which concern the service branches of the armed forces and types of troops within a service branch or special troops."[49] In a 1976 article, Marshal Iakubovskii wrote that meetings of the WTO Chiefs of Staff and heads of WTO service branches have become "traditional."[50] His volume on the WTO documents meetings of WTO Chiefs of Staff in 1969, 1971, 1973, and 1974 and notes that the WTO Staff attended at least one of these meetings, the 1974 session in Prague.[51]

A joint Soviet-Bulgarian study published in 1969 said that by 1968 the WTO had conducted more than 2,500 meetings of military specialists devoted to military-technical, military-political, and military-historical questions. This study added:

> At the meetings of the leading staffs of the [WTO] armed forces, there is a summing up of the operational training of troops and staffs, new educational tasks are designated, and the basic directions of the development of types of troops are defined. . . .
>
> A creative exchange of opinions and acquired experience takes place on a broad range of questions of the development of national defense systems, and of the training and upbringing of troops which are of mutual interest for all the fraternal armed forces.
>
> Results achieved and shortcoming are evaluated in a principled and self-critical manner.[52]

The WTO Technical Committee

The 1969 meeting of the Political Consultative Committee may have established an agency to coordinate weapons research. In 1975, the Soviet military press began mentioning the name of such an agency, the WTO Technical Committee,[53] but these sources do not indicate just when this agency was created. According to the *Soviet Military Encyclopedia,* the head of this agency is chosen "by mutual agreement of the representatives of the WTO countries."[54] The representatives of the WTO states involved in this selection process have yet to identify either themselves or the officer they have chosen to head the Technical Committee. The Polish vice admiral who served as deputy chief of the WTO Staff in 1975 wrote that the Technical Committee had East European representatives on it.[55] The Iakubovskii text implies that the Technical Committee is covered by the 1973 Convention, which permits the Soviet government to appoint personnel to the Staff "and other organs" of the WTO.[56] This text also suggests that the Technical Committee is concerned with weapons research but not weapons production.[57] Warsaw Pact sources do not reveal any additional information on the work of the Technical Committee, but they do note extensive joint efforts in the production of weapons and military goods.[58] These discussions suggest that the coordination of armaments manufacture takes place in the agencies of the Council for Mutual Economic Assistance and the corresponding national economic agencies, rather than in the Technical Committee or any other agency of the Warsaw Pact.[59]

The Sports Committee of the WTO

The Sports Committee of the Friendly Armed Forces (SCFAF) is "the authoritative international sports organization" for the Warsaw Pact, according to a colonel general of the Soviet Main Political Administration.[60] When the SCFAF was established in 1958, its membership included all the Warsaw Pact states and China, Mongolia, and Korea. According to the *Soviet Military Encyclopedia,* during the early 1960s both Albania, a Pact member, and China ceased participating in the work of the SCFAF. Eventually the SCFAF recovered from these defections by adding several new members, Cuba (1969), South Yemen (1974), and Angola (1977).[61]

Every four years the members of the Sports Committee of the Friendly Armed Forces elects a bureau which administers the activities of the SCFAF. Soviet sources have identified at least one Soviet officer who served as head of the bureau, a Colonel Bragin.[62] According to the *Soviet Military Encyclopedia* both the bureau and the SCFAF itself make decisions by majority voice with open ballots, a procedure that may permit a majority within the SCFAF to conduct joint activities without being impeded by the vetoes or noncooperation of some members.

In the period from 1958 to 1978, the SCFAF had conducted 10 Spartakiads (Olympic-style competitions in several sports) and 306 championships in individual sports. Eight of the Spartakiads came after the 1969 reorganization of the Pact.[63] The bureau of the SCFAF also organizes the exchange of information on the teaching of physical culture and monitors the implementation of recommendations of the SCFAF.[64] The Soviet Armed Forces served as the host for at least one SCFAF conference, a meeting of 1972 devoted to "Psychological Preparation of Military Personnel Through Physical Culture and Sports."[65]

"Other Organs of Administration" of the WTO

The significance of the information available on the Sports Committee of the Friendly Armed Forces is in what it suggests about the "other organs of administration" of the WTO: if corresponding agencies in national defense ministries have engaged in frequent, publicized joint activities, there is a good chance that a WTO agency exists to coordinate their joint activities. It is unlikely that a military alliance run by Soviet officers on the basis of Leninist principles would rely on the spontaneous coordination of joint activities. The phrase "other organs of administration of the WTO" appears in the 1973 Convention, the Iakubovskii text on the Warsaw Pact, and the *Soviet Military Encyclopedia*.[66] One of these agencies is probably a military intelligence agency, but only one Pact source even hints at the coordination of Pact security agencies.[67] The available evidence suggests that three of the "other organs of administration" are a directorate for military doctrine, a directorate for the WTO political administrations, and a directorate for officer education in the Warsaw Pact. This evidence consists of: (1) frequent, publicized joint activities among the corresponding national agencies charged with responsibilities in these three areas; (2) frequent public statements from the highest-ranking military officers of the Pact calling attention to the importance of the coordinated programs in these three areas; (3) in the case of the Pact political administrations, regular meetings of the heads of these agencies, comparable to the regular meetings of the Council of Defense Ministers and the Military Council.

The question of whether or not formal Pact agencies exist to coordinate joint programs in these three areas is less important than the fact that evidence exists to document the functioning of the joint programs. The loyal members of the Warsaw Pact may have decided not to identify these agencies publicly because they may not wish to call attention to the fact that Romania does not participate in these three programs of joint activities. For their part, the Romanians may have concluded that participation in the joint activities sponsored by the unidentified Pact agencies will enhance the capability of the central Pact administrative structure to compete effectively with national agencies for control of the separate components of East European armed forces. Romania appears to have agreed to participate fully only in those agencies in which Romania has the right to veto measures affecting Romania: the Political Consultative Committee, the Council of Foreign Ministers, the Council of Defense Ministers, the Military Council and perhaps the Technical Committee and the Sports Committee of the Friendly Armed Forces.

The United Armed Forces

The military-administrative agencies of the WTO preside over the United Armed Forces (UAF) of the Warsaw Pact. Soviet sources claim that each member of the alliance decides for itself the forces it assigns to the UAF after taking into consideration "the decrees of the PCC and the recommendations of the WTO Commander in Chief."[68] In its annual publication, *The Military Balance,* the International Institute of Strategic Studies (IISS) puts the number of Soviet divisions in East Europe at 31. Of these divisions, 20 are in the Group of Soviet Forces in Germany, which consists of 10 tank divisions and 10 mechanized infantry divisions. The Northern Force Group in Poland consists of 2 tank divisions; the Central Force Group in Czechoslovakia consists of 2 tank and 3 mechanized infantry divisions; the Southern Force Group in Hungary is made up of 2 tank and 2 mechanized infantry divisions.[69]

The Military Balance distinguishes among divisions in Category I (three-quarters to full strength), Category II (half to three-quarters strength), and Category III (about one-quarter full strength). The IISS places all 31 Soviet divisions in East Europe in Category I.[70] The IISS counts 50 Soviet divisions in the seven European military districts of the USSR and places half of these divisions in Category III, but does not specify how many of the remaining divisions are in Categories I or II. By combining its unspecified totals for the Soviet forces in East Europe and the western military districts of the USSR, *The Military Balance* arrives at a figure of 785,000 Sovit troops assigned to the Warsaw Pact.[71] Without specifying the individual contributions of East European Pact members, the IISS puts the total non-Soviet Warsaw Pact forces at 546,000.[72]

Subtracting the figure of 546,000 East European troops assigned to the UAF from 1,093,500, the total of the *Military Balance* figures for the regular armed forces of the East European WTO states,[73] leaves a total of 547,000 East European regular forces not assigned to the UAF. These figures suggest that each East European WTO member assigns roughly half its regular armed forces to the UAF. According to Soviet sources, the UAF contingent is the better half.[74] *The Military Balance* also lists figures for the regular reserves of the East European Pact members. Excluding the Romanian total of 345,000, the regular reserve forces of the five loyal East European WTO members number 1,638,000.

The Military Balance also gives figures for the paramilitary forces of each WTO member. These forces consist of small detachments of border troops and internal security forces and large groups of militia, known as People's or Workers' or Citizen's Militia. In every WTO state except Romania, these parttime militia forces consist largely of Communist party members who serve as low-grade reserves for both the regular military forces and internal security forces. In Romania and Yugoslavia, the paramilitary forces play a much different role in national defense: they are vital components of the territorial defense systems and are closely linked to the regular armed forces, which draw upon them both as auxiliaries and as reserves. In Romania, the Patriotic Guard numbers about 700,000;[75] in Yugoslavia, the Territorial Defense Forces comes to 1,000,000.[76] Excluding the Romanian total of 737,000 paramilitary forces, the total paramilitary forces of the East European members of the Pact comes to 1,412,500. The Military Balance figures for regular forces, regular reserves and paramilitary forces are as follows:[77]

Table No. 2 — Military Manpower of the Non-Soviet Warsaw Pact States

Country/Forces	Number	Composition	Number	Country/Forces	Number	Composition	Number
Bulgaria				**Hungary**			
Regular forces:	150,000	Ground Forces	115,000	Regular forces:	114,000	Ground Forces	91,000
		Navy	10,000			Air Force	23,000
		Air Force	25,000				
Reserves:	235,000	Ground Forces	200,000	Reserves:	143,000	Ground Forces	130,000
		Navy	15,000			Air Force	13,000
		Air Force	20,000				
Paramilitary forces:	189,000	Border Guards	15,000	Paramilitary forces:	75,000	Border Guards	15,000
		Construction	12,000			Workers' Militia	60,000
		Security Police	12,000				
		People's Militia	150,000				
Czechoslovakia				**Poland**			
Regular forces:	186,000	Ground Forces	140,000	Regular forces:	306,500	Ground Forces	222,000
		Air Force	46,000			Navy	22,500
						Air Force	62,000
Reserves:	350,000	Ground Forces	300,000	Reserves:	605,000	Ground Forces	500,000
		Air Force	50,000			Navy	45,000
						Air Force	60,000
Paramilitary forces:	132,500	Border Guards	10,000	Paramilitary forces:	450,000	Border Troops	18,000
		Civil Defense	2,500			Internal Security	77,000
		People's Militia	120,000			Citizen's Militia	350,000
German Democratic Republic				**Romania**			
Regular forces:	157,000	Ground Forces	105,000	Regular forces:	180,500	Ground Forces	140,000
		Navy	16,000			Navy	10,500
		Air Force	36,000			Air Force	30,000
Reserves:	305,000	Ground Forces	250,000	Reserves:	345,000	Ground Forces	300,000
		Navy	25,000			Navy	20,500
		Air Force	30,000			Air Force	25,000
Paramilitary forces:	571,000	Border Troops	46,000	Paramilitary forces:	737,000	Border Troops	17,000
		Security Troops	25,000			Internal Security	20,000
		Workers' Militia	500,000			Patriotic Guard	700,000

Source: International Institute of Strategic Studies (IISS), *The Military Balance, 1978–79* (London: IISS, 1978), pp. 13-15

The 547,000 regular troops not assigned to the UAF, the 1,638,000 reserves (excluding the Romanian total of 345,000), and the 1,402,500 paramilitary forces (excluding Romania's total of 737,000) are rough indicators of the additional troop strength the elite regular armed forces of East Europe could draw upon if they were to plan for wars of territorial defense. In the case of Poland, the existing military troops outside the Polish UAF contingent numbers slightly over one million. One function of the military-administrative agencies of the WTO is to insure that such possibilities remain purely theoretical. For a national defense ministry to develop a credible capability for territorial defense, the elite regular armed forces must provide the leadership, organizational structure, and strategy for the larger masses of lower-quality forces.

The military-administrative agencies of the UAF place the 546,000 East European troops assigned to the UAF under the same command structure as the 785,000 Soviet troops assigned to the UAF. The United Command of the UAF appears to drill its forces mainly for offensive actions outside the home territory of each national army. In accepting the missions defined by the military-administrative agencies of the Pact, the national forces assigned to the UAF permit the WTO agencies to exert a strong influence on their relationship to national military reserves and national paramilitary forces. The policies of WTO administrative agencies also prevent the formation of a military-political bloc of East European states which excludes the USSR. These policies also preserve a system of bilateral Soviet-East European military relationships in which each East European Pact member faces an overwhelming combination of Soviet forces. In the cases of Hungary, Czechoslovakia, and Poland, some of these forces are based in the country itself, but most of them are stationed to the west in the Group of Soviet Forces in Germany and to the east in the military districts of the USSR. The participation of these Soviet forces in the program of joint alliance activities probably eliminates the possibilities of planning wars of territorial defense in Hungary, Czechoslovakia, Poland, and East Germany.

The most important of these alliance activities is the system of joint exercises and coordinated training programs. Other important joint activities linking the Soviet and East European forces assigned to the UAF are the regular exchanges of military delegations between corresponding formations and units. These "exchanges of experience" involve commanders, technical specialists, political officers, military journalists, and personnel concerned with the sports and cultural activities. Soviet forces also maintain regular ties with local governments and economic enterprises in East Europe and regularly receive visits from the highest-ranking East European political leaders. The major concentration of Soviet troops in East Europe, the Group of Soviet Forces in Germany, conducts the most extensive program of joint activities with the other fraternal armies.[78]

The Carpathian, Belorussian, and Odessa Military Districts of the USSR maintain similar networks of contacts with the East European forces assigned to the United Armed Forces. Some or all of the Soviet forces in these three military districts may be assigned to the UAF and may be directly under the military-administrative agencies of the Pact. The Carpathian Military District borders on Poland, Czechoslovakia, Hungary, and Romania. This district has been the site of at least one multilateral WTO military exercise.[79] A Soviet history of the Carpathian Military District notes that the district participates in "the systematic exchange of military delegations with other socialist states," including Poland, Czechoslovakia, Hungary, and Bulgaria.[80] The delegations consist of commanders, technical specialists, political officers, and military journalists.[81] The district also maintains ties with economic enterprises and local governments in the border districts of the neighboring socialist states.[82] According to the Soviet volume on the Carpathian Military District, political work among the soldiers of the district focuses on the Warsaw Pact countries, the armed forces of these states, and the obligation of Soviet soldiers to defend East European socialism against its external and internal enemies.[83]

The Belorussian Military District borders on Poland. A Soviet history of this district declares that the district's soldiers and Polish troops "have more than once participated in joint exercises and maneuvers."[84] According to this text, one of these maneuvers was the "Neman" exercise of July–August 1968,[85] during which the Commander of the Soviet Rear Services, General S.S. Mariakhin, directed the movement of several Soviet divisions to Poland where they joined forces with Polish and East German units in preparation for the invasion of Czechoslovakia on the night of August 20. This text also notes that in addition to regularly participating in military exercises with Polish troops, "The soldiers of the Belorussian Military District participate in many [other] joint measures conducted in the framework of the Warsaw Pact."[86] These activities include the exchange of "tens of delegations" from the armed forces of Poland, the GDR, and Czechoslovakia.[87] The delegations include commanders and political officers from the command of the district down to the command of individual sub-units. This district has frequently been host to WTO sports competitions[88] and to frequent ceremonies involving Polish and Soviet troops in the joint commemoration of political and martial anniversaries. One such ceremony of October 1968 brought to the Belorussian town of Lenino the chief of the Soviet Main Political Administration, General A.A. Epishev, and the Polish Defense Minister, General Vojtech

Jaruzelski, to dedicate a memorial to Polish-Soviet military friendship.[89] According to the Soviet study of the Belorussian Military District, the political officers of the district educate their troops in the traditions of Soviet military aid to East European states struggling against imperialism.[90] Officers from the fraternal armed forces play an important role in the political education program of the district. In the period from 1968 to 1970, East European officers delivered "about 200" speeches to the troops of the district. These officers included the military attaches to the USSR of unspecified socialist countries, lecturers from the Main Political Administration of the Polish Armed Forces, and historians from the East German Institute of Military History.[92]

The Odessa Military District borders directly on Romania and has naval access to Bulgaria through the services of the Red Banner Black Sea Fleet of the Soviet Navy. The Soviet history of this district does not mention the participation of the district's troops in any joint WTO exercises, but the proximity of this district to Bulgaria would make it a likely candidate for supplying the Soviet ground forces and airborne personnel which periodically participate in maneuvers in Bulgaria. According to the Soviet volume on the district, its troops did participate in the 1968 intervention in Czechoslovakia.[92]

This text notes that the exchange of military delegations has become "traditional" between the district and the armed forces of Bulgaria and Romania. In 1973, the Military Council of the district, in a review of the training of personnel in internationalism, noted that "recently" there had been "about 40 mutual exchanges" with unspecified socialist armies.[93] The only exchanges specifically identified by this text were with Bulgaria and Czechoslovakia; these included delegations of commanders, political workers, and military journalists.[94] The Soviet history of the district adds that in 1974 the Bulgarian ambassador, in commemoration of the 30th anniversaries of the Bulgarian revolution and the founding of the Bulgarian People's Army, presented decorations to the commander and staff of the Odessa Military District. This text does not explain why the Bulgarian ambassador chose to honor this particular military district.[95] It does note, however, that one of the principal goals of political work in the district is to acquaint Soviet soldiers with the organization and special features of the armed forces of the Warsaw Pact.[96] The Odessa Military District has also regularly provided facilities for WTO sports competitions and film festivals.[97]

Conclusion

The military-administrative agencies of the Warsaw Pact, particularly the WTO Staff, play a critical role in drawing the East European forces assigned to the United Armed Forces into military-political activities conducted jointly with the Soviet Force Groups in East Europe and the Soviet forces in at least three of the western military districts of the USSR. The charters of the central WTO administrative agencies are agreements concuded by six of the Pact members outside the Political Consultative Committee and the Council of Defense Ministers. The 1973 Convention on the privileges and immunities of these agencies enables them to compete with East European defense ministries for control over the East European forces assigned to the UAF. In designating the joint missions of the UAF, the military-administrative agencies of the WTO pre-empt the development of territorial defense capabilities by the elite regular forces of East Europe and impede the mobilization of the reserve forces necessary to sustain a strategy of territorial defense.

Chapter Six
The Warsaw Pact Directorate for Military Doctrine

Six of the Warsaw Pact states synchronize and standardize the writing of their military doctrines. Common views on military doctrine serve as the basis of the joint military exercises and the coordinated training programs of the WTO armed forces. Common views on military doctrine also serve as the texts for the party-political work conducted by the main political administrations of the Warsaw Pact and as the texts for the curriculum of the synchronized programs of officer education in the Warsaw alliance. The available evidence suggests that one of the "other organs of administration" of the WTO is an agency that monitors and coordinates the activities of the national agencies responsible for the formulation of military doctrine. The primary mission of the WTO directorate for military doctrine is to defend the armed forces of East Europe against the doctrinal heresies of the Romanians and Yugoslavs.

If there is no six-member directorate for military doctrine in the WTO United Command, the Military Science Directorate of the General Staff of the Soviet Armed Forces[1] may serve as the clearinghouse for the publishing of the military doctrines of individual Pact members. In either case, the WTO does synchronize the writing of the military literature of six of its members. In its discussion of the forms of cooperation among Pact states[2] Marshal Iakubovskii's article in the *Soviet Military Encyclopedia* notes:

> One of the most important directions of socialist military cooperation is the coordination of efforts in the further development of military theory and in a working out of a unity of views on the character and methods of waging war on the basis of Marxist-Leninist ideology.
>
> For these purposes business-like contacts have been established among military-scientific institutions, theoretical conferences are regularly conducted, and there is a joint working out of military-historical studies.[3]

These scholarly activities are not mere academic exercises. A Soviet authority on the Warsaw Pact observes, "As a result of cooperation in the area of military theory, very important standards have been adopted in the armed forces of the socialist confederation. These norms synchronize the basic development of regulations, of military administration and of training manuals."[4]

The Iakubovskii text on the Warsaw Pact points out an extensive program of WTO conferences that bring together specialists from corresponding agencies and service branches of the WTO.[5] This text also calls attention to systematic exchanges among the faculties of the WTO military academies responsible for the writing and teaching of military doctrine.[6]

According to the Iakubovskii study of the Warsaw Pact, the defense ministries of East Europe have received large quantities of Soviet military literature, especially on the conduct of nuclear war.[7] Heinz Hoffmann, the East German defense minister, wrote in 1976 that since 1956 the GDR military publishing house had translated 333 Soviet military texts and published a total of 11 million copies of Soviet military works.[8]

The Iakubovskii text on the WTO notes that Soviet military doctrine plays the central role in defining the common propositions shared by the doctrines of the WTO states.[9] In a 1972 article, Marshal Grechko explained the reasons for Soviet preeminence in the formulation of the doctrinal axioms of the Pact:

> The working out of the questions of modern military theory is the result of the close cooperation of the scholars of the allied armed forces.
>
> The availability of the extremely rich military experience of the Soviet Armed Forces and of its first-class material-technical base and of its well-trained military cadres—all this guarantees Soviet military scholars an avante-garde role in the resolution of the problematic tasks of military science.[10]

The *Soviet Military Encyclopedia* suggests that Soviet military scholars formulate their doctrinal propositions partly out of consideration of how Soviet doctrine will affect the relations between the Soviet defense ministry and the defense ministries of other socialist states. In its unsigned article on military doctrine the *Encyclopedia* declares, "Soviet military doctrine accords paramount importance to the close cooperation of the Soviet armed forces with the armed forces of the fraternal socialist countries."[11] The *Encyclopedia*'s article on military strategy, which is signed by Marshal Ogarkov, declares: "The formation of the Warsaw Treaty Organization in 1955 placed before [Soviet] military strategy a new task— the formulation of the common bases of the military strategy of the countries of the socialist confederation in which the international and national interests of the allied countries are organically combined."[12]

Several other Soviet texts also emphasize the close connection the Soviets see between formulating Soviet military doctrine and maintaining Soviet military alliances.[13]

The Role of Soviet Military Doctrine in the Warsaw Pact

In the Warsaw Pact the primary function of Soviet military doctrine is to prevent Bulgaria, Hungary, East Germany, Poland, and Czechoslovakia from adopting military doctrines of territorial defense similar to those of Romania and Yugoslavia. The administrative agencies of the WTO rely on Soviet military doctrine as the charter for all joint Pact activities which prevent the members of the Warsaw alliance from developing the capability to wage a war of territorial defense. Soviet doctrine serves this function by defining specific policies in virtually all areas of military affairs. Soviet military doctrine has two mutually dependent components: the military-political and the military-technical. The authors of Soviet doctrine claim that the military-political component is the more decisive component in the formulation of military doctrine. The military-technical component consists of four principal subcategories: the theory of military art, the theory of troop training, the theory of military economics and rear services, and the theory of the organization and development of a national defense system.

The theory of military art consists of three subtheories, those of strategy, operational art, and tactics. These three subfields of military art are mutually dependent on each other but each has its particular laws of development.[14] Strategy is the entire complex of measures undertaken to plan, prepare and lead armed forces in military operations aimed at the complete destruction of the military forces of a political opponent. The requirements of strategy mainly determine the development of operational art.[15] Operational art is the planning, preparation, and conduct of joint or individual operations by formations (a force consisting at least of one division or its equivalent) and superformations (a military "front") within a theater of military operations. Each service branch has its own operational art. The requirements of operational art mainly determine the development of tactics.[16] Tactics works out the optimal combat techniques for formations (a force consisting of at least a division) and smaller groupings. Each service branch and each type of troops has its own tactics.[17]

According to the *Soviet Military Encyclopedia,* the theory of Soviet military art specifically addresses "the problems of the preparation and conduct of military action by the United Armed Forces of the countries of the Warsaw Pact."[18] The Iakubovskii text on the WTO says that the WTO General Staffs and the commanders of the national service branches of the WTO formulate the military art of the Warsaw Pact.[19] Other WTO texts specifically declare that the Pact members have adopted common views on strategy, operational art and tactics.[20] The military exercises of the Pact suggest that the common propositions of military art of the WTO states require preparation for both nuclear and conventional war. The limited information available suggests that the Pact exercises train the WTO forces mainly for the conduct of offensive rather then defensive actions.[21]

The publishing house of the Soviet defense ministry has published discussions of the military art of offensive nuclear war. Western analysts have documented in these discussions Soviet plans to use both nuclear weapons and large conventional forces to destroy the nuclear arsenals and conventional forces of the probable enemy and to seize the enemy's principal economic and administrative centers with a minimum of destruction.[22] The military art discussed in these Soviet works could serve several objectives, including the planning, preparation and conduct of Soviet military interventions against East European members of the Warsaw Pact.

If the WTO states have accepted the treatises of Soviet military art on the conduct of offensive nuclear war as the sole military art of the Warsaw Pact, then they have provided the Soviet forces in Europe with a doctrine of intervention and denied themselves doctrines of the defense of national territory with conventional weapons. Because each subtheory of Soviet doctrine complements the other subtheories of doctrine, adopting a particular theory of Soviet military art entails adoption of the corollary Soviet theories in the other subfields of the military-technical component of Soviet doctrine. These subfields are the theory of troop training and education, the theory of military economics and rear services, and the theory of the organization and development of a national defense system.

The theory of troop training and education is designed to prepare Soviet military personnel for the conduct of the actions required by Soviet military art. The theory of troop training and education consists of three overlapping subtheories.[23] The subtheory of troop training is a set of views on the organization and training of armed forces personnel.[24] The subtheory of troop education is a set of views on how to inculcate heroism, self-sacrifice, and other martial virtues in individual soldiers; it is also a set of views on how to develop cohesion and morale within military units.[25] The subtheory of the Communist education of troops is a set of views on how to foster devotion both to the Soviet fatherland and to "proletarian and socialist internationalism, the principles of Communist ideology and high vigilance and constant readiness to step forward in defense of the gains of socialism."[26] The large body of Soviet literature on these three subtheories may serve as the basis for the coordinated WTO training programs and joint programs of political education.

The Soviet theory of military economics and rear services considers not only the specific questions of the organization of defense production and rear services but also the more general questions of the mobilization of economic and social resources for national defense.[27] The Soviet theory of military economics and rear services may provide the WTO states with a blueprint for the integration of their defense industries and rear reserves with those of the Soviet Union.

The theory of *voennoe stroitel'stvo* is usually translated as the theory of "military construction," or "military administration," but these translations do not convey the Soviet sense of the term, which is the organization and development of a national defense system. The theory of *voennoe stroitel'stvo* summarizes the Soviet experience in the organization of a national defense ministry and its service branches, the recruitment, deployment and training of military personnel, both active and reserve, and in the organization of the auxiliary services necessary to support national military forces. The article on *voennoe stroitel'stvo* in the *Soviet Military Encyclopedia* declares that in a socialist state the theory of *voennoe stroitel'stvo* encompasses ". . . the totality of economic, political, moral and purely military measures directed at the securing of armed defense which are carried out under the leadership of a Communist party."[28] The principal component of the theory of *voennoe stroitel'stvo* is the subtheory of *stroitel'stvo vooruzhennykh sil,* or "the organization and development of armed forces." This subtheory is a specific set of views on how to organize and manage a national defense ministry.[29]

Marshal Grechko identified one of the fundamental bases of the Warsaw Treaty Organization as "a unity of views in the theory and practice of *voennoe stroitel'stvo*."[30] The Soviet conception of the organization and development of a national defense system plays the central role in the achievement of a unity of views among the WTO states on *voennoe stroitel'stvo*. According to the Czechoslovak Minister of Defense, Martin Dzur, "We consider as one of the most important traditions and factors of the organization and development of our armed forces the fact that from the very beginning we learned from the rich experience of the glorious Soviet Armed Forces."[31]

According to a Soviet study of the National People's Army of the German Democratic Republic, the East Germans have also based the organization and development of their national defense system on the

Soviet experience.[32] A joint Soviet-Bulgarian study declares:

> The Bulgarian Communist Party, in carrying out the leadership of the armed forces, relies on the enormous experience of the leadership of the CPSU in the organization and development of a national defense system.
>
> It undeviatingly makes a reality of the instructions of Georgi Dimitrov, the leader of the Bulgarian people, who declared, "Our armed forces must be just like the Soviet Armed Forces. We must have identical tasks, identical organization, identical weaponry and an identical military science."[33]

This text notes that the current Bulgarian leadership avoids being carried away with Dimitrov's enthusiasm: "However, the experience of the Soviet Union is not mechanically introduced into the organization and development of the national defense system of Bulgaria, but wisely, creatively, taking into account the historical and national peculiarities which have arisen in each country."[34]

Neither the Bulgarian national defense system nor that of any other WTO member exactly duplicates the much larger and more complex Soviet national defense system. But the available evidence suggests that, with the exception of Romania, each of the principal agencies of the defense systems of the WTO states has a Soviet analogue.[35] The existence of parallel agencies facilitates the conduct of an extensive network of regular bilateral exchanges at virtually every level between the Soviet defense ministry and the defense ministries of East Europe.[36] These exchanges incude frequent visits of defense ministers, commanders of service branches,[37] chiefs of political administrations,[38] and extend down to the level of army youth organizations,[39] military sports and cultural organizations,[40] and the paramilitary organizations that give military training to youth in factories and schools.[41] The WTO also conducts regular exchanges among the journalists of analogous military newspapers and journals.[42] The Soviet force groups in Europe and the forces of at least three of the western military districts of the USSR maintain an extensive network of ties with their WTO analogs.[43]

The Alternative Military Doctrines of Yugoslavia and Romania

The Yugoslavs and the Romanians both reject the theories and practice of the military-technical component of Soviet doctrine in favor of doctrines of territorial defense.[44] Both states assume that the likely aggressor will use conventional rather than nuclear weapons. The military art (strategy, operational art and tactics) of each of these two states addresses the problem of ensuring the survival of national military forces and the national political leadership in the event of the occupation of either country by an enemy force estimated at 700,000–2,000,000 soldiers. The troop training of each country emphasizes the training of regular and paramilitary forces for "people's war" actions adapted to the specific conditions of each country. The military-economic and rear service policies of each state emphasize the domestic production of small and medium sized weapons and the limited purchase of weapons, transport and reconnaissance equipment from sources outside the Warsaw Pact. The organization of the national defense system of each country is directed at maintaining the continuity of national political authority over civilians during an enemy occupation.

According to the Yugoslavs, the formulation of postwar Yugoslav military doctrine on territorial defense began in 1958.[45] The Romanians developed their postwar territorial defense system sometime between 1958, when Soviet troops withdrew from Romania, and 1968, when President Ceausescu mobilized the system the day after the Soviet intervention in Czechoslovakia. The available evidence suggests that the critical years in the development of Romania's territorial defense system were the late 1950s and early 1960s.[46] A former Polish military intelligence officer who emigrated to the West has written that in the late 1950s General Zygmunt Dusynski headed a group of high-ranking Polish officers who unsuccessfully attempted to draw up plans for establishing within the Warsaw Pact "a separate, compact, well-defined 'Polish Front,' intended as an exclusive theater of operations for the Polish armed forces. . . ."[47] According to this account, Dusynski's plans called for the formulation of a specifically Polish military doctrine, a Polish national defense system and an independent Polish defense industry.[48] In the late 1950s, the East German defense ministry faced the task of developing a national military doctrine for the newly formed (1956) National People's Army. At the same time the pro-Soviet remnants of the Hungarian officer corps were in need of a Hungarian military doctrine that rejected Imre Nagy's policy of withdrawal from the Warsaw Pact.

To borrow a Soviet expression, perhaps it is not accidental that in the late 1950s when one or more East European states was developing a national military doctrine of territorial defense, the Soviets also began a major reformulation of military doctrine.[49] There may also be a connection between the appearance of Marshal V.D. Sokolovskii's *Military Strategy* in 1962 and the introduction of the Warsaw Pact's system of multilateral exercises. The first of these took place in late 1961; four more took place in 1962. Sokolovskii's text specifically called for the incorporation of East European forces in joint theater actions under Soviet command[50] and declared that the next war fought in Europe would be a nuclear war which would require the development of a new military art.[51]

The Military-Political Axioms of the Warsaw Pact

The authors of Soviet doctrine claim that the military-political component is the more decisive component of military doctrine. In the case of the Warsaw Pact, this claim is completely justified. For the five loyal East European members of the Warsaw Treaty Organization, accepting a common set of military-political axioms is the prerequisite for accepting the Soviet theories of military art, of troop training and education, of military economics and rear services, and of the organization and development of a national defense system. For Yugoslavia and Romania, the basis for rejection of the military-technical component of Soviet doctrine is rejection of the military-political component of Soviet doctrine and the diplomatic policies linked to it. The military-political axioms of Romanian and Yugoslav doctrines declare that the sole mission of their national armed forces is to defend the sovereignty of the existing socialist regimes. The Communist parties of these two states derive their popular legitimacy primarily from their zealous defense of the political independence of their nations against the claims of larger polities to the east and west. The military-political axioms shared by the military doctrines of the loyal WTO states accept the Soviet argument that the ideologically correct expression of the national sovereignty of a socialist state is the acceptance of a series of binding obligations, including military obligations, to the larger socialist confederation headed by the Union of Soviet Socialist Republics.

The Soviets do not depend on the intrinsic logic of their military-political axioms to persuade East European defense ministries to accept these axioms and their military-technical corollaries. The Soviets depend on the force of the bilateral treaties and party programs into which these axioms have been written. Reincarnated as articles of international treaties and sections of party programs, the military-political axioms of Soviet doctrine are binding on the officers of five East European WTO countries in their capacities as state officials and party members.[52]

The military scholars of the Soviet Armed Forces have produced a voluminous literature which traces the WTO's military-political axioms back to Lenin. These axioms form a circular Maginot Line in which each axiom is defined as a basic element of the others: joint defense of the gains of socialism in each fraternal country against external and internal enemies; proletarian internationalism; socialist internationalism; the Leninist teaching on defense of the socialist fatherland; the Marxist-Leninist teaching on war and armed forces; the Marxist-Leninist conception of the necessity of the military-political unity of the armed forces of the socialist states; the concept of the "combat confederation" (*boevoe sodruzhestvo*) of the armed forces of the "socialist confederation" (*sotsialisticheskoe sodruzhestvo*); the concept of the joint defense of socialism and peace.[53]

In discourses on their military-political axioms the framers of Soviet military doctrine demonstrate a distinct preference for vague enemies: imperialism, reaction, the enemies of peace and socialism.[54] Soviet analysts assert that these hostile forces threaten not only the Soviet Union but the entire socialist confederation; they also claim that the hostile forces are invariably organized in a coalition. This axiom leads Major General Samoilenko to a conclusion shared by all his Soviet colleagues: "The military unity of the socialist states is vitally necessary because a new world war, if the enemies of peace and socialism unleash it, will be a coalition war."[55] According to General A.A. Epishev, chief of the Main Political Administration of the Soviet Armed Forces, it is not only Soviet doctrine which views the military unity of the socialist states as vitally necessary. In a work entitled *Ideological Struggle in Military Questions* General Epishev declares, "The military doctrines of the socialist confederation proceed from the fact that it is possible to prevent the possible outbreak of a new world war only by joint efforts of the fraternal socialist countries."[56] In his article on military strategy for the *Soviet Military Encyclopedia,* the Chief of the Soviet General Staff notes not only that one of the tasks of Soviet strategy is to formulate "the common bases of the military strategy of the countries of the socialist confederation,"[57] but that Soviet military strategy is a strategy of waging a coalition war against an opposing coalition:

> Soviet military strategy considers a future world war, if the imperialists succeed in unleashing it, as a decisive conflict between two opposing world socio-economic systems—the socialist and the capitalist.
>
> It is assumed that in such a war a majority of the states of the world would be drawn in simultaneously or consecutively.
>
> This will be a global conflict unprecedented in extent and severity, a conflict of multi-million coalition armed forces which will be conducted with no quarter, with the most decisive political and strategic objectives.[58]

The authors of Soviet doctrine insist that the socialist confederation has taken up arms only because the aggressive forces of imperialism and reaction have consistently rejected Soviet proposals for general and complete disarmament. They also insist that no small or medium-sized socialist state can stand alone against the hostile coalition of imperialist forces because such states lack the economic and scientific resources to fend off the imperialist armies preparing for wars conventional and nuclear, local and global.[59] The bilateral treaties of the Soviet Union with the five loyal members of the Warsaw Pact all contain articles specifying the need for socialist unity in response to the "aggressive forces of imperialism and reaction"; they also contain articles pledging the signatories to the pursuit of general and complete disarmament.[60]

The military-political axioms of Soviet doctrine advance from their discourses on the need for socialist unity against the imperialist threat to discussions of the internal functions of a socialist army. Colonel Timorin writes that the internal function of a socialist military has three aspects: (1) as a psychological deterrent against anti-socialist forces; (2) as a back-up for internal security forces; (3) as a combat force "in those cases when the opposition of the enemies of socialism within a country acquire significant scale, intensity, duration, and sharpness (a counterrevolutionary uprising, mutiny, banditry, the unleashing of civil war)."[61] Marshal Iakubovskii's volume on the Warsaw Pact points out that in executing its internal function a socialist army will not have to rely on its own forces but can count on fraternal assistance from other socialist armies. The Iakubovskii text specifically declares that one of the missions of the WTO is "joint defense of the gains of socialism in each fraternal country when these gains are threatened by danger from internal or external reaction."[62] General Epishev has identified the principle of joint defense of the gains of socialism as a law of history. In *Ideological Struggle in Military Questions,* the chief of the Main Political Administration of the Soviet Armed Forces declares, "In the epoch of the transition from capitalism to socialism a new aspect of the theory of socialist revolution has arisen. . . ." General Epishev explains:

> First, defense of the gains of socialism is a general law of socialist revolution in whatever form or whatever country it has been carried out. . . .
>
> Second, the defense of socialism embraces not only the sphere of military affairs, but includes all other areas of social life as well—economics, culture, politics and ideology. . . .
>
> Third, the law of the necessity of the defense of socialism applies as long as imperialism exists, which is a constant threat to socialism. Moreover, as historical experience shows, this threat exists not only in the form of a direct attack on the socialist countries, but in the form of the so-called "peaceful counterrevolution."
>
> Fourth, the defense of socialism in an exceptionally important international task.[63]

The obligation of the WTO states to honor the principle of joint defense of the gains of socialism is not only a frequent topic of discussion in the works of General Epishev and his subordinates in the Soviet Main Political Administration but is also a commitment accepted by the USSR and the five loyal Pact members in their bilateral treaties.[64] Iakubovskii's text on the Warsaw Pact declares that the Soviet action in Hungary in 1956 and the WTO action in Czechoslovakia in 1968 are examples of the joint defense of the gains of socialism in each fraternal country against internal and external enemies.[65] Virtually every other detailed discussion of the law of joint defense of the gains of socialism cites the same examples.[66]

In his *Ideological Struggle in Military Questions,* General Epishev explains that imperialists seek to put socialist states on an anti-Soviet course by attacking the principle of the necessity for the joint defense of the gains of socialism. According to General Epishev, "In bourgeois military sociology there is often an attempt to portray the principles of the international defense of socialism as 'an attack on national sovereignty,' as *diktat,* and 'the hegemony of certain countries.' "[67] The chief of the Soviet Main Political Administration continues:

> It is not difficult to see that the basic direction of the attack of bourgeois propaganda on the consciousness of the personnel of the armed forces of the socialist countries sets the goal of emphasizing national differences and opposing some socialist countries to others.
>
> All this is done to loosen the unbreakable moral-political unity of the socialist countries and their armed forces and to disrupt the fraternal relations which exist among them.[68]

M.S. Kirichenko, the author of a Soviet study of the Warsaw Pact, identifies some of the slanders used to loosen the unbreakable unity of the armed forces of the socialist states: (1) the Soviet army exported socialist revolutions to Eastern Europe; (2) the Soviet forces stationed in East Europe are occupation troops; (3) Soviet military specialists interfere in the internal affairs of East European forces; and (4) Soviet troops crushed "liberalization" in Hungary in 1956 and in Czechoslovakia in 1968.[69]

The authors of Soviet military doctrine see the greatest danger to the unity of the armed forces of the Warsaw alliance in the possibility that the nationalism of the armed forces will merge with an ideological deviation of the ruling party to carry out a program of national Communism. The Iakubovskii text warns:

> In wagering on the nationalist elements within the socialist countries, bourgeois ideologists try to poison the consciousness of peoples and sow the seeds of distrust among them.
>
> The danger of contemporary nationalism consists in the fact that it often hides under the banner of socialism.
>
> The preaching of the ideas of "national models" of socialism, the assertion that each country can supposedly proceed to socialism by a special path, is in fact a negation of the social laws of development and a rejection of Marxism-Leninism and proletarian internationalism.[70]

According to the authors of Soviet military doctrine, the Communist parties which combine nationalism with an ideological deviation inevitably distort the relationship between national sovereignty and proletarian internationalism. The Iakubovskii text declares, "The enemies of socialism try to oppose proletarian internationalism to the sovereignty of states and nations. They depict the matter in such a way that the solidarity of the socialist states is supposedly incompatible with state and national sovereignty. . . ."[71]

In a 1972 article, Marshal Grechko, former commander of the Pact, noted that although it was axiomatic that socialist states based their relations on "respect for sovereign rights and noninterference in internal affairs,"

> The sovereignty of a socialist state presupposes not only the right to independence but also the responsibility before the confederation of fraternal countries and before the international Communist and workers movement for the fate of socialism.
>
> The collective defense of socialism is the international duty of Communists and consequently the primary task of the armed forces of the socialist confederation.[72]

The principal threat to the military-political axioms of the Warsaw Pact and their military-technical corollaries is the challenge posed by the military doctrines of Romania and Yugoslavia. These doctrines are standing invitations to the defense ministries of East Europe to adopt strategies of territorial defense. The authors of Soviet doctrine have chosen not to attack Yugoslav and Romanian military doctrines by name. They have instead confined themselves to denunciations of Maoist military doctrine as unsuitable for small socialist countries. The Iakubovskii text declares:

> The experience of the political cooperation of the socialist countries shows that their unity is a natural phenomenon and that the course of building socialism in isolation from the world confederation of socialist countries, one basis of which is the theory of 'reliance on one's own forces' propagated by the Mao Zedong group, is reactionary and harmful to the world socialist system.

> The course of building socialism in isolation is advantageous to the reactionary imperialist forces, which are striving, by the means of stirring up nationalist, anti-Soviet moods, to wreck the unity of the socialist countries, to isolate them from the most powerful socialist country, the USSR, and to deal with the socialist countries one by one.

> The 20-year experience of the Warsaw Pact shows that each socialist state can develop most successfully with the aid of the other socialist countries, most of all the Soviet Union, and in close unity with each other.[73]

The bilateral treaties of the loyal WTO members with the USSR and the party programs of these states share Marshal Iakubovskii's commitment to the principle of the unity of the Warsaw Pact states.[74] In a 1974 article in *Krasnaia Zvezda,* the Bulgarian defense minister also denounced the Maoist threat to the unity of the Warsaw alliance: "We are . . . deeply convinced that the collective defense of socialism is impossible without unity and military alliance with the armed forces of the socialist countries. Therefore we condemn with indignation the crude anti-Sovietism of the Maoists as well as their slander of the Warsaw Pact."[75] Without specifically mentioning either the Maoists, the Yugoslavs or the Romanians M.S. Kirichenko, author of a Soviet study of the WTO, calls for a "sharp class struggle with the forces which propagandize various theories of 'neutralism,' 'non-alignment,' 'an inter-block position' and 'reliance on one's own forces.'"[76]

The Soviet military-political axioms shared by the armed forces of the loyal members of the Warsaw Pact require a military art that eschews "reliance on one's own forces" and facilitates multilateral WTO interventions in East Europe. The common views of the loyal WTO members on military art serve as the basis of the alliance's joint military exercises. In turn, the joint exercises provide the United Command of the Warsaw Pact with the capability of enforcing the conformity of the East Europeans to the military-political and military-technical components of Soviet doctrine.

Chapter Seven
The Political Directorate of the Warsaw Pact

One of the "other organs of administration" of the Warsaw Pact appears to be a political directorate in charge of organizing regular exchanges among the officers of the main political administrations of the WTO. These exchanges facilitate the conduct of joint political activities, most of which are bilateral Soviet-East European programs. The exchanges among WTO political officers also facilitiate the coordination of political education among the soldiers and officers of the Pact. There are two prerequisites for the integration of the fraternal political administrations: common sets of military-political axioms and common versions of East European military history on which to base joint programs in political education; and a set of corresponding political agencies within the WTO defense ministries to carry out the particular programs agreed to by the political officers of the alliance. Romania, which lacks both political axioms and political organs corresponding to those of the loyal Pact members, does not participate in the joint activities and coordinated political education programs of the other WTO states. When officers of the Czechoslovak Main Political Administration proposed in 1968 a revision of Czechoslovakia's relationship to the WTO along the path first charted by Romania, they also proposed a revision of Czechoslovakia's military-political axioms and a reorganization of the political agencies in the Czechoslovak armed forces. If the United Command of the Warsaw Pact does not have a political directorate responsible for arranging the exchanges that facilitate the conduct of joint political activities and coordinated programs of political education, then the Soviet Main Political Administration probably serves as the clearinghouse for the joint activities of the WTO political agencies.[1]

The Structure of the WTO Political Administration

The chief of the Soviet Main Political Administration (MPA) enjoys the "rights" of a Central Committee secretary but is the deputy of the minister of defense. The Soviet MPA is subdivided into "administrations" and "departments." There are at least three central administrations: one for agitation and propaganda; a second for organizational and party work; a third for cadres. Each service branch has a separate administration. There are also separate administrations for each military district, each force group in Europe, each naval fleet and each air-defense district. There are "departments" for special troops such as the Airborne Troops. There are at least two central "departments": one for the party youth organizations in the military, the Komsomol; and one in charge of military research. Departments also exist in each "formation" (*soedinenie*)—a grouping at least the size of a division; in the staff of each service branch; and in each of the higher-level military-educational institutions. Below the departments are the primary party organizations responsible for the direct conduct of party-political work among military personnel. At each level of the MPA structure, the head of the MPA apparatus is the deputy commander for the corresponding regular officer. The bureau of the MPA coordinates the work of the political agencies. The bureau consists of the chief of the MPA, the deputy chiefs, the heads of the central administrations, the heads of the administrations of the service branches, the secretary of the party commission of the MPA, and the editor of *Krasnaia Zvezda*. The Soviet MPA not only conducts all party-political work in the military but also administers all Soviet military newspapers and journals, and the publishing house of the Ministry of Defense. It also monitors the activities of the instruction and research staffs of the social science faculties of all military educational institutions.[2]

According to Soviet sources, the East European political administrations, with the exception of the Romanian party apparatus in the military, have structures and functions virtually identical with those of the Soviet Main Political Administration.[3] The similarity is not surprising in light of the fact that the Soviet MPA organized the political administrations of the East European armies in the postwar period.[4] The Soviet and East European political administrations carry out political work among officers mainly through the party organizations in the military, which are subordinate to the MPA. According to the former chief of staff of the WTO, General S.M. Shtemenko, the percentage of party membership among WTO officers in 1976 was 97 percent for East Germany, 83 percent for Bulgaria and Hungary, and 60 percent for Poland.[5] The figure of 60 percent for the Polish army in 1976, contrasts with a figure of 70 percent in 1973 and 1974, given by two generals of the Soviet MPA.[6] No Soviet discussion during the early and mid-1970s of party membership among the WTO officer corps gave a specific figure for the

Czechoslovak officer corps, which had been depleted by large-scale resignations after the 1968 invasion and an extensive purge of those officers who chose to remain in the military.[7] In 1977, a Czechoslovak political officer reported in *Krasnaia Zvezda* that party membership among the Czechoslovak officer corps had reached "almost 75 percent."[8] In his 1974 discussion of party membership in the WTO, General A.A. Epishev, chief of the Soviet MPA, wrote that "almost all senior officers and generals" of the Soviet armed forces were party members and that 66.2 percent of "younger officers" were party members.[9]

According to the chief of the Soviet MPA, the parallel structures of the WTO political administrations maintain regular contacts from the highest to the lowest levels. General Epishev writes that WTO exchanges on the political training of officers and enlisted personnel takes place during "meetings of the representatives of the Main Political Administrations, of the political administrations of service branches of the armed forces, of military districts and of force groups, and meetings of the political workers of formations and units and at conferences and seminars."[10] In the translation by the Central Intelligence Agency of an article attributed to the restricted-circulation Soviet journal, *Military Thought,* a passage suggests that meetings of the chiefs of the WTO political administrations took place frequently before 1969.[11] Evidence from open Soviet sources indicates that after Marshal Iakubovskii's reorganization of the Pact in 1969, the highest-ranking political officers of the WTO have met frequently. The Iakubovskii text on the Warsaw Pact reports that from August 31 to September 2, 1970, "generals and officers" of the Pact political administrations met in Dresden to "exchañge opinions on current questions of party-political work in the allied armed forces."[12] Another Soviet source reports a WTO meeting in April 1972 of "generals and officers of the political administrations."[13] The Iakubovskii study mentions a meeting in Dresden on Oct. 18–19, 1973 at which "the leaders of the political organs of the WTO armed forces discussed ideological work, raising the combat capabilities of the WTO armed forces and the ideological diversions of imperialism."[14] At least two articles in the Soviet military press noted a June 1976 meeting in the Bulgarian resort town of Varna of the "leading political workers of the armed forces of the member countries of the WTO."[15]

The apparently irregular meetings of the highest-ranking MPA officers of the Warsaw Pact may be the equivalent of the occasional meetings of the WTO defense ministers that took place before the establishment of the Committee of Defense Ministers in 1969. If the 1969 reorganization of the Pact established a political directorate comparable to the Committee of Defense Ministers, Military Council and Technical Committee, its sessions may be more regular than the sources cited above indicate. If such a Pact agency exists, Romania has probably declined membership on the grounds that it has no main political administration. In 1964, the Romanians abolished their main political administration and replaced it with a system of party committees evidently modeled on the system of party committees in the Yugoslav armed forces. The highest political agency in the Romanian armed forces, the Higher Political Council, which consists of both political officers and regular officers, has no analogue in any of the other WTO armed forces.

In 1967, the Hungarians created a separate system of party committees in the military outside the MPA hierarchy, but this system does not replace the Hungarian Main Political Administration or even compete with it. The primary purpose of the Hungarian party committees appears to be to involve Hungarian officers in the affairs of corresponding party committees of civilian officials and vice versa. In the event of mobilization, the party committees organized at the regimental level and above dissolve and those below the regimental level become subordinate to MPA bodies. The Hungarian Main Political Administration participates actively in joint political activities with the political administrations of other Pact members and in coordinated programs of political training.

In addition to the meetings of the highest-ranking political officers of the Pact, the system of contacts among the WTO political officers also entails, according to Colonel General P.I. Efimov of the Soviet MPA, "participation of the responsible workers of the party-political apparatus of the fraternal armed forces in various conferences, symposia, colloquia and seminars on military-theoretical problems and on practical questions of party-political work."[16] An article by Marshal Iakubovskii mentioned two such conferences, one in Sofia in 1973 and another in Moscow in 1975. According to the late WTO commander, both conferences examined "the importance of an active, aggressive struggle against bourgeois ideology and the necessity of the further strengthening of contacts in this area."[17]

The meetings mentioned by General Epishev among the political officers of service branches, military districts and force groups appear to take place mainly on a bilateral Soviet-East European basis, as do the joint political activities of the WTO. A section below discusses the bilateral meetings and joint activities of the Soviet Main Political Administration with the political administrations of each of the East European armies. The most important of the multilateral joint political activities are those that take place during the joint military exercises, which a section of a previous chapter discussed. In an examination of the political activities conducted during the joint exercises, Colonel Semin notes that "usually" the main political administration of the commander of the exercise organizes the program of political activities.[18] This leaves open the possibility that a central WTO political directorate may organize the political activities of some exercises, probably those conducted by officers of the United Command, such as the WTO commander, chief of staff, and commander of the WTO Anti-Aircraft Forces.

In his study of the Warsaw Pact, Colonel General Efimov noted several other forms of multilateral activity among the political administrations of the Pact. According to Efimov's text, in the 1973 training year the Soviet MPA sent lecturers to East Europe to speak on "The All-World Historical Significance of the Half Century of the Development of Communism in the USSR, a United Multi-National Socialist State"; "The Successes of the Development of Communism in the USSR"; and "The Soviet Armed Forces—The Armed Forces of the Friendship of Peoples and the Reliable Defender of the Cause of Socialism and Peace." Efimov's text also reported that during the same year East European lecturers spoke to units of the Soviet armed forces on the political and military affairs of East Europe.[19] A Soviet study of the Belorussian Military District of the USSR noted that during the period from 1968 to 1970 "generals and officers" from the fraternal armies delivered "about two hundred speeches" to the soldiers of the district. According to this study, the speakers included military attaches posted to Moscow, lecturers from the Main Political Administration of the Polish Armed Forces, and historians from the East German Institute of Military History.[20] A Soviet study of the Odessa Military District reported that in 1973 the Military Council of the district noted that in the conduct of "patriotic and internationalist training" the district and neighboring East European armies had carried out "about 40 recent mutual exchanges of delegations of commanders, political organs, party and Komsomol organizations."[21] According to the Iakubovskii text, during 1971–72 some 70 East European military journalists visited the editorial offices of Soviet military publications and some 60 Soviet military journalists paid reciprocal visits. The Efimov volume adds that during 1971–73 "more than 100" East European military journalists visited the Soviet Union and "about as many" Soviet military journalists visited East Europe.[22] The military journalists of the WTO armies are subordinate to the main political administrations of the Pact. A Soviet study of the USSR's military press notes that there are regular contacts among Soviet and East European military journalists.[23]

The extent of the interaction among the political administrations of the Warsaw Pact has led General Epishev of the Soviet MPA to conclude: "The ties of the fraternal political organs, their cooperation and the wealth of joint forms of internationalist training have become an organic part of the general complex of relations among the armed forces of the fraternal socialist countries.''[24]

General Epishev and the Warsaw Pact

In making this evaluation General Epishev is probably commenting on his own creation: his background and his tenure in office suggest that he is the principal designer of the network linking the political administrations of the Warsaw Pact. After joining the party in 1929, Alexei Alexeevich Epishev entered the Red Army in 1930 and rose to the position of the chief of the personnel section of a Soviet division. After being graduated in 1938 from the Academy of Motorization and Mechanization, he took a position as the military inspector of a Kharkov factory. In 1940, he became the first secretary of the Kharkov party committee. He then held a number of important civilian posts in various parts of the Ukraine and southern Russia under assault by the Nazi armies and participated as a civilian administrator in the great battles of Stalingrad and Kursk and in the campaigns that drove the Germans out of the Ukraine.

He then entered upon a phase of his career that may have prepared him for his work as chief of the Soviet MPA. In October 1943, Epishev became the chief political officer of the 38th Army of the First Ukrainian Front and participated in the conquest of Lvov and the western Ukraine, an ethnically diverse and politically volatile area, parts of which had been Polish and Czechoslovak rule before World War II. Epishev also participated in the liberation of southern Poland, of Slovakia, of Moravia and the central Bohemian region around Prague.[25] These campaigns probably brought him into frequent contact with the political officers of the Polish and Czechoslovak armies which the Soviets had raised on Soviet soil to participate in the occupation of Poland and Czechoslovakia.

Epishev held a series of important party positions in the Ukraine from 1946-51, a period of complex political and economic reconstruction. From 1951-53 he served as a deputy USSR minister of state security. From 1953-55 he served as the first secretary of the Odessa oblast party committee. In 1955, he returned to duty in East Europe that further prepared him for his work in the Soviet MPA: from 1955 to 1961 he served as Soviet ambassador to Romania, the period during which Khrushchev and Gheorghiu-Dej engaged in a struggle over Romania's pursuit of autonomy from the Soviet Union. In 1961, Ambassador Epishev was reassigned to Belgrade, the capital of East European heresy. In 1961, Tito was again contesting Soviet ideological formulas and was organizing

the nonaligned movement of Third World states. After one year in Yugoslavia, Epishev left East Europe to become chief of the Main Political
Administration of the Soviet Armed Forces in 1962.[26]

Roman Kolkowicz has argued that Khrushchev appointed Epishev
in order to quash criticism of the MPA by the regular officer corps of the
Soviet army.[27] But an equally important reason for his appointment, or
perhaps more important reason, may have been his experience in the
military-political affairs of Poland and Czechoslovakia and his exposure
to the tactics used by Romania and Yugoslavia to disengage themselves
from the Soviet bloc. Epishev's appointment as chief of the Soviet MPA
in the spring of 1962 coincides with the first full-year of regular joint
exercises in the Warsaw Pact. By the fall of 1962, *Krasnaia Zvezda* was
reporting on the conduct of joint political activities during WTO exercises in Romania and Poland.[28] During the first several years of Epishev's
tenure in office the Soviet MPA developed an extensive series of bilateral
ties between the political administrations of the Soviet force groups in
Europe and of the western military districts of the USSR with the political
administrations of the loyal East European states.[29] Epishev's predecessor, General F.I. Golikov, may have tolerated too much independence
on the part of regular officers, as Kolkowicz argues, but another, perhaps
more important defect, may have been his virtual lack of exposure to
East European affairs prior to his appointment as chief of the Soviet
MPA in 1958.[30]

The Military Institute in Leningrad (originally the Military Institute
of Foreign Languages) provides undergraduate training for Soviet political officers specializing in the affairs of foreign countries. The Military
Institute graduates military translators/readers, teachers of foreign languages, officers trained in both the languages and military affairs of
foreign countries and jurists specializing in the military law of foreign
armies.[31] The Institute was formed in 1942 by combining the faculty of
the Second Moscow State Pedagogical Institute of Foreign Languages
with one of the faculties of the Institute of Eastern Studies,[32] at the time
the principal Soviet institute studying the affairs of East Europe. The
establishment of the Military Institute coincides with the formation on
Soviet soil of East European military detachments recruited from prisoners of war and Comintern personnel.[33] The Institute was reorganized in
1956 and 1963. In 1974, it annexed the military-jurisprudence faculty of
the Lenin Military-Political Academy in Moscow.[34]

The East European armies train junior political officers in East
European undergraduate colleges, but mid-career political officers
receive graduate-level training at either an East European academy or
the Lenin Military-Political Academy. The Voroshilov General Staff

Academy in Moscow appears to enjoy a monopoly on the training of East European political officers for the highest-level MPA positions in the Warsaw Pact.[35]

The Missions of the WTO Political Directorate

Western analysts of the Soviet Main Political Administration have debated for some time whether the MPA is the adversary or ally of the regular Soviet officer corps in the training and administration of military personnel. Roman Kolkowicz has argued that the professional officer corps of the Soviet Union finds that the MPA drills in proletarian internationalism are antithetical to the values of nationalism, elitism and technical professionalism which he maintains are the values of the regular officer corps of the Soviet Union.[36] Timothy Colton has assembled evidence from which he draws the conclusion that the professional and political officers of the Soviet armed forces provide each other with support in the execution of common tasks.[37] Dale Herspring and other analysts of party-military relations in East Europe have come to a range of intermediate conclusions between the Kolkowicz and Colton theses.[38] Alex Alexiev, who accepts the Kolkowicz view on the inherent antagonism between political and professional officers, has noted that in Romania the party and the military have united around a program of nationalism and assertion of autonomy in Romania's foreign policy. In Alexiev's analysis, the party and the army in Romania have resolved their feud because the Romanian party has abandoned much of its Marxist-Leninist ideology in order to accommodate itself to the nationalism and professionalism of the Romanian military.[39] The evidence cited by Alexiev to support his conclusion can just as well support the conclusion reached by an earlier chapter in this study: the Romanian party has not surrendered its ideological values to the military but instead has captured the Romanian defense ministry.[40]

This chapter argues that the principal mission of the political directorate of the Warsaw Pact is to prevent the party and military hierarchies of another WTO member from uniting on a program of territorial defense designed to offer nationalist resistance to Soviet military hegemony in East Europe. The MPA system of the Warsaw Pact carries out this mission by monitoring the practical applications of the shared military-political axioms of the WTO in every command of East Europe except those of Romania. The WTO program of joint political activities and coordinated programs of ideological education enable the political directorate of the Warsaw Pact or the Soviet MPA to make a legitimate claim on the obedience of East European officers to the central Pact agencies controlled by Soviet officers. The bilateral ties of the fraternal political administrations to the Soviet MPA probably also enable the Soviets to monitor the political reliability of East European military personnel and to influence officer promotion to the higher levels of the East European armed forces. In addition, the WTO MPA network may also provide an administrative cover for Soviet intelligence agencies to penetrate into every military command of the WTO, except Romania's.

The joint political activities conducted by the WTO political administrations, particularly the multilateral political drills of the joint exercises, also prepare the soldiers of the Warsaw Pact for intervention in each other's states and perhaps also for war with NATO. The ranking Soviet commanders of the Force Groups in East Europe, the western military districts of the USSR, the air defense districts of the WTO, and the Baltic and Black Sea fleets probably find that Soviet capabilities for military action against either East European or West European states depend as much on the political work conducted by the Soviet MPA with the political administrations of East Europe as on the technical professionalism of the regular military personnel of the Soviet armed forces.

The political administrations of the Warsaw Pact appear to conduct political work on three basic themes: (1) socialist patriotism, defined as loyalty to the party and state hierarchies of the respective socialist fatherlands; (2) proletarian internationalism, defined as the joint defense of the gains of socialism in each fraternal country by Soviet and other WTO forces against both internal and external enemies; (3) class hatred for the imperialists, who are defined in the case of each WTO member according to its historical experience with the West in general and Germany in particular.[41] The source materials for these three themes come from the shared military-political axioms of the WTO and the national military histories of the Soviet Union and other Pact states, many of which have been jointly written by Soviet and East European military historians.

Political drills on these three themes attempt to divert the attention of the soldiers of the United Armed Forces from the facts that Russians and Poles have been fighting each other for the last six centuries; that the German-Russian battles of the First and Second World Wars were probably the most bloody conflicts of modern times; that Hungarians fought Russians in two world wars and endured interventions by Moscow which suppressed the popular insurrections of 1848 and 1956; and that Romanians fought Russians in both world wars and still harbor muted claims to the Moldavian Soviet Socialist Republic. These three themes may also serve in the Soviet military to divert attention from historical, religious, and cultural conflicts among the nations that make up the USSR.

General Epishev appears fully aware of the difficulties of conducting ideological-political work among military personnel with long histories of fighting each other. In his *Ideological Struggle in Military Questions,* the Chief of the Soviet MPA observes, "In order to form an internationalist consciousness it is necessary to go beyond the limits of a nationalist world view. And this presupposes enormous ideological-educational work. . . ."[42] The Main Political Administration of the Soviet Armed Forces has both the historical experience and the organizational resources to conduct enormous ideological-educational work among the Soviet personnel assigned to the United Armed Forces and to assist East European political administrations in the conduct of complementary programs. The history of the Soviet MPA is in large part a history of using Marxist-Leninist ideology to mobilize Russian and non-Russian military personnel to carry out combat missions which have been passively or actively opposed by the majority of the civilian population in any given theater of action from the Civil War of 1918 to the intervention of 1980 in Afghanistan. The body of literature which Soviet political officers describe as the "Marxist-Leninist teaching on war and armed forces" is in part a system of views on the practical administrative problems of recruiting, deploying and disciplining multinational military formations, both those of one state and those of a coalition of states.[43] The Marxist-Leninist teaching on war and armed forces is also a set of views, based on specific historical experiences, on the complex conditions that affect the political reliability of multinational personnel, from the level of the individual unit to the level of national armed forces and to the level of socialist military alliances. This set of views recognizes different national traditions that affect the capabilities of national groups for particular kinds of military missions, like that of invading Czechoslovakia in 1968.[44]

Many of the treatises on "internationalism" written by leading Soviet political officers address the interrelated problems of commanding the multinational personnel of the Soviet army and of commanding the multinational personnel of the Warsaw Pact.[45] Soviet military writers often date back to the Civil War in two aspects of "internationalism": (1) Lenin's realization that the Bolshevik military detachments formed in the Ukraine, Belorussia, Latvia, and Lithuania were made up largely of non-Russian personnel who resisted central control by Moscow and pursued their own local objectives. Lenin concluded that a Red Army made up of national-territorial formations was an unreliable and ill-disciplined military force. He reorganized the main body of Bolshevik forces into a centrally directed army with a central political apparatus to enforce discipline.[46] The Bolsheviks did retain some national-territorial formations during and after the Civil War. In the 1920s, the Red Army fielded four Ukrainian divisions, one Belorussian division, two Georgian divisions, one Armenian division, one Azerbaidzhani division, and smaller national units made up exclusively of Turkmen, Uzbeks, Bashkirs, Buriat-Mongols, Karazkhs, Khirghiz, Tadzhiks, Tatars, Yakuts, "and others."[47] According to the *Soviet Military Encyclopedia,* the Soviet Defense Ministry abolished all national-territorial formations in 1938 and incorporated their personnel into integrated formations, but beginning in 1941 reorganized national units of Kazakhs, Bashkirs, Tatars, Kalmyks and created division-level formations made up exclusively of Estonians, Latvians, Georgians, Armenians, Azerbadzhani, and Turkmen. The Soviets also organized division-size formations based on the union republics of the Caucasus, Kazakhstan and Central Asia in which "local nationalities" made up 50–70 percent of all personnel.[48] According to the *Encyclopedia,* divisions and units drawn entirely or mainly from national territories were not disbanded until the mid-1950s,[49] but it is possible that sub-units made up exclusively of certain nationalities continue to exist inside large units and formations.

(2) The Bolshevik recruitment for the Civil War of prisoners of war captured by the Imperial Russian armies of World War I. These prisoners provided some of the recruits for the Communist movements of East Europe. These recruits included Bela Kun, the leader of the Hungarian Soviet Republic of 1919 and Josip Broz, a Croat-Slovenian who had served in the Austro-Hungarian army and later became a Yugoslav Communist leader better known by his underground name of Tito. According to Soviet sources, the Red Army of the Civil War included 250,000 foreigners, mainly East European prisoners of war, but also some Asians. These personnel were organized into five international divisions, three international bridages, 55 international regiments, 40 international battalions and 46 other separate international military units.[50] The Bolsheviks also acquired experience in the organization of international formations during the Spanish Civil War.[51] One of the veterans of the international brigades of the civil war in Spain was Heinz Hoffmann, who later became the East German minister of defense.

During the Second World War, the Soviet Defense Ministry organized on Soviet soil national formations of Poles, Czechs, Slovaks, and Romanians, for combat on Eastern Europe. The Soviets recruited these soldiers mainly from prisoners of war and Comintern members who had fled to the USSR. Soviet personnel served directly in these national formations. According to a Soviet study, as of August 1944, there were 204 Soviet officers and 419 Soviet sergeants and soldiers among the 12,000 personnel of the Czechoslovak Army Corps.[52] By the middle of July 1944, the Polish forces organized by the Soviet numbered 57,355. Of these personnel, 85 percent were Poles and a contingent of Russians, Belorussians and Ukrainians made up 10 percent. Of the officers, Poles made up only 60 percent; the Russian-Belorussian-Ukrainian contingent (presumably recruited from the Soviet army) made up 35 percent. According to the Soviet study that published these statistics, the majority of the Soviet officers serving in the Polish forces served as staff officers, heads of central administrations, commanders of formations and regiments, and the heads of special services.[53] This study also noted that the party-political apparatus of the Polish force was modeled on the Soviet party-political apparatus.[54]

During World War II the Soviets organized two Romanian divisions in the USSR. As of March 1944, the Tudor Vladimiriscu Division had 9,589 soldiers. Of the 895 officers, 383 were Romanian officers captured by the Soviets and 408 were noncommissioned Romanian officers who had been graduated from a two-month course at the Riazin infantry school.[55] The remaining 105 officers were probably Soviets. The Second Romanian Infantry Division, formed in 1945, had "more than 100 Soviet officer-instructors," according to a Soviet study.[56] This volume also reported that the Main Political Administration of the Soviet Army provided the Romanians with "great assistance" in the organization of the political apparatus of each of the two Romanian divisions.[57]

The Polish, Czechoslovak, and Romanian military forces recruited and organized by the USSR played symbolic roles in the liberation of East Europe to which the historians of the WTO have devoted great attention. In the postwar period they played extremely important political roles in the establishment of Communist regimes in East Europe.[58]

The officers of the Soviet MPA make persuasive cases for their assertions that the solution to the task of integrating the multinational personnel of the Soviet forces stationed in East Europe into the multinational Warsaw alliance has its roots in the October Revolution and in the Great Fatherland War of 1941–45. In the immediate postwar period the Soviets solved the problem of integrating the Soviet forces in East Europe with the East European armies by placing Soviet officers directly in the key commands of East Europe. After the political upheavals of 1956, the Soviets began to withdraw their officers from East European armed forces and to develop indirect but effective controls over the armies of their allies. Marshal Grechko and General Epishev presided over the refinement of indirect controls through the reorganization of the Warsaw Pact that began in 1961–62. In a 1976 article in a Soviet military journal, Admiral Verner, chief of the East German Main Political Administration, called attention to the general process of replacing direct Soviet controls with indirect controls:

Before 1958 as advisors to the commanders and chiefs of the National People's Army and afterwards as representatives of the United Command of the United Armed Forces of the Warsaw Pact, and as military specialists and, after the establishment of the Friedrich Engels Military Academy, as guest lecturers, Leninists in military uniform have always rendered our young army multi-faceted support in the spirit of proletarian internationalism and respect for sovereignty.''[59]

The political education programs of the WTO attempt to transform the nationalisms of Warsaw Pact personnel from a threat to Soviet military power in East Europe into a justification for military policies that enhance the capabilities of the Soviet armed forces for action in Europe both East and West. The loyal political officers of the Pact argue that nationalism, "correctly understood" is compatible with internationalism, "correctly understood."[60] One of the most typical devices used to proclaim this compatibility is the frequent practice of naming units of one national army after the military heroes of another army. A *Krasnaia Zvezda* article of 1977 focused on three such units: a Soviet tank regiment stationed in East Germany which bore the name of Sukhe Bator, the Mongolian revolutionary; a Polish tank regiment named in honor of "The Anti-Fascist Fighters of Germany"; and an East German tank regiment named for Karol Sverchevskii, the Polish hero.[61]

The minimum objective of the political education programs of the WTO is to proscribe publicly the doctrine of territorial defense, the military-political axioms of the Romanians and Yugoslavs and the episodes of East European history incompatible with the history of the proletarian internationalism. The political education programs of the Pact may prove persuasive to some WTO personnel: probably among the aging veterans of the Spanish Civil War and World War II; perhaps among some of the advisors sent to aid revolutionary and guerrilla movements in the Third World; and perhaps among Bulgarian officers and soldiers, who have legitimate historical reasons for allying themselves with the Soviet Union. If the political education programs of the WTO fail to win the hearts and minds of East European soldiers, they at least make clear to all personnel of the Warsaw Pact that the Soviets are determined to enforce external acceptance of the shared versions of the military histories of Pact states and of the shared military-political axioms of the alliance. The WTO political exercises also demonstrate that the political directorate of the Warsaw Pact has identified as the more probable enemy not the armies of NATO but the historians and political philosophers of East Europe.

Bilateral MPA Contacts: Soviet Ties with Bulgaria, Hungary, East Germany, and Poland

The practical focus of the multilateral activities of the WTO political administrations is on maintaining bilateral contacts between the Soviet MPA and its East European analogues. Specific information on the links of the Soviet MPA to the political administrations of Bulgaria, Hungary, East Germany, and Poland varies from case to case. Taken collectively, this information confirms General Epishev's claim that MPA links at every level of the WTO armed forces are an organic part of the Warsaw Pact. In 1964, the Romanians abolished their main political administration and greatly reduced the contact between the political agencies of the Soviet and Romanian forces. In 1968, several high-ranking officers of the Czechoslovak Main Political Administration proposed the reoganization of the political agencies of the Czechoslovak armed forces and the adoption of a new military doctrine based on Czechoslovakia's withdrawal from active participation in the Warsaw Pact. The dissolution of the Romanian political administration in 1964 and the proposals made by Czechoslovak political officers in 1968 suggest that East Europeans seeking to disengage their military forces from control by the Warsaw Pact command find it wise to eliminate or greatly reduce the bilateral ties of their political agencies with those of the Soviet army. The bilateral ties of the WTO political administrations with the Soviet MPA may be the single most important device used by the Soviets to monitor the practical military applications of the shared military-political axioms of the WTO.

Soviet-Bulgarian Ties

Reciprocal visits of the officers of the Bulgarian and Soviet main political administrations date back at least to the mid-1960s. According to a joint Soviet-Bulgarian study published in 1969, there were an unspecified number of exchanges of political officers in the period from 1966 to 1968. In 1966, Lieutenant General Velko Palin, Chief of the Bulgarian Main Political Administration, led a delegation of political officers to the USSR. Following this trip there was "a series of visits" to Bulgaria by delegations of Soviet political officers, at least one of which was led by Colonel General N.A. Nachankin, a deputy chief of the Soviet MPA. One of the 1968 exchanges involved the political officers of Soviet and Bulgarian anti-aircraft forces.[62] A Soviet study published in 1974 noted that in 1973 General Epishev and Colonal General Kiril Kosev, Palin's successor as chief of the Bulgarian MPA, had led delegations on reciprocal visits. This study also noted an unspecified number of exchanges among the political officers of Soviet and Bulgarian military districts and of the Black Sea fleets of both countries.[63] A 1977 article in *Communist of the Armed Forces* mentioned in passing that Epishev and Kosev regularly exchange visits, although the article did not mention any specific visits.[64]

According to the joint Soviet-Bulgarian study of 1969, during his visit to the Soviet Union in 1966 Lieutenant General Palin and his colleagues held discussions with General Epishev, with the bureau of the Soviet MPA, and with the heads of political administrations and departments. The Bulgarians studied the forms and methods of political training in the Soviet armed forces and examined how the resolutions of the CPSU were translated into practical political work among personnel. In a visit to a division of the Moscow military district, the Bulgarians became acquainted with the techniques used by party youth organizations to conduct ideological work. The visitors from Sofia also toured industrial plants, scientific and cultural institutes and visited historical monuments.[65]

Although this study did not discuss in similar detail the reciprocal visits of Soviet political officers, alliance protocol would require an equally thorough Soviet inspection of political work in the Bulgarian armed forces. This study did note, however, that "generals and officers" of the Soviet MPA have examined Bulgarian methods for teaching Marxism-Leninism to military personnel and have visited individual units and formations of the Bulgarian armed forces.[66] In one of the exchanges of 1968 Soviet officers delivered lectures to groups of Bulgarian political officers. They spoke on "The Work of Political Departments and Deputy Commanders for Political Work and Party Organizations in the Raising of the Combat Readiness of Troops"; "The Basic Laws of the Process of Education and Training"; and "The Work of the Komsomol Organizations in the Soviet Armed Forces in the Training of Youth." In turn, lecturers from the Bulgarian MPA toured units and ships of the Red Banner Black Sea Fleet of the Soviet Navy to deliver lectures on "The Bulgarian People's Army — the Reliable Guard of Socialist Bulgaria" and "The Success of the Bulgarian People in Socialist Development."[67]

During his 1973 visit to Bulgaria, General Epishev met with Bulgarian political officers from the central administrations and departments of the Bulgarian MPA, from line units and from military-educational institutions. He joined several of his Bulgarian colleagues in a joint discussion of "defense of the gains of socialism" and of "the ideological diversions of imperialism." During his visit, General Epishev also learned that fully one third of the political education work in the Bulgarian armed forces was directly devoted to the study of "internationalism."[68] According to

Krasnaia Zvezda, the texts for the study of internationalism in the Bulgarian army include materials from the party congress of both Bulgaria and the Soviet Union.[69] A volume on the WTO edited by Colonel General P.I. Efimov of the Soviet MPA also noted that political education work in the Bulgarian armed forces used materials from Soviet party congresses.[70] According to a Bulgarian study of party-political work in the Bulgarian army, political offices seek to inspire in soldiers

> a feeling of national pride, a consciousness of duty and responsibility to fatherland, and love for the revolutionary traditions and socialist gains of the Bulgarian people; responsibility to internationalist duty, to boundless trust in and brotherhood with the great Soviet Union and the invincible Soviet army, to the fraternal armed forces of the Warsaw Pact; and responsibility to the world socialist system and to the international Communist movement and to solidarity with the peoples who are struggling against imperialism for peace and social progress.[71]

Soviet-Hungarian Ties

Compared to the information available on bilateral ties of the Soviet MPA to the political administrations of the other loyal WTO members, there is relatively little material on the ties of Hungarian and Soviet political agencies in the armed forces. The available information focuses almost entirely on joint political activities between the Southern Force Group in Hungary and the Hungarian armed forces. These joint activities are devoted to the themes of socialist patriotism and joint defense of the gains of socialism. A Western analyst of party-political relations in the Hungarian armed forces, Ivan Volgyes, concludes that there is "an obvious conflict" in this attempt to train soldiers in both nationalism and proletarian internationalism.[72]

An article in a Soviet military journal explains how Hungarians and Soviet political officers overcome such difficulties: they conduct joint readings from the party programs of the two fraternal parties. According to this account in *Communist of the Armed Forces* of such a joint reading, the officers of one of the sub-units of the Southern Force Group decorated the Lenin room of their sub-unit with bilingual banners which read, "Let Us Strengthen Unbreakable Friendship Between the Soviet Armed Forces and the Hungarian People's Army!" and "Long Live Friendship Between the Soviet and Hungarian Peoples!" After the fraternal soldiers had filed into the room, they listened to a tape recording of Leonid Brezhnev reading a passage from his speech to the 25th Congress of the CPSU on proletarian internationalism and "the sacred obligation of Marxist-Leninists" to defend the concept of proletarian internationalism against class enemies.

Following Brezhnev's recorded remarks a Soviet officer delivered a speech in which he pledged Soviet loyalty to the principles of proletarian internationalism and joint defense of the gains of socialism. Several Hungarian officers then declared their loyalty to proletarian internationalism. A Hungarian concluded the meeting with a speech on the forms and methods of agitation and propaganda work in the Hungarian armed forces. At another joint political meeting of the Hungarian and Soviet forces, Hungarian and Soviet political officers read each other passages from their respective party programs. At a third meeting, Soviet and Hungarian officers staged a dramatic reading of a radio conversation conducted between Lenin and Bela Kun, just before the collapse of Kun's Hungarian Soviet Republic of 1919. According to *Communist of the Armed Forces,* these three meetings received extensive coverage in the Hungarian military press.[73]

In a 1974 article for *Krasnaia Zvezda,* two Soviet officers reported that "broad and multi-faceted contacts between the Soviet and Hungarian political administrations play an important role in relations between the two fraternal armed forces."[74] They did not, however, offer specific examples of such contacts. These two Soviet offices were part of a delegation of political workers from the Soviet MPA who toured installations of the Hungarian armed forces. The two, Major General Balakirev and Colonel Gromov, a frequent contributor of articles on Hungarian military affairs to Soviet publications, sought to learn about the work of MPA organs, and party and youth organizations in the Hungarian army. In pursuit of this information, they met with generals and officers of the central administrations of the Hungarian MPA and visited formations and units where they spoke with commanders, political officers, non-commissioned officers, and enlisted personnel. They learned that in honor of the 25th anniversary of the liberation of Hungary by the Soviet army, 10 army youth organizations had renamed themselves in honor of 10 Soviet soldiers who had received the decoration of Hero of the Soviet Union for their roles in the liberation of Hungary. The two Soviet officers also discovered that Hungary had built a large number of war memorials to honor Soviet soldiers killed during the liberation. The visiting officers reported to the readers of *Krasnaia Zvezda* that the party and government of Hungary were devoting great attention to raising the combat capabilities of the Hungarian armed forces and to strengthening their combat cooperation with the Soviet armed forces and the armies of the other Warsaw Pact states.[75]

Colonel General Efimov's study of the WTO also notes that the Soviet and Hungarian political administrations engage in "broad and multi-faceted contacts" but this study does not mention any details of these contacts.[76] The former commander of the Southern Force Group in Hungary noted in 1975 that his forces conducted "regular exchanges" with Hungarian soldiers, "including political activities." The only such activity which General Ivanov specifically mentioned was a series of joint visits of the youth organizations of the two fraternal armies to Hungarian monuments dedicated to Soviet soldiers.[77]

The reorganization of the political agencies of the Hungarian armed forces in 1967 does not appear to have impeded contacts between the Soviet and Hungarian main political administrations. The changes of 1967 established alongside the MPA structure a system of party committees corresponding to every level of the MPA system. These party committees replaced the party organizations formerly subordinate to the MPA. The party committees were placed under the direction of the All-Army Party Committee, which is directly subordinate to the party Central Committee.[78] The MPA remained officially the "highest political organ" of the Hungarian army. In the event of mobilization, the party committees at the regimental level and above dissolve and the lower-level party committees become subordinate to the corresponding MPA agencies.[79]

The primary reason for the establishment of the system of party committees seems to have been to involve corresponding civilian party committees in ideological work among party members in the armed forces and to draw party members from the military into the work of civilian party organizations, particularly during elections to party and state bodies. Military officers often serve in these bodies.[80]

Soviet-East German Ties

The ties between the political administrations of the Group of Soviet Forces in Germany and the Main Political Administration of the GDR National People's Army are probably the most publicized of the bilateral ties of the WTO political administrations.[81] It would be unconstitutional for the East Germans not to maintain extremely close links between the corresponding structures of the two fraternal armies. Article 7 of the GDR constitution reads, "In the interest of the preservation of peace and the guaranteeing of the security of the socialist state, the National People's Army maintains close military cooperation with the Soviet Army and the armies of the other socialist countries. . . ."[82] The military oath required of each East German soldier demands that the soldier fulfill his constitutional duty of loyalty to the Soviet army. The oath reads, "I swear as a soldier of the National People's Army always to be ready to defend socialism on the side of the Soviet Army and of the armies of the socialist states allied with us against all enemies, not sparing my own life for the attainment of victory."[83]

According to the volume on the WTO edited by Colonel General Efimov of the Soviet MPA, there are "regular meetings and exchanges of experience" between representatives of the corresponding central administrations of the MPA, corresponding administrations of service branches, corresponding political departments of troop formations and among the political organs of youth groups, newspapers and journals.[84] These meetings include regular exchanges of delegations of political workers, such as the one led by Admiral Verner, chief of the GDR MPA, to the Soviet Union in 1972.[85] In addition, lecturers from the Soviet MPA regularly tour the National People's Army and East German lecturers regularly visit the military personnel of the Group of Soviet Forces in Germany, and of the Belorussian, Baltic, Leningrad, and Moscow military districts. According to the Efimov study, there are regular contacts between the political officers of Soviet and East German troops units. This volume notes, "it is hard to find a [GDR] military unit which does not maintain multi-faceted ties with a neighboring unit of the Group of Soviet Forces in Germany."[86] The difficulty of finding such units is evident in the reports of *Krasnaia Zvezda* correspondents, who have discovered such ties even at the level of the sub-units they have visited.[87]

Soviet and East German units frequently engage in a large number of joint political activities, including friendship evenings, and joint visits to industrial enterprises, military museums, and cultural institutions.[88] The highest ranking party and state officials of the GDR and USSR regularly visit the personnel of the Group of Soviet Forces in Germany to express their gratitude to the soldiers for their devotion to proletarian internationalism.[89] The exercises in fraternal good will annually culminate in the traditional "Week of Combat Friendship," during which there are frequent bilingual choruses of the military hymn, *Druzhba-Freundschaft* ("Friendship-Friendship").[90] A Soviet journalist reports that when East German soldiers are not engaged in combat and political training or in joint activities with their Soviet comrades, they often relax by reading the war memoirs of the Soviet officers who liberated Germany.[91]

According to the chief of the East German Main Political Administration, political work in the National People's Army seeks to inspire friendship for the Soviet army and a correct understanding of the imperialist threat:

> The internationalist training of the personnel of the National People's Army (NPA) strives to inform our soldiers well about the successes of the Soviet Union, about the concrete conditions in which they have been achieved, and about the self-sacrificing service of the soldiers and sailors of the Soviet Armed Forces.

This promotes the raising of the responsibility of the NPA for the fulfillment of its military class duty and of its allied obligations to unbreakable brotherhood in arms with the Soviet Armed Forces and with the other socialist armed forces.

As long as the imperialists have not renounced their goal of the destruction of socialism, the most important basic task of our ideological work is and will continue to be the unmasking of the aggressive essence of the military policy of imperialism. . . .

In the offensive struggle against the ideological diversions of the enemy, we are implanting a profound understanding among soldiers of the necessity for a further raising of combat capabilities and combat readiness. . . ."[92]

Polish-Soviet Ties

A joint study written by the institutes of military history of the Polish and Soviet defense ministries notes that there are "systematic meetings of political workers at all levels . . . every year there are visits to Poland and the USSR of tens of delegations of groups of Soviet and Polish political workers at the most diverse levels."[93] Among these contacts are an unspecified number of Soviet delegations to Poland led by General Epishev. Epishev's delegations have included Colonel General P.I. Efimov, a deputy chief of the Soviet MPA and editor of a Soviet study of the WTO; another deputy chief of the MPA, General G.V. Sredin; the chief of the political administration of the Soviet Air Foce, General I.M. Moroz; and the chief of the political administration of the Soviet Anti-Aircraft Troops, General I.F. Khalipov. In addition, other Soviet service branches and Soviet military districts have frequently sent delegations of political officers to Poland to meet with their opposites.[94]

The joint Soviet-Polish text on military friendship notes that the exchanges of delegations of political officers help to maintain "traditional ties" between the Moscow and Warsaw military districts, the Baltic Military District of the USSR and the Maritime Military District of Poland, between a series of Polish and Soviet tank divisions and between a series of unidentified Polish and Soviet military units.[95] This study specifically mentioned a Soviet delegation of 1971 that visited the Heroes of the Soviet Union 10th Polish Tank Division. During this visit, the personnel of the Polish division declared their "true friendship" for the USSR and their determination to defend jointly "the revolutionary gains of our peoples."[96] A Soviet study of the Belorussian Military District of the USSR noted that the personnel of this district, including political officers, engaged in a wide range of contacts and joint activities with unspecified Polish units.[97]

The political administrations of Poland and the USSR regularly send officers on lecture tours among the units of each other's armed forces. The officer clubs of the two armies participate in a regular exchange of lecturers, films, "oral newspapers," thematic evenings and artistic and cultural exhibits. Many of these exchanges are prepared by the staffs of the military museums of each country, in particular by the staff of the Museum of Polish-Soviet Military Friendship in the Belorussian city of Lenino. This museum draws a large number of military visitors every year.[98] Its exhibits are mainly devoted to the aid given by the Soviet Union in the formation of the Polish army which assisted the Soviet army in the liberation of Poland. According to the chief of the Polish Main Political Administration, by the end of the war the Communist forces of Poland numbered 400,000, among whom served 19,000 Soviet generals and officers and an additional 13,000 noncommissioned officers and technical specialists from the Soviet army.[99]

The political administrations of the Polish and Soviet armed forces also assist in the scheduling of sport competitions, song and dance festivals, and regular exchanges among military cinematographers and journalists, including the journalists of corresponding military districts.[100]

The Northern Force Group in Poland maintains an extensive series of political contacts with the Polish units in the Silesian Military District and with civilian administrative and economic agencies in the district.[101] According to a 1974 *Krasnaia Zvezda* article, "There is not a single unit of the Northern Force Group which does not maintain friendly contacts with the troop collectives of the Polish Armed Forces." The Soviet army newspaper continued, "Each year they draw up joint plans for the conduct of measures for the strengthening of friendly ties, for the exchange of experience of combat training, of party-political work, and of ideological and cultural work. And these plans are undeviatingly put into effect."[102] The author of this article noted that one such activity was a "permanently functioning seminar" for the leaders of political study groups of officers in each army. This particular correspondent also reported on a meeting he had attended in the Lenin room of a Soviet unit where a bilingual discussion was taking place on the theme, "V.I. Lenin on the Defense of the Socialist Fatherland." He wrote that despite the language barrier, both Soviet and Polish personnel appeared thoroughly familiar with the contents of the speeches delivered by foreign officers.[103] In this article, the *Krasnaia Zvezda* correspondent noted that the head of the Polish Council of Ministers had recently visited the Northern Force group to express Poland's gratitude to Soviet soldiers for "fulfilling their internationalist duty on the territory of a fraternal socialist state." The Soviet correspondent also noted that so many workers and peasants had written so many letters of thanks to the Northern Force Group that a Warsaw publishing house was bringing out a collection of such letters in a volume entitled *Just A Friend.*[104] *Krasnaia Zvezda* has not provided any information on the sales of this volume. In a 1975 article in *Krasnaia Zvezda,* a Polish officer reported that units of the Northern Force Group and of the Silesian Military District had recently introduced a special two-week summer program of joint military-political study by Polish and Soviet personnel.[105]

The broad range of joint political activities conducted by Polish and Soviet political officers testifies to the faithfulness of the Polish MPA in carrying out the resolution of the Sixth Congress of the Polish United Workers' Party:

> The Party will strengthen ideological ties and brotherhood in arms of the soldiers of the People's Polish Armed Forces with the heroic Soviet Army and will strive to ensure that Polish soldiers, conscientiously carrying out their duty, have increased the forces of the defensive alliance of the Warsaw Pact—the guarantee of peace and security on our continent.[106]

Contacts Between Soviet and Romanian Political Agencies

After the 1969 reorganization of the Warsaw Pact Romania continued to participate in the multilateral activities of the Political Consultative Committee and of the Sports Committee of the Friendly Armed Forces. Romania also regularly attended the sessions of the new Pact agencies, the Committee of Defense Ministers, the Military Council, the Committee of Foreign Ministers and probably the Technical Committee as well. Romania even agreed to the conduct of two "joint exercises" in Romania, each of which was a "command-staff map exercise"[107] which took place in a map room of the Romanian Defense Ministry.[108]

After the reorganization of the Pact in 1969, Romania also participated in a series of bilateral exchanges of delegations of political officers from the Soviet and Romanian armed forces. In 1971, the deputy directors of the higher political organs of each army exchanged visits.[109] In 1973, the highest-ranking Romanian political officer, Major General Gheorghe Gomoiu, led a delegation of Romanian political officers to the USSR where they visited the headquarters of the Soviet MPA, the offices of the political administration of a military district, and the political sections of several academies and institutes.[110] In 1975, General Epishev led a delegation of Soviet political officers on a return visit.[111]

Leading Romanian military officers have frequently pointed out that it is official policy for Romanian officers to engage in a variety of exchanges with the armed forces of all socialist states.[112] These exchanges include regular meetings with military officers from China and Yugoslavia.[113] The available evidence indicates that the exchanges between the political officers of the Romanian and Soviet armies have not led to any joint political activities with the other political organs of the WTO. The Romanian-Soviet exchanges of political officers may permit each side to honor the protocol of the Warsaw Treaty while continuing their mutual disagreements over WTO affairs. The exchanges may even enable the political officers of each army to obtain first-hand information of interest to each side. Yugoslavia engages in a comparable series of military exchanges with the Soviet Union. At least one Soviet military delegation to Yugoslavia included General Epishev, although it is not clear whether Epishev headed a subdelegation of political officers.[114]

There are probably two objections raised by the Romanians to the conduct of joint political activities and coordinated political education programs by the Soviet and Romanian armies. One is that the structure of the Romanian political organs in the military rules out the coordination of political activities by parallel agencies; the other is that the Romanians reject the WTO's shared military-political axioms and shared versions of East European military history which serve as the basis of the political education programs of the loyal WTO political officers.

As the leading Soviet specialist on the Romanian military, Colonel D.V. Diev, noted in a 1970 article, "The structure of the [Romanian] political organs is different from the structure of the party-political apparatus in the armed forces of the other countries of the Warsaw Pact, although their functions are one and the same."[115] The Romanians abolished their Main Political Administration in 1964. By abolishing the MPA, Ceausescu, who had been chief of the Romanian MPA in the early 1950s, may have sought to sever the party-political links through which the Soviet MPA could make a claim on the loyalty of Romanian officers. The April 1964 statement issued by the Romanian Central Committee shortly after Ceausescu came to power declared Romanian policy toward any such Soviet claims: "No party is allowed to go over the heads of the party leaders of one country and even less to launch appeals for the removal or the change of leadership of a party."[116]

Ceausescu replaced the Main Political Administration with a system of party committees very much like that of Yugoslavia. The directing body of the party committees is the Higher Political Council, a 35-member body made up of the highest-ranking regular officers from the service branches and central agencies of the Ministry of Defense and of the political officers who serve as the heads of the more important party councils within the armed forces. Each service branch has its own political council (where formerly it had an MPA administration). There are also political councils in certain larger formations, in each military district and in military-education institutions. Below the political councils are party committees organized at the level of regular military organizations—divisions, regiments, etc. At each level of military organization, the regular commanding officer is officially in charge of political work. The head of the corresponding party committee or party council is his deputy for political work.[117]

The Higher Political Council has a bureau, headed by a secretary, who also has the title of deputy minister of defense. The Higher Political Council reports to the State Defense Council, which in turn is subordinate in peacetime to both the Central Committee and the Grand National Assembly. Ceausescu is the chairman of the State Defense Council.[118] At every level of the system of party committees, the party bodies report to corresponding civilian party organizations about political work in the military.[119] The links of the party bodies in the military to civilian party organizations complement the overall program of the mobilization of the civilian population for territorial defense.[120]

The military-political axioms of Romania use some of the terms of the military-political axioms of the other members of the Warsaw Pact. But like the Yugoslavs, Albanians and Chinese, the Romanians define these terms to justify rejection of Soviet policies. Romania's military-political axioms avoid any mention of Romania's obligations to the Warsaw Pact or the Soviet Union and specifically reject the Soviet definition of joint defense of the gains of socialism. Romania's 1972 Law on the Organization of National Defense declares:

> The organization of the national defense of the Socialist Republic of Romania is based on the general policy of the Romanian Communist Party of building socialism and Communism, of strengthening friendship, cooperation and alliance with the socialist countries in conformity with the principles of Marxism-Leninism and proletarian internationalism, of promoting good neighborly relations, respect for national sovereignty, non-interference in internal affairs and mutual advantage, as well as eliminating force or the threat of force in settling disputes, with the aim of defending peace and security in the world.
>
> The right to decide on the problems of the defense of the Socialist Republic of Romania is a sovereign attribute of the Romanian state.[121]

When discussing Romania's obligations to the Warsaw Pact, Ceausescu and spokesmen for the Romanian defense ministry frequently point out that the Warsaw Treaty and the series of bilateral treaties with WTO members require only immediate consultations about military aid in the event of war rather than immediate military aid. After his disagreements with the Soviets at the 1978 session of the Political Consultative Committee in Moscow, Ceausescu delivered an address to the Romanian Central Committee in which he noted, ". . . in the case of an aggression in Europe against a country in the membership of the Warsaw Pact, we will fulfill our obligations taken under the Pact and also under the bilateral pacts of mutual assistance, according to the respective provisions."[122] Article Four of the Warsaw Treaty defines the obligations of WTO members to each other:

> In the event of an armed attack in Europe on one or several of the members states of this Treaty on the part of any state or group of states, each member of this Treaty in order for the realization of the right of individual or collective self-defense, in accordance with article 51 of the United Nations Charter, will render the state or group of states subject to such attack immediate aid, individual or collective in concert with the other member states of the Treaty with all means it deems necessary, including the use of armed force.

> The member states of the Treaty will immediately consult in regard to the joint measures which must be adopted for the purpose of restoring and preserving international peace and security.[123]

Romania's bilateral treaty of 1970 with the Soviet Union also requires only consultations in the event of war and specifically limits the mission of the WTO to defense against NATO.[124] In the volume on Romanian military doctrine published by the Romanian Defense Ministry, Colonel Traian Grozea called attention to the limited obligations of Romania to its allies:

> A characteristic, fundamental trait of the treaties concluded between Romania and other socialist countries is the fact that they provide for respect for national independence and sovereignty.

> Military assistance will be granted only at the request of the state which is the victim of imperialist aggression, and the forms and volume of such assistance are established by agreement between the legal leaderships.

> Since the elected party and state bodies alone have the responsibility for the destinies of socialist nations, it is only they who can decide whether the cause of socialism and the revolutionary gains of the people are threatened.[125]

A Soviet specialist on the WTO, Colonel V.F. Samoilenko, correctly noted in a discussion of the military-political axioms incorporated into the party programs of the WTO states, "In the documents of the Romanian Communist party are statements about the importance of the development of cooperation among the member states of the Warsaw Pact and among the armed forces of these states."[126] Colonel Samoilenko did not, however, comment on the text of these statements, such as that made by Ceausescu to the party congress that met after the Soviet intervention in Czechoslovakia:

> By the world system of socialism we understand not a bloc of states which are fused into a whole, giving up their national sovereignty, but the assertion of socialism as an international force by its victory in several independent states, which develop independently. . . ..
>
> The development and consolidation of the new socialist system, the defense of the revolutionary gains of socialism, represent the sacred right and duty of every people, of every Communist party in the socialist countries.
>
> Naturally, in the spirit of proletarian internationalism, in the case of an imperialist attack, the peoples of the socialist countries must aid each other, fighting shoulder to shoulder for the defeat of the aggressor.
>
> The establishing of the forms and ways of mutual aid in such cases must be the result of agreement between the leading party bodies, between the constitutional leading bodies of each country.
>
> The solidarity and mutual aid of socialist countries presupposes relations of equality between all the socialist nations; it must not lead to interference in the internal affairs of any people. . . .[127]

Romanian military historians have produced a sizeable literature which purports to trace back to the Middle Ages a Romanian tradition of patriotic resistance to foreign domination and even a tradition of fighting wars of territorial defense.[128] Romanian military historians date the formation of the modern Romanian concept of territorial defense to the Romanian General Staff of the 1930s.[129] They also take issue with Soviet historians over the credit due the Romanian army both for the installation of the Romanian Communist Party in power in 1944 and for the expulsion of Nazi forces from Romania.[130]

The military-political axioms and military history texts of the Romanians suggest not only that the Soviets have failed to impose the preferred WTO versions on the Romanian armed forces but that the Soviet MPA may discourage contacts of the loyal political administrations of the Pact with Romanian political officers in order to avoid contamination by Bucharest's military heresies.

Rebellion and Reconstruction in the Czechoslovak
Main Political Administration

During the spring of 1968 the rector, vice rector, and several leading staff members of the Gottwald Military-Political Academy in Prague attacked the military-political axioms of the Warsaw Treaty Organization. They charged that the practical application of these axioms denied Czechoslovakia sovereignty over its own armed forces. They proposed as an alternative to Czechoslovakia's continued membership in the Warsaw Pact that Czechoslovakia work out an independent military doctrine based either on the concept of "reliance on one's own forces" or on the creation of a Central European security system outside the framework of the WTO. They suggested that such a security system could be made up either of Communist states, excluding the USSR, or a bloc of Communist or non-Communist states. The command of the assault on the military-political axioms of the WTO passed from the Gottwald Academy to Lieutenant General Vaclav Prchlik, the chief of the Main Political Administration of the Czechoslovak People's Army, who in June of 1968 was promoted to the post of secretary of the eighth department of the Central Committee, a department in charge of political work not only in the armed forces but in the internal security organs as well. Lieutenant General Prchlik drew upon the proposals of the Gottwald Academy to draft resolutions for the 14th Party Congress on the revision of Czechoslovak military doctrine. Some of these resolutions proposed the reorganization of the political organs of the Czechoslovak armed forces to accord with the new doctrinal concepts advocated by Prchlik.

Within a few days of the drafting of the proposals by the faculty of the Gottwald Academy, Marshal Iakubovskii came to Prague to arrange for large-scale WTO military exercises on Czechoslovak soil in the immediate future. About two weeks after Marshal Iakubovskii's visit Marshal Grechko and General Epishev also came to Prague where they elicited a formal pledge from the Czechoslovak Defense Ministry to preserve the policies and administrative structures linking the Czechoslovak armed forces to the Warsaw Pact. Lieutenant General Prchlik and Marshal Iakubovskii then engaged in a quasi-public dispute which culminated in the intervention of August 21.

After the intervention, the Soviets overhauled the administrative agencies of the WTO in a manner designed to disarm Lieutenant General Prchlik's criticisms of the Warsaw Pact. The Soviets and Czechoslovaks also negotiated a series of party and state charters which facilitated the reintegration of the Czechoslovak armed forces into the WTO. These developments took place during a large-scale exodus of officers from the

Czechoslovak military consisting of those who resigned their commissions in protest over the invasion and those who were purged during 1969 and 1970 as politically unreliable. Probably the single most important element in the reconstruction of Soviet-Czechoslovak military ties was the reestablishment of the capability of the Soviet MPA to monitor the loyalty of the Czechoslovak political officers responsible for monitoring the loyalties of regular military personnel. The political re-education programs of the Czechoslovak MPA in the period after the WTO intervention focused specifically on rejection of the proposals of Prchlik and the Gottwald Academy and on reaffirmation of the military-political axioms of the WTO.

The mutiny of several prominent officers of the Czechoslovak Main Political Administration in 1968 suggests that the political officers of the WTO may be the first to understand that the military-political axioms of the Warsaw Pact determine the military capabilities of East European armed forces and that these capabilities in turn have great influence on Soviet-East European political relations.[131]

The Gottwald Memorandum

After the Czechoslovak Central Committee adopted in early April of 1968 the "Action Program," which served as the charter for the Prague Spring, the staff of the Klement Gottwald Military-Political Academy in Prague drafted a 100 page document entitled "Notes on the Action Program of the Czechoslovak People's Army." In early May the Gottwald Academy drafted a shorter, ten-page document, "How Czechoslovak State Interests in the Military Sphere Are to Be Formulated," a document that became known as the "Gottwald Memorandum." The authors of the memorandum were the rector of the Academy, Colonel Professor Vojtech Mencl; the vice rector, Lieutenant Colonel Dr. Borivoi Svarc; a department head at the Academy, Colonel Vladimir Rehak; and a staff member, Lieutenant Colonel Milan Zdimal. An additional 21 members of the Gottwald staff signed the memorandum, as did 5 staff members of the Zapotocky Military Academy in Brno.[132] According to Colonel Milan Matous, head of the ideological department of the Czechoslovak Main Political Administration after Gustav Husak replaced Alexander Dubcek as first secretary of the party, the staff of the Gottwald Academy also drew up a proposal to split the Czechoslovak MPA into a "service organization" and a separate party organization.[133]

The Gottwald Memorandum identified three possible defense strategies for Czechoslovakia:

1. The coalition principle (the alliance with the Soviet Union and the other states of the Warsaw Pact) on which our defense system is currently based, is subject to development and it is necessary to reconsider its validity in the coming 10 to 15 years;

2. It is possible to think about co-ordinated defense in Central Europe without the military potential of the USSR (some kind of military analog to the political Little Entente 'in a socialist form' or some kind of collective security organization without a class determination;

3. The possibility of neutralizing one's territory or pursuing a policy of neutrality and relying on one's own means of defense.[134]

In his dissection of the Gottwald Memorandum, Colonel Matous of Czechoslovak MPA specifically focused on the Gottwald Memorandum's rejection of the military-political axioms of the Warsaw Pact:

According to the 'Memorandum,' our military policies were not based on an analysis of the real requirements and interests of the nation and the state. . . .

The authors tried to prove in this and other connections that military policy was dictated by outside interests, the interests and requirements of the Warsaw alliance.

So, these policies were supposed to be dictated by the interests of the Soviet Union, as clearly emerges also from other more cautious formulations. . . .[135]

Colonel Matous added in further criticism of the memorandum:

The memorandum belittles the military threat from the West, chiefly from the Western countries allied in NATO and from German militaristic circles. In section 2, point 2, it is expressly said that: "The threat of German aggression increasingly plays the role of an additional, external factor, which is to strengthen the cohesion of the socialist community. The military factor is intended to compensate for inadequate economic cooperation and development of other ties among the socialist countries after the original idea about a universal political and economic model had to be revised. . . ."

As the authors of the memorandum see our basic military-political situation, therefore, there is no threat from West German militaristic circles and from NATO, but a fictitious threat created by the Soviet Union as a result of its great-power ambitions.

In this connection, the authors of the memorandum have no qualms about leveling the crudest possible accusations at the foreign and military-political orientation of the Soviet Union. In section 2, point 2, the possibility of a strategic attack for the purpose of ensuring the absolute hegemony of the Soviet Union over Europe is expressly mentioned.

The orientation as outlined by the memorandum aims at the disruption of the Warsaw Pact and at the withdrawal of Czechoslovakia from the defensive coalition with the other socialist countries. It is expressly stated in one of the sections of the memorandum that "practical measures which are feasible in this situation aim at the conclusion of international agreements with potential adversaries." And in another section possible agreements between Czechoslovakia and members of the Atlantic Pact, specifically between Czechoslovakia and the German Federal Republic, are also expressly mentioned.[136]

Another post-1968 Czechoslovak critic of the Gottwald Memorandum, Jiri Heckho, also concluded that the memorandum advocated Czechoslovakia's withdrawal from the Warsaw Pact.[137] Hechko described the Gottwald Academy as "the principal base for the working out of a new military policy of the party and state."[138] Several other public documents of the Husak era explicitly condemned the proposals of the Gottwald Memorandum and the attempts of Lieutenant General Prchlik to act upon these proposals. These documents include the official history of the events of 1968 adopted as a resolution by Husak's Central Committee, statements by both of Prchlik's successors as chief of the Czechoslovak Main Political Administration and several articles by Czechoslovak and Soviet military journalists.[139]

In early May of 1968, the authors of the Gottwald Memorandum sent copies of their document to Alexander Dubcek, the first secretary of the Central Committee; to Ludvik Svoboda, the president of the Republic; to Oldrich Cernik, the chairman of the Council of Ministers; and to members of the Central Committee, the National Assembly, the Foreign Ministry, and to the Higher Party School in Prague.[140] The Soviets appear to have responded almost immediately.

In an article of May 9 devoted to the 23rd anniversary of the liberation of Czechoslovakia, *Krasnaia Zvezda* noted in passing that Marshal Iakubovskii had recently returned from Prague where he and Defense Minister Martin Dzur had agreed on the conduct of a large-scale WTO exercise in Czechoslovakia in the near future.[141] The same issue also contained a reprint of an interview with Dubcek in which he endorsed the principle of Czechoslovakia's participation in the joint military exercises of the WTO.[142] This same issue also contained an article by Marshal Iakubovskii in which the WTO commander declared that Bonn was making military preparations for the revision of its European borders; that Maoists were attempting to undermine their contacts and cooperation; and that at the Dresden meeting in March the leaders of the WTO states had agreed to take immediate measures to strengthen the organization of the Warsaw Pact.[143]

From May 10 to 14, a delegation of retired Soviet marshals visited Czechoslovakia to commemorate the 23rd anniversary of the Soviet liberation.[144] In its enthusiasm for celebration of the anniversary, the Soviet Defense Ministry sent another delegation, which arrived on May 17. This delegation included Marshal Grechko, General Epishev, V.G. Kulikov, then commander of the Group of Soviet Forces in Germany, and N.V. Ogarkov, then deputy chief of the Soviet General Staff. According to *Krasnaia Zvezda,* the delegation exchanged views with the Czechoslovak comrades on *voennoe stroitel'stvo* ("the organization and development of national defense systems"). The Soviet army newspaper also reported that both sides had agreed to "concrete measures for the further development of friendship between the Soviet army and the Czechoslovak People's Army and the strengthening of their interaction in the framework of the Warsaw Pact."[145]

The next Soviet military delegation to visit Czechoslovak consisted of units of the Group of Soviet Forces in Germany which crossed the Czechoslovak border on May 31 in an unannounced exercise designed to be "as close as possible to reality."[146] From June 20 to 30, Marshal Iakubovskii commanded a large scale command-staff exercise covering the territories of Czechoslovakia, East Germany, Poland, the USSR and involving troops from each of these states plus Hungarian forces as well.[147] Following the completion of the exercise, Soviet troops remained in Czechoslovakia. The timing of the exercises coincided with the first round of the election of delegates to the 14th Party Congress. The "progressives" in the Czechoslovak party hoped to elect a majority of delegates to the party congress in order to purge the Central Committee of its "conservative" members.[148] On July 2, shortly after the completion of the WTO maneuvers and shortly before the final round of election of delegates to the 14th Congress, the Czechoslovak army newspaper, *Lidova Armada,* published the complete text of the Gottwald Memorandum. According to one of the later critics of the Gottwald Memorandum, the publication of the memorandum in *Lidova Armada* constituted a public declaration of "the program of the rightist forces in the army." This critic added, "The rightists intended to force this program through the 14th Congress of the party."[149]

On July 15, Lieutenant General Prchlik took the unusual step of holding a press conference. In his prepared statement Prchlik summarized the various points made by the Gottwald Memorandum and then proceeded to list the practical implications of these points for the 14th Congress of the party. In his prepared remarks,[150] Prchlik raised the question of Czechoslovakia's relations with the Warsaw Pact only in connection with the principal purpose of his speech, that of outlining ". . . the necessary conditions for working out a Czechoslovak military doctrine."[151] As *Krasnaia Zvezda* later charged, Prchlik discussed the possibilities of organizational changes within the Warsaw Pact in order to adopt a deliberately false pose of loyalty to the Pact.[152]

Lieutenant General Prchlik proposed that the forthcoming Party Congress adopt a resolution requiring the revision of Czechoslovak military doctrine. He also proposed that the specific details of Czechoslovakia's new military policy should be worked out by the new Central Committee to be elected at the Congress and by the new National Assembly to be elected in late 1968. He noted the Czechoslovakia's previous military policy was based on the military-political axioms written into the programs of the last several party congresses and that these axioms could no longer serve as the basis for Czechoslovakia's military posture. He emphasized that the working out of a new military doctrine depended upon the election of "progressives" to the new Central Committee and the new National Assembly. He proposed that these two bodies establish a State Defense Council to formulate the new doctrine. He may have had in mind a body that would be identical to Romania's State Defense Council not only in name but in purpose. General Prchlik made these points in the circumlocutory style so favored by East European bureaucrats:

> We further think that in the forthcoming period, the party, particularly its supreme organs, that is, the Congress and the Central Committee, should work out the concepts of military and defense policy, develop them in a creative way, and implement them.
>
> In view of the significance of this sector of party activity we are trying to ensure that the Congress adopt a special independent resolution on the problem of military and security policy or at least one of the next plenums after the Congress deal with the state of affairs of these institutions and give concrete shape to the general resolution of the Congress.
>
> Why do we make this request?
>
> We do so because so far the Congress has dealt with the problem of military security only on the most general level. If you look at the individual Congress decisions, you know that the Congresses have adopted only a few short sentences, formulated in the most general way, which without any change might have been adopted as well by the 9th, 13th or 14th Congresses. . . .
>
> In the National Assembly a military and security affairs committee has been set up . . . however, it will not help us to settle anything so long as the qualification structure of the plenum of the National Assembly is not changed too.
>
> This is a question connected with the quality of the deputies and with the preparation of the forthcoming elections to the National

Assembly which should provide safeguards that people are elected to the National Assembly who will be able to implement these functions.

We are preparing a proposal on the creation of a state defense council. We are still discussing its relation to the government and the question of the work and function of the secretariat of this council.

We hold the view that the state defense council should be an organ of the government and . . . serve the government as an expert organ in this field.

Its primary task will be to discuss the necessity, possibilities and necessary conditions for working out a Czechoslovak military doctrine.

We suppose the 14th Congress will also express its view on this problem.[153]

This discussion of the practical steps necessary to work out a new Czechoslovak military doctrine brought Lieutenant General Prchlik to his pro forma suggestions for improving the Warsaw Pact: strengthening the role of the Political Consultative Committee, giving each member state genuine equality in the alliance, and creating "clear guarantees . . . preventing fractionalist activities . . . which . . . would lead in the last analysis to violating the basic items of the Pact, particularly the items concerning the state sovereignty of members."[154] After having declared his desire for reforms within the Pact, Lieutenant General Prchlik then concluded his remarks by reiterating his intention to submit draft resolutions to the 14th Congress on the redefinition of Czechoslovak military doctrine. He added that he would also submit proposals on the reorganization of the Czechoslovak Main Political Administration and the party apparatus in the security police: "It stands to reason that in our preparations of Congress materials we will also deal with a number of other problems, such as the structure of the party and other institutions in the army and security organs, the system of their management, and many other problems."[155]

Immediately after reading his prepared statement Lieutenant General Prchlik accepted questions from the reporters present. According to a Western transcript of the press conference, none of the journalists asked about Prchlik's detailed plans for the revision of Czechoslovak military doctrine by the 14th Party Congress and the future session of the National Assembly. The transcript of the press conference available in the West indicates that all of the reporters' questions focused on Prchlik's brief proposals for reorganizing the Warsaw Pact and on his reaction to the "Warsaw Letter" of July 14. A previous chapter discussed both the Warsaw Letter and Lieutenant General Prchlik's reaction to it.[156] Prchlik replied to the questions on the Warsaw Pact as follows:

To the group of questions which concern the joint command of the Warsaw Pact itself: So far the situation is that this command is formed by marshals, generals and officers of the Soviet Army and that the other member armies have only their representatives in this joint command.

These representatives, however, have so far held no responsibilities nor had a hand in making decisions, but rather played the role of liaison organs.

This is why our party presented proposals in the past for the creation of the required prerequisites for the joint command to competently discharge its functions.

One of these prerequisites is the demand that the allied command also be composed of appropriate specialists of the individual armies and their incorporation in this command be of such a nature as to enable them to co-create and to participate in the whole process of learning and deciding, in the whole command system. So far the proper conclusions have not been made.

From the viewpoint of the further work of this joint command, we believe that it also will be necessary to clarify the position of the ministers of the individual countries who have been holding so far the functions of deputy commanders of the joint command.[157]

At no point in either his prepared remarks or his answers to questions did Lieutenant General Prchlik suggest that his plans for the reformulation of Czechoslovak military doctrine would depend on the reorganization of the command structure of the Warsaw Pact. Throughout his press conference, Prchlik made it quite clear that he intended to press for a revision of Czechoslovak military doctrine no matter what changes, if any, were made in the Warsaw Pact. One week after the press conference, a *Krasnaia Zvezda* editorial sharply rebuked Prchlik for his criticisms of the Warsaw Pact but refrained from commenting on his proposals for the revision of Czechoslovak military doctrine.[158] On July 25, the Presidium of the Czechoslovak Communist Party responded ambiguously to the Soviet criticism by abolishing the eighth department of the Central Committee, which Prchlik headed, and transferring the general back to his previous past of chief of the Main Political Administration.[159] On July 27, the Czechoslovak press agency released an unattributed statement to the effect that Prchlik's remarks had not contributed to the strengthening of the friendship of the Warsaw Pact armed forces.[160] The intervention of August 21 cut short any debate within the Czechoslovak leadership over the question of how to respond to Soviet criticisms of Lieutenant General Prchlik.

Reconstruction in the Czechoslovak Main Political Administration: The Theoretical Legacy of V.I. Lenin

After the intervention the Soviets faced a problem of reconstruction of the officer cadre of the Czechoslovak armed forces probably similar in scope to the reconstruction of the Czechoslovak officer corps following World War II. According to a Czechoslovak publication cited by Robert Dean, a former analyst for Radio Free Europe, by the end of 1968, 57.8 percent of the military officers under the age of 30 had resigned their commissions.[161] As further proof of the crisis of morale which he detected in the Czechoslovak army after 1968, Dean cited another document of the Husak era which published the results of a survey of political attitudes among Czechoslovak military recruits in the summer of 1969. According to this survey, 81 percent of the recruits opposed strengthening Czechoslovakia's ties with the Soviet Union and 56 percent saw no danger of an attack by either NATO or West Germany.[162]

In order to render fraternal assistance to the Czechoslovak Main Political Administration in improving the political attitudes of officers and enlisted personnel, the Soviets first established several legal-political charters on which to rebuilt the links between the Soviet and Czechoslovak armed forces. The first was the treaty that Czechoslovakia signed on October 18, 1968, which established the legal basis for the formation of the Central Force Group on Czechoslovak soil. In March 1969, the Political Consultative Committee of the WTO approved Marshal Iakubovskii's proposals for the reorganization of the Warsaw Pact. The establishment of the Committee of Defense Ministers, the Military Council and the Technical Committee was at least in part an attempt to respond to General Prchlik's proposals that the position of the WTO defense ministers in the alliance be clarified and that the technical specialists of the East European armies be involved in working out the policies of the central Pact agencies.[163]

On May 6, 1970, the Soviet Union and Czechoslovakia signed a new treaty of friendship. The new treaty declared that "support, strengthening and defense of the gains of socialism, which have been achieved at the cost of the herioc efforts and self-sacrificing labor of each people, is the common internationalist duty of socialist countries." The treaty also declared that both sides would "strictly observe the responsibilities deriving from the Warsaw Treaty. . . ."[163] In December 1970, Gustav Husak's Central Committee adopted a document entitled "The Lessons of Crisis Development." This document specifically condemned the Gottwald Academy for producing "an official memorandum which demanded a revision of the principles of the military policy of our party and state, which had been confirmed by the 13th Congress of the Czechoslovak Communist Party, and a change in Czechoslovak military doctrine on the basis of a revision of our relationship to the Warsaw Pact."[165]

The Czechoslovak Party Congress in 1971 provided the authoritative charter for party-political work in the Czechoslovak armed forces. The resolution on foreign policy read in part:

> The Czechoslovak Socialist Republic will contribute to the utmost to the constant strengthening of the Warsaw Treaty Organization and will actively participate in the deepening of cooperation and in the development of economic integration of the socialist countries in the framework of the Council for Mutual Economic Assistance.
>
> Our party will unswervingly safeguard firm friendship and alliance with the Soviet Union.
>
> We will do everything in order that the new Treaty of Friendship, Cooperation and Mutual Aid between the CSSR and USSR will become fruitful and will provide the point of departure for the further development of cooperation in all areas.[166]

The brief resolution on the Warsaw Pact was emphatic in its commitment to the WTO but vague as to the details of Czechoslovakia's participation in the Pact, except for the resolution's endorsement of the 1970 Treaty, which was much more specific about Czechoslovakia's obligations to the alliance. The brevity of the Congress resolution on military affairs was in keeping with the spirit of the resolutions on military affairs of previous Congresses, about which Prchlik had complained in his press conference. Despite the brevity of the resolution on the WTO of the 14th Congress, a study of the WTO edited by Colonel General Efimov of the Soviet MPA reached the following conclusions:

> The 14th Congress of the Czechoslovak Communist Party placed before the armed forces and the whole Czechoslovak people a most important task—the guaranteeing of the reliable armed defense of the gains of socialism of the workers of Czechoslovakia.
>
> The resolution of the Congress emphasized that this could take place only in the framework of joint efforts in full correspondence with the interests of all the member states of the Warsaw Pact and in unbreakable union and friendship with the Soviet Union.
>
> The resolution required the military cadres of the Czechoslovak People's Army to be guided in the organization and development of the national armed forces and in the training of the officer crops by the conclusions of Marxist-Leninist military science and by the experience of the fraternal socialist countries.[167]

According to an article by a colonel in the Czechoslovak MPA, cited by Robert Dean, Czechoslovak political officers in the postinvasion period took the party-political work in the Soviet armed forces as the model for the work of the Czechoslovak MPA.[168] One of the first steps in the reconstruction of political training was the closing of the Gottwald Academy in early July 1969 and the establishment of a new military-political faculty at the Zapotocky Military Academy in Brno. Sometime before 1974, the military-political faculty was promoted to the status of a new Gottwald Military-Political Academy, also located in Brno.

Another part of process of reconstruction took place during the spring of 1970. In conjunction with a general inquisition into the records of all party members, each officer in the armed forces had to give an account of his activities during the period of 1968–69.[169] In December 1970, the resolution adopted by the Husak Central Committee reported that as a result of this process, "a significant number of party members in military units were ejected from the Czechoslovak Communist Party and many of them had to retire from military service."[170] The volume on the WTO edited by Colonel General Efimov of the Soviet MPA noted that the Czechoslovak Defense Ministry established special one-year officer schools in 1970 to train personnel to replenish an officer corps which had been "purged of alien elements." In 1971, the curriculum of these schools was expanded to two years.[171]

According to the public discussion by Czechoslovak officers of the reorganization of party-political work cited by Robert Dean, the MPA officials of Czechoslovakia were in a quandary during 1970 and 1971 over the selection of materials to be used for political education.[172] By 1972, the new chief of the Czechoslovak Main Political Administration, Lieutenant General Vaclav Horachek, had found a solution. He reported in a 1972 interview that the personnel of the armed forces had just embarked upon a three-year study program devoted to the theoretical legacy of V.I. Lenin. During the initial year of the study of Lenin's legacy, Czechoslovak military personnel read materials from the 14th Congress of the Czechoslovak party and the 24th Congress of the Communist Party of the Soviet Union.[173] In his 1972 interview, Horachek, without mentioning the Gottwald Memorandum by name, noted that conceptions identical to those of Gottwald Memorandum had found broad support in the armed forces. He added that these ideas had resulted in "deformation of the concept of the probable enemy," a euphemism worthy of his cashiered predecessor, Lieutenant General Prchlik.

Question: Western ideological centers have been leading an assault for many years on our population—including the members of the armed forces—for the purpose of blunting their understanding of the world in terms of classes, and creating illusions about worldwide imperialism—above all, about the Federal Republic of Germany and the United States. For example, 'theories' appeared in the past alleging that the Federal Republic of Germany should not be used as a scarecrow. The purpose of all this was to disarm our people ideologically and, among other things, also to create a negative attitude toward the defense of the socialist fatherland. What are your intentions in this respect?

Answer [Horachek]: It is a fact that particularly in 1968–69 there was the problem of imperialism. . . .From this there was only a small step to such fantastic allegations as the claim that the North Atlantic Pact is outspokenly of a defensive character, and that there are no militarists or revanchists in West Germany. . . .There can be doubt that this ideological-political diversion had and always has had its clearly military-political aspects. . . .With regard to the members of the armed forces, such a trend is particularly dangerous, because it may result in a deformation of the concept of the probable enemy.[174]

To prevent the reoccurrence of the deformation of the concept of the probable enemy, Soviet political officers of the Central Force Group in Czechoslovakia began directly assisting officers of the Czechoslovak MPA in the conduct of political work. According to a 1970 article in *Krasnaia Zvezda* by a Czechoslovak major, "We devote great attention to the political and internationalist training of army youth . . . such work proceeds with the aid and participation of our Soviet comrades, Communists and Komsomol members."[175] This officer noted that joint political work took place regularly, both during regular joint exercises and during national training exercises.[176] In 1974, Colonel Jan Khmelik, editor of the Czechoslovak army newspaper, reported to the readers of *Pravda,*

Our army has the possibility to draw directly upon the rich experience of the Soviet armed forces through direct cooperation with commanders, political organs and party and Komsomol organizations in the Central Force Group.

We make good use of such possibilities on the basis of a joint plan of the Main Political Administration of the Czechoslovak People's Army and the Political Administration of the Central Force Group.[177]

In a 1975 article entitled "Shoulder to Shoulder with the Soviet People and Their Army," the Chief of the Czechoslovak Main Political Administration gratefully acknowledged that the political officers of the Central Force Group had been providing their Czechoslovak colleagues with "great aid."[178]

A study of Soviet-Czechoslovak military cooperation published jointly in 1975 by the military history institutes of the Soviet Union and Czechoslovakia noted that during joint political exercises the fraternal soldiers engaged in a wide variety of activities, including visits to industrial enterprises, historical museums and population centers. The two armies also regularly received visits from the highest-ranking party and state figures of Czechoslovakia.[179] This study also noted that the Czechoslovak MPA maintained regular ties not only with the political officers of the Central Force Group but with Soviet political offices in the central administrations of the Soviet MPA, the administrations of Soviet military districts, the departments of Soviet formations (divisions or larger groupings), and with the personnel of Soviet military-education institutions.[130] These ties included regular contacts between the Lenin Military-Political Academy and the rehabilitated Gottwald Military-Political Academy in Brno.[181] The two fraternal political administrations also exchange lecturers, cultural workers and journalists.[182]

In August 1974, *Krasnaia Zvezda* published an article about the visit of a group of Soviet "ideological workers" who had come to Czechoslovakia "at the invitation of the Main Political Administration of the Czechoslovak People's Army." One of the members of the Soviet group was Major General S.K. Il'in, the author and co-author of a number of political texts used by the Soviet MPA,[183] who had also reported for *Krasnaia Zvezda* on a 1973 inspection of political work in the Bulgarian armed forces by General Epishev.[184] The delegation of Soviet ideological workers visited the "leading staff" of the Czechoslovak Main Political Administration, the political administration of the Eastern Military District of Czechoslovakia, the soldiers of a Czechoslovak formation, and the leaders of local party and state bodies in Slovakia. Major General Il'in and his colleagues also visited the new Gottwald Academy.[185]

Il'in reported to the readers of *Krasnaia Zvezda* that, just as in the Soviet Armed Forces, ideological work in the Czechoslovak People's Army was directed at inculcating the ideas of Marxism-Leninism in order to foster the development of "the spiritual qualities of patriot-internationalists." Major General Il'in also reported that he had examined the methods used in ideological work, which included readings from the speeches of Gustav Husak and L.I. Brezhnev.[186] In his article Il'in noted that he had also visited Czechoslovakia in 1972. He declared that, compared to 1972, party-political work in the Czechoslovak armed forces had become "much more purposeful."[187]

In a study also published in 1974, General Epishev observed that the "moral-political situation" of the Czechoslovak armed forces had "recently improved."[188] General Epishev made this observation in a discussion of party membership among the officer corps of the Warsaw Pact, a discussion during which he declined to give a specific figure for party membership of the Czechoslovak officer corps. In 1977, Colonel

Khmelik, the editor of the Czechoslovak army newspaper, reported in *Krasnaia Zvezda* that party membership among Czechoslovak officers stood at "almost 75 percent." Speaking of the political education work in the Czechoslovak army, he noted, "We are striving first of all to form in soldiers a socialist conviction and patriotic and internationalist feelings."[189]

Ten years after the Gottwald Memorandum, the political officers of the Czechoslovak People's Army had been reintegrated into the network of WTO political administrations. The re-establishment of close links between the Soviet and Czechoslovak political administrations once again enabled Soviet officers to monitor and even participate in the political education of Czechoslovak military personnel. The mission assigned by the Soviets to the Main Political Administration of the Czechoslovak People's Army has not been so much persuasion in the military-political axioms of the WTO as proscription of the alternative military-political axioms of the Gottwald Memorandum.

Chapter Eight
The Warsaw Pact Directorate for Educational Exchanges

Another of the "other organs of administration" of the United Command of the Warsaw Pact appears to be a directorate for coordinating exchanges among the military-educational institutions of the WTO, except for those of Romania. In these exchanges, East Europeans send students to study in the USSR and the Soviets send lecturers and instructional materials to East Europe. The Soviets may also train faculty for East European military schools and academies.[1] If the United Command of the WTO does not have a directorate for coordinating educational exchanges within the WTO, then the Main Administation of Higher Military-Educational Institutions of the Soviet Defense Ministry may serve as the Warsaw Pact clearinghouse for educational exchanges.[2]

The military-educational system of the WTO has three levels, each of which trains officers for the corresponding field of the three components of military art: tactics, operational art, and strategy. Undergraduate colleges, known as higher military schools, train future lieutenants in the tactics of individual types of troops. Military academies train captains and majors for responsibilities as senior officers in command of tactical-operational combined arms actions at the level of divisions and smaller formations. The Voroshilov General Staff Academy in Moscow trains colonels and generals from Bulgaria, Hungary, East Germany, Poland, Czechoslovakia, and the Soviet Union for command responsibilities in operational-strategic combined arms actions consisting of larger formations, superformations, armies, and fronts.

The loyal East European members of the WTO train most of their junior military officers in local higher military schools. East European captains and majors seeking promotion to senior ranks must acquire a post-graduate degree in military science from either an East European mid-career academy or a Soviet mid-career academy. The Soviet Union maintains a series of mid-career academies that offer highly specialized degrees that do not appear to be available from East European mid-career academies, with the possible exception of the mid-career academies of Poland. The Frunze Academy in Moscow for combined arms commanders and the Lenin Military-Political Academy in Moscow compete with their East European counterparts for East European applicants and appear to offer the more prestigious degrees. Only the Voroshilov General Staff Academy in Moscow is qualified to train the officers of Bulgaria, Hungary, East Germany, Poland, Czechoslovakia, and the Soviet Union for operational-strategic level commands in WTO ministries of defense, general staffs, political administrations, service branches and military districts.

The majority of serving officers in the WTO armies do not have higher military educations. According to figures published in a 1974 volume edited by General of the Army E.E. Mal'tsev, commandant of the Lenin Military-Political Academy, "more than 40 percent" of the Soviet officer corps has a higher or special technical education; "more than 40 percent" of the Bulgarian officer corps; 20 percent of the Hungarian officer corps; and 33 percent of the Polish officer corps. General Mal'tsev did not give an overall figure for the East German officer corps, but noted that all commanders of formations had a higher military education, as did 85 percent of the commanders of "units," which make up formations.[3] Marshal Iakubovskii's 1975 text stated that 33 percent of the East German officer corps had a higher education and declared that "all commanders of formations" in the East Germany army had higher educations as did "the overwhelming majority" of the commanders of units. Marshal Iakubovskii added that "many" of the commanders of the East German army had received degrees from the Voroshilov General Staff Academy.[4]

Neither Mal'tsev's study of 1974, Efimov's study of 1974, nor Iakubovskii's study of 1975 gave a figure for the percentage of officers with a higher military education in the Czechoslovak People's Army. Their collective reluctance to cite a figure for the Czechoslovak officer corps may be due to the depletion of qualified officers which resulted from the resignations of many officers following the 1968 invasion and the purges of politicially unreliable officers in 1970.[5] In his volume on the WTO, Marshal Iakubovskii did say that 85 percent of the Czechoslovak officer corps had completed a secondary-school level education.[6]

An article in a Soviet publication noted that during the five years from 1971–76 "more than six thousand" East German officers had been graduated from unidentified higher military schools and "almost three thousand" East German officers had received degrees from unidentified military academies during the same period.[7] This suggests that in the East German army, slightly less than half the officers commissioned in the higher military schools will advance into military academies. Information on the careers of individual officers in East Germany and other WTO states indicates that promotion to the highest military commands of East Europe is restricted to the elite which passes through the three levels of the alliance's officer education system.[8]

This system inducts the East European graduates of Soviet military academies into a greater socialist officer corps bound together by old-school ties, trained in a common military doctrine addressed to the conduct of joint missions, and accustomed to using Russian as the language of military communication. The members of the greater socialist officer corps preside over different national contingents, each of which may harbor sentiments toward the other contingents ranging from friendship to enmity. The East European officers trained in the Soviet Union command their troops in joint WTO exercises and other joint alliance activities, such as the invasion of Czechoslovakia in 1968.

If the WTO military-educational system does not induct the highest-ranking East European officers into a greater socialist officer corps subordinate to the Soviet defense ministry then this system at least carries out two missions: (1) the denial of formal training in the theory and practice of territorial defense to any "domestic faction" of an East European officer corps; (2) the cultivation of a pro-Soviet faction among the upper echelons of East European officers corps. These pro-Soviet officers can compete for authority over national armed forces with the officers loyal to the indigenous party leadership. The pro-Soviet officers can justify their political orientation by citing the bilateral treaties and East European party programs which have incorporated the military-political axioms of Soviet doctrine.

The evidence to support the argument that the WTO military-educational system detaches high-ranking East European officers from the local defense ministries and binds them to the Soviet defense ministry consists of the following:

1. The fact that Romania, a WTO member, insists on educating Romanian officers only in Romanian institutions. The Romanian Defense Ministry trains its officers to execute the strategy, operational art, and tactics of a war entirely different from that for which the WTO military-educational system trains its officers. The Romanian leaders claim that national education of military officers is one of the fundamental manifestations of national sovereignty in military affairs. Albania, a former WTO member, and Yugoslavia also forego the hospitality offered by Soviet military academies to East European officers and insist on training their military officers at home.

2. The likelihood, demonstrated by the limited evidence available, that Soviet control devices in the WTO favor the promotion of East European officers with mid-career degrees from Soviet academies. It is doubtful that the Soviets rely on the educational process itself to implant pro-Soviet loyalties in the East European alumni of Soviet academies who are candidates for senior command positions. It is more likely that

the Soviets use the admissions processes to Soviet academies to identify those East European officers who have decided to advance their careers by openly demonstrating their acceptance of Soviet hegemony over the alliance. To attend a Soviet mid-career academy means to acquire proficiency in the Russian language, to spend several years living in the USSR and to develop a capacity for practical daily cooperation with Soviet officers. If postgraduate education in a Soviet military academy fails to generate loyalty to the Soviet Defense Ministry, it probably generates expectations of Soviet patronage after graduation. The Soviet officers who administer the central agencies of the WTO have ample opportunity to reward the East European officers who chose to study in Soviet academies. These opportunities arise in the course of joint exercises, the activities of the joint agencies of the alliance and in the bilateral activities of Soviet and East European forces.

3. The fact that the Voroshilov Academy of the Soviet General Staff enjoys a monopoly on the teaching of strategic doctrine to senior WTO officers and the fact that the East European graduates of Voroshilov, particularly those graduated with honors, appear to enjoy a virtual monopoly in the WTO on the posts of defense ministers, chiefs of staff and chiefs of main political administrations. At the very least, the Voroshilov program denies senior WTO officers training in any strategy other than that defined by Soviet doctrine. The available evidence suggests that the admissions office at the Voroshilov Academy is partial to East European officers who have already acquired at least one Soviet degree. The available evidence also suggests that only Voroshilov alumni are qualified to fulfill command and staff responsibilities in the administration of multinational forces in joint exercises. Such experience may in turn be a prerequisite for promotion to the positions in East European defense ministries which require interaction with the fraternal armed forces.

The Romanian Military-Educational System

Since the early 1960s the Romanian government has trained all its military officers only in Romania.[9] According to a Soviet study, the postwar Romanian higher military education system was first reorganized in 1949. The Defense Ministry created military colleges to train lieutenants for various types of troops and established four mid-career institutions: a combined arms academy, a military-political academy, a military-technology academy, and a rear services academy.[10] A Romanian study notes that these four academies were formed by breaking up the Higher War College, which had been founded in 1889.[11] According to both Soviet and Romanian sources, Romanian officers began studying in Soviet higher military schools and mid-career academies in the 1949–50 academic year.[12]

During the period from 1957–59,[13] when the Romanians successfully negotiated the withdrawal of Soviet troops from Romania, the Romanians also reorganized their higher military-education system. The Romanians merged most of their undergraduate officer colleges into the Nicolae Balescu Military Officer College. They also merged the four mid-career academies and several military institutes into the General Military Academy,[14] an institution which can trace itself back to the prewar Higher War College. In 1961, the Defense Ministry reorganized the curricula at the officer colleges.[15] A Soviet study claims that the merger of the four mid-career academies into the General Military Academy did not take place until 1961.[16] Perhaps what the Soviet study documented was a change in the curriculum of the mid-career academies that ruled out sending Romanian officers to Soviet academies. In its coverage of the graduation ceremonies of Soviet mid-career academies from 1960 to 1980, *Krasnaia Zvezda* noted award of diplomas to officers from Bulgaria, Hungary, East Germany, Poland, and Czechoslovakia and even, in 1960, to an Albanian officer. The only mention of Romanian officers was in a discussion of the 1965 graduates of the Zhukovskii Military-Air Engineering Academy.[17] Because the curriculum at the mid-career engineering academies of the Soviet Union is generally four to five years in length, the Romanian officers may have entered in 1960 or 1961 and stayed to complete training for operation of Soviet aircraft, at the time the only aircraft used by the Romanian military. At present the Romanians jointly manufacture aircraft with the Yugoslavs and have purchased Western aircraft as well.

The Romanians may have decided to educate their officers only in Romanian military-educational institutions for technical as well as political reasons. In the late 1950s and early 1960s, Soviet academies began training officers for the conduct of both nuclear war and conventional wars.[18] At some point before the late 1960s when Romania openly adopted a doctrine of territorial defense, the Romanians began training their officers to wage a different kind of war than that for which other WTO armies train their officers. Romanian military education emphasizes conduct of small-scale infantry actions by independent units trained to operate with minimal logistical support. Romanian training also requires that even noninfantry troops be fully trained for the conduct of infantry actions.[19]

At the present time the Romanian officer colleges train lieutenants in programs that last from three to four years depending on the particular specialty they are studying. The General Military Academy also trains lieutenant-engineers in a special five-year curriculum.[20] The General Military Academy trains mid-career officers no older than 35 with a minimum rank of major for command posts on the general staff, in service branches, and in political organs. The courses for the combined-arms commanders are two years in length; courses for higher-level engineering officers last from three to five years.[21] The General Military Academy also offers separate postgraduate courses and a four-year doctoral program in military science.[22]

In a speech to the graduating classes of the General Military Academy on August 14, 1968, about a week before the Warsaw Pact invasion of Czechoslovakia, President Ceausescu declared that there was a direct connection between educating Romanian officers only in Romania and maintaining Romanian control over the Romanian armed forces. In a discussion of Romania's obligations to the Warsaw Pact, Ceausescu told the graduates:

> We proceed from the idea that the responsibility and obligation for the endowment, education and instruction of each national army belongs—and cannot but belong—to the Party and Government of the respective country. . . .
>
> By perseveringly preoccupying itself with strengthening and developing the national army and with raising its fighting potential, the Party fulfills one of its supreme obligations to its own people.
>
> At the same time it also fulfills a higher internationalist duty, to the general cause of socialism, security and peace in the world.
>
> The better each national army is endowed, the more thoroughly it is trained, the more devoted it is to the interests of its own people, the more resolutely it supports the policy of the Party and of the socialist State, then the more powerful is the might of the whole world socialist system.
>
> Each army answers to the people of its country and to its Party and State leadership for its capabilities and its level of military training.
>
> This is an essential and inalienable attribute of national sovereignty, a necessary expression of the functions of the socialist State to defend and consolidate the people's revolutionary gains.
>
> The full responsibility of the Party and State bodies in each country for the organization of the armed forces, for their endowment, instruction and education, is the guarantee for the strengthening of the defense capacity of each socialist country and for the strengthening of the might of the whole community of socialist countries.
>
> It also creates the prerequisites for the fruitful development of their military cooperation.

This shows clearly that the command of the armed forces cannot be exercised by any outside body; this is a sovereign attribute of the leadership of our Party and State.[23]

The Undergraduate Military-Educational Institutions of the Loyal WTO Members

The loyal East European members of the Warsaw Pact appear to educate most of their junior officers at local East European military colleges, known as higher schools, which graduate officers as lieutenants or lieutenant-engineers. The curriculum at most engineering schools is four to five years; at the higher schools for commanders and political officers, the curriculum is three to four years. Bulgaria has four undergraduate institutions which train junior officers: the Vasilii Levskii Higher Command School, the Georgii Dimitrov Higher Command-Engineering School, the Georgi Penkovskii Higher Engineering School, and the Nikolai Vaptsarov Higher Political School. Bulgaria also has a school for reserve officers. Hungary has three undergraduate colleges: the Kossuth Higher Combined Arms School, the Zalki Higher Engineering School, and the Killian Higher Aviation Engineering School. The German Democratic Republic has four higher military schools: the Ernst Telemann Military School, the Karl Liebknecht Higher Naval School, the Wilhelm Pick Military-Political School, and the Franz Mehring Air Force School. Poland has ten higher military schools for ground forces, aviation, navy, and engineering specialties. At five of these, political officers are trained along with command officers. Czechoslovakia has six undergraduate military colleges: the Hero of the Soviet Union Captain Otakar Jarosh Higher Military School of Ground Forces, the Slovak National Uprising Higher Military-Aviation School, the Higher Military-Command Technical School, the Soviet-Czechoslovak Friendship Higher Military-Technical School, the Hero of the Czechoslovak Socialist Republic Jan Sherma Higher Military School of Rear Services and Technical Logistics, and the Higher Military-Political School.[24]

According to the information collated by William F. Scott, the Soviet Defense Ministry operates 133 higher military schools.[25] His figures are as follows:

Strategic Rocket Forces.................................... 7
Ground Forces
    Combined Arms...................................... 9
    Tanks 9
    Artillery and Rockets.............................. 12

Artillery Engineers...................................... 3
Air Defense for Ground Forces......................... 5
Airborne... 5

Air Defense Forces
Surface-to-Air Missiles............................... 6
Flying Training...................................... 3

Air Force
Flying Training....................................... 13
Aviation Engineering and Technical................... 10

Navy 10

Main Political Administration............................ 9

Rear Services and Logistics............................... 6
Signals (communications).................................. 12
Military Engineering...................................... 3
Motor Transport... 4
Chemical Defense.. 3
Military Technical.. 2
Civil Defense... 1
Building and Construction................................. 4
Finance 1
Total   133

There is limited evidence that East European officer candidates study in some Soviet higher military schools, perhaps to obtain technical training unavailable in East Europe, but the evidence is not extensive enough to indicate any pattern.[26] A 1977 article in *Krasnaia Zvezda* suggests that an officer seeking to make a career as a professional officer in East Europe might find it helpful to receive an undergraduate military education in the Soviet Union. This article discussed what it called a "dynasty" in the Hungarian People's Army consisting of Major General Ene Kovacs and his two sons, Andras and Ene. Ene Kovacs senior entered the army in 1949 after completing his secondary education. After serving in the ranks, he enrolled in a Hungarian higher military school. At the urging of a Soviet officer stationed near his unit, Lieutenant Kovacs attended the Zrini Military Academy in Budapest for mid-career officers. Ene Kovacs eventually enrolled in the Voroshilov General Staff Academy in Moscow. After receiving a doctoral degree from Voroshilov, Kovacs became the deputy commandant of an unidentified Hungarian military academy and then the commander of an unidentified Hungarian formation. *Krasnaia Zvezda* noted that both of the sons of the founder of the dynasty had enrolled in higher military schools. The Soviet army newspaper partially identified the school Andras had chosen: an artillery-engineering higher school in the Soviet Union.[27]

The Mid-Career Academies of the WTO

After several years of active duty and promotion to the rank of captain or major by the age of the early 30s, a WTO officer is eligible for enrollment in the postgraduate military academies that serve as the gateways to the higher commands of East Europe. There are eleven mid-career military academies among the five loyal East European members of the WTO. The courses of study at these academies range from three to five years. In Bulgaria, the Georgii Rakovskii Military Academy offers postgraduate degrees to officers from all service branches, as does the Zrini Military Academy in Hungary and the Engels Military Academy in the German Democratic Republic.[28] Poland maintains five mid-career academies: the Sverchevskii General Staff Academy which, despite its name, does not offer training on the same level as the Voroshilov General Staff Academy,[29] the Dombrovskii Military-Technical Academy, the Dzershinsky Military-Political Academy, and the Military Medical Academy. According to the Efimov text, the Heroes of Westerpliatte Higher Naval School also offers a mid-career degree at the Academy level.[30] Czechoslovakia trains mid-career officers from all service branches at the Zapotocky Military Academy and political officers at the Gottwald Military-Political Academy. The Purkin Military-Medical Institute trains doctors.[31] The Soviet Union maintains at least seventeen military academies:[32]

> The Voroshilov General Staff Academy in Moscow
> The Frunze Military Academy (for combined arms commanders) in Moscow
> The Lenin Military-Political Academy in Moscow
> The Malinovskii Armed Troops Academy in Moscow
> The Dzerzhinsky Military Academy (for engineering specialities) in Moscow
> The Budennyi Military Communications Academy in Leningrad
> The Military Academy of Rear Services and Transport in Leningrad
> The Timoshenko Military Academy of Chemical Defense in Moscow
> The Kalinin Military Artillery Academy in Leningrad
> The Govorov Military-Engineering Radio-Technical Academy of Air Defense in Kharkov
> The Zhukov Military-Command Academy of Air Defense in Kalinin
> The Zhukovskii Military Air Engineering Academy in Moscow
> The Gagarin Military Air Academy in Moscow province
> The Kuibishev Military Engineering Academy in Leningrad
> The Kirov Military Medical Academy in Leningrad
> The Grechko Naval Academy in Leningrad
> The Mozhaiskii Military Engineering Academy in Leningrad

The Efimov text on the WTO notes in its chapters on Bulgaria, Hungary, East Germany, Poland, and Czechoslovakia that part of the officers corps of each of these states studies in Soviet military-educational institutions.[33] Efimov's study also declares that the East Germans have decorated fifteen unidentified Soviet military-educational institutions for their services in training German officers.[34] Marshal Iakubovskii and his Soviet and East European colleagues have frequently called attention to the importance of the system of educational exchanges in the WTO and to the central role of Soviet mid-career academies in these exchanges. In his article for the *Soviet Military Encyclopedia* on the combat confederation of the armed forces of the socialist confederation Marshal Iakubovskii declared:

> Mutual aid in the training of cadres is of fundamental importance.
>
> Its basic form is the education of military personnel in the military-educational institutions of the allied countries and most of all in the Soviet Union and in the rendering of aid to national commands in the establishment and improvement of the educational process and the sending of military specialists to the military-educational institutions of the fraternal countries.[35]

A volume on the Voroshilov General Staff Academy edited by Marshal V. G. Kulikov, Iakubovskii's successor as WTO Commander, notes:

> One of the main channels of the transfer of military experience and military-scientific knowledge is aid in the training of national command cadres in the military-educational institutions of the Soviet Union.
>
> Highly qualified generals and officers of the socialist states successfully apply the knowledge acquired in the Soviet Union to the organization, development and training of their national armies.
>
> At the present stage of the development of military art, when an uninterrupted modernization of military technology and the improvement of the means of conducting war proceeds on the basis of scientific-technical progress, the education and advanced training of command cadres takes on exceptional significance.[36]

Two studies written jointly by Soviet and East European officers have concurred with Marshals Iakubovskii and Kulikov on the importance of training East European military officers in the Soviet Union. A joint Soviet-Bulgarian study published in 1969 noted: "The Soviet Union has a broad network of military-educational institutions and the authority of Soviet military schools grows from year to year. Thus it is fully understandable that the socialist countries have striven to send their military personnel to study in the USSR."[37] This study adds that the military-educational institutions of the USSR have been "a veritable forge of highly qualified military cadres for the Bulgarian People's Army."[38] A joint Polish-Soviet study published in 1975 noted that the Soviet Union provides Poland with aid "in the training of the command and engineering cadres necessary for the administration of sub-units, units and formations. . . ." This volume explained:

> In the first post-war years Soviet military specialists directly participated in the establishment of military academies in the Polish People's Republic and in the training of highly qualified cadres in these academies.
>
> But in the first half of the 1950's the Soviet Union broadly opened to the officers of the Polish Army and of the other allied armies the doors of its higher military-educational institutions.
>
> Many generals and officers of the Polish Armed Forces acquire in Soviet academies a higher qualification while mastering the achievements of advanced military science so that, upon returning to their homeland, they successfully apply the experience and knowledge they have gained to the cause of improving their armed forces.[39]

According to an East German professor of military science: "The education of the officers, generals and admirals of the German Democratic Republic in Soviet military academies permits the National People's Army to fulfill successfully its tasks in the framework of the Warsaw Pact on the basis of the latest achievements of Marxist-Leninist military thought and Soviet military art."[40]

As a result of the aid of the Soviet Union in educating the officer corps of the socialist states, there are, according to General Mal'tsev, Commandant of the Lenin Military-Political Academy, "hundreds of generals who have completed Soviet military academies and other military-educational institutions."[41] Marshal Iakubovskii's study of the Warsaw Pact takes issue with General Mal'tsev on this question. According to the volume edited by the former WTO Commander, the figure is not hundreds but thousands: "Thousands of officers and generals of the fraternal armed forces have studied in Soviet military academies and higher military-educational institutions. These generals and officers constitute the backbone of national military cadres and have played an important role in the establishment and development of their national armed forces."[42] Colonel Semin offers some support for Marshal Iakubovskii's figures. In a 1970 article, Semin declared that in the GDR National People's Army alone "hundreds of generals and officers have completed Soviet military academies."[43]

Evidence from Soviet sources specifically identify seven of the Soviet military academies that train officers from the socialist countries. They are:

The Voroshilov General Staff Academy[44]
The Frunze Military Academy[45]
The Lenin Military-Political Academy[46]
The Malinovskii Military Academy of Armored Troops[47]
The Budennyi Military Academy of Communications[48]
The Kuibishev Military Engineering Academy[49]
The Grechko Naval Academy[50]

According to Soviet sources, each of these seven academies has been decorated by socialist countries for its services in training officers.[51] The *Soviet Military Encyclopedia* notes that the five following additional Soviet military academies have received decorations from socialist countries for unspecified reasons:

The Military Academy of Rear Services and Transport
The Gagarin Military Air Academy
The Zhukovskii Military Air Engineering Academy
The Timoshenko Military Academy of Chemical Defense
The Kalinin Military Artillery Academy[52]

In light of the fact that seven Soviet academies received foreign decorations for training foreign officers, it is likely that the five academies which have received foreign decorations for unspecified reasons received them for training foreign officers. It is also possible that some Soviet academies which have not received decorations for training foreign officers nevertheless educate East European military personnel.

The Soviet-Bulgarian study of 1969 notes that East European officers pursue the same course of study in Soviet academies as Soviet officers. This study adds that foreign students who are fluent in Russian attend classes jointly with Soviet officers. Foreign students who are less than fluent study separately in classes that use simplified Russian-language texts. This study also notes that Bulgarian and other non-Soviet officers do course work and write diploma papers on topics of practical significance for their national armed forces and for the cooperation of the socialist armed forces.[53] The Soviet-Bulgarian volume of 1969 points out that this curriculum enables the fraternal officers to arrive at common positions on the questions of tactics, operational art, and military technology. These common positions in turn serve as the basis for conduct of joint military exercises.[54] This volume further notes that foreign officers are organized into separate national groups to which specially trained Soviet instructors are assigned. The host academies of the Soviet Union observe the national holidays of each group of foreign students, conduct frequent friendship evenings to acquaint them with Soviet officers, and take them on frequent excursions to points of interest in the USSR. The Soviets also ensure that the wives and children of foreign officers studying in the Soviet Union are able to enroll in Soviet schools, universities, and institutes.[55]

In the case of East European officers serving in highly technical services, there do not appear to be East European academies qualified to confer mid-career degrees in these fields. The credentials necessary for promotion may be available only in the Soviet Union, with the possible exception of Poland's engineering academy. For mid-career combined arms commanders and political officers, there is a choice between local academies and the Frunze and Lenin academies. The Frunze Academy, which formulates the WTO doctrines on tactics and operational art, and the Lenin Academy, which formulates the military-political axioms of the WTO, may offer degrees that are better passports to high commands in East Europe than the degrees of the national academies for combined-arms commanders and political officers. The Frunze and Lenin academies appear to be the only WTO academies in which aspiring commanders and political officers from several WTO armies study together in a curriculum designed to prepare them to carry out joint WTO actions.

Harriet Fast Scott and William F. Scott report that graduates of Soviet military academies are assigned to command posts under a *nomenklatura* system that reserves certain positions for the graduates of certain academies.[56] It is possible that a similar *nomenklatura* system reserves for East European graduates of the Frunze, Lenin and other mid-career academies certain positions in the central agencies of the WTO and certain command positions in the East European contingents assigned to the United Armed Forces. It is also possible that an informal old-boy network may enable Soviet officers in the central WTO agencies to show favoritism to their fellow alumni in the evaluation of East European officers.

Even before the establishment of the WTO a special relationship existed between the Soviet Defense Ministry and the East European officers trained in the Soviet Union. After the Cominform called for Tito's removal from power *Pravda* printed an "open letter" from Yugoslav army officers studying in Moscow to the delegates of the Yugoslav party congress that convened shortly after the Cominform denunciation of Tito. In this letter, the Yugoslav officers in Moscow urged the delegates "to choose a new leadership capable of leading our party on to the correct Leninist-Stalinist path. . . ."[57] General Bela Kiraly, one of the Hungarian officers who deserted to the rebels during the 1956 revolution, later wrote that Hungarian officers who had studied in the Soviet Union "were usually given high positions in Hungary." He added:

This was especially true for graduates of the Frunze Academy for general staff officers and, after 1954, the Voroshilov Academy, which was the most advanced of the institutes.

In most cases, Soviet training proved to quite effective, and in their new positions at home the graduates strove to carry out what they had learned, some of them even attempting to outshine the Soviet military advisors in their loyalty to Moscow.

The Soviet graduates, especially those who had married Russian women, began to form a separate caste in Hungary.[58]

The Frunze Academy trained many of the leading Soviet generals of World War II, several Soviet defense ministers and three of the four commanders of the WTO.[59] A Soviet history of the Frunze Academy notes that "the Academy has always regarded as its internationalist duty the training of officers for the armies of the socialist confederation."[60] At the fiftieth anniversary celebration of the Frunze Academy the combined-arms academies of East Europe sent delegations to mark the anniversary. At these ceremonies General Chaplevskii, commandant of Poland's Sverchevskii General Staff Academy, spoke on behalf of the fraternal delegations. He declared:

The services and the authority of the M. V. Frunze Academy and great recognition and respect for it have long ago gone beyond the boundaries of the Soviet army and the Soviet state.

The Academy is especially close to the armies of the socialist states. Many officers of these countries have studied and continue to study within its walls.

Just as in the Soviet army, the graduates of the M. V. Frunze Academy hold responsible leading posts in the armed forces of the socialist states.[61]

The very limited information available on East European military officers reveals some distinguished Frunze graduates: Heinz Hoffmann, the current East German Defense Minister, who attended Frunze during the 1930s after fleeing from the Nazis; Dobri Dzhurov, the current Bulgarian Defense Minister; Atanas Semerdzhiev, the current Bulgarian chief of staff; and the current Czechoslovak chief of staff, Karel Rusov, who also attended the Lenin Academy.[62]

Krasnaia Zvezda reported in 1975 on the process by which one Czechoslovak officer, Ludvik Sokhor, entered the Frunze Academy. Sokhor's father had been decorated with the order of Hero of the Soviet Union for his part in the Soviet-Czechoslovak campaign against the Nazis. Ludvik had attended the Hero of the Soviet Union Otakar Jarosh Higher Military School of Ground Forces in Czechoslovakia and had been commissioned as a lieutenant. After several years of active duty he had risen to the rank of captain. *Krasnaia Zvezda* reported that in 1970 Captain Sokhor received a telephone call in which he was told that he had one hour to decide if he wanted to accept an opening at the Frunze Academy. Before deciding, Captain Sokhor called his wife. "You," she reminded him, "are a Sokhor." While studying at Frunze, Sokhor junior worked under faculty members who had fought in some of the same battles as had Sokhor senior. At Frunze, Ludvik also met Soviet officers who had served in the Central Force Group in Czechoslovakia. When he received his Frunze degree in 1973, four other Czechoslovak officers were graduated with him. Three of them were already regimental commanders. *Krasnaia Zvezda* reported that soon after his graduation Ludvik was promoted to the rank of major and given command of his own regiment. The Soviet army newspaper also reported at some length on the outstanding work of Major Sokhor in commanding his troops.[63]

General Mal'stev, commandant of the Lenin Military-Political Academy, has reported that "a series of socialist countries" have decorated the Lenin Academy for training their officers, but he did not indicate which countries.[64] Other Soviet sources reveal that one of these socialist countries was Bulgaria and another was Czechoslovakia.[65] *Krasnaia Zvezda* has mentioned three graduation speeches by foreign students at the Lenin Academy—one by a Czech in 1977, one by a Cuban in 1976, and one by an Albanian in 1960. The Soviet army newspaper also noted the award of a gold medal to a Mongolian graduate of the Lenin Academy in 1965.[66] The *Soviet Military Encyclopedia* reports that in the period from 1939 to 1975, the Lenin Academy awarded 1400 degrees of candidate of military science and 100 doctoral degrees.[67] This averages out to about 57 degrees a year, not allowing for the likely possibility that the classes of the 1960s and 1970s were considerably larger than the earlier classes. In 1970, *Krasnaia Zvezda* reported that the graduating class of the Lenin Academy in that year numbered 106, but did not identify the size of the foreign contingent.[68] The *Soviet Military Encyclopedia* reports that the Lenin Academy has eight faculties but does not identify them. In his article for the *Encyclopedia*, General Mal'stev writes that the Academy trains its students in the history of the CPSU, the history of the international Communist and workers' movement, and the history of the national liberation movements. It also teaches Marxist-Leninist philosophy, politics, economics, and scientific communism and courses on party-political work in the Soviet armed forces, including work in specialized types of troops. The Academy in addition teaches military pedagogy and military psychology.[69] Mal'tsev also notes that texts written by the Lenin Academy have won acclaim abroad, but he did not indicate exactly where.[70]

The Voroshilov General Staff Academy

Since 1958, the Voroshilov General Staff Academy has trained generals, admirals, and senior officers of the Soviet Armed Forces for the top command posts of each service branch, the Soviet General Staff and the central administrations of the Ministry of Defense.[71] It also serves as the collator and synthesizer of doctrine on operational art and strategy.[72] A Soviet history of the Voroshilov Academy says openly that the Academy plays the same role for the five loyal East European members of the WTO:

> The level of military preparedness both of national armies and of the United Armed Forces of the member states of the Warsaw Pact depends greatly on scientific knowledge, practical experience and organizational capabilities.
>
> The Central Committee of the CPSU and the Soviet Government, in attaching great significance to this question and acceding to the wishes of the governments of the socialist states, has organized the training and improvement of the leading command staff of the fraternal armed forces in the Academy of the General Staff.[73]

As the oracle of operational-strategic doctrine and the anointer of its practitioners, the Voroshilov Academy stands at the very center of the greater socialist officer corps. The Soviet history of the Academy, published in 1976, listed among its alumni four of the defense ministers of the five loyal East European WTO members: Dobri Dzhurov of Bulgaria, Heinz Hoffmann of East Germany, Vojtech Jaruzelski of Poland, and Martin Dzur of Czechoslovakia. All five of the loyal East European Pact members had Voroshilov graduates as chiefs of general staffs: Atanas Semerdzhiev of Bulgaria, Istvan Olah of Hungary, Heinz Kessler of East Germany, Florian Sivitskii of Poland, and Karel Rusov of Czechoslovakia. Four of five of these states have Voroshilov alumni as chiefs of their main political administrations: Kiril Kosev of Bulgaria, Waldemar Verner of East Germany, Voldimezh Savchuk of Poland, and Vaclav Horacheck of Czechoslovakia.[74]

Neither the Hungarian defense minister, Laoish Csinege nor the Hungarian MPA chief, Ferenc Karpati, has a Voroshilov degree, according to this study. But the fact that Csinege was appointed defense minister in 1960 and Karpati was appointed as MPA Chief in 1959 suggests that each of these officers had successfully passed the examinations of 1956 and did not need a Voroshilov degree.[75] The current Romanian defense minister, Ion Coman, is a graduate of the General Military Academy in Bucharest, as is his chief of staff.[76] The Soviet history of the Voroshilov

Academy also included in its partial list of distinguished alumni the defense minister of Mongolia, the chief of staff of Mongolia, the defense minister of Vietnam and the chief of staff of Cuba.[77]

Each of the five loyal East European WTO members has decorated the Voroshilov Academy for its services in training personnel.[78] When he presented a medal to the Voroshilov Academy for training Bulgarian officers, the Bulgarian ambassador to the USSR declared, "In this most authoritative educational institution there has taken place the training of almost all the leading staff of the Bulgarian People's Army."[79] Romania has not decorated the Voroshilov Academy and *Krasnaia Zvezda* has never reported a valedictory speech by a Romanian graduate of Voroshilov. *Krasnaia Zvezda* has reported valedictory addresses at Voroshilov commencements by officers from Bulgaria (1974, 1968, 1962); Hungary (1977, 1970, 1965); East Germany (1977, 1972, 1966); Poland (1973, 1967, 1963); Czechoslovakia (1975, 1969, 1964); and Mongolia (1971, 1978).[80]

The high incidence of Voroshilov alumni in the top commands of East Europe is not the result of a Soviet policy of inundating the armies of the WTO with Voroshilov graduates and relying on the laws of probability. According to the U.S. Central Intelligence Agency translation of an article in the restricted journal, *Military Thought,* during the period from 1945 to 1966 the Voroshilov Academy graduated "nearly 300" officers of whom "nearly 30" received the degree of doctor of military science.[81] This averages out to only 14 graduates a year. Even allowing for an increase in enrollment following the 1958 reorganization, the Academy probably does not graduate more than two or three East European officers from a given WTO member in any one year. If the small numbers of Voroshilov graduates are not the beneficiaries of a *nomenklatura* system that reserves the top command posts of East Europe for them alone, they may be the beneficiaries of a *nomenklatura* system that reserves for them command and staff positions in Warsaw Pact exercises. These positions in turn could be the only gateways to the top posts in East European defense ministries.

If the previous chapter on WTO military exercises is correct in concluding that Warsaw Pact exercises require the interaction of national sub-units and units organized in multinational formations and superformations, Voroshilov training for staff and command positions in these exercises may be a technical as well as political requirement. The Soviet history of the Voroshilov Academy notes that the East European officers in residence at Voroshilov study the problems of organizing joint TWO exercises:

> One of the forms of operational training of [foreign] students is their working out of the organizational and conduct of troop and command-staff exercises.
>
> In the resolution of these practical tasks great attention is devoted to the questions of joint planning and organization of the armed forces of the allied socialist states.
>
> In papers and diploma dissertations students as a rule work out those problems which in the greatest degree correspond to the tasks decided upon by national armed forces or by the United Command of the Warsaw Pact.[82]

Another passage from this study declares that the fraternal generals and officers trained at the Academy "skillfully command formations and superformations." The passage continues, "This is clearly demonstrated in the joint troop and command-staff exercises conducted according to the plan of the command of the member countries of the Warsaw Pact."[83] This text cites two examples of the work of Voroshilov alumni in conducting joint WTO exercises: a Soviet-Czechoslovak exercise of August 1970, commanded by Vasil Valo, the commander of the western military district of Czechoslovakia and a deputy Czechoslovak minister of defense; and the Brotherhood in Arms exercise of 1970 conducted by Heinz Hoffmann, the GDR defense minister. The history of the Voroshilov Academy added:

> A great contribution to the preparation and conduct of the Brotherhood in Arms exercises was made by generals and officers of the armies of the socialist countries who are graduates of the [Voroshilov] Academy and who occupy responsible duties in the central apparati of ministries of defense, branches of the armed services, of military districts and who command general staffs, divisions, regiments and units.[84]

According to the Soviet history of the Academy, most of the foreign students have passed through the network of undergraduate higher schools and postgraduate academies. As of 1976, 91 percent of the foreign students had completed a higher military education. The Soviet history of the Academy adds, "Moreover, some of them have completed Soviet military academies."[85] Perhaps the primary incentive for an East European officer to study in a Soviet mid-career academy is to enhance the likelihood of admission to Voroshilov. The nine percent of the 1976 Voroshilov students who lacked a higher military education may have come directly from commands in the Vietnamese and Cuban armies. The history of the Academy notes that in the postwar period only 35–40 percent of the foreign students had completed a higher military education, but that many of the foreign students admitted to Voroshilov had served in command positions in the Polish and Czechoslovak armies recruited on Soviet soil during World War II and also in partisan and resistance movements throughout East Europe.[86] The Voroshilov Academy first began training foreign students in 1939 and educated them separately from Soviet officers until the 1961-62 academic year, when they were placed in the same course of study as Soviet officers.[87] The 1961-62 academic year coincides with the introduction of joint WTO exercises by Marshal Grechko.

The Voroshilov Academy tailors its program for each foreign officer according to the officer's fluency in Russian. For those who speak Russian well, there is a special course to familiarize them with both military and scientific terminology. These students attend lecture courses along with Soviet officers and are required to read both the assigned and supplementary texts. For those who are less fluent, the Soviets organize special lecture courses with shortened, simplified texts. Professors deliver lectures slowly, pausing to explain carefully each new term and frequently to ask questions of the students so as to involve them directly in discussion of the topic under consideration. The faculty who work with foreign students make maximum use of charts, diagrams, maps, pictures, and other visual aids. If a student has difficulty in reading the simplified texts, instructors go over the principal points of the assigned reading in seminars and then summarize the conclusions reached by the seminars.[88]

All foreign officers and their families participate in a program to familiarize them with Soviet life. Officers and their families meet Soviet celebrities from the fields of science, culture, art, and politics. The commander of the WTO and his chief of staff regularly deliver lectures to the foreign students. The Soviets take their guests to visit a large number of points of interest in the Moscow vicinity and send them on "traditional visits" to some of the sites of the great battles of World War II: Leningrad, Stalingrad, Sevastopol. The Soviets also mark the national holidays of the students studying at Voroshilov.[89]

At Voroshilov the two-year program of study includes not only lecture courses but seminars, independent study projects, consultations with faculty, practical projects requiring the application of theoretical concepts, command-staff map exercises, and participation in actual troop exercises. Officers from the same army work in national study groups led by Voroshilov faculty of general officer rank, many of whom are veterans of the World War II campaigns of the Soviet army in East Europe. The history of the Academy notes that the leaders of the study groups remain with their students for the duration of a student's assignment to Voroshilov. The history explains:

> This affords them the possibility of thoroughly studying not only the individual peculiarities of each student, but also the history of the country, its achievements in the area of socialist development, the training of its armed forces, and also its culture and customs.
>
> All this permits the leaders of the study groups more quickly to make contact with the students and to choose the most effective methods of their education. . . .
>
> Work of the instructor with each of the students occupies a major place in the study process. In this regard, the instructor studies the level of knowledge of the student of the Russian language, his general and specific training and his individual peculiarities.[90]

National party organizations formed in each national study group are responsible for liaison between foreign officers and the Academy's administrative command, professor-instructional staff and the MPA political department. The national party organizations discuss the progress and problems of each foreign student with the Voroshilov hierarchy. According to the Soviet history of the Academy, one of the forms of supervision used by the national party organization is the regular posting of the grades received by East European officers in their examinations, seminars, and groups assignments on practical problems.[91]

The Voroshilov program requires that officers study military history, Marxist-Leninist philosophy, strategy, and tactical arts. The Voroshilov program on military history includes a course on the history of the Soviet armed forces, a course on World War II, a course on the development of Soviet operational art and strategy in the post-war period, and a course entitled "Military Art in Local Wars After the Second World War."[92] In the study of World War II the fraternal officers pay particular attention to the origins of the socialist alliance system:

> In this course there is an especially convincing demonstration of the decisive role of the Soviet Armed Forces in the defeat of the fascist aggressor and the great aid of our army to the peoples of East and South-Eastern Europe in the liberation from fascist enslavement. . . .
>
> There is widely used as a most important means of inculcating patriotism and proletarian internationalism examples of the joint actions of the Soviet army with the partisan detachments and armed forces of Poland, Czechoslovakia, Romania, Bulgaria, Hungary, Yugoslavia and Albania and there is revealed the contribution of all countries to the victory over fascism.[93]

The course on Marxism-Leninism demonstrates the legitimacy of the combat confederation of the WTO members as a part of the greater socialist confederation. In this course, the Voroshilov history notes:

"Special attention is devoted to the character of the world socialist system as a new type of socialist organization and of inter-state relations and to the manifestation of the natural law of the confederation of the armed forces of the member states of the Warsaw Pact."[94]

As an extracurricular activity, the national study groups examine the sections of the most recent CPSU congress devoted to "the further development of friendship and cooperation among the socialist countries."[95] The Soviet text on the Voroshilov Academy notes that these passages from Soviet congress materials are closely linked with the decisions of the party congresses of Bulgaria, Hungary, East Germany, Poland, Czechoslovakia, and Mongolia.[96] This text made no references to documents of Romanian party congresses.

The courses on tactics and strategy address the problems of planning joint actions, including joint exercises.[97] The Soviet history of the Voroshilov Academy is probably accurate in concluding that as a result of their studies at the Soviet General Staff Academy foreign officers arrive at a "unity of views" on the questions of tactics, operational art, strategy, national military training, and the organization of national defense systems.[98] Foreign students at Voroshilov take USSR state examinations in all subjects, including political and historical topics, and are eligible to receive gold medals for outstanding diploma dissertations.[99]

Krasnaia Zvezda reported that at the 1977 graduation cermonies three East Europeans received gold medals for their work at Voroshilov: Colonel L. G. Toshkov of Bulgaria, Colonel H. Zaidel of East Germany, and Lieutenant Colonel T. Noskovskii of Poland.[100] These three officers joined a company of other East European recipients of Voroshilov gold medals, which includes the defense minister of Bulgaria, the chief of staff of Bulgaria, the chief of the Bulgarian Main Political Administration, the defense minister of Czechoslovakia and the chief of the Polish Main Political Administration.[105] At the 1977 Voroshilov graduation, Colonel Zoltan Soradi of Hungary delivered the valedictory address on behalf of the foreign officers being graduated from the Academy:

> During the course of our studies . . . we, the officers of the armies of the Warsaw Pact countries, have constantly felt fatherly concern and attention from the Communist Party of the Soviet Union, the Soviet Government and the whole Soviet people.
>
> We have deeply studied Marxist-Leninist theory, advanced Soviet military science and the experience of the Armed Forces of the USSR.
>
> Wherever we are, we will never forget our Soviet teachers, tutors, and friends.[102]

For its part, the Voroshilov Academy goes to some lengths not to forget its East European graduates. According to the Soviet history of the Academy, every year Voroshilov faculty tour East Europe. During these visits they regularly meet with their graduates to aid them in the "further development of their political and military knowledge." The Soviet text adds, "These ties are broadened every year and have a planned and purposefully directed character."[103] In addition, Warsaw Pact exercises, meetings of the Committee of Defense Ministers and sessions of the Military Council probably provide regular opportunities for holding Voroshilov alumni reunions.

Conclusion

The Soviets have drawn Bulgaria, Hungary, East Germany, Poland, and Czechoslovakia into a WTO network which controls officer education in these countries. Romania has escaped from this network and educates all its officers only in Romanian institutions for the missions defined by the Romanian doctrine of War of the Entire People.

East European undergraduate military schools train the great majority of East European junior officers. These institutions teach "tactics," the conduct of actions by lower-level military units. Some East European officer candidates attend Soviet undergraduate institutions but the principal points of entry into the Soviet old-boy network in the WTO are the mid-career academies of the Soviet Union. These academies teach WTO captains and majors "operational art"—the command of regiments, divisions and equivalent formations in various service branches. Soviet and East European mid-career academies compete for East European applicants. The Soviet mid-career academies appear to offer the degrees more likely to advance an officer's career and also appear to offer special programs to prepare WTO officers for participation in joint missions.

The WTO officer education system limits formal training in strategic doctrine to the Voroshilov General Staff Academy in Moscow. The strategy taught by Voroshilov faculty to WTO officers is that of waging war by a coalition of national armies using nuclear weapons and conducting actions on a continental scale. The only WTO institution which offers instruction in an alternative strategic doctrine is the General Military Academy in Bucharest. The available evidence suggests that Voroshilov alumni enjoy a monopoly on the highest-ranking military posts in East Europe and on command and staff positions involving the administration of multinational forces in WTO exercises.

Admission to a Soviet mid-career academy or to the Voroshilov Academy requires commitments to achieve proficiency in the Russian language, to live in the Soviet Union for several years and to work closely with Soviet officers. The Soviet officers who command the central agencies of the WTO are in a position to influence the promotion of the East European alumni of Soviet academies. These Soviet officers evaluate the performance of WTO personnel in joint exercises, joint agencies and in bilateral activities.

At a minimum, the military-educational network of the WTO enables the Soviets to deny East European officers training in the theory and practice of territorial defense. At a minimum, this network also enables the Soviets to compete with East European political leaders for the obedience of the upper echelons of the East European officer corps. At most, the military-educational network of the WTO inducts high-ranking East European officers into a greater socialist officer corps commanded by Soviet marshals and assigned the joint missions defined by Soviet doctrine.

Chapter Nine
Conclusion

The Soviets have relied on the agencies and programs of the Warsaw Treaty Organization (WTO) to secure a Soviet capability for military interventions in East Europe to prevent either the capture of an East European party by a domestic faction of the party or the destruction of the party by local anti-Communist forces. The Soviets had formed the WTO in 1955 as a diplomatic gambit to the entry of the Federal Republic of Germany into the North Atlantic Treaty Organization and as a device to provide the legal bases for the stationing of Soviet troops in East Europe after the signing of the Austrian State Treaty in 1955. Since then, the Political Consultative Committee of the WTO has developed into a clearinghouse for foreign policy declarations, as has the WTO Council of Foreign Ministers, which was established in 1976.

One year after the formation of the Warsaw Pact, political upheavals in Hungary and Poland badly damaged the network of political, military, economic, and cultural controls with which Moscow had attempted to bind the leaders of the East European Communist parties to the Soviet party. During the late 1950s and early 1960s domestic factions of the Communist parties of Albania and Romania took advantage of the temporary disintegration of the Soviet control mechanisms in East Europe to establish their independence of the Communist Party of the Soviet Union. Like the leaders of the domestic faction of the Yugoslav party, who had been the first to establish an independent Communist regime in East Europe, the Albanian and Romanian leaders based their regimes on a combination of domestic and foreign support. The leaders of each party sought domestic support by claiming to defend the sovereignty of the nation against domination by the Soviet Union. The Romanian party sought foreign support both from the West and from the People's Republic of China. The Albanian party sought foreign support almost exclusively from the Chinese during the early years of Albania's rebellion against the Soviet Union.

In 1961, Albania, a member of the WTO, asserted its complete independence of the Soviet Union and reverted to a strategy of territorial defense based mainly on the experience of the Albanian party in organizing a national liberation struggle against the Italians during the Second

World War. It is impossible to assess the degree to which this strategy forced Khrushchev to confine himself to verbal assaults against Tirana. Several other factors, which the Albanian leaders deliberately linked to this military strategy, were probably more important deterents to Soviet intervention than the strategy itself: (1) the lack of any staging area for a Soviet intervention, since no WTO state bordered on Albania; (2) the fact that in 1961 the Adriatic coastline of Albania was a province of the United States Navy; (3) the fact that China, which shared a disputed border with the Soviet Union, gave direct military assistance to the Albanian defense ministry.

Romania, not only a WTO member but a state bordering directly on the Soviet Union and two other Pact members, Bulgaria and Hungary, began sometime in the late 1950s or early 1960s to develop a strategy of territorial defense to reinforce its independent stand against the Soviet Union. The Romanians, though claiming that the prewar Romanian General Staff had developed a national strategy of territorial defense, appear to have borrowed directly from the territorial defense strategy of Yugoslavia, Romania's neighbor across the Danube. After the resumption of Soviet-Yugoslav polemics in 1958, Belgrade had undertaken a modernization of its territorial defense strategy as a necessary military support for its foreign policy of nonalignment. Yugoslav diplomacy in turn complemented its military strategy by soliciting diplomatic support for a possible war of national liberation against the Soviet army. Both the Yugoslav and Romanian strategies of people's war seek to defend the national Communist leaders against any rival leaders championed by the Soviet army. Both the Yugoslav and Romanian governments have relied on their independent military capabilities as the bases of their political sovereignty.

For Romania, there were two crucial prerequisites for the adoption of a strategy of territorial defense: (1) the withdrawal of Soviet troops in 1958; (2) the securing of diplomatic support and potential logistical support from Yugoslavia, China, and the West in the event of a Soviet intervention. These preconditions enabled the Romanians to refine a military strategy directed against the vulnerability of the multinational Soviet armed forces and the multinational Warsaw Pact to the political strains of waging a prolonged guerrilla war against an army planning to mobilize its entire population by appealing to anti-Russian nationalism.

The Joint Exercises of the Warsaw Pact

In the early 1960s the Soviet Commander of the Warsaw Pact, Marshal A.A. Grechko, activated the military agencies of the WTO in order to try to halt Romania's movement toward adoption of a strategy of territorial defense and to pre-empt the possibility that rebellious Communists in the parties of other Pact members might try to imitate the Albanian and Romanian examples. The device Marshal Grechko used to restore Soviet domination over the armed forces of the WTO was the system of multilateral military exercises, which he introduced in 1961-62. In a public declaration, which he published on the eve of the first joint WTO maneuvers, Marshal Grechko specifically identified one of the missions of the Warsaw Pact as that of carrying out internal interventions in East Europe like the one the Soviet army had conducted against "the counterrevolutionary putsch inspired by the imperialists in Hungary in 1956." The WTO Commander added, "Then, as is well known, Soviet troops, true to their internationalist duty, at the request of the Revolutionary Workers' and Peasants' Government of Hungary, helped the Hungarian people to vanquish the mutineers."[1]

By drawing the East European armies into frequent joint exercises with the Soviet forces in East Europe and the western military districts of the USSR, Grechko forestalled the development of territorial defense capabilities by the East European defense ministries which agreed to participate in the exercises. The offensive drills practiced in the joint exercises also enhanced Soviet capabilities for massive, rapid intervention in all East European states, in particular in the three WTO members which lacked Soviet garrisons in 1961: Romania, Bulgaria, and Czechoslovakia. Marshal Grechko's system of military exercises further established a Soviet capability for mobilizing token detachments of East European forces for symbolic participation in military interventions by the Soviet army.

The prospective targets of Soviet military interventions in East Europe have been the opponents of the ruling Muscovite factions of the local Communist parties, either inside or outside the parties. The Muscovite factions of the East European parties have consciously chosen not to adopt national strategies of territorial defense, because these factions have been as anxious as the Soviets to preserve a WTO capability for military intervention on behalf of the Muscovites. Once an East European party has permitted its defense ministry to deploy a national territorial defense system, the local officer corps could elect to defend whatever political authority the officer corps chose to recognize as the legitimate bearer of national sovereignty. The Muscovite factions of East Europe and their Soviet patrons have also relied on the offensive posture of the WTO to keep NATO forces in a defensive configuration which minimizes the possibility of Western assistance to anti-Soviet rebels within an East European Communist party or anti-Communist rebels in a Warsaw Pact state.

The Military-Political Mechanisms of the Warsaw Pact

The system of joint exercises introduced by Marshal Grechko also served as the catalyst for the crystallization of five interlocking control mechanisms that denied each WTO member except Romania and Albania the possibility of "relying on its own forces":

1. The United Command of the WTO. The joint exercises activated this body, formally created in 1955, by giving it a focus for practical organizational activities. To conduct joint exercises the United Command began to detach the individual service branches and elite combat detachments from the East European defense ministries and to assign them to configurations in which each national component became dependent on other allied forces for the execution of any large-scale sustained military action. The United Command also used the conduct of joint exercises to claim the right to regulate the type of training programs conducted by East European armed forces.

2. The common arsenal of Soviet weapons. The joint exercises required the close interaction of allied forces which in turn justified standardization of weaponry. The dependence of each WTO army, except Romania's, on Soviet arms made it difficult if not impossible for any of these armies to contemplate any long-term action without securing Soviet logistical support.

3. The common propositions of the military doctrines of the WTO states. The conduct of joint exercises required the adoption of common doctrinal axioms. In the early 1960s Soviet military theorists elaborated a comprehensive military doctrine that established well-defined norms for the organization of all aspects of a nation's defense system. The states that have accepted Soviet doctrinal propositions as their own have agreed to the creation of a set of agencies parallel to those of the Soviet defense ministry. They also agreed to the interaction of these national agencies with their Soviet counterparts. The adoption of common concepts of strategy, operational art, and tactics by the WTO states has required the Warsaw Pact armies to prepare for nuclear and conventional wars on a continental scale, rather than for small-scale actions confined to the national territory. The common military-political axioms of the WTO doctrines have justified the fragmentation of national armed forces into units and formations assigned to the United Command and have also justified the right of the WTO states to intervene in each other's territories in joint defense of the gains of socialism.

4. An integrated network of political administrations. The joint exercises of the Pact members required the conduct of joint political activities by the allied political administrations. In the early 1960s, under the direction of General A.A. Epishev, Chief of the Soviet Main Political Administration, the WTO political officers have developed a system of regular multilateral and bilateral Soviet-East European political activities ostensibly focused on the conduct of joint combat actions. The network of WTO political administrations has enabled the Soviets to monitor the military-technical applications of the military-political axioms of the WTO. It has also facilitated the interaction of the multinational personnel of the alliance and prepared them for the political strains likely to arise in the conduct of joint actions in defense of the gains of socialism.

5. An integrated system of officer education. The joint exercises appear to have led to the designation of certain Soviet military academies as the only institutions qualified to prepare WTO officers for the command of the large multinational formations and specialized services that participate in the joint exercises. Soviet military doctrine has evidently served as the basis for the curriculum of officer education both at the Soviet and East European institutions which train military officers. The WTO has educated most of its East European junior officers in local East European military colleges but has required that mid-career East European officers aspring to senior commands receive their advanced training in Soviet military academies.

The interaction of three of these control devices, the WTO system of officer education, the WTO network of political administrations, and the WTO United Command, appears to enable the Soviets to control the promotion of officers to the senior command posts of the East European armed forces. Control over the promotion of senior officers may in turn permit the Soviets to maintain the devices which assure control over promotion.

The Warsaw Pact and the Combat Confederation

The mechanisms which the Soviets have used to bind the national detachments of the WTO to the United Command of the Warsaw Pact appear to be the same mechanisms with which the Soviets are attempting to bind to the Soviet Defense Ministry the non-European armies of what the Soviets call the "combat confederation" (*boevoe sodruzhestvo*). The Soviets recruit the armies of the combat confederation from the states of what the Soviets refer to as the "socialist confederation" (*sotsialistiche-skoe sodruzhestvo*). According to the leaders of the CPSU, the same political, military, economic, and cultural mechanisms which have integrated 15 union republics into the Union of Soviet Socialist Republics are gradually integrating the fraternal states into the socialist confederation.

The socialist confederation appears to have three distinct sets of members: the inner members of the confederation, consisting of the union republics of the USSR; the outer members of the confederation, consisting of the republics of Bulgaria, Hungary, East Germany, Poland, Czechoslovakia, Mongolia, and Afghanistan; and the overseas members of the confederation, Cuba, Vietnam, and probably South Yemen, Ethiopia, Mozambique, and Angola. The combat confederation has three corresponding sets of members. The national armed forces of the combat confederation appear to share (1) a Soviet arsenal and logistical supply system; (2) common propositions of military doctrine, both military-technical and military-political; (3) a network of political administrations which conducts ideological work in the various national languages of the confederation on the common theme of joint defense of the gains of socialism; (4) a network of officer education systems which trains junior officers in local institutions, often with Soviet assistance, and sends mid-career officers to Soviet academies for advanced training.

In his public declaration just prior to the first WTO joint exercises Marshal Grechko traced the "brotherhood of the peoples of the socialist countries and of the combat confederation of their armies" to the mobilization of different nationalities in the Civil War of 1918–21 and to the mobilization of the peoples of the Soviet Union and East Europe to fight against Hitler.[2] In his capacity as Grechko's successor, Marshal I.I. Iakubovskii also served as the chief editor of the principal Soviet study of the Warsaw Pact, *The Combat Confederation of the Fraternal Peoples and Armies (Boevoe sodruzhestvo bratskikh narodov i armii)* and as the official author of the *Soviet Military Encyclopedia* entry for the "Combat Confederation" (*Boevoe sodruzhestvo*). This article identified the Warsaw Pact as the core of the combat confederation but did not restrict the membership of the confederation to East Europe. Iakubovskii's article defined the combat confederation as

> . . . a form of relations among the armed forces of the socialist states, a qualitatively new socio-historical phenomenon which developed naturally as a result of the establishment and development of the world system of socialism.
>
> The Combat Confederation is characterized by broad all-round cooperation and close links embracing all aspects of the life and activity of the fraternal armed forces.

The Combat Confederation is part of the general collaboration of the fraternal states, is one of the sources of their power, and is the reliable guarantee of the security of their peoples.

It serves as an important means of securing the conditions favorable to the development of socialism and Communism in the countries of the socialist system.[3]

After Iakubovskii's death in 1977, Marshal V.G. Kulikov, First Deputy Minister of Defense of the USSR and Chief of the General Staff of the Soviet Armed Forces, succeeded to the post of First Deputy Defense Minister of the USSR and Commander in Chief of the United Armed Forces of the Warsaw Treaty Organization. Western analysts have usually concluded that Kulikov had been demoted in favor of Marshal N.V. Ogarkov, the new Chief of the Soviet General Staff, who had previously served as Kulikov's deputy. But it is just as likely that Marshal Kulikov had assumed new responsibilities as the first deputy defense minister for Soviet military alliances, a position that carries with it the command of the Warsaw Pact. The *Soviet Military Encyclopedia* entry on Marshal Kulikov notes that since becoming the WTO commander Kulikov has been making "a great contribution to the strengthening of the combat confederation of the armed forces of the socialist countries."[4] Marshal Kulikov's primary mission as First Deputy Defense Minister of the USSR may be to secure Soviet capabilities to mobilize the armed forces of the combat confederation for joint defense of the gains of socialism against the internal and external enemies of the socialist confederation.

In his study, *Ideological Struggle in Military Questions,* General A.A. Epishev, chief of the Main Political Administration of the Soviet Armed Forces, explains why it is incumbent upon the armies of the combat confederation to prepare for joint defense of the gains of socialism against internal and external enemies. In this book General Epishev argues that the historical experience of Communist parties in seizing power and governing their societies leads to four military-political conclusions:

First, defense of the gains of socialism is a general law of socialist revolution in whatever form or whatever country it has been carried out. . . .

Second, the defense of socialism embraces not only the sphere of military affairs, but includes all other areas of social life as well—economics, culture, politics and ideology. . . .

Third, the law of the necessity of the defense of socialism applies as long as imperialism exists, which is a constant threat to socialism. Moreover, as historical experience shows, this threat exists not only in the form of a direct attack on the socialist countries, but in the form of the so-called "peaceful counterrevolution. . . ."

Fourth, the defense of socialism is an exceptionally important internationalist task. A powerful socialist system now stands in opposition to imperialism. The socialist system possesses inexhaustive material resources and enormous ideological power. In order to guarantee favorable conditions for the construction of socialism and Communism in the face of the threat of the aggressive imperialist blocs, the objective necessity has arisen to unite the efforts of all socialist countries for the military defense of the world socialist system.[5]

Epishev's law, which the Soviet army is presently trying to enforce in Afghanistan, brooks no distinctions among the inner, outer and overseas members of the socialist confederation. Securing the defense of the gains of socialism within the socialist confederation may be a more critical mission for the commanders of the combat confederation than recruiting additional members. In either case, the military requirements are the same: very large ground forces, air forces and navies combined with a strategic nuclear capability sufficiently fearsome to deter Western intervention againt joint actions by the armies of the combat confederation to defend socialism against its internal enemies. Such joint actions, past and future, depend on the military-political mechanisms first developed by Marshal Grechko for the Warsaw Pact. General Epishev, Marshal Kulikov and their comrades-in-arms have justified the military-political mechanisms which link together the national armies of the combat confederation by proclaiming the common necessity to develop military barriers which prevent aggressors from breaking into the socialist confederation. These barriers serve just as well to prevent the defenders from breaking out.

NOTES

Notes to Chapter One

1. Milovan Djilas, *Lenin on Relations Between Socialist States* (New York: Yugoslav Information Center, 1949), p. 32. This essay was first published in the Yugoslav Communist party journal *Komunist,* September 1949.

2. "Secret Speech of Khrushchev Concerning the 'Cult of the Individual,' Delivered at the Twentieth Congress of the CPSU, February 25, 1956" in Russian Institute of Columbia University, *The Anti-Stalin Campaign and International Communism* (New York: Columbia University Press, 1956), p. 63.

3. "Address by Wladyslaw Gomulka Before the Central Committee of the Polish United Workers' Party, October 20, 1945," in *National Communism and Popular Revolt in East Europe,* ed. Paul E. Zinner (New York: Columbia University Press, 1957), pp. 228-29.

4. Imre Nagy, "Ethics and Morals in Hungarian Public Life," *Nagy On Communism* (New York: Praeger, 1957), p. 51

5. "Declaration by the Government of the USSR on the Principles of Development and Further Strengthening of Cooperation Between the Soviet Union and other Socialist States, October 30, 1956" in *National Communism,* ed. Zinner, p. 486.

6. "Statement by the Government of the People's Republic of China on the Declaration of the Soviet Government on Relations Among Socialist States, November 1, 1956," in *National Communism,* ed. Zinner, p. 493.

7. *Pravda* editorial, July 16, 1956: "The International Forces of Peace, Democracy and Socialism Are Growing and Gaining in Strength" in *National Communism,* ed. Zinner, p. 63

8. "Declaration of the Conference of the Representatives of the Communist and Workers' Parties of the Socialist Countries, November 14-15, 1957" in *The Second Soviet-Yugoslav Dispute,* eds. Vaclav Benes, et al. (Bloomington: Indiana University Press, no date), p. 19

9. Ibid.

10. "Communique of the Conference of Representatives of Communist and Workers' Parties," *Pravda,* December 2, 1960, p. 1

11. See Leo Gruliow, ed., *Current Soviet Policies, Vol. IV: The Documentary Record of the Twenty-Second Congress of the CPSU* (New York: Columbia University Press, 1962), p. 223: (Resolution of the Congress): "An implacable and consistent fight on two fronts—against revisionism, as the main danger, and against dogmatism and sectarianism—is of decisive importance for the triumph of Marxism-Leninism. The CPSU sees as its internationalist duty to strengthen the monolithic solidarity of the international Communist movement in every way possible and to wage a struggle against all who try to weaken the unity of the Communists of all countries. It is necessary to continue exposing the theory and practice of latter-day revisionism, which has found its most concentrated expression in the program of the Yugoslav League of Communists."

12. *Report of the Central Committee of the Communist Party of the Soviet Union to the 23rd Congress of the CPSU* (Moscow: Progress Publishers, 1966), pp. 30-31.

13. *The 24th Congress of the Communist Party of the Soviet Union* (Moscow: Novosti Publishing House, 1971), p. 9

14. *XXV S''ezd Kommunisticheskoi partii Sovetskogo Soiuza,* [The 25th Congress of the Communist party of the Soviet Union], (Politizdat, 1976), p. 29.

15. *Mezhdunarodnoe soveshchanie kommunisticheskikh i rabochikh partii: dokumenty i materialy* [International meeting of the Communist and Workers' parties: documents and materials], (Moscow: Izdatel'stvo politicheskoi literatury, 1969), p. 181. On p. 327, the resolution of this meeting specifically mentions and endorses the resolutions of the meetings of 1957 and 1960 on relations among Communist parties.

16. "Speech by Todor Zhikov" in *Current Digest of the Soviet Press,* (July 28, 1976): pp. 7–8.

17. *Materialy XXV S''ezd KPSS* [Materials of the 25th Congress of the CPSU] (Moscow: Politizdat, 1976), p. 5.

18. "Speech by Comrade L. I. Brezhnev," *Pravda,* June 30, 1976, p. 1.

19. See the book review signed "Moravus" entitled "Shawcross' *Dubcek*" in *Survey,* 17 (Autumn, 1971).

20. Nagy, "Ethics and Morals in Hungarian Public Life," *Nagy On Communism,* pp. 54–55.

21. Adam Wasyk, "Poems for Adults," in *National Communism,* ed. Zinner, pp. 45–46.

22. "Address by Wladyslaw Gomulka Before the Central Committee of the Polish United Workers' Party," October 20, 1957, in *National Communism,* ed. Zinner, p. 210.

23. Radoslav Selucky, *Czechoslovakia: The Plan That Failed* (London: Thomas Nelson and Sons, 1970), p. 84.

24. Ivan Svitak, "Heads Against the Wall," April 10, 1968, *The Czechoslovak Experiment, 1968–69* (New York: Columbia University Press, 1971), pp. 29–30.

25. "Rapport sur l'etat de la Republique et sur les voies menant a son assainisement," *L'Alternative* (Paris January 1980), p. 30.

26. "The International Forces of Peace, Democracy and Socialism...," *Pravda* editorial, July 16, 1956 in *National Communism,* ed. Zinner, p. 27

27. "Speech of Comrade L. I. Brezhnev," *Pravda,* November 13, 1968, p. 1.

28. Ignacy Szenfeld, "The Reminiscences of Wladyslaw Gomulka," *Radio Liberty Research Paper No. 50, 1974* (New York: Radio Liberty Committee).

29. Quoted in William E. Griffith, *Albania and Sino-Soviet Rift* (Cambridge: MIT Press, 1963), p. 71.

Notes to Chapter Two

1. For these accusations see The Royal Institute of International Affairs, *The Soviet-Yugoslav Dispute* (London: Oxford University Press, 1948), pp. 48–52.

2. Reshenja plenuma TS. K. KPJ o sasivu V Kongresa Kommunistichke Partije Jugoslavije," *Borba,* May 25, 1948, p. 1.

3. "The Soviet government's Note No. 208 of August 18, 1949," in, Ministry of Foreign Affairs, Federal People's Republic of Yugoslavia, *White Book* (Belgrade: Ministry of Foreign Affairs 1951), p. 125: The Soviet note read, "The Resolution of the Cominform, which was published on the eve of the party congress in Yugoslavia, said in part, *as though addressed to the congress* (my

emphasis), 'The Information Bureau does not doubt that inside the Communist Party of Yugoslavia there are sufficient healthy elements, loyal to Marxism-Leninism, to the internationalist traditions of the Yugoslav Communist Party....'"

4. "Resolution of the Information Bureau...," in Royal Institute, *The Soviet-Yugoslav Dispute,* p. 70.

5. "S"ezd Iugoslavskoi kompartii" [Congress of the Yugoslav Communist Party], *Pravda,* July 25, 1948, p. 3.

6. "Zaiavlenie chlenov Iugoslavskogo posolstva i predstavitelei Iugoslavii pri OON" [Declaration of the members of the Yugoslav embassy and of the Yugoslav representatives at the UN], *Pravda,* July 22, 1948, p.3.

7. "Otkrytoe pis'mo piatomu s"ezdu Kommunisticheskoi partii Iugoslavii" [Open letter to the Fifth Congress of the Yugoslav Communist party], *Pravda,* July 23, 1948, p. 4. See also "Gruppa Iugoslavskikh kommunistov prisoediniatsia k otkrytomu pis'mu" [A group of Yugoslav Communists endorse the open letter], *Pravda,* July 24, 1948, p. 4.

8. *Pravda,* July 25, 1948, p. 3.

9. Josip Broz Tito, *Political Report of the Central Committee of the Communist Party of Yugoslavia; Report Delivered at the Fifth Congress of the YCP* (Belgrade, 1948), p. 136.

10. Ibid., p. 135.

11. Ibid., p. 128.

12. "Ts. Ka. [Central Committee), "Kuda vedet natsionalizm gruppy Tito v Iugoslavii?" [Where is the Nationalism of the Tito Group in Yugoslavia Leading?] *Pravda,* September 8, 1948, p. 2.

13. "Soviet Government's Note No. 208 of August 18, 1949," in Yugoslav Foreign Ministry, *White Book,* p. 125.

14. Adam Bromke, *Poland's Politics: Idealism vs. Realism* (Cambridge, Mass: Harvard University Press, 1967), p. 65.

15. Konrad Syrop, *Spring in October: The Polish Revolution of 1956* (London: Weidenfeld and Nicolson, 1957), p. 84.

16. "Polish People Brand Organizers of Provocation," *Pravda,* July 1, 1956, in *National Communism,* ed. Paul E. Zinner, (New York: Columbia University Press, 1957), pp. 136–38.

17. Bulganin's speech of July 21, 1956, in *National Communism,* ed. Zinner, p. 144.

18. "Resolution Adopted by the Central Committee of the Polish United Workers' Party...," July 18–26, 1956, in *National Communism,* ed. Zinner, p. 146.

19. Ibid., p. 148.

20. Quoted in Syrop, *Spring in October,* p. 94; also in Flora Lewis, *A Case History of Hope* (New York: Doubleday, 1958), p. 209.

21. Zawadski's remarks from the transcript of the Eighth Plenum, October 20–21, 1956, in the Journal of the Polish Central Committee, *Nowe Drogi,* October 1956, quoted in Syrop, *Spring in October,* p. 92.

22. See Imre Nagy, "The Five Basic Principles of International Relations and the Question of Our Foreign Policy," Chap. 3; "Ethics and Morals in Hungarian Public Life," Chap. 4, *Nagy On Communism* (New York: Praeger, 1957).

23. L.N. Nezhinskii, *Ocherk istorii narodnoi Vengrii* [Outline of a history of People's Hungary] (Moscow: Izdatel'stvo Nauka, 1969), pp. 207–10.

24. Paul Kecskemeti, *The Unexpected Revolution: Social Forces in the Hungarian Uprising* (Stanford: Stanford University Press, 1961), p. 56.

25. "Resolution Adopted by the Central Committee of the Hungarian Workers' Party, June 30, 1956," in *National Communism,* ed. Zinner, pp. 328–92.

26. Paul E. Zinner, *Revolution in Hungary* (New York: Columbia University Press, 1962), p. 147.

27. Ibid., p. 124; see also Ferenc Vali, *Rift and Revolt in Hungary* (Cambridge, Mass.: Harvard University Press, 1962), p. 147.

28. Vali, *Rift,* p. 239.

29. "Resolution of the Executive Committee of the Party Organization in the Hungarian Writers' Union," in *National Communism,* ed. Zinner, pp. 391–92.

30. See Vali, *Rift,* p. 266.

31. "Radio Address by Erno Gero. . . , October 23, 1956," in *National Communism,* ed. Zinner, p. 526.

32. Ibid.

33. Vali, *Rift,* pp. 292–95; see also *Report of the Special Committee on Hungary* (New York: United Nations, 1957), chap. 11.

34. P.O. Bezushko, *Konsolidatsiia revoliutsionnykh sil i stroitel'stvo sotsializma v Vengrii* [The consolidation of revolutionary forces and the development of socialism in Hungary] (Moscow: Izdatel'stvo Nauka, 1971), pp. 43–53, 69.

35. William E. Griffith, *Albania and the Sino-Soviet Rift* (Cambridge: MIT Press, 1963), p. 24.

36. Ibid., p. 47; see also Nicholas C. Pano. *The People's Republic of Albania* (Baltimore: Johns Hopkins, 1968), pp. 137–38.

37. See "N. Khrushchev Has Been Devoting His Time to Aggravating the Divergencies with Our Party and State Instead of Solving Them," *Zeri i Popullit,* March 25, 1962, in Griffith, *Albania,* p. 339: ". . . [in 1960] the personnel of the Soviet embassy in Tirana, acting on N. Khrushchev's instructions regarding a radical change of policy toward Albania, began feverishly to attack the Marxist-Leninist line of the APL, to divide our party and to sow panic and confusion within its ranks, to detach the leadership from its party, and to turn against it the army cadres and the other cadres who had studied in the Soviet Union."

38. "Khrushchev's comments on Albania. . ." in Griffith, *Albania,* p. 228.

39. "Declaration of the Central Committee of the Albanian Party of Labor . . . October 21, 1961," in Griffith, *Albania,* p. 229.

40. Ibid.

41. "Khrushchev's speech . . . October 27, 1961," in Griffith, *Albania,* p. 233.

42. "Albanian Leaders' Refusal to Discuss Differences," Radio Moscow in Albanian, Feb. 8, 1962 in Griffith, *Albania,* p. 319.

43. "Khrushchev's speech . . . October 27, 1961," in Griffith, *Albania,* pp. 234–35.

44. Ibid., pp. 234–35.

45. "Speech by M.A. Suslov," in *The Documentary Record of the 22nd Congress of the Communist Party of the Soviet Union,* eds. Charlotte Saikowsky and Leo Gruliow (New York: Columbia University Press, 1962), p. 144. During the Soviet-Albanian polemics of 1961 and 1962 Radio Moscow broadcast in Albanian Soviet complaints about the composition of the Albanian Central Committee. According to Radio Moscow, a total of 53 persons, constituting slightly more than half of the members of the Albanian Central Committee, were relatives of either Hoxha, Shehu or two other Politburo members, Hysni Kapo and Josif Pashko. Radio Moscow traced the complicated family trees of these four leaders,

whose relatives also held key posts not only in the Central Committee but in the military, security, and party youth organizations as well. According to the Soviet broadcast to Albania, "The system for the selection for the organs of the party and state creates the disease of nepotism and makes office a family right. . . . Striving to keep power in their hands and to control the organs of the party and state, the Albanian leaders do their best to keep out of these organs people whom they do not like. How can one speak about collective leadership when all important decisions are taken by Albanian leaders secretly and in a close family circle?" See "Nepotism in Albania," Radio Moscow, February 10, 1962," in Griffith, *Albania,* pp. 320-21.

46. "Speech Delivered at a Celebration of the 20th Anniversary of the Founding of the Albanian Party of Labor. . .," Nov. 8, 1961, in Griffith, *Albania,* p. 252 for the first question cited in the text and p. 267 for second quotation cited in the text.

47. "Statement of the Stand of the Romanian Workers' Party, April 1964," in William E. Griffith, *Sino-Soviet Relations, 1964-1965* (Cambridge, Mass.: MIT Press, 1967), pp. 292-94.

48. Ghita Ionescu, *Communism in Romania, 1944-1962* (New York: Oxford University Press, 1964), pp. 5, 7, 49; Jacques Levesque, *Le conflit sino-sovietique et l'Europe de l'Est* (Montreal: Les Presses de l'Universite de Montreal, 1970), pp. 183 and ff.

49. Levesque, *Le conflit,* pp. 102-3.

50. Stephen Fischer-Galati, *The New Romania* (Cambridge, Mass: MIT Press, 1967), pp. 49-50, 59-61, 67.

51. Levesque, *Le conflit,* pp. 11-12.

52. David Floyd, *Romania, Russia's Dissident Ally* (New York: Praeger, 1965), pp. 92-98. See also Fischer-Galati, *The New Romania,* p. 75.

53. See Floyd, *Romania,* pp. 85-86. "The Romanian dispute with Russia was not purely nor in fact primarily, a matter of economics. It was simply that Comecon had been the best and most convenient battleground on which the Romanians could make their stand and it was natural, especially after June, 1962, when the Russians launched their offensive, that the Romanians should extend their campaign to other fields. In doing so they took skillful advantage of the situation developing inside the Communist camp and inside Russia itself. At the same time, they took care to exploit their own success in the dispute with Moscow to consolidate the Communist regime in Romania."

54. "Statement of the Romanian Workers' Party," in Griffith, *Sino-Soviet Relations,* pp. 282-83.

55. Fischer-Galati, *The New Romania,* pp. 80-81; Levesque, *Le conflit,* pp. 123-24.

56. "Statement of the Romanian Workers' Party," in Griffith, *Sino-Soviet Relations,* p. 285.

57. Ibid., p. 286.

58. "Statement of the Romanian Workers' Party," in Griffith, *Sino-Soviet Relations,* pp. 292-94.

59. See Pavel Tigrid, *Why Dubcek Fell* (London: MacDonald, 1971); Phillip Windsor and Adam Roberts, *Czechoslovakia, 1968* (New York: Columbia University Press, 1969); William Shawcross, *Dubcek* (London: Wiedenfeld and Nicolson, 1970); H. Gordon Skilling, *Czechoslovakia's Interrupted Revolution* (Princeton: Princeton University Press, 1976); and Jiri Valenta, *Soviet Intervention in Czechoslovakia, 1968* (Baltimore: Johns Hopkins, 1979).

60. *Pravda pobezhdaet* [The truth shall prevail] (Moscow: Izdatel'stvo politicheskoi literatury, 1971), p. 4.

61. "The Lessons of Crisis Development" in *Pravda pobezhdaet,* pp. 19–21.

62. Zdenek Hejzlar, "Changes in the Czechoslovak Communist Party, 1968," in *The Czechoslovak Reform Movement,* ed. V.V. Kusin (Santa Barbara, California: ABC-Clio, 1973), p. 118.

63. Vojtech Mencl and Frantisek Ourednik, "What Happened in January," in *Winter in Prague,* ed. Robin A. Remington (Cambridge: MIT Press, 1969), p. 39.

64. "Why Was Alexander Dubcek Expelled From the Ranks of Our Party?" *Rude Pravo,* July 16, 1970. Reprinted in *Pravda pobezhdaet,* p. 348. Dubcek completed Soviet secondary schools and in the mid-1950s returned to the USSR to study at the Higher Party School in Moscow.

65. Hejzlar, "Changes in the Czechoslovak Communist Party, 1968," in *Czechoslovak Reform,* ed. Kusin, p. 118.

66. Ibid.

67. "Why Was Alexander Dubcek Expelled," *Pravda pobezhdaet,* p. 352.

68. Shawcross, *Dubcek,* pp. 101–5.

69. Interview with Drahomir Kolder, "It is Impossible to Keep Facts Silent," *Rude Pravo,* September 10, 199 in *Pravda pobezhdaet,* p. 155.

70. For a list of these resignations see *CSSR: The Road to Democratic Socialism: Facts on Events from January to May, 1968* (Prague: Pragopress, 1968), pp. 25–26.

71. Interview with Vasil Bilak, "From Dresden to Bratislava," *Rude Pravo,* Sept. 3, 1969, in *Pravda pobezhdaet,* p. 134.

72. Ibid.

73. Interview with Alois Indra, "August 1968 and the September Plenum of the CSCP," *Svet Socialismu,* Oct. 15, 1969 in Radio Free Europe, *Czechoslovak Press Survey,* Nov. 12, 1969, p. 3.

74. The following people lost their Presidium seats: Novotny, Michal Chudik, Bohuslav Lastovicka, Jaromir Dolansky, Otakar Simunek, and Jiri Hendrych. Other positions lost included: Novotny—chairmanship, National Front; Lastovicka—chairmanship, National Assembly; Chudik—chairmanship, Slovak National Council and vice chairmanship, National Assembly. Novotny, Hendrych and four others were also deprived of their posts as CC secretaries. See *CSSR: The Road to Democratic Socialism,* pp. 38–45.

75. Ibid.

76. See the "Lessons of Crisis Development" in *Pravda pobezhdaet,* p. 29: "At the April plenum and in public speeches the rightist forces attempted to express no confidence in the Central Committee of the CSCP. At the same time they made a demand for the convening of an extraordinary, so-called 'cadre congress' with the intention of gaining control of the highest organs of the party."

77. "On Current Problems of the International Situation and the CPSU's Struggle for the Solidarity of the World Communist Movement," resolution of the CPSU CC Plenum of April 10, in *Pravda,* April 11, 1968, p. 1.

78. "The March-April Plenum of the CPSC CC," in *Pravda,* April 12, 1968, p. 4.

79. See *CSSR: The Road to Democratic Socialism,* p. 56.

80. J. Malik, "How the Rightist-Opportunist Center in Brno [the capital of South Moravia] was Formed," *Rude Pravo,* December 29, 1969, in *Pravda pobezhdaet,* p. 279–82.

81. "The Lessons of Crisis Development" in *Pravda pobezhdaet*, pp. 30–32.

82. Bilak interview in *Pravda pobezhdaet*, pp. 140–41.

83. "The visit of the CSSR Delegation in Moscow," *Pravda*, May 6, 1968, p. 1.

84. Bilak interview in *Pravda pobezhdaet*, p. 142.

85. "Conference of the Party Aktiv of the Czechoslovak Communist Party," *Pravda*, May 15, 1968, p. 4.

86. See chapter 7 of this book for a discussion of the military delegations.

87. "Celebration on the Border," *Pravda*, May 26, 1968, p. 6.

88. Alois Indra, "The Truth, Not Myths," *Rude Pravo*, Sept. 24, 1969 in *Pravda pobezhdaet*, p. 190.

89. Pavel Tigrid, the emigre Czech journalist, claims that on May 24 Alexei Kosygin, the Soviet premier, agreed while in Prague to the convening of the extraordinary party congress. See Tigrid, *Why Dubcek Fell*, p. 68.

90. "The Lessons of Crisis Development" in *Pravda pobezhdaet*, p. 33.

91. Michel Tatu, "Arrivee des premieres troupes sovietiques qui doivent participer aux 'exercises' de pacte de Varsovie," *Le Monde*, May 31, 1968, in Tatu, *L'Heresie Impossible* (Paris: Editions Bernard Grasset, 1968), p. 115.

92. Ibid., p. 116, Tatu quoting *Literarni Listy*.

93. "Plenum of the Czechoslovak Party Central Committee," *Pravda*, June 8, 1968, p. 1.

94. "Strengthen the Positions of Socialism and Peace," *Pravda*, July 19, 1968, p. 1.

95. "The Lessons of Crisis Development" in *Pravda pobezhdaet*, p. 33.

96. Hejzlar, "Changes," in *Czechoslovak Reform*, ed. Kusin, p. 128.

97. Bilak interview in *Pravda pobezhdaet*, pp. 143–44.

98. Ludvik Vaculik, "The 2000 Words Manifesto," in *Winter in Prague*, ed. Remington, p. 199.

99. Kolder interview in *Pravda pobezhdaet*, p. 154.

100. A progressive journalist later complained of the "irritating failure to understand the '2000 Words' by those very people whom it was meant to assist." See A.J. Liehm, "War of Nerves," *Literarni Listy*, July 11, 1968, in Radio Free Europe, *Czechoslovak Press Suvey*, July 17, 1968. p. 5.

101. Kolder interview in *Pravda pobezhdaet*, p. 159.

102. I. Alexandrov, "Attack on the Socialist Foundations of Czechoslovakia," *Pravda*, July 11, 1968, p. 4.

103. "Why Was Alexander Dubcek Expelled," *Rude Pravo*, July 16, 1970, in *Pravda pobezhdaet*, p. 357.

104. "The Lessons of Crisis Development," in *Pravda pobezhdaet*, p. 34.

105. "'Two Thousand Words'—A Counterrevolutionary Leaflet," Radio Prague Commentary by Karel Tisar, 1739 GMT, Sept. 29, 1969, excerpts translated in *Studies in Comparative Communism* 3 (January 1970): 110.

106. Ibid., p. 111.

107. "The Lessons of Crisis Development" in *Pravda pobezhdaet*, p. 34.

108. The CSCP CC Free Information, Plans, and Management Unit, "Report on the Current Political Situation in the CSSR and the Conditions under which the CSCP Pursues Its Activity," a document presented at the Presidium meeting of August 20, 1968. First published in *Rude Pravo*, July, 1969. Translated in Radio Free Europe, *Czechoslovak Press Survey*, No. 2244, July 30, 1969. Citation from p. 32 of the RFE translation.

109. A. Svaroska and J. Rous, "The Protocol Testifies: Concerning the Prague City Committee Conference, July 1968" in *Tribuna*, Nos. 38, 39, October, 1969, in *Pravda pobezhdaet*, pp. 213–14.

110. Quoted in Jiri Smrcina, "The Dictatorship of the Prague Intellectuals," *Rude Pravo,* Sept. 16, 1969, in *Pravda pobezhdaet,* p. 173.

111. See Svarovska and Rous, "The Protocol," in *Pravda pobezhdaet,* pp. 215–16; and the unsigned article, "The Attempt of the Rightist Center to Bring About an Upheaval in the Party," *Rude Pravo,* Nov. 6, 1969, in *Pravda pobezhdaet,* p. 234.

112. "To the Czechoslovak Communist Party Central Committee," *Pravda,* July 15, 1968, p. 1.

113. "Strengthen the Positions of Socialism and Peace," *Pravda,* July 19, 1968.

114. "Information Report on the Plenum of the Central Committee of the Communist Party of the Soviet Union," *Pravda,* July 18, 1968, p. 1.

115. Kolder interview in *Pravda pobezhdaet,* p. 163.

116. Ibid.

117. Ibid., pp. 241–42.

118. Bilak interview in *Pravda pobezhdaet,* p. 146.

119. Alexander Dubcek, "Address to the Special CSCP CC Plenum, July 19, 1968 in *Winter in Prague,* ed. Remington, p. 246.

120. Kolder interview in *Pravda pobezhdaet,* p. 165.

121. The CPSU delegation consisted of L.I. Brezhnev, A.N. Kosygin, N.V. Podgorny, G.I. Voronov, K.T. Mazurov, A.J. Pel'she, M.A. Suslov, A.N. Shelepin, P. Ye. Shelest; two candidate members of the Politburo, P.N. Demichev and P.M. Masherov; and two CC secretaries, B.M. Ponomarev and K.F. Katushev. See *Pravda,* July 30, 1968, p. 1.

122. Tigrid, *Why Dubcek Fell,* p. 88.

123. "Statement of the Communist and Workers' Parties of the Socialist Countries," *Pravda,* August 4, 1968, p. 1.

124. See Chapter 6 of this study, footnote no. 52.

125. "In the CPSU Central Committee" (despite the title, the article speaks only of the Politburo), *Pravda,* August 7, 1968, p. 1.

126. "Letter of Warning from the CPSU Politburo," in *Studies in Comparative Communism,* (January 1970): 143.

127. Roger Littell, editor, *The Czech Black Book* (prepared by the Institute of History of the Czechoslovak Academy of Sciences) (New York: Praeger, 1969), p. 83. For a transcript of the proceedings of the Congress see Jiri Pelikan, ed., *The Secret Vysocany Congress* (London: Allen Lane: The Penguin Press, 1971).

128. Ibid.

129. See "The Attempt of the Rightist Center to Bring About an Upheaval in the Party," and "The Protocol Testifies . . . ," both in *Pravda pobezhdaet,* p. 234 and pp. 206–22.

130. "Illegal Assemblage," *Pravda,* August 24, 1968, p. 4.

131. For a listing of these, see Christopher D. Jones, "Autonomy and Intervention: The CPSU and the Struggle for the Czechoslovak Communist Party," *Orbis,* (Summer, 1975): 620.

132. "The Moscow Protocol," from Tigrid's *Svedectvi,* (Paris) reprinted in *Winter in Prague,* ed. Remington, p. 379.

133. Ibid.

134. Ibid., p. 380.

135. Pelikan, *The Secret Vysocany Congress,* p. 282.

Notes to Chapter Three

1. Soviet discussions of relations among socialist states frequently cite Lenin's observation that a "correct understanding" of national interests will lead to the unity of the international proletariat. See the argument of F. T. Konstantinov and A. P. Sertsova in Akademiia Nauk, SSSR, Institute filosofii [The Academy of Sciences, USSR, Institute of Philosophy] and The Higher Party School of the Central Committee of the Communist Party of Czechoslovakia, *Sovremennyi pravyi revizionizm* [Modern Rightist Revisionism] (Moscow: Izdatel'stvo Mysl, 1973, and Prague: Izdatel'stvo Svoboda, 1973), pp. 397–98; "The rightist revisionists generally attempt to put national interests in opposition to international interests while slipping to a position of bourgeois nationalism. The betrayal of internationalism is also inherent in Maoism. Nationalists consider patriotism and internationalism as mutually exclusive concepts. They try to speculate on the fact that patriotism and internationalism outwardly appear as forces which seem to go in different directions. . . . However, life shows that in a socialist society there is not only no antagonism between patriotism and socialist internationalism, but, on the contrary, there is a deep dialectical unity. Under the conditions of socialism, fundamental national interests, correctly understood, objectively unite with the international interests of the entire socialist confederation."

2. For an examination of Soviet military doctrine on these points, see Christopher D. Jones, "Just Wars and Limited Wars: Restraints on the Use of the Soviet Armed Forces," *World Politics,* 27 (October, 1975): 44–68.

3. 'Ministry of Foreign Affairs, Federal People's Republic of Yugoslavia, "Yugoslav Government's Note of Protest No. 49023 of May 23, 1949" in *White Book* (Belgrade: Ministry of Foreign Affairs 1951), p. 107.

4. "Soviet Government's Note No. 125 of May 31, 1949," Yugoslav Foreign Ministry *White Book,* p. 109.

5. See the text of the resolution in *Pravda,* November 29, 1949, p. 3. See also the issues of *Pravda* of November 30, p. 1, and December 3, p. 2, for commentary on the resolution.

6. B. Gribanov, *Banda Tito—orudie amerikano-angliskikh podzhigatelei voiny* [The Tito bank—the tool of the Anglo-American instigators of war] (Moscow: Gospolitizdat, 1952), p. 167. For a review of these newspapers, see "Klika Tito-Rankovicha prevraschaet Iugoslaviiu v platsdarm agressi (po stranitsam gazet iugoslavskikh revoliutsionnykh emigrantov")] [The Tito-Rankovich clique is transforming Yugoslavia into a staging ground for aggression (From the pages of the newspapers of the Yugoslav revolutionary emigres)] *Bol'shevik* 7 (April 1951).

7. See extracts from these journals in the Yugoslav Foreign Ministry, *White Book,* pp. 267, 271, 275 and 277.

8. *Pravda,* December 6, 1949, p. 1.

9. Pietro Rossi, "The Struggle Against Tito is the International Duty of Communists" in "For a lasting peace, for a people's democracy" 33, (December 30, 1949), in Yugoslav Foreign Ministry, *White Book,* p. 278.

10. I. Medvedev, "Klika Tito na sluzhbe u podzhigatelei novoi voiny" [The Tito clique in the service of the instigators of a new war], *Bol'shevik* 11 (June 1950): 64.

11. Yugoslav Foreign Ministry, *White Book,* p. 472.

12. Vladimir Dedijer, *The Battle Stalin Lost: Memoirs of Yugoslavia, 1948–1953* (New York: Viking Press, 1971), p. 278.

13. Ibid., p. 208.

14 .Marguerite Higgins, "Tito Interview: He'd Fight for West," New York *Herald-Tribune,* August 27, 1951, p. 1.

15. Ibid.

16. Col. Gen. Savo Drljevic, "The Role of Geo-Political, Socio-Economic and Military-Strategic Factors" in *The Yugoslav Concept of General People's Defense* eds. Maj. Gen. Alexander Vukotic, et al., (Belgrade: Medunarodna Politika, 1970), pp. 198-99.

17. Maj. Gen. Mirko Vranic, "The Strategic Employment of the Armed Forces in a General People's Defensive War," in *Yugoslav Concept,* p. 244, quotes Tito as saying: "A country that is alone in preparing for war, that relies on its own modest resources, is in a very difficult position and therefore must pay attention to other aspects, particularly to partisan warfare and to the participation of the entire people in the war. Even in 1948 I pinned great hopes on this particular aspect and still do so today [mid 1960s]."

18. "The Role and Character of the Yugoslav People's Army" (interview with *People's Army,* December 22, 1953), Josip Broz Tito, *Selected Military Works* (Belgrade: Vojnoizdavacki zavod, 1966), p. 216.

19. "The Specific Features of the Liberation Struggle and the Revolutionary Transformation of the New Yugoslavia," October, 1946, in Tito, *Selected Military Works,* p. 204.

20. Dedijer, *Battle,* p. 279.

21. "Secret Speech of Khrushchev...," in Russian Institute of Columbia University, *The Anti-Stalin Campaign and International Communism* (New York: Columbia University Press, 1956), p. 63.

22. See Konrad Syrop, *Spring in October: The Polish Revolution of 1956* (London: Weidenfeld and Nicolson, 1957), pp. 94 and ff. Flora Lewis, *A Case History of Hope* (New York: Doubleday, 1958), p. 209 and ff.; Adam Bromke, *Poland's Politics: Idealism vs. Realism* (Cambridge, Mass.: Harvard University Press, 1963), p. 90 and ff.; Zbigniew Brzezinski, *The Soviet Bloc* (Cambridge, Mass.: Harvard University Press, 1976), p. 256 and ff.; Richard Hiscocks, *Poland: Bridge For the Abyss* (New York: Oxford University Press, 1963), p. 212 and ff.

23. Syrop, *Spring,* pp. 86-7; Brzezinski, *Soviet Bloc,* p. 256; Hiscocks, *Poland,* pp. 212-3.

24. Ignacy Szenfeld, "The Reminiscences of Wladislaw Gomulka," *Radio Liberty Research Paper No. 50* (New York: Radio Liberty Committee, 1974), p.3.

25. Syrop, *Spring,* p. 95.

26. Our Own Correspondent, "Antisotsialisticheskie vystupleniia na stranitsakh pol'skoi pechat'" [Antisocialist statements on the pages of the Polish press], *Pravda,* October 20, 1956, p. 3.

27. Syrop, *Spring,* pp. 95-6; Bromke, *Poland's Politics,* pp. 91-2; Hiscocks, *Poland,* p. 212; Lewis, *Case History,* pp. 209-13.

28. Ibid.

29. Ibid.

30. Lewis, *Case History,* p. 214.

31. Syrop, *Spring,* p. 97.

32. Lewis, *Case History,* p. 214.

33. Hiscocks, *Poland,* p. 214.

34. Bromke, *Poland's Politics,* pp. 91-94.

35. Adam B. Ulam, *Expansion and Coexistence* (New York: Praeger, 1968), pp. 591-94.

36. "Address by Wladyslaw Gomulka Before the Central Committee of the Polish United Workers' Party, October 20, 1956" in *National Communism and Popular Revolt in East Europe,* ed. Paul E. Zinner (New York: Columbia University Press, 1957), pp. 227–28.

37. Ibid., passim.

38. Syrop, *Spring,* pp. 112–15.

39. Edward Ochab, *Nowe Drogi,* October 1956 quoted in Syrop, *Spring,* p. 116.

40. Ibid., p. 134.

41. Ibid., pp. 139–43.

42. Brzezinski, *Soviet Bloc,* pp. 261 and ff.

43. "Declaration by the Central Committee of the Hungarian Workers' Party, October 26, 1956," in *National Communism,* ed. Zinner, pp. 420–26.

44. "Polozhenie v Vengrii," [The situation in Hungary], *Pravda,* October 29, 1956, p. 4.

45. "Krushenie antinarodnoi avantiury v Vengrii," [The crushing of the antipopular adventure in Hungary], *Pravda,* October 28, 1956, p. 6.

46. The four were Joszef Bognar, Ferenc Erdei, Bela Kovacs, and Zoltan Tildy. Bognar and Erdei were politicians who had worked for years within the Communist regime as the representatives of the prewar parties which still retained seats in the national parliament but always voted with the Communists. Bela Kovacs, a former leader of the Smallholders party, refused to accept his appointment as minister of agriculture. Zoltan Tildy, also a leader of the Smallholders party, and a former president of the post-1945 republic, in effect withdrew from Nagy's cabinet by immediately calling for the abolition of the one-party system. See Ferenc Vali, *Rift and Revolt in Hungary* (Cambridge, Mass.: Harvard University Press, 1961), p. 290.

47. "Polozhenie v Vengrii," [The situation in Hungary], *Pravda,* October 30, 1956, p. 4.

48. See Elie Abel, New York *Times,* October 30, 1956, p. 10.•

49. See Elie Abel, New York *Times,* October 28, 29 and 30, 1956.

50. "Declaration of the Government of the USSR on the Principles of Development and Further Strengthening of Friendship and Cooperation Between the Soviet Union and Other Socialist States, October 30, 1956" in *National Communism,* ed. Zinner, p. 488.

51. John MacCormac, "Tanks Seal Off Budapest," New York *Times,* October 28, 1956, p. 1, and "Soviets Reported Pouring in Troops," *National Communism,* ed. Zinner, p. 31.

52. William T. Jordan, "Moscow States Hungary Policy," New York *Times,* October 30, 1956, p. 1.

53. "Declaration, October 30," in *National Communism,* ed. Zinner, p. 485.

54. Vali, *Rift,* p. 301. See also William E. Griffith, "The Revolt Reconsidered," *East Europe* 9 (July, 1960): 18–19.

55. "Proclamation by Imre Nagy on the Restoration of a Multi-Party System and Coalition Government" in *National Communism,* ed. Zinner, pp. 453–54.

56. Vali, *Rift,* p. 299.

57. Vali, *Rift,* pp. 364–67. Paul Zinner, *Revolution in Hungary* (New York: Columbia University Press, 1962), p. 331, agrees with Vali that Nagy's reason for withdrawing from the Pact was to win diplomatic support from the West for his new government. Zinner does not, however, explicitly say that the threat of Soviet military intervention prompted Nagy to seek foreign support by withdrawing

from the Pact. In his study, Raymond Garthoff, *Soviet Military Policy* (New York: Praeger, 1966) argues that the Soviet decision to intervene preceded Nagy's formal withdrawal from the Warsaw Pact. See pp. 155–72.

58. United Nations, *Report of the Special Committee on Hungary* (New York: United Nations, 1957), p.27.

59. Vali, *Rift,* p. 370.

60. "The Formation of a New Communist Party: Radio Address to the Nation by Janos Kadar, November 1, 1956," in *National Communism,* ed. Zinner, pp. 464–67.

61. Ibid.

62. "Program and Composition of the Hungarian Revolutionary Worker-Peasant Government: Announcement by Janos Kadar, November 4, 1956," in *National Communism,* ed. Zinner, pp. 474–78.

63. See Brzezinski, *The Soviet Bloc,* Ch. 10: "Hungary: The Test Case of National Communism," especially p. 232.

64. See *Pravda,* November 5, 1956, pp. 1 and 3, for identical statements by the Soviet government and by Kadar's government.

65. "Doklad tovarishcha Janosha Kadara va VII S"ezde vengerskoi sotsialisticheskoi rabochei partii," [Speech of Comrade Janos Kadar at the VII Congress of the Hungarian Socialist Workers Party], November 30, 1959, in *Pravda,* December 1, 1959, p. 2.

66. "Pregradit put' reaktsii v Vengrii," [Close Off the Path of Reaction in Hungary], *Pravda,* November 4, 1956, p. 1.

67. General Bela Kiraly: "Hungary's Army: Its Part in the Revolt," *East Europe* 7 (June 1958).

68. Vali, *Rift,* pp. 374–76.

69. *Report of the Special Committee on Hungary,* p. 27. Vali, *Rift,* p. 318: "The regular armed forces of Hungary were not in any way prepared to resist a new Soviet attack. When, at last, orders were issued to put up reistance, the widely scattered units of the regular army participated only sporadically in the renewing battle, because effective centralized leadership was lacking (orders had generally not reached the troops) and because pro-Soviet officers sabotaged these efforts and others hesitated. The police were also unfitted to take part in open or street battles. Only the National Guard, some workers' units, some cadets and a few small military units stood at the disposal of the revolutionary command when the combat opened on November 4."

70. Maj. General Mirko Vranic, "The Strategic Employment of the Armed Forces in a General People's Defensive War" in *Yugoslav Concept,* eds. Vukotic et al., p. 244: "After 1948, thinking on military problems showed a tendency to evolve. Nevertheless, the territorial forces and the partisan methods of waging war were more or less reduced, in substantive part, to their tactical values. A decisive turning point took place only in 1957."

71. Col. Drago Nikolic, "The League of Communists of Yugoslavia and General People's Defense" in *Yugoslav Concept,* ed., Vukotic et al., p. 92.

72. Col. Pajo Samardzija, "The Economy in General People's Defense" in *Yugoslav Concept,* eds. Vukotic et al., pp. 306–12.

73. See the relevant sections of the National Defense Law and of the Ninth Congress of the LCY in *Yugoslav Concept,* eds. Vukotic et al.

74. International Institute of Strategic Studies (IISS), *The Military Balance, 1980–81,* (London: IISS, 1980) p. 38.

75. See A. Ross Johnson, "Yugoslav Total National Defense," *Survival,* (March/April 1973): 56. See also Dusko Doder, *The Yugoslavs* (New York: Random House, 1978) pp. 138–56.

76. Maj. Gen. Dusan Dozet, "The Social Basis of People's Defense" in *Yugoslav Concept,* eds. Vukotic et al., p. 73.

77. Col. General Savo Drljevic, "The Role of Geo-Political, Socio-Economic and Military-Strategic Factors," in *Yugoslav Concept,* eds. Vukotic et al., p. 209.

78. Ibid.

79. Ibid.: ". . . an act of aggression, regardless of which of the two blocs were involved, would inevitably be aimed not only at occupying our territory but primarily at changing the character of our social system."

80. See article 254 in *Yugoslav Concept,* eds. Vukotic et al., p. 317.

81. See Drljevic in *Yugoslav Concept,* eds. Vukotic et al., p. 209.

82. Johnson, "Yugoslav Defense," p. 54.

83. See *Yugoslav Concept,* eds. Vukotic et al., pp. 281–311.

84. Johnson, "Yugoslav Defense," p. 55.

85. See Col. Gen. Pavle Jaksic, "On Mutual Transformations Between Frontal and Partisan Warfare" in *Yugoslav Concept,* eds. Vukotic et al. and also Col. Gen. Bogdan Orescanin, "Liberation Wars and the Historical Awakening of Nations."

86. Ibid.

87. Ibid., p. 36.

88. Col. Andro Gabelic, "The Universal Substance of General People's Defense," in *Yugoslav Concept,* eds. Vukotic et al., p. 147.

89. Dozet, *Yugoslav Concept,* ed. Vukotic et al., p. 126.

90. Col. Gen. Danilo Lekic, "Introduction," in *Yugoslav Concept,* eds. Vukotic et al., p. 12.

91. Gabelic in *Yugoslav Concept,* eds. Vukotic et al., p. 149.

92. "Balcony Speech by Nicolae Ceausescu . . ." August 22, 1968, in *Winter in Prague,* ed., Robin A. Remington (Cambridge, Mass.: MIT Press, 1969), pp. 358–59.

93. For documentation of the mobilization, see Mary Ellen Fischer, "Ceausescu and the Romanian Political Leadership," Ph.D. thesis (Harvard University, 1974), pp. 315 and ff.

94. See *Pages from the History of the Romanian Army* (in English) (Bucharest: Military Publishing House, 1975); see also Colonel Iulian Cernat et al., eds., *National Defense: The Romanian View* (in English) (Bucharest: Military Publishing House, 1976), chap. 2; *Romania si traditule luptei armate a intrereguleii popor* (Bucharest: Editura Militara, 1972); see also *File din istoria militara a poporului roman Vol. 3* (Bucharest: Editura Militara, 1977).

95. Stephen Fischer-Galati, *The New Romania* (Cambridge, Mass.: MIT Press, 1967), pp. 70–71.

96. Jacques Levesque, *Le conflit sino-sovietique et l'Europe de l'est* (Montreal: Les Presses de l'Universite de Montreal, 1970), pp. 116–17.

97. With the author of this book.

98. See Chapter 8 of this book.

99. See Chapter 4 of this book.

100. See Chapter 7 of this book.

101. "Statement of the Romanian Workers' Party . . .," April 1964, in William E. Griffith, *Sino-Soviet Relations* (Cambridge, Mass.: MIT Press, 1964), p. 280.

102. Ibid.

103. See the English text of this law in Joint Publications Research Service (JPRS), *Translations on East European Political, Sociological and Military Affairs No. 58017,* January 18, 1973, from *Scinteia* (December 24, 1972): 4; see also the Decree on the Reorganization of the Defense Ministry in JPRS, *Translations on East European Political, Sociological and Military Affairs No. 57812,* December 19, 1972, from *Buletinul Oficial al Republici Socialiste Romana,* Part I, No. 130 (November 21, 1972) 1048–1051, Decree No. 444/1972.

104. See Colonel Mihai Arsintsescu, "The People's War of Defense: Its Theory and Practice" in *National Defense,* ed. Cernat; see also *Studii social-politice asupra fenomenului militar contemporan* (Bucharest: Editura Militara, 1972) and *Guerila, resistenta, razboi popula* (Bucharest: Editura Militara, 1972). See also, David P. Burke, "Defense and Mass Mobilization in Romania," *Armed Forces and Society* 7 (Fall 1980).

105. Col. Gheorghe Stanculescu, "The Resistance Movement," in *National Defense,* ed. Cernat, p. 142. See also Col. Cernat's remark in "The Political and Strategic Aims of the War of the Entire People" in *National Defense,* ed. Cernat, p. 113: "The political strategy of the imperialist, aggressive and hegemonic states utilizes a variety of procedures for the 'alignment' of the peoples against whom it has launched aggression, such as the organization of puppet regimes present in different political-strategic formulas as exemplified by the 'Vietnamization' of the war, 'Asians against Asians,' the break-up of national unity...."

106. "Law Concerning the Organization of the National Defense of the Socialist Republic of Romania" in JPRS, *Translations on East European Political, Sociological and Military Affairs, No. 58017,* January 18, 1973, Article 1.

107. Col. Traian Grozea, "The Socio-Political Foundations of National Defense" in *National Defense,* ed. Cernat, p. 98: "It can be expected that a war unleased by the aggressor against this country would be waged in the main with classical armament. This hypothesis has in view that the enemy, having great superiority as to the number of troops and technical means, would be certain of a balance of forces on the basis of which he could believe that he is capable of obtaining a military victory without having resort to nuclear weapons (if he has such weapons)....The fundamental political nature of the type of conflict to which the riposte is the war of the entire people is not very favorable to the deployment of the rocketry and nuclear weapon arsenal from the viewpoint of the propaganda aims pursued by a possible aggressor. At the same time it should be noted that the use of nuclear weapons would produce the danger of generalizing the war, of increasing its area, whereby the publicly declared aims of the aggressor at the start of the hostilities, which as a rule refer to a local war, would lose all meaning."

108. See Cernat, "The Political and Strategic Aims of the War of the Entire People" in *National Defense,* ed. Cernat, pp. 109–110.

109. Ibid., pp. 100 and 113.

110. Ibid., p. 110.

111. Ibid., p. 111.

112. Grozea in *National Defense,* ed. Cernat, pp. 92–93. A Soviet officer, writing in the restricted journal *Voennaia Mysl'* notes the tendency of modern wars to draw the majority of a state's population into different aspects of the war effort. He produces figures roughly in the same range as those specified by Colonel Cernat. See Maj. Gen. Kh. Dzhelaukhov, "Human Resources in Modern Warfare," CIA FBIS FPD 0087/69 *Translations from Voennaia Mysl'* 1 (1969): 27.

113. See Col. Gheorghe Stanculescu, "The Resistance Movement," in *National Defense,* ed. Cernat, pp. 157–58.

114. Ibid., pp. 153–54.

115. Ibid., pp. 148–53.

116. Ibid., pp. 147–48.

117. Cernat, "General Features of the Armed Struggle Waged against the Aggressor" in *National Defense,* ed. Cernat, p. 113: "The second stage of the armed conflict can also be the last if the aggressor has been unable to achieve his political aims by force. If, as a result of the confrontation between the occupier and the resistance movement, the occupation forces have been continuously worn out and exhausted, then what we would call a 'strategic stalemate' is realized. Such a situation can be a step to the final act of a war concluded by a political settlement, accompanied by the withdrawal of the occupation troops and the re-establishment of national independence and sovereignty and of territorial integrity."

118. Ibid., pp. 113–14.

119. Grozea, "General Characteristics of National Defense" in *National Defense,* ed. Cernat, pp. 96–97.

120. Cernat, "General Features of the Armed Struggle," in *National Defense,* ed. Cernat, p. 130.

121. Colonel Mihai Arsintescu, "The People's War of Defense" in *National Defense,* ed. Cernat, p. 20: "However courageously the masses are fighting, their efforts and sacrifice do not lead to the desired results if they do not have the military training and skills which are absolutely necessary for combat action. History actually proves that quite a few revolutionary wars for defense of the homeland were lost because, although fighting with great enthusiasm, the popular forces did not have or did not create suitable means of struggle, transport and communication."

122. See Article 11 of the 1972 law on national defense in JPRS, *Translations on East European Political, Sociological and Military Affairs, No. 58017,* January 18, 1973.

123. See Alex Alexiev, *Party–Military Relations in East Europe: The Case of Romania* (Los Angeles: University of California Center for International and Strategic Affairs, 1979), p. 35.

124. See Colonel Bela Iani, "Preparing the Economy for Defense," in *National Defense,* ed. Cernat, pp. 211–29.

125. Alexiev, *The Romanian Case,* pp. 25–26.

126. Ibid.

127. International Institute for Strategic Studies (IISS), *The Military Balance, 1978–79,* (London: IISS, 1979), p. 15.

128. Cernat, ed., *National Defense,* p. 188.

129. See the 1972 defense law, article 16 in JPRS, *Translations on East European Political, Sociological and Military Affairs, No. 58017,* January 18, 1973; see also Cernat, ed., *National Defense,* pp. 255–61.

130. Alexiev, *The Romanian Case,* p. 35.

131. Ibid.

132. IISS, *The Military Balance, 1978#79,* p. 15.

133. Cernat, ed., *National Defense,* pp. 175–76.

134. Ibid., p. 173.

135. Ibid., p. 177.

136. Ibid.

137. Ibid., p. 176.

138. Lt. General Constantin Petcu, "Organization of the Territory for Defense, *National Defense,* ed. Cernat, p. 231.

139. Ibid., pp. 178–79.

140. Ibid., p. 176.

141. Ibid., p. 173.

142. Ibid., pp. 170–71.

143. IISS, *The Military Balance, 1978–79,* p. 15.

144. Cernat, ed., *National Defense,* pp. 185–89.

145. Ibid., pp. 189–196, 201–9.

146. Ibid., pp. 179–82.

147. Stanculescu, "The Resistance Movement," in *National Defense,* ed. Cernat, p. 140.

148. See Alexiev, *The Romanian Case,* pp. 15–20, for a discussion of the Romanian effort to use the military as a school for patriotic indoctrination.

149. See the texts cited in footnote 94.

150. Col. Mihai Arsintescu, "The People's War of Defense: Its Theory and Practice in Retrospect," in *National Defense,* ed. Cernat, p. 21.

151. William E. Griffith, *Albania and the Sino-Soviet Rift* (Cambridge, Mass.: MIT Press, 1963), p. 3.

152. Peter R. Prifti, *Socialist Albania since 1944* (Cambridge, Mass.: MIT Press, 1978), p. 207.

153: Mehmet Shehu, *A propos de l'experience de la guerre de liberation nationale et du developement de notre armee nationale* (Paris: Editions GIT, LeCoeur, 1969), (First Albanian edition, 1947, revised edition 1962), pp. 14, 78, 98, esp. p. 98: "The Soviet army has an extensive experience of war on mountainous terrain and it has an entire doctrine of war in the conditions of mountainous terrain. The second world war demonstrated that the Soviet army is the best organized, the most advanced and the strongest in the world. It fought the fascist army not only in winter in defense of Moscow but also during the spring and summer and not only on the vast plains of Russia but also on her highest mountains, in the Caucasus, on the mountainous terrain of the Crimea, in the Carpathians, in the Balkans, on the polar rocks of Norway and on the desert summits of the Far East. Its basic experience has a universal character and is the best experience in all cases." Earlier in this study Shehu drew a distinction between Soviet military doctrine of the Stalin era, which he still accepts, and Soviet doctrine of the Khrushchev era, which he rejects. See p. 14.

154. Ibid., pp. 16–17.

155. Prifti, *Albania,* p. 207.

156. Ibid., p. 208.

157. Ibid., pp. 212–17.

158. Enver Hoxha, "Speech Delivered at the Celebration of the 20th Anniversary of the Founding of the Albanian Party of Labor" in Griffith, *Albania,* p. 224.

159. "Whom Do N. Khrushchev's Views and Actions Serve?" *Zeri i Popullit* (March 2, 1962), in Griffith, *Albania,* p. 339.

160. Prifti, *Albania,* p. 204.

161. Both citations from Michael Checinski, "The Post-War Development of the Polish Armed Forces" (Santa Monica, Calif.: RAND Corp., forthcoming).

162. See Hansjakob Stehle, *The Independent Satellite* (New York: Praeger, 1965), pp. 220–51.

163. Ibid.

164. J. Hechko, "Scientific Hypothesis or Political Speculation," *Rude Pravo,* January 8, 1970, reprinted in *Pravda pobezhdaet* [The truth shall prevail] (Moscow: Politizdat, 1971), p.292.

165. Quotation of the Gottwald Memorandum from Colonel Milan Matous, "The So-Called 'Memorandum'—What It was and the Purpose It Served," *Zivot Strany* 42 October 15, 1969, in Radio Free Europe, *Czechoslovak Press Survey* 2272 November 18, 1969 (New York: Radio Free Europe Research).

166. Ibid.

167. Cited in Miroslav Starosta, "How the Postulate of Neutrality Arose," *Tribuna,* August 20, 1969, in RFE, *Czechoslovak Press Survey* 2257, September 10, 1969, p. 2.

168. Quoted in RFE, *Czechoslovak Press Survey* 2257, p. 3.

169. J. Hecho, "Scientific Hypothesis," p. 292: "In one of the sections of the memorandum the position of Czechoslovakia in the Warsaw Pact was characterized as the position of a victim of processes on which we were not able to exercise influence. The authors of the memorandum put forward arguments against the participation of Czechoslovakia in the Warsaw Pact."

170. Matous, "The So-Called 'Memorandum,'" p. 7.

171. See Chapter 5 for a discussion of these and other matters related to Soviet intervention in Czechoslovakia in 1968.

172. Hechko, "Scientific Hypothesis," p. 287.

173. According to Matous, "The So-Called 'Memorandum,'" p. 10, Prchlik relied upon officers of the Gottwald Academy, in particular a Colonel Blizek, for drawing up unspecified documents and for preparing Prchlik's speeches. It is likely that one of the speeches Matous had in mind was Lieutenant General Prchlik's press conference of July 15; it is also likely that the documents to which Prchlik referred in his press conference were the documents which Matous accused Col. Blizek of drafting.

174. See Chapter 7 of this study for a further discussion of Prchlik's press conference.

175. "Report on the Press Conference of Lt. General Vaclav Prchlik . . . ," in *Winter in Prague,* ed. Remington, p. 217.

176. Ibid., pp. 216–17.

177. Ibid., p. 217.

178. See the editorial of July 23 in *Winter in Prague,* ed. Remington, pp. 220–23. In this editorial *Krasnaia Zvezda* declared: "First General Prchlik assured his audience at the press conference that 'Czechoslovakia supports efforts aimed at a further strengthening and improving of the Warsaw Pact.' But he immediately followed this with arguments whose meaning belies this."

179. Pavel Tigrid, *Why Dubcek Fell* (London: MacDonald, 1971), pp. 106–7.

180. "Two Thousand Words," in *Winter in Prague,* ed. Remington, p. 201.

181. "The Gordian Knot," lecture delivered at Yale University, November 17, 1968, in Ivan Svitak, *The Czechoslovak Experiment, 1968–1969* (New York: Columbia University Press, 1971), pp. 180–81.

182. See William Shawcross, *Dubcek* (New York: Simon and Schuster), pp. 191–203.

183. Dedijer, *Battle.*

184. Adam Roberts, "Czechoslovakia: Invasion and Resistance," in Roberts and Phillip Windsor, *Czechoslovakia, 1968* (New York: Columbia University Press, 1969), p. 97. See also, Adam Roberts *Nation in Arms: The Theory and Practice of Territorial Defense* (New York: Praeger, 1976).

185. Ignacy Szenfeld, "The Reminiscences of Wladislaw Gomulka," Radio Liberty Research Paper No. 50, 1974. John Erickson claims that Lieutenant General Prchlik had actually drawn up plans for military defense against a Soviet intervention. In John Erickson, "International and Strategic Implications of the Czechoslovak Reform Movement" in *The Czechoslovak Reform Movement, 1968,* ed. V. V. Kusin, (Santa Barbara, California: ABC Clio, 1968), p. 46: "After the invasion of Czechoslovakia General Prchlik was tried for this press conference [of July 15, 1968] but it should be noted that the original charge of 'betraying military secrets' was dropped. What was not a part of the public indictment was that General Prchlik was the man behind the contingency plans to defend the state frontiers against other members of the Warsaw Pact, principally the USSR. Such a plan was undoubtedly drawn up, one envisaging Czechoslovak resistance. But this document was immediately withdrawn as a 'provocation' to the Russians; nevertheless the Soviet command learned of it, possibly through Bilak, and thus the 'anonymous' source of opposition to Prchlik proves to be less mysterious. This seems to have been Prchlik's real crime, after his involvement with the removal of the previous military leadership."

186. Dedijer, *Battle,* p. 108.

187. All of the information given above comes from the account of the invasion of Czechoslovakia prepared by the Institute of History of the Czechoslovak Academy of Sciences in the period immediately after the invasion. See p. 5 of the English translation of this work, Robert Littell, ed., *The Czech Black Book* (New York: Praeger, 1969).

188. Josef Smrkovsky, "In the Eye of the Storm," The Washington *Post,* March 2, 1975, p. B-1.

189. Ibid.

190. Ibid., p. B-5.

191. "Appeal by a group of members of the Czechoslovak Communist Party Central Committee, the CSSR Government and the National Assembly," *Pravda,* August 22, 1968, in *Winter in Prague,* ed. Remington, p. 297.

192. Roberts, "Invasion and Resistance," pp. 107–8.

193. For the details of Pavel's activities, see Littel, ed., *The Czech Black Book,* pp. 133–34, 177–78, 191–92.

194. Tigrid, *Why Dubcek Fell,* p. 110.

195. See Christopher Jones, "Autonomy and Intervention: The CPSU and the Struggle for the Czechoslovak Communist, 1968," in *Orbis* (Summer 1975): 619–20.

196. Ibid., p. 620.

197. "The Moscow Protocol," in *Winter in Prague,* ed. Remington.

198. Jiri Pelikan, *The Secret Vysocany Congress* (London: Allen Lane: The Penguin Press, 1971), p. 298.

Notes to Chapter Four

1. See the biography of A. A. Grechko in *Sovetskaia voennaia entsiklopediia* [Soviet military encyclopedia] Vol. 3, pp. 48–49.

2. V. A. Muradian, *Boevoe bratstvo* [Combat brotherhood] (Moscow: Voenizdat, 1978), pp. 73–74.

3. Christopher D. Jones, "Just Wars and Multi-National Armies" in *The Military-Political Mechanisms of the Warsaw Pact,* unpublished paper, a study written for the National Council for Soviet and East European Research (Washington, D. C., 1980).

4. A. P. Artem'ev, *Bratskii boevoi soiuz narodov SSSR v Velikoi otechestvennoi voine* [The fraternal combat union of the peoples of the USSR in the Great Fatherland War] (Moscow: Mysl', 1975), pp. 44–46.

5. Muradian, *Boevoe bratstvo,* p. 116.

6. K. Tskitishvili, *Na frontakh Velikoi otechestvennoi* [On the fronts of the Great Fatherland War] (Tibilisi: Izdatel'stvo Sabchota Sakartvelo, 1975), p. 283.

7. Artem'ev, *Bratskii boevoi soiuz,* pp. 121–42. Artem'ev documents the participation in the battle of Moscow in 1941–42 of five rifle divisions from Kzakhstan, two cavalry divisions from the Uzbek republic, and one rifle division and one rifle brigade from the Kirghiz republic. (pp. 116–21). He avoids revealing the names and numbers of divisions from the Caucasus, Kazakhstan, and Central Asia that participated in the battles for the Caucasus and for Stalingrad. However, his discussion of the military contributions of these divisions to the war effort in 1941 and 1942 is in fact almost exclusively a discussion of action on the Caucasus and Stalingrad fronts.

8. Muradian, *Boevoe bratstvo,* p. 74.

9. Artem'ev, *Bratskii boevoi soiuz,* p. 52.

10. Ibid.

11. M. I. Semiriaga, A. S. Antosiac, P. M. Derevianko, eds., *Zarozhdenie armii stran-uchastnits Varshavskogo dogovora* [The Birth of the Peoples Armies of the Member Countries of the Warsaw Pact] (Moscow: Nauka, 1975), p. 117.

12. Ibid., p. 61.

13. Ibid., pp. 73–91; 118–160.

14. Ibid., pp. 359–61.

15. Jones, "Just Wars."

16. Ibid.

17. "In the middle 1950s there began a new stage of development in the life of the multi-national Soviet armed forces. This stage was conditioned by the formation of the world system of socialism and by the further strengthening of the political and economic might of the USSR. Soviet society had made a new major step forward in its socio-political, economic and cultural development. A further drawing together of all the nations and nationalities of the country took place. In these conditions, the necessity for national detachments in the union republics and autonomous republics fell away. The existing republic formations and units were disbanded and their personnel went into the ranks of the multi-national formations of the Soviet Army and Navy" (*Sovetskaia voennaia entsiklopediia* Vol. 5, p. 553).

18. ". . . the composition of our armed forces was and continues to be multi-national. Our country's multi-national nature is practically expressed in the units and formations of the army and navy. This stems from the specific peculiarities of their recruitment. Each nation lives in a definite social and geographical milieu. It has its own history and its own culture and traditions. The situation demands a

tactful, differentiated approach by the teachers to the students and a necessary consideration of their national features, languages, peculiarities of character, experience, educational levels and labor skills. It must also be remembered that national features and traditions do not remain unchanged. They are developed, perfected and filled with new socialist content and become the great moving force of Communist development and its armed defense. . . . Internationalist indoctrination acquires special significance for the troops who are beyond the boundaries of the homeland and for the border districts and fleets. Considerable work is being carried out among the Soviet troops stationed temporarily on the territory of the GDR, Poland and Hungary to explain the basic principles of military organization in the fraternal socialist countries, and the successes achieved by the workers of these countries in the construction of socialism are graphically demonstrated. The troops familiarize themselves with the culture, community life and traditions of the German, Polish, and Hungarian peoples and with the life and combat experiences of their armies" (Colonel V. Koniukhovskii and Rear Admiral F. Chernyshev, "The Army of the Friendship of Peoples and Proletarian Internationalism," *Voennaia Mysl'*, [Military Thought] 11 (1967) in CIA FBIS FPD 0157/68 Nov. 18, 1968 *Selected Translations from Voennaia Mysl'* (available from the Library of Congress, Washington, D.C.) pp. 87–8).

Lt. Gen. I.S. Mednikov, chief, in 1972, of the political administration of the Group of Soviet Forces in Germany (GSFG) notes that the current policy of placing soldiers of all Soviet nationalities in multinational integrated units and formations obtains in the staff of the GSFG. He observes that such staffing is intended to emphasize that all Soviet soldiers have one common homeland. He implies that making this claim may be very important to the conduct of joint political work and joint military activities of the GSFG and the National Peoples Army of the German Democratic Republic. (Later chapters in my study note the extent of interaction between these two national armies.) Mednikov makes these observations in a brief article in a collection of short articles by leading Soviet military officers and party officials of the union republics of the USSR. These articles all deal briefly with aspects of the service of different nationalities in the Soviet armed forces and with the relationships of civilian personnel in individual republics to the Soviet Armed Forces. The significance of these articles is probably not in their specific contents, but rather in the identification of "themes" or issues which the Soviets have identified as important ones in maintaining cohesion and morale among the different nationalities serving in the armed forces. Mednikov's article may be read as a random juxtaposition of topics whose interrelationships are not defined. But this article by the chief of the political administration of the GSFG may also be read as a statement that the Soviets see a relationship between the question of how non-Russians are placed into the GSFG and other Force Groups in East Europe (in national units or in integrated, multinational units) and the question of how the Soviets organize joint political and military activities with the East European armies of the Warsaw Pact.

Mednikov writes: "When it is a matter of the friendship of soldiers and of their internationalist upbringing one frequently hears that in such and such a unit representatives of many nationalities serve. What is unusual about that? Such facts shouldn't surprise anyone. One has to consider very thoughtfully the specific manifestation of the multi-nationality of units and sub-units. It is extremely important and significant that in any of our troop collectives the sons of various peoples have approximately equal proportionate representation in the leadership nucleus, in the party organization, and in the ranks of the soldiers officially recognized as outstanding in combat and political training. That commanders and senior leaders have a respectful, considerate attitude toward the soldiers of various nationalities is both fully natural but at the same time extremely significant. And this does not involve just the designated service relationships, but the fact that all officers and soldiers are qualitatively, if one can use such an expression, identical; they have good general education and military training and are competent in a very broad spectrum of matters. The recruit from the distant village or settlement of Central Asia or the Caucasus in no way stands out from the recruit from the big city—both have studied in Soviet schools, both are accustomed to good living conditions and a high level of culture.

"One thinks about all this with joy and pride when one encounters the multi-national family of whatever unit. One sees the whole country in microcosm, a country which is a beautiful and beloved homeland for all peoples.

"Soldiers of various nationalities serve in a Guards Tank Division, the Ural-L'vov Red Banner Order of Suvorov and Kutuzov Volunteer Division named in honor of Marshal of the Soviet Union R. Ia. Malinovskii. Here one can meet a Tatar major, A. Aidarov, and they will tell you that this officer skillfully and responsibly executes his service duties. They will point out among the officially designated group of the best soldiers the Ukrainian commander of a company, Senior Lieutenant A. Matseichuk, who was decorated for successes in service ahead of the normal schedule; the Kazakh commander of a platoon, Lieutenant B. Kerimbaev; the Lithuanian commander of a battery, Senior Lieutenant, M. Tomashaitis, and many other officers, non-commissioned officers, and soldiers. . . .

"Commanders and political organs, party organization and the political administration of the Group of Soviet Forces in Germany in every way broaden and enrich the arsenal of the forms and methods of the internationalist training of soldiers. A prominent place in this effort is taken by propaganda of the tradition of the joint struggle of the peoples with the enemies of socialism. A prominent place is taken also by popularization of the transformations which have taken place in the socialist countries and also by the achievements of the various republics of our Homeland during the years of Soviet power. Work in internationalist education in the units and sub-units begins with the first day that a young soldier puts on a military uniform. Great attention is devoted to the spiritual questions and needs of young soldiers, their national peculiarities and characteristics are taken into account, and everything is done in order that proper military relationships develop among military personnel and troop comradeship is strengthened.

"The soldiers of the Group of Soviet Forces in Germany serve on the territory of the GDR. Right next to our garrisons are deployed the garrisons of the National People's Army of the German Democratic Republic. The defense of socialism has become the state policy not only of our one country but the general policy of all the countries of the Warsaw Pact and of the friendly armed forces. We are class brothers and comrades in arms. The soldiers of the GSFG and the soldiers of the NPA shoulder to shoulder fulfill their patriotic and internationalist duty in the defense of the western borders of the socialist confederation. Literally all events of life and service testify to the close ties of combat brothers—from joint evening meetings conducted in one sub-unit or another to major troop exercises like 'Brotherhood in Arms' which took place on the territory of the GDR." The next three pages of Mednikov's article then itemize various forms of contacts between the GSFG and East German troops. In the chapter on the Political

Directorate of the Warsaw Pact, later in my study, is a discussion of the types of activities briefly mentioned here by Mednikov (Lt. Gen. I.S. Mednikov. "Dryzhboi narodov sil'nyi" [Strong because of the friendship of peoples] in S.M. Isachenko, comp., *Armiia bratstva narodov* [Army of the brotherhood of peoples] (Moscow: Voenizdat, 1972), p. 159-61).

19. "In the first years [of the existence of the Warsaw Pact] joint exercises were conducted primarily on a tactical level, then beginning in 1961 they began to take place regularly on the operational and strategic scale, with the participation of almost all types of armed forces and types of troops" (I.I. Iakubovskii, ed., *Boevoe sodruzhestvo bratskikh narodov i armii* [The combat confederation of the fraternal peoples and armies] (Moscow: Voenizdat, 1975), p. 151).

20. Semiriaga, *Zarozhdenie,* pp. 363-64.

21. A.A. Epishev (USSR) and Velko Panin (Bulgaria), eds., *Naveki vmeste* [Forever together] (Moscow: Voenizdat, 1969), p. 287.

22. A.A. Grechko, "Patrioticheskii i internatsional'nyi dolg Vooruzhennykh sil SSSR" [The patriotic and internationalist duty of the armed forces of the USSR] *Krasnaia Zvezda,* October 6, 1961, p. 3.

23. Frank Gibney, ed., *The Penkovskii Papers* (New York: Doubleday, 1965), p. 245. In the "memoirs" attributed to Col. Oleg Penkovskii, a Soviet officer who allegedly worked for Western intelligence services, Penkovskii offers the following comment on the first WTO joint maneuver of 1961: "Soviet troop maneuvers will be conducted jointly with the troops of the people's democracies. During maneuvers the divisions of the satellite countries are included in the T/O of the Soviet Army. This is necessary because we still do not trust them; they might turn their guns against the Soviets or run to the West." If this statement, attributed to Penkovskii, is genuine, and if it actually reflects official military thinking on the exercises, it would logically follow that the Soviets might be equally concerned about the reliability of divisions or regiments of Lithuanians, Latvians, Estonians, Moldavians and other Soviet nationalities operating on East Europe soil.

24. *Dictionary of Basic Military Terms: A Soviet View* (Washington: U.S. Government Printing Office, no date), p. 219.

25. Ibid., p. 128.

26. Ibid., p. 144.

27. Ibid.

28. Ibid., p. 213.

29. Graham H. Turbiville, Jr., "Soviet Bloc Maneuvers," *Military Review* 58, (August 1978).

30. In the GDR *Volksarmee* 25 (1969), Maj. Gen. Fleisswehr of the GDR lists a total of 40 joint exercises in the period from 1964-68 conducted between the National People's Army of the GDR and the Group of Soviet Forces in Germany. Turbiville, who cites this article in his study, does not speculate how many, if any, of these 40 are included in his list of 36; I am not able to guess how many are included in my list of 72. Fleisswehr, a GDR Deputy Minister of Defense in 1969, breaks down the 40 as follows: 10 joint command staff exercises for higher staffs; 10 staff-command exercises using one German and one Soviet division; 16 joint ground forces maneuvers and 4 joint naval and air exercises. My list of 72 indicates that for the period of 1964-68 the service branches of the GDR participated in 13 WTO exercises, but I cannot determine if the Soviet forces which participated in the ground forces exercises always included units from the Group of Soviet Forces in Germany, as specified by Fleisswehr.

Epishev and Palin, eds., *Naveki vmeste,* p. 289, reports that "in recent years" joint Soviet-Bulgarian exercises have been conducted "on the most diverse scales with the participation of ground forces, air forces and navies." But, apart from the 1958 Soviet-Bulgarian exercises in Bulgaria, the Soviets have reported only those in which they have claimed that Romania participated, a total of five.

A Soviet study of the Belorussian Military District noted that during the summer of 1967 one of the formations, the Irkutsk-Pinsk division, had participated in an exercise conducted on Polish soil with the Polish armed forces. This text also reported that "formations *[soedinenie]* and units *[chasti]* of the Belorussian Military District and the Polish armed forces have "more than once taken part in joint exercises and maneuvers" (A.G. Ovchinnikov, ed., *Krasnoznamennyi Belorusskkii voennyi okrug* [The red banner Belorussian Military District] (Minsk: Belarus, 1973), p. 501.) This study did not indicate however, how many times more than once. An article in *Krasnaia Zvezda,* October 12, 1975, p. 21, mentioned in passing the conduct of a joint exercise of Soviet and Polish tank companies in the Silesian Military District of Poland but did not indicate whether such exercises had taken place more than once.

A Czech officer mentioned an incident in a Soviet-Czechoslovak joint tactical exercise and then added, "Frequently the sub-units (*podrazdelenie*—translation: a battalion, a company, a platoon or a squadron) of the two friendly armies act in combat actions, constituting a monolithic striking force. See *Krasnaia Zvezda* October 10, 1972. On at least one other occasion (August 2, 1979), *Krasnaia Zvezda* has mentioned joint Soviet-Czechoslovak exercises at the *podrazdelenie* level and on at least one occasion (July 14, 1971) has mentioned the conduct of low-level Soviet-Hungarian tactical exercises.

31. See Table 1 for the exercises of May 14–19, 1969 and the exercises in the Carpathian Military District during the summer of 1973.

32. *Krasnaia Zvezda,* July 17, 1964.

33. Ibid., Sept. 21, 1966, p. 1.

34. See Chapter 7 for a discussion of the attempts of Czechoslovak political officers in 1968 to disengage their forces from the WTO in order to prepare them for independent combat missions.

35. For a further discussion of this and related events, see Christopher Jones, "Autonomy and Intervention: The CPSU and the Struggle for the Czechoslovak Communist Party, 1968," *Orbis* 19 (Summer, 1975).

36. Michel Tatu, "Arrivee des premieres troupes sovietiques qui coivent participer aux 'Exercises du pacte de Varsovie,'," *Le Monde,* May 31, 1968 in Tatu, *L'Heresie Impossible* (Paris: Editions Bernard Grassett, 1968), p. 115.

37. Ibid. Tatu cites as his source an article in the Czech journal *Literarni Listy.*

38. I.I. Iakubovskii, ed., *Boevoe sodruzhestvo bratskikh narodov i armii* [The Combat Confederation of the Fraternal Peoples and Armies] (Moscow: Voenizdat, 1975), p. 154.

39. See Chapter Two of this study.

40. See Chapter Two of this study.

41. See Chapter Two of this study.

42. *Pravda,* July 15, 1968, p.1.

43. *Pravda,* July 19, 1968, p. 1.

44.For a further discussion, see Jones, "Autonomy and Intervention."

45. *Krasnaia Zvezda,* July 24, 26, 31 and August 9, 1968.

46. *Krasnaia Zvezda,* August 20, 1968, p. 1.

47. Malcolm Mackintosh, "The Evolution of the Warsaw Pact," *Adelphi Paper,* 58 (June, 1969): 41.

48. For a further discussion of the role of WTO exercises in preparing for this invasion see General James H. Polk, "Reflections on the Czechoslovak Invasion," *Strategic Review* 5 (Winter, 1977).

49. *Pravda,* August 22, 1968, p.2.

50. See Jones, "Autonomy and Intervention."

51. Ibid.

52. *Krasnaia Zvezda,* October 19, 1962, p. 1. *Krasnaia Zvezda* stated the exercise was conducted "according to the plan of preparation of the United Armed Forces of the Warsaw Pact."

53. Ibid.

54. Col. D. Diev, Lt. Col. K. Spirov, "Combat Collaboration of the Armies of the Warsaw Pact States," *Voennaia Mysl'* 2 (1968) in CIA FBIS FPD 0049/69 *Selected Translations from Voennaia Mysl'* 25 April, 1969," p. 64. It is possible that because of typographical or other errors in either the original Soviet edition or the CIA translation the 1963 exercise referred to was in fact the 1962 exercise, which was not mentioned by Colonels Diev and Spirov, even though *Krasnaia Zvezda* reported this exercise. However, the list presented by Colonels Diev and Spirov mentions selected exercises in chronological order; in this order the Romanian-Soviet-Bulgarian exercise of 1963 is listed *after* the Sept. 1963 exercise in the GDR commanded by Heinz Hoffmann. Diev's list, like all other lists presented by WTO sources, is presented as a "for example" citation. A given WTO source invariably omits exercises mentioned by another WTO source.

55. See Table 1. These are the exercises of Feb. 1972 as cited by Turbiville (I have not been able to find Soviet or Romanian sources to confirm this); the exercise of February 12–21, 1973, and the exercise of February 17–22, both documented in Iakubovskii, ed., *Boevoe sodruzhestvo,* p. 293. Turbiville does not list either of these two exercises.

56. *Krasnaia Zvezda,* Sept. 22, 1964, p. 1.

57. Epishev and Panin, eds., *Naveki vmeste,* p. 290.

58. Ibid.

59. Epishev and Panin, eds., *Naveki vmeste,* p. 287.

60. Table 1: exercises of June 4–14, 1974.

61. Table 1.

62. See footnote No. 30.

63. See footnote No. 30.

64. See footnote No. 30.

65. See footnote No. 30.

66. Iakubovskii, ed., *Boevoe sodruzhestvo,* p. 158.

67. See the biography of P.F. Batitskii, *Sovetskaia voennaia entsiklopediia,* Vol. I. See also the discussion of the United Command in Chapter 4 of this study.

68. *Krasnaia Zvezda's* coverage of the exercises of October 16–22, 1965 and of the exercises of Sept. 21–28, 1969; see also Mackintosh, "The Evolution of the Warsaw Pact," p. 8. Also: "In the course of the maneuvers great attention is paid to the improvement of the interaction of allied armies, to carrying out marches in complex conditions; to the organization of counterblows, to the conduct of attacks, to the parrying of counterblows, *to the use of nuclear weapons* (my emphasis) and of paratroops" (Iakubovskii, *Boevoe sodruzhestvo,* p. 152).

69. Iakubovskii, *Boevoe sodruzhestvo,* p. 145.

70. P.A. Zhilin (USSR), E. Jadziac (Poland), eds., *Bratstvo po oruzhiiu* (Brotherhood in Arms] (Moscow: Voenizdat, 1975), p. 352.

71. Iakubovskii, *Boevoe sodruzhestvo,* p. 146 and pp. 290–93 for exercises of June 24–July 2, 1971; July 12–21, 1971; Feb. 28–March 4, 1972; Sept. 4–16, 1972; and Feb. 12–21, 1973. See also Table 1.

72. *Krasnaia Zvezda,* Sept. 29, 1969 and Sept. 10, 1976.

73. See Zhilin and Jadziak, eds., *Bratstvo po oruzhiiu,* pp. 353–55, and P.A. Zhilin (USSR) and F. Gefurt (Czechoslovakia), *Na vechnye vremena* [For Eternity] (Moscow: Voenizdat, 1975), pp. 306–7.

74. Iakubovskii, *Boevoe sodruzhestvo,* p. 152.

75. Ibid., p. 155.

76. *Krasnaia Zvezda,* Sept. 26, 1969.

77. N. Taratorin, "V ediom stroiu—k edinoi tseli" [In One Battle Order— For a One Purpose] in *Na boevom postu: kniga o voinakh Gruppy sovetskikh voisk v Germanii* [At the battle station: a book about the soldiers of the Group of Soviet Forces in Germany], ed. E.F. Ivanovski, (Moscow: Voenizdat, 1975), p. 291.

78. Zhilin and Gefurt, eds., *Na vechnye vremena,* p. 307.

79. *Krasnaia Zvezda,* October 10, 1970.

80. Col. V. Semin in S.K. Il'in et al. eds., *Partiino-politicheskaia rabota v Sovetskikh vooruzhennyhj silakh* [Party-Political Work in the Soviet Armed Forces] (Moscow: Voenizdat, 1974), p. 591.

81. The Iakubovskii text declares that "according to the results of the exercises theoretical conclusions are reached and practical recommendations are made for introduction into the conduct of troop training" (Iakubovskii, *Boevoe sodruzhestvo,* p. 150). Some of the other sources which testify to this link read as follows: "During this time [1955–70] in the mutual relations among the fraternal armies there has developed an harmonious system of the coordination of the training of the troops and staffs in which a special role is assigned to the joint exercises" (Editorial, *Krasnaia Zvezda,* October 21, 1970); "Joint exercises take place annually according to an agreed-upon plan. It is necessary to emphasize that great attention is devoted in the United Armed Forces to the exchange of experience of the training of soldiers and sailors. The national and United Commands, the commanders and staffs of the allied armies share everything which is best in the combat and political training of personnel, and in the method of training and in the educational-material base. The United Command and the Staff of the United Armed Forces generalize the leading experience of the allied armed forces and share it for the achievements of all commanders, staffs and troops" (Iakubovskii, *Boevoe sodruzhestvo,* p. 160); "According to the results of exercises and maneuvers, necessary conclusions are drawn and then recommendations are made for introduction into the practice of troop training" (Gen. Josef Kaminski of Poland, deputy Chief of Staff of the UAF in *Krasnaia Zvezda,* Sept. 8, 1976); "The goal of these exercises is the evaluation of the training of troops in 1969..." (Communique on the Oder-Neisse exercise of 1969 in *Krasnaia Zvezda,* Sept. 20, 1969); "The United Command accords great significance to the conduct of joint measures in the operational and combat training of the allied forces because these measures and especially troop exercises permit us to decide the important questions of the working out of interaction, the exchange of experience and the achievement of mutual understanding....This exercise was preceded by the all-round training of troops, fleets, and aviation and of generals and officers and of organs of the rear..." (Editorial, *Krasnaia Zvezda,* Sept. 28, 1969).

82. The Iakubovskii text usually describes each of these meetings as assemblies of the "leading staff" of the WTO armies who meet to discuss "combat and operational training." The wording used to describe these meetings from 1963–69 is virtually identical with the wording used to describe joint sessions of the "leading staff" of the WTO armies and the Military Council in the period beginning in 1969. These post-1969 sessions are specifically identified as discussion of the exercises of a given year for the purpose of preparing the training programs and exercises of the coming year. For the descriptions of the post-1969 sessions see p. 144 and pp. 288–93. The descriptions of the pre-1969 meetings are as follows in the Iakubovskii text: p. 283: Feb. 28, 1963, in Warsaw, a meeting of WTO defense ministers to consider "plans for measures for coordinating military training in 1963." No meeting is mentioned for 1964. On p. 284: Meeting of Nov. 24–25, 1965, in Warsaw of "Representatives of the leadership of the armies of the member states of the Warsaw Pact at which were discussed questions of combat training and combat readiness." See p. 285 for meeting of Nov. 14–17, 1966, in Budapest "of representatives of the armed forces of the member states of the Warsaw Pact at which were discussed questions connected with the operational activity, combat training and combat readiness of troops." See p. 285 for meeting of Nov. 13–17, 1976, in Dresden of "the leading staff of the armed forces of the Warsaw Pact at which were discussed questions of the raising of combat readiness and the level of operational and combat readiness of troops . . . and tasks were designated for 1968." See p. 286 for meeting of Nov. 26–29, 1968 in Bucharest "of the leading staff of the armies of the member states of the Warsaw Pact at which were considered questions of the combat training of troops and the further strengthening of the defensive capabilities of the allied states."

83. "It has already become a tradition that at the end of each year there are combined sessions of the Military Council to which in an all-round manner are considered the results of combat and operational training during the preceding year and the tasks are designated for troops and fleets for the subsequent training year. Such sessions are conducted jointly with meetings of the leading staff of the allied armies" (*Ibid.,* p. 145).

84. See Chapter 5 of this study.

85. Iakubovskii, *Boevoe sodruzhestvo,* p. 144. See also discussion of these officers in Chapter 5 of this study.

86. Ibid.

87. See Chapter 5 of this study for a discussion of this convention and related devices assuring Soviet control over the central agencies of the WTO.

88. Iakubovskii, *Boevoe sodruzhestvo,* p. 151.

89. *Krasnaia Zvezda,* Oct. 7, 1970.

90. *Ibid.,* October 20, 1970. See also the editorial of July 10, 1978: "An exercise is the highest form of training and education, and the most important means of raising field, air and naval mastery. It is difficult to overestimate their role in the improvement of the mastery of commanders and staffs in the administration of troops, the forces of the fleets and in the increase of the coordination of subunits, units and ships in the strengthening of discipline and organization."

91. *Krasnaia Zvezda,* Oct. 23, 1965; several issues during the coverage of the Shield 76 exercises, Sept. 9–15, 1976; several issues during the 1969 Oder-Neisse exercises, Sept. 21–28, 1969; and several issues during the Brotherhood in Arms exercises, Oct. 12–18, 1970.

92. *Krasnaia Zvezda,* October 7, 1980.

93. Western observers of WTO exercises either ignore the political aspects of the exercises or mention them only in passing. "From 1961 onwards the Pact organized a series of multi-lateral military exercises, many of which were well publicized . . . most of them amounting in practice to large-scale politico-military demonstrations emphasizing the enthusiasm, interalliance solidarity and friendship of the component national armies" (Malcolm Mackintosh, "The Warsaw Pact Today," *Survival* 16 [May–June 1974] p. 122).

94. See *Krasnaia Zvezda*, October 10, 1962 for an account of the exercises in Poland; see *Krasnaia Zvezda*, October 20, 1962 for an account of the exercises in Romania.

95. See Grechko's article in *Krasnaia Zvezda*, Oct. 6, 1961, p. 3. See also Chapter 7 of this study on the political directorate of the Warsaw Pact.

96. Semin in Il'in et al. eds., *Partiino-politicheskaia rabota*, p. 599.

97. P.I. Efimov, ed., *Boevoi soiuz bratskikh armii* [The combat union of the fraternal armies] (Moscow: Voenizdat, 1974), p. 29.

98. Semin in S.K. Il'in et al. eds., *Partiino-politicheskaia rabota*, p. 599.

99. Iakubovskii, ed., *Boevoe sodruzhestvo*, p. 263.

100. Semin in S.K. Il'in et al. eds., *Partiino-politicheskaia rabota*, pp. 600–1.

101. Zhilin and Jadziac, eds., *Bratstvo po oruzhiiu*, p. 355.

102. Zhilin and Gefurt, eds., *Na vechnye vremena*, p. 309.

103. *Krasnaia Zvezda*, July 14, 1971.

104. *Krasnaia Zvezda*, October 8, 1970.

105. Ibid.

106. *Krasnaia Zvezda*, Feb. 8, 1979.

107. *Krasnaia Zvezda*, October 8, 1970.

108. "My stali lushche videt" [We have begun to see better] *Krasnaia Zvezda*, Sept. 10, 1968, p. 3.

109. N.T. Panferov et al. eds., *Odesskii krasnoznamennyi* [The red banner Odessa Military District] (Kishinev, Kartiia Moldoveniaske, 1975), p. 280.

110. Ibid., p. 90.

Notes to Chapter Five

1. I.I. Iakubovskii et al., eds., *Boevoe sodruzhestvo bratskikh armii i narodov* [The combat confederation of the fraternal armed forces and peoples] (Moscow: Voenzidat, 1975), p. 286.

2. Ibid.

3. N.N. Rodionov et al., eds., *Organizatsiia Varshavskogo dogovora, 1955–75: dokumenty i materialy* [The Warsaw Treaty Organization, 1955–75: documents and materials] (Moscow: Politizdat, 1975), p. 114.

4. Ibid.

5. The Pact foreign ministers met as a body on Oct. 31, 1969; June 22, 1970; Feb. 19, 1971; Dec. 1, 1971; Jan. 17, 1973. The vice foreign ministers of the Pact met on May 22, 1969; Jan. 28, 1970; April 24, 1973; Feb. 1, 1975. For the communiques of these meetings see the materials in Rodionov et al. eds., *Organizatsiia*.

6. For example, at the November 1978 session of the PCC.

7. For a discussion of Romania's obduracy, see Robin Remington, *The Warsaw Pact* (Cambridge, Mass: MIT Press, 1971).

8. See the text of the Convention in Rodionov et al., eds., *Organizatsiia*, pp. 160–64.

9. Ibid.

10. A number of statements by Ceausescu suggest that the Romanians have used the ratification procedure for backing out of the commitment made by the Romanian vice foreign minister in 1973 when he signed the Convention. These statements may also apply to other documents agreed to by other Pact members. At the November 1978 session of the Political Consultative Committee, Romania refused to endorse the Mid-East policy adopted by the other six members of the Pact. For the first time in the history of the Pact, the other six, acting as six states rather than as a majority in the Warsaw Pact PCC, issued a separate statement at a PCC session. Judging by Ceausescu's other statements (See Patrick Moore, "The Ceausescu Saga," Radio Free Europe Research RAD Background Report, Romania, 275, Dec. 20, 1978) the six other members of the PCC also adopted a resolution, binding on the six only, to increase defense expenditures and to further tighten integration of the WTO command structure. In justifying Romania's refusal to accept these decisions as binding on the Romanian armed forces, Ceausescu repeatedly referred to the supremacy of Romanian constitutional procedures over Romanian military forces. In remarks to Romanian workers on November 25, Ceausescu said that he could not commit the Romanian army to any joint actions in the WTO "except on the basis of laws, the constitution and approval by the party–state bodies and approval, in the final analysis, by all our people." (Moore, "Ceausescu Saga," p. 3.) In an address to the Romanian Central Committee on Nov. 29 he said, ". . . I wish to say most clearly, [here] at the Plenary Meeting of the Central Committee . . . that nobody can sign documents which commit our State, our army otherwise but in conformity with the provisions of the Constitution, with the Defense Law, with the laws of the country. Neither the General Secretary, nor the President of the country, nor the Supreme Commander and nobody else can sign documents or pledges on behalf of the country unless they accord with the Constitution of the country, with the laws of the state!" ("Speech by Nicolae Ceausescu, General Secretary of the Romanian Communist Party at Plenary Meeting of the CC of the RCP" in *Romania: Documents/Events,* 48, Nov. 1978 (Bucharest: Agerpress.), p. 12.)

11. *Organizatsiia,* Rodionov et al., eds., pp. 160–64.

12. Ibid.

13. Ibid.

14. Ibid.

15. See Article 11 of the original Warsaw Treaty in Rodionov et al., eds., *Organizatsiia,* p. 9.

16. *Organizatsiia,* Rodionov et al., eds., pp. 160–64.

17. "The composition of the CDM inclues ministers of defense, the Commander-in-Chief and the Chief of Staff of the United Armed Forces" (*Sovetskaia voennaia entsiklopediia (SVE)* Vol. 5, (Moscow: Voenizdat, 1978), p. 682). The communiques issued by sessions of the CDM usually mention the presence of the WTO Commander-in-Chief and Chief of Staff. For these communiques from 1969 to 1975 see Rodionov et al., eds., *Organizatsiia,* pp. 123, 124, 142, 158, 159, 170, 182.

18. Iakubovskii, *Boevoe sodruzhestvo,* p. 142.

19. S.M. Shtemenko, "Bratsvo rozhdennoe v boiu," [Brotherhood Born in Battle] *Za rubezhom [Abroad]* 19 (1976): 7.

20. See the chronology of CDM Sessions in Rodionov et al., eds., *Organizatsiia,* pp. 187–93.

21. Iakubovskii, *Boevoe sodruzhestvo,* p. 142.

22. Ibid., p. 145.

23. Ibid.

24. See these communiques in Rodionov et al., eds., *Organizatsiia,* pp. 123, 124, 142, 158, 159, 170, 182. The chronology in the Iakubovskii text gives a shorter, but essentially identical account of each of these sessions, as does the text's brief discussion of the CDM on p. 142.

25. See the discussion of the United Command later in the chapter.

26. Iakubovskii, *Boevoe sodruzhestvo,* p. 144.

27. See the communique in *Krasnaia Zvezda,* July 27, 1960. This statement did note that the Political Consultative Committee had granted Konev's request that he retire, but it did not indicate whether the PCC formally appointed Grechko. There is no record of the PCC having met during 1960 to accept Konev's resignation or to appoint Grechko.

28. See *Krasnaia Zvezda,* July 8, 1967 and January 9, 1977.

29. Iakubovskii, *Boevoe sodruzhestvo,* p. 143; *SVE,* Vol. 5, p. 682.

30. Ibid.

31. Ibid.; for a listing of these personnel in 1975 see Lawrence Caldwell, "The Warsaw Pact: Directions of Change," *Problems of Communism* 24 (Sept.-Oct., 1975): 8.

32. Central Intelligence Agency, "USSR: Organization of the Ministry of Defense CR 78-15257, Dec., 1978."

33. *SVE,* Vol. 1, p. 408.

34. "Reshenie o sozdanii ob"edinennogo komandovaniia...." [Resolution on the establishment of the united command....] May 14, 1955, in Rodionov et al., eds., *Organizatsiia,* p. 11.

35. See Appendix to this volume.

36. P.A. Zhilin (USSR) and E. Jadziak (Poland), eds., *Bratstvo po oruzhiiu [Brotherhood in arms]* Moscow: Voenizdat, 1975), p. 369.

37. Iakubovskii, *Boevoe sodruzhestvo,* p. 161.

38. *SVE,* Vol. 2, p. 615.

39. See Appendix to this volume.

40. Ibid.

41. Iakubovskii, *Boevoe sodruzhestvo,* p. 158.

42. Ibid., pp. 143-44.

43. See Central Intelligence Agency, "Organization of the Ministry of Defense CR 78-15257 Dec. 1978." For Bulgaria: Col. Gen. Kh. M. Ambarian; for the GDR: Gen. I. Ye. Shavrov; for Poland, Gen. A.F. Shcheglov; for Romania: Lt. Gen. V.K. Diatlenko; for Czechoslovakia: Gen. D.I. Litovtsev. The Sept. 21, 1971, issue of *Krasnaia Zvezda* identified the liaison representative to the GDR at that time as Col. Gen. A.S. Burdeinyi; *Rude Pravo* of Sept. 14, 1974 identified the representative to Czechoslovakia at that time as Col. Gen. K.G. Kozhanov. H.F. Scott, *Armed Forces of the USSR,* (Boulder, Colo.: Westview Press, 1979), p. 205, lists all the liaison representatives for 1979, but does not give the source of this information.

44. Iakubovskii, *Boevoe sodruzhestvo,* p. 145.

45. Ibid., p. 145 and *SVE,* Vol. 5, p. 682.

46. See A.A. Grechko et al., eds., *Velikaia pobeda Sovetskogo naroda 1941-1945* [The great victory of the Soviet people, 1941-1945] (Moscow: Nauka, 1976), p. 574.

47. Z. Studzinski, "Nash neruzhimyi boevoi soiuz" [Our unbreakable combat alliance], *Krasnaia Zvezda,* March 28,1975, p. 3.

48. Iakubovskii, *Boevoe sodruzhestvo,* p. 148.

49. Ibid., p. 161.

50. Iakubovskii, "XXV s"ezd KPSS i ukreplenie boevogo sodruzhestva armii stran varshavskogo dogovora" [The 25th Congress of the CPSU and the strengthening of the combat confederation of the armed forces of the countries of the Warsaw Pact] *Voenno-istoricheskii zhurnal* [The Military Historical Journal] 8 (1976): 12.

51. Iakubovskii, *Boevoe sodruzhestvo,* p. 148.

52. A.A. Epishev (USSR) and Velko Panin (Bulgaria), eds., *Naveki vmeste* (Moscow: Voenizdat, 1969), p. 296.

53. Studzinski in *Krasnaia Zvezda,* March 28, 1975, p. 3; Iakubovskii, *Boevoe sodruzhestvo,* (1975), p. 146; Maj. Gen. M. Titov, "Nadezhnyi oplot sotsializma" [The reliable bulwark of socialism] *Krasnaia Zvezda,* January 9, 1976, p. 3.

54. *SVE,* Vol. 5, p. 682.

55. See Studzinski, "Nash neruzhimyi boevoi soiuz," *Krasnaia Zvezda,* March 28, 1974, p. 3.

56. Directly following its brief mention of the Technical Committee, the text declares in the next paragraph: "For the successful fulfillment of the tasks placed on the Staff and other organs of leadership of the United Armed Forces, these organs have been accorded legal competence, privileges and immunities which have been designated by a special convention concluded among the member governments of the Warsaw Pact in 1973" (Iakubovskii, *Boevoe sodruzhestvo,* p. 146).

57. "The Technical Committee is mainly concerned with the tasks connected with the development and improvement of weapons and technology, and the coordination of the efforts of the allied armies in the area of scientific research and experimental design work" (Ibid.).

58. Ibid. Also: "With the Soviet Union's assistance, there is being set up in Poland the manufacture of various types of arms and military equipment.Poland's defense industry is now producing ships, jet aircraft, tanks, trucks, radar sets and so forth" (I.I. Iakubovskii, "The Fraternal Polish Troops After Half a Century," in the classified journal *Voennaia Mysl'* 10 (1968) translated and released by the Central Intelligence Agency in CIA FBIS FPD 00844/69 Sept. 4, 1969, *Selected Translations from Voennaia Mysl',* p. 65).

59. Iakubovskii, *Boevoe sodruzhestvo,* chap. 8, pp. 170–242.

60. Col. Gen. P.I. Efimov et al., eds., *Boevoi soiuz bratskikh armii* [The combat union of the fraternal armed forces] (Moscow: Voenizdat, 1974), p. 30. Iakubovskii, *Boevoe sodruzhestvo,* pp. 167–68 discusses the SCFAF as if it were exclusively a Warsaw Pact agency.

61. *SVE,* Vol. 7, p. 499.

62. See *Sovetskii sport,* July 19, 1974.

63. *SVE,* Vol. 7, p. 499 lists the total of sports competitions in the period 1958–78; Iakubovskii, *Boevoe sodruzhestvo,* p. 167 and *Krasnia Zvezda,* Feb. 20, 1977, p. 4 provide information indicating the upsurge of SCFAF activity after 1969.

64. *SVE,* Vol. 7, p. 449.

65. Iakubovskii, *Boevoe sodruzhestvo,* p. 168.

66. See the text of the Convention in *Organizatsiia,* eds. Rodionov et al., pp. 160-64; see Iakubovskii, *Boevoe sodruzhestvo,* p. 146; see *SVE,* Vol. 5, p. 682.

67. "The Marxist-Leninist parties organize exchanges of experience not only among the armies and navies of the allied states, but also with the troop formations of the people's militia, the organs of security and the border troop" (M.S. Kirichenko, *Na strazhe mira* [Guarding the peace] (Minsk: Belarus, 1975), p. 146).

68. *SVE,* Vol. 5, p. 682.

69. International Institute of Strategic Studies (IISS), *The Military Balance, 1978-79* (London: IISS, 1978), p. 9.

70. Ibid.

71. Ibid., pp. 9, 108, 109.

72. Ibid., p. 109.

73. Ibid., pp. 13-15.

74. "The formations and units of each country which are best prepared and best equipped make up the corpus of the UAF" (*SVE,* Vol. 5, p. 682).

75. Ibid., p. 15.

76. Ibid., p. 33.

77. Ibid., pp. 13-15.

78. See E.F. Ivanovskii et al., eds., *Na boevom postu: kniga o voinakh Gruppy sovetskikh voisk v Germanii* [At the battle station: a book about the soldiers of the Group of Soviet Forces in Germany] (Moscow: Voenizdat, 1975), pp. 268-318. See also P.I. Efimov et al., eds., *Boevoi soiuz,* pp. 127-28 for a discussion of the joint alliance activites of the Group of Soviet Forces in Germany; pp. 160-61 for a discussion of the similar activities of the Northern Force Group in Poland; p. 95 for the Southern Force Group in Hungary; see p. 254 and 262-63 for discussion of the activities of the Central Force Group in Czechoslovakia.

79. See Table 1 in Chapter 4 for the exercise in the summer 1973.

80. V.I. Varennikov et al., eds., *Krasnoznammenyi pricarpatskii* [The red banner Carpathian military district] (L'vov: Izdatel'stvo 'Kameniar', 1976), p. 188 and ff.

81. Ibid.

82. Ibid.

83. "The fraternal ties between our country and the countries of the socialist confederation and among the armed forces of the member states of the Warsaw Pact have become an important part of the political life of the soldiers of the district. Using these ties, the commanders, political workers and party organizations constantly conduct extensive work in the training of soldiers in the spirit of patriotism and socialist internationalism and of high responsibility for the security of our Fatherland and of the fraternal countries in the spirit of constant readiness to come to the defense of the gains of socialism" (Ibid., p. 188).

84. I.M. Tretiak et al., eds., *Krasnoznammenyi Belorusskii voennyi okrug* [The red banner Belorussian military district] (Minsk: Izdatel'stvo 'Belarus', 1973), p. 501.

85. Ibid., p. 505.

86. Ibid., p. 501

87. Ibid., p. 502.

88. Ibid.

89. Ibid., p. 503.

90. "The growing ties between our country and the other socialist countries, and among the armed forces of the Warsaw Pact have had a direct and deep

influence on the political training of the troop personnel of the Red Banner Belorussian Military District. The most important direction of the ideological work of commanders, political organs and party organizations is the formation in soldiers, non-commissioned officers and officers of the noble qualities of patriot–internationalists and of cultivation of a high responsibility for the peace and security of the fraternal countries and of the readiness to render aid to the friendly peoples and governments which are struggling against imperialism. For example, this work is consciously and purposefully carried out in the Rogachevskii Guards Division. Here, active propaganda is carried out concerning the successes of the workers of the fraternal countries. In political activities, in lectures and discussions, propagandists discuss in detail with the troops the struggle of the party for the strengthening and unification of the world system of socialism; they also discuss in detail the life, military training and special features of the armies of the socialist states. In the Lenin rooms and clubs thematic evening programs and afternoon programs are systematically conducted and there are meetings with participants of the liberation of the fraternal countries . . . The Guards Rogachevskii Division personnel actively maintain ties with one of the divisions of the Polish Army and the workers of the Lublin district, which was liberated by units of the [Rogachevskii] Division from the German-Fascist invaders" (Ibid., p. 504).

91. Ibid., p. 505.

92. I.M. Voloshin et al., eds., *Odesskii krasnoznamennyi* [The red banner Odessa military district] (Kishinev: Izdatel'stvo 'Kartia moldoveiaske', 1975), p. 278.

93. Ibid., p. 283.

94. Ibid., pp. 280, 281, 283.

95. Ibid., p. 283.

96. "Following the decrees of the party, the Armed Forces of the USSR at all stages of their development strive to be a model of devotion to the principles of proletarian internationalism. Multi-faceted and purposefully directed political education work among the personnel is carried out. It is conducted by commanders, political workers and party and *komsomol* organizations. A definite experience in the internationalist training of soldiers has been acquired among the troops of the Red Banner Odessa Military District . . ." (Ibid., p. 276) and "In political exercises artillery personnel have become thoroughly acquainted with the life and work of the fraternal peoples of the countries of socialism and with the special features of the military service of their armed defenders. A good source for the deepening of the knowledge of soldiers are political information meetings, thematic evening programs devoted to important dates and events in the histories of the socialist confederation, collective viewing of films and corresponding television broadcasts, and the substantive lectures and speeches of experienced propagandists" (Ibid., p. 277).

97. Ibid., p. 281.

Notes to Chapter Six

1. For a discussion of the role of this agency in the Soviet Armed Forces see Harriet Fast Scott, "The Making of Soviet Doctrine," an unpublished paper presented at a Harvard University seminar, March 13, 1978 sponsored jointly by the Center for Science and International Affairs, the Center for International Affairs and the Russian Research Center. According to Scott, the Military Science Directorate of the Soviet General Staff serves as a clearinghouse for the doctrinal treatises produced by the General Staff, the staffs of the Soviet service branches, the faculty of the Voroshilov General Staff Academy, and the faculties of other military academies, in particular, the Frunze and Lenin academies. Much of the material in this paper is available in H.F. Scott and W.K. Scott, *The Armed Forces of the USSR,* (Boulder, Colorado: Westview Press, 1979), chaps. 2, 3.

2. See A.A. Grechko, ed., *Sovetskaia voennaia entsiklopediia (SVE)* [Soviet Military Encyclopedia], Vol. 1, pp. 525-28 for the article on *boevoe sodruzhestvo.* This is a technical term. An accurate translation is "the combat confederation of the armed forces of the members of the socialist confederation." WTO sources, such as Marshal I.I. Iakubovskii's *Boevoe sodruzhestvo bratskikh narodov i armii* [The combat confederation of the fraternal armed forces and peoples (Moscow: Voenizdat, 1975) use this term interchangeably with the term "Warsaw Pact," but prefer the term "boevoe sodruzhestvo" because it specifies commitments and obligations more binding than those required in the text of the Warsaw Treaty of 1955. In its article on "boevoe sodruzhestvo," *Sovetskaia voennaia entsiklopediia,* Vol. 1 (Moscow: Voenizdat, 1976) which is signed by Marshal Iakubovskii, states on p. 525: "Boevoe sodruzhestvo is a form of relations among the armed forces of the socialist states. . . . The combat confederation of the armed forces of the socialist confederation is characterized by all-round cooperation and close ties embracing all sides of the life and activity of the fraternal armed forces. . . . The combat confederation of the armed forces of the members of the socialist confederation is clearly manifested in the relations among the armed forces of the fraternal defensive alliance — the Warsaw Pact."

3. Ibid., p. 527.

4. Col. V.F. Samoilenko, "Voennoe sodruzhestvo stran sotsializma." [The military confederation of the countries of socialism] in *Voina i armiia* [War and Armed Forces] eds., S.A. Tiushkevich et. al. (Moscow: Voenizdat, 1977), p. 373.

5. The great majority of the publicly identified conferences are on military-political themes, which by definition, are intended for public distribution. See Iakubovskii, *Boevoe sodruzhestvo,* pp. 160-63, which mentions a 1971 conference of the UAF Staff on "The Historical Significance of the World System of Socialism and the Necessity of the Strengthening of the WTO in Light of the Decisions of the Congresses of the Fraternal Communist and Workers Parties"; an October, 1973 conference of the UAF Staff on "The Further Development of the Leninist Teaching on the Defense of the Socialist Fatherland and on the Decisions of the 24th Congress of the CPSU and the Congresses of the Communist and Workers' Movement" (p. 178); a 1970 conference in Prague of more than 100 Pact officers on rear services (p. 167). See also B. Bochkov, "Sfera bratskogo sotrudnichestva — ideologicheskaia rabota" [A Sphere of Fraternal Cooperation — Ideological Work] *Kommunist vooruzhennykh sil* [Communist of the armed forces] 6, (1977); 14 for mention of two military-political conferences to mark the

20th anniversary of the WTO; one in Moscow and another in Sofia. P.A. Zhilin (USSR) and F. Gefurt, (Czechoslovakia) *Na vechnye vremena* [For all time] (Moscow: Voenizdat, 1975), p. 304, mentions a 1970 conference in Prague devoted to the 15th anniversary of the WTO and the 25th anniversary of the victory of socialism in Czechoslovakia. P.A. Zhilin (USSR) and E. Jadziac (Poland), eds, *Bratstvo po oruzhiiu* [Brotherhood in arms] (Moscow: Voenizdat, 1975), p. 364, mentions a 1972 conference in Moscow on "The Military Cooperation of the Peoples of the USSR and Poland in the Struggle with Fascism During the Years of the Second World War and Its Significance for the Strengthening of Soviet-Polish Friendship." More general references to the regular conduct of conferences on military doctrine are in the following: Zhilin and Gefurt, eds., *Na vechnye vremena*; p. 303: "Czechoslovakia and the other socialist countries jointly work out the important questions of the Marxist-Leninist teaching on war and armed forces and in this regard work out the problems of the essence, origins, character and contents of modern war and of the dependence of wars and armed forces on politics, economics and social conditions. They also work out the problems of the means and forms of armed struggle. On these and other important problems there is a broad exchange of opinions at military-scientific conferences, symposiums, and on the pages of military-theoretical publications and in the course of business-like contacts." See also A.A. Epishev (USSR) and Velko Panin (Bulgaria), eds., *Naveki vmeste* [Forever together] (Moscow: Voenizdat, 1969), p. 296: "Every year in accordance with the policy of the Staff of the United Armed Forces, the Ministry of Defense of the USSR, the General Staff of the USSR, and the Main Political Administration of the USSR [note that this quotation refers to the period before the 1969 reforms, which probably established a WTO directorate for doctrine, a directorate for political administrations and strengthened the staff of the UAF] a great quantity of consultations are conducted for the military specialists of the socialist countries...." See also the article by the UAF Deputy Chief, Vice Admiral Studzinski of Poland, "Nash neruzhimyi boevoi soiuz" [Our unbreakable combat alliance] *Krasnaia Zvezda*, March 28, 1975, p. 3. The Admiral briefly identifies cooperation in military theory as one of the main forms of WTO activity then adds, "It should be mentioned again that there are military-scientific and scholarly conferences at which questions of the revolution in military affairs [technological changes] are examined."

6. Iakubovskii, *Boevoe sodruzhestvo,* p. 164.

7. "There is great significance for the purpose of improving the training of troops of such forms of exchange among the allied armies as training manuals, regulations, periodicals, textbooks and the lecturers of military-educational institutions. After the allied armed forces began the study of the conduct of the military actions of troops in the conditions of the application of weapons of mass destruction by the probable enemy, the Armed Forces of the Soviet Union gave them a great quantity of military literature in which is revealed the experience of the training of troops in new conditions. The most recent Soviet manuals, regulations and programs which express the up-to-date achievements of science and technology and also the experience of the education of Soviet soldiers and sailors have been given. In recent times, in connection with the transmittal to the allied armed forces of new, more modern forms of weapons and combat technology, they have been given a significant quantity of military-technical literature. During the period from 1955-59 alone, they received about 100,000 titles of military and

military-technical literature" (Iakubovskii, *Boevoe sodruzhestvo*, p. 161).

8. H. Hoffmann, "Vernost 'internatsional' nomu dolgu" [Fidelity to internationalist duty] *Krasnaia Zvezda,* March 1, 1976, p. 3.

9. "...the allied armed forces rely most of all on Soviet military science, on the military-scientific base of the Soviet armed forces, which possess the greatest possibilities for the development of the theory and practice of military affairs" (Iakubovskii, *Boevoe sodruzhestvo,* p. 162).

10. A.A. Grechko, "Boevoe sodruzhestvo armii sotsialisticheskikh gosudarstv" [The combat confederation of the armed forces of the socialist states] *Kommunist* 15 (1972); 47.

11. *SVE,* Vol. 3, p. 229: The quotation continues: "The military doctrines of the socialist confederation, their views on the character and goals of a future war, and on the basic questions of the organization and development of national defense systems and military art have common social, economic, political, and moral bases." These terms have very specific meanings, which this chapter will examine below.

12. *SVE,* Vol. 7, p. 563.

13. In some issues of the classified Soviet journal, *Voennaia Mysl'* [Military thought], which the Central Intelligence Agency translated and made public, several authors discuss how Soviet doctrine serves to integrate the Soviet Armed Forces with the militaries of East Europe. In the article, *"Honvedele* — The Military Organ of the Hungarian People's Army," *Voennaia Mysl'* 7 (1967) translated in CIA FBIS FPD 0120/68 *Selected Translations from Voennaia Mysl',* July 30, 1968, V. Kutsenko reviews an article on military doctrine in a Hungarian military journal. Kutsenko writes on p. 93 of the CIA translation: "In this same [Hungarian] article it is stated that the military doctrines of the socialist confederation express a common point of view on the responsibility for the defense of the camp of socialism. Its basis is the military doctrine of the Soviet Union, the leading state of the camp of socialism. It comprehensively and most completely reflects the views of socialist states regarding the development of the armed forces and their use in the event of necessity. Soviet military doctrine takes into account the integration of the countries of the socialist camp in the struggle against imperialist aggression and thus has definite influence on the execution of these countries' general military tasks. The military doctrines of the socialist states are common to each other on the basis of their socio-political content, because they are all based on the foundation of Marxist-Leninist teaching on war and the military and on socialist military science. But this does not exclude the fact that each of them chooses its own doctrine. Furthermore, the doctrine can have differences in the military-technical sense. This is caused by the level of development of productive forces in a given country as well as by its historical, geographical and national peculiarities."

In "Soviet Military Doctrine and Strategy," *Voennaia Mysl'* 5 (May 1969), translated in CIA FB is FPD 0116/69 *Selected Translations from Voennaia Mysl'* Dec. 18, 1969. General S. Ivanov writes on pp. 44-45 of the CIA translation, "Soviet military doctrine is a system of scientifically based views on questions of military policy, the organization of the armed forces and the preparation of the country for the triumphant waging of any war in defense of the interests of the Soviet Union and the countries of the socialist confederation. Our armed forces have been created and are being maintained for the protection of the Soviet state and other socialist states from imperialist aggression."

In "The Ideological Foundation of the Military Unity of Socialist Countries," *Voennaia Mysl'* No. 5, May 1969 in CIA FBIS FPD 0116/69 Dec. 18, 1969, p. 29, Maj. Gen. N. Kirayeyev and Col. A. Beshentsev write: "A strictly-scientific Marxist-Leninist methodology makes it possible productively to resolve the major problems of the military doctrines of the socialist states, the fundamental tenets of which are the same, for they express the common laws of development of the armies of the nations of the socialist confederation."

In a joint Soviet-Bulgarian study of Soviet-Bulgarian military cooperation, the bilateral editorial commission of this study writes: "A strictly scientific Marxist-Leninist approach to the working out of the question of the military affairs permits the resolution of the most important problems of the military doctrine [singular] of the fraternal socialist states, the principal postulates of which are common for all of them. The interests of the defense of the socialist confederation from the aggression of imperialist states demands the working out of a common view of the following basic questions: for what kind of war must the allied countries and their armed forces be prepared; what and how must be prepared in peacetime for the event of war; how to conduct a joint armed struggle in order to achieve victory over the united forces of an aggressor" (Gen. A.A. Epishev and Lt. Gen. Velko Palin, *Naveki Vmeste/Naveki Zaedno* [Together forever] (Moscow: Voenizdat, 1969, p. 284).

14. For a discussion of the relationship among these subfields, see the discussion of military art in *SVE*, Vol. 2, pp. 211-18; see also the separate discussion of military strategy, *SVE*, Vol. 7, pp. 555-65; operational art, *SVE*, Vol. 6, pp. 53-57; and tactics *SVE*, Vol. 7, pp. 628-33.

15. *SVE*, Vol. 7, p. 556.

16. *SVE*, Vol. 6, p. 53.

17. Ibid.

18. *SVE*, Vol. 2, p. 188.

19. Iakubovskii, *Boevoe sodruzhestvo*, p. 162.

20. See eds. *Bratstvo po oruzhiiu*, eds. Zhilin and Jadziac, p. 352: "In the framework of the Warsaw Pact...questions linked with the collective working out of military strategy are decided, as are questions of operational art and tactics." See also Col. A. Dmitriev, "Po puti stroitel'stva razvitogo sotsializma" [On the path of the development of developed socialism], *Kommunist vooruzhennyk sil* [Communist of the armed forces] 15 (1976); 75: "...in the framework of the Warsaw Pact...there is a collective working out of common views in the areas of strategy, operational art and tactics..."

21. See Chapter 4 of this study.

22. See three works by Joseph Douglass, *The Soviet Theater Nuclear Offensive* (U.S. Government Printing Office, 1976) and *Soviet Strategy for Nuclear War* (Stanford, Calif.: Hoover Institution Press, 1979). *Soviet Military Strategy in Europe* (New York: Pergamon, 1980) See also Richard Pipes, "Why the Soviet Union Thinks It Could Fight and Win a Nuclear War," *Commentary* (July, 1977) 64. Much of the Soviet material on which these studies are based appears in the following: Harriet Fast Scott, ed., *Soviet Military Strategy* (English translation and collation of the three editions of V.D. Sokolovskii, *Voennaia strategiia*) (New York: Crane and Russak, 1975), A.A. Sidorenko, *The Offensive* (U.S. Air

Force translation of the Soviet work, *Nastuplenie*) (Washington: U.S. Government Printing Office, no date); also the "Selected Translations of *Voennaia Mysl'*, " a Soviet classified military journal, released by the CIA and FBIS. Available on microfilm from the Library of Congress.

23. See the article on military science in *SVE*, Vol. 2, p. 184; see the article on troop training in *SVE*, Vol. 5, p. 675.

24. *SVE*, Vol. 5, pp. 675-76.

25. *SVE*, Vol. 2, pp. 368-69.

26. *SVE*, Vol. 4, pp. 283-84.

27. *SVE*, Vol. 2, p. 184.

28. *SVE*. Vol. 2, p. 219.

29. *SVE*, Vol. 7, p. 580.

30. A.A. Grechko, "Boevoe sodruzhestvo armii sotsialisticheskikh gosudarstv" [The combat confederation of the armed forces of the socialist states], *Kommunist*, 15 (1972); 47: "An important element of the combat confederation is the unity of views on the theory and practice of *voennoe stroitel'stvo....*"

31. Dzur is quoted in Col. S. Sokolov, "Zhivotvornye idei boevogo bratstva" [The vital ideas of combat brotherhood] *Voenno-istoricheskii zhurnal* [The Military-Historical Journal] 6 (1977); 71.

32. "The military administration of the National People's Army is based on principles identical with Soviet military administration and the military administration of the armed forces of the other socialist countries" (P.I. Efimov, ed., *Boevoi soiuz bratskikh armii* [The combat alliance of the fraternal armed forces] (Moscow; Voenizdat, 1974), p. 106).

33. Epishev and Palin, eds., *Naveki vmeste*, pp. 284-85.

34. Ibid.

35. For an outline of the Soviet defense ministry and the Soviet service branches see the article on the USSR Ministry of Defense, *SVE*, Vol. 5, pp. 295-96; see also the article on the main and central administrations of the Soviet Defense Ministry in *SVE*, Vol. 2, p. 565. For partial identification of corresponding agencies in the East European armed forces see P.I. Efimov, ed., *Boevoi soiuz*, p. 47 for Bulgaria; pp. 72-72 for Hungary, pp. 103-4 for the GDR; pp. 142-44 for Poland; p. 252 for Czechoslovakia.

36. Ibid., p. 27: "There is a broad mutual exchange of military delegations on the most diverse levels..." See also M.S. Kirichenko, *Nadezhnyi strazh mira* [Reliable Guard of Peace] (Minsk: Belarus, 1975), p. 138: "In the armed forces of the countries of the Warsaw Pact there are all the objective and subjective conditions for the exchange of the theoretical and practical activity of commanders, political organs, party and youth organizations."

37. For example, see *Krasnaia Zvezda*, Oct. 11, 1977, for identification of a delegation to Moscow led by the Bulgarian Defense Minister, Dobri Dzhurov; see *Kommunist vooruzhennykh sil*, 77 (1977); 79 for mention of the visit of an analogous delegation to Sofia led by the Soviet Defense Minister, D.F. Ustinov; See Efimov, ed., *Boevoi soiuz*, p. 95 for mention of a 1973 visit to Hungary by A.A. Grechko; See Zhilin and Jadziac, *Bratstvo po oruzhiiu* for mention of visits

to the Soviet Union of the Polish defense minister in 1969 and 1974 and a visit to Poland in 1970 by the Soviet defense minister.

38. See Chapter 7 of this study.

39. See the volume on the youth organizations of the Warsaw Pact armies, *Soiuz boevoi* [The combat union] (Moscow: Voenzidat, 1975).

40. Efimov, ed., *Boevoi soiuz,* p. 29.

41. See Zhilin and Gefurt, eds., *Na vechnye vremena,* p. 308, for mention of the ties between the Soviet organization, DOSAAF, and its Czechoslovak counterpart, SVAZARM. See also the DOSAAF newspaper, *Sovetskii patriot* [Soviet Patriot] for occasional articles on the ties of DOSAAF to its analogous agencies in the Warsaw Pact.

42. See Efimov, ed., *Boevoe soiuz,* p. 29 where the author notes that during 1971-73 more than 100 East European military journalists studied the work of the Soviet military press and "about as many" Soviet journalists paid reciprocal visits to East European military press organs. Epishev and Palin, eds., *Naveki vmeste,* p. 205 mentions exchanges between analogous newspapers and journals of the Soviet and Bulgarian armed forces; Zhilin and Jadziac eds., *Bratstvo po oruzhiiu,* p. 363 mention regular exchanges between certain press organs of the Polish and Soviet armed forces. For a listing of the principal military periodicals of the WTO states see *SVE,* Vol. 3, p. 352-53.

43. See the discussion of these exchanges in Chapter 5 of this study.

44. See Chapter 3 of this study.

45. Maj. Gen. Aleksandr Vukotic, et. al., eds., *The Yugoslav Concept of General People's Defense* (Belgrade: Medunarodna Politika, 1970), p. 61.

46. See Chapter 3 of this study.

47. Michael Chechinski, "The Postwar Development of the Polish Armed Forces," (RAND Corp., forthcoming).

48. Ibid.

49. H.F. Scott and W.K. Scott in *The Armed Forces of the USSR,* pp. 41-42, date the reformulation of Soviet doctrine in its present form to December 1959.

50. V.D. Sokolovskii, ed., *Soviet Military Strategy* (in English) (Englewood Cliffs, N.J.: Prentice Hall, 1963), p. 495.

51. Ibid., Chapter 6.

52. The force of the military-political axioms of the Warsaw Treaty Organization (WTO) derives from that fact that these axioms have been incorporated into bilateral Soviet-East European treaties and into the party programs of Bulgaria, Hungary, the German Democratic Republic, Poland, and Czechoslovakia. Soviet military leaders have frequently called attention to the importance of this interlocking network of party and state documents that bind the WTO states to each other. See Iakubovskii, *Boevoe sodruzhestvo,* p. 110 and A.A. Epishev, *Partiia i armiia* [The party and the army] (Moscow: Politizdat, 1977), p. 321.

The bilateral treaties of the Soviet Union with the five loyal East European members of the Warsaw Pact contain five sets of commitments which endorse the military-political axioms of Soviet military doctrine. The single most important of these five sets of commitments is the commitment to the principle of the joint defense of the gains of socialism. The five sets of treaty commitments are:

1. commitments to "eternal and unbreakable" bilateral friendship and to membership in the socialist confederation on the basis of the shared principles of socialist internationalism. These commitments are proclaimed fully compatible with mutual respect for national independence and sovereignty.

2. commitments to observe the "obligations deriving from the Warsaw Treaty," which undoubtedly include the protocols to the Treaty such as the 1973 Convention, discussed in the chapter on the administrative agencies of the WTO.

3. commitments to give immediate military aid in the event of an armed attack on the other signatory of a bilateral treaty.

4. commitments to resist "the intrigues of imperialism and reaction" as part of a commitment to mutual pursuit of international peace and security. These commitments also oblige the signatories of bilateral treaties to work toward "general and complete disarmament."

5. commitments to "joint defense of the gains of socialism."

The bilateral treaties of the Soviet Union with the other members of the Warsaw Pact are contained in the series of volumes entitled *Sbornik deistvuiushchikh dogovorov, soglashenii i konventsii zakliuchennykh SSSR s inostrannymi gosudarstvami* [Collection of current treaties, agreements and conventions concluded by the USSR with foreign states] (Moscow: Ministerstvo inostrannykh del SSSR). This discussion below will cite the volumes of the series and the numbers of the treaty articles under consideration.

For the Soviet treaties with Bulgaria, Hungary, East Germany, Poland and Czechoslovakia the text of the relevant treaty articles is usually identical although the number of the treaty article may vary from treaty to treaty. The text of the Soviet-Bulgarian treaty is in Volume 25; of the Soviet-Hungarian treaty in Volume 25; of the Soviet-German Democratic Republic treaty in Volume 31; of the Soviet-Polish treaty in Volume 24; of the Soviet-Czechoslovak treaty in Volume 26.

For the treaty articles which establish the five sets of commitments mentioned above see the bilateral treaties of the USSR with the following:

Bulgaria. First set of commitments: Preamble and Article One. Second set of commitments: Article Six. Third set of commitments: Article Seven. Fourth set of commitments: Article Four. Fifth set of commitments: Bulgarian signature of the Bratislava Declaration of August 4, 1968.

Hungary. First set of commitments: Preamble and Article One. Second set of commitments: Article Five. Third set of commitments: Article Seven. Fourth set of commitments: Article Four. Fifth set of commitments: Hungarian signature of the Bratislava Declaration of August 4, 1968.

German Democratic Republic. First set of commitments: Preamble and Article One. Second set of commitments: Preamble and Article Six. Third set of commitments: Article Eight. Fourth set of commitments: Article Five. Fifth set of commitments: East German signature of the Bratislava Declaration of August 4, 1968, and from bilateral treaty, Preamble and Article Four.

Poland. First set of commitments: Preamble and Article One. Second set of commitments: Preamble. Third set of commitments: Articles Six and Seven. Fourth set of commitments: Article Four. Fifth set of commitments: Polish signature of the Bratislava Declaration of August 4, 1968, and Polish signature of the Joint Soviet-Polish Declaration of 1976, the text of which is available in *Vneneshnaia politika Sovetskogo Soiuza i mezhdunarodnye otnosheniia 1976 goda* [The foreign policy of the Soviet Union and international relations in 1976] (Moscow: Izdatel'stvo mezhdunarodnye otnoshenii, 1977), p. 153.

Czechoslovakia. First set of treaty commitments: Preamble and Article One. Second set of commitments: Preamble. Third set of commitments: Article Ten. Fourth Set of commitments: Article Seven. Fifth set of commitments: Czechoslovak signature of the Bratislava Declaration; Czechoslovak signature of the Soviet-Czechoslovak Treaty of October 18, 1968; and, in the 1970 Soviet-Czechoslovak treaty, Preamble and Article Five.

For restatements of most and usually all of these five sets of commitments in the party programs of the loyal East European parties see *X S"ezd Bolgarskoi Kommunisticheskoi partii* [10th Congress of the Bulgarian Communisty Party] (Moscow: Politizdat, 1972), p. 288 and ff. *XI S"ezd Vengerskoi sotsialisticheskoi rabochie partii* [11th Congress of the Hungarian Socialist Workers Party] (Moscow: Politizdat, 1975), pp. 252, 254, 255. *Dokumente des VII Parteitages der Sozialistischen Einheitspartei Deutchlands* [Documents of the 7th Party Congress of the Socialist Unity Party of Germany] (Berlin: Deitz Verlag, 1971), p. 13 and ff. *VII S"ezd Pol'skoi ob"edinnenoi rabochei partii* (7th Congress of the Polish United Workers Party] (Moscow: Politizdat, 1977), pp. 235-37. *XIV S"ezd Kommunisticheskoi partii Chekhoslovakii* [14th Congress of the Communist Party of Czechoslovakia] (Moscow: Politizdat, 1971), p. 259.

For the text of the treaty articles and party programs cited above see Christopher D. Jones, *The Military-Political Mechanisms of the Warsaw Pact,* unpublished study for the National Council for Soviet and East European Research, Washington, D.C., appendix.

The Romanian Exception. The 1970 Soviet-Romanian treaty, in conjunction with the Warsaw Treaty of 1955 and various other party and state documents of Romania, define a bilateral relationship between Romania and the Soviet Union different than that of the other bilateral relationships between the Soviet Union and the Warsaw Pact states. The legal definitions of this relationship ensure Romanian control over the Romanian armed forces and reject the legal right of WTO armed forces to intervene in Romania. Romanian party and state documents reject the Soviet concept of the joint defense of the gains of socialism. They also narrow the legal obligations of WTO members to joint actions against a NATO attack. They have also defined socialist internationalism and the socialist confederation in a way that places primary emphasis on the absolute sovereignty of individual socialist states and the absolute obligation of other socialist states to observe strictly the territorial integrity of each socialist state. President Ceausescu has firmly and frequently expressed Romania's positions on these matters, for instance, in his address to the 10th Party Congress in 1969, shortly after the WTO intervention in Czechoslovakia. See Nicolae Ceausescu, *Report at the 10th Congress of the Romanian Communist Party* (Bucharest: Agerpress, 1969), pp. 107-11.

The Soviet-Romanian bilateral treaty of 1948 expired in 1968. The two states could not agree upon a new treaty until 1970. This treaty does not endorse the five sets of military-political axioms endorsed by the other members of the WTO. There is no reference at all in this treaty to the concept of the joint defense of the gains of socialism. Unlike the Soviet treaties with East Germany, Poland, and Czechoslovakia, the Soviet treaty with Romania does not commit the signatories to observing the "obligations deriving from the Warsaw Treaty of May 14, 1955." (Volume 26).

The Soviet treaties with Bulgaria and Hungary, both signed in 1967, also refer only to "obligations stipulated in the Warsaw Treaty of May 14, 1955." But this oversight is, in my opinion, made up for by the fact that Bulgaria and Hungary each signed the Bratislava Declaration of 1968, which Romania did not sign. It is also made up for, in my opinion, by references in the party programs of Bulgaria and Hungary to joint defense of the gains of socialism.

The Soviet-Romanian treaty of 1970 not only limits Romania's obligations to those stipulated in the Warsaw Treaty of May 14, 1955, it also states that the Warsaw Treaty is directed only against NATO. The preamble declares that the signatories ". . . will undeviatingly observe the obligations stipulated in the Warsaw Treaty of Friendship, Cooperation and Mutual Aid of May 14, 1955, for the period of validity of this Treaty, which was concluded in response to the threat from NATO." The Warsaw Treaty of May 14, 1955, does not require its signatories to give each other immediate military assistance in the event of an armed attack on one of them; it only requires that the signatories consult with each other. Article Four of the Warsaw Treaty states: "In the event of an armed attack in Europe on one or several of the member states of this Treaty on the part of any state or group of states, each member of this Treaty in order for the realization of the right of individual or collective self-defense, in accordance with article 51 of the United Nations Charter, will render the state or group of states subject to such attack immediate aid, individual or collective in concert with the other member states of this Treaty with all means it deems necessary, including the use of armed force. The member states of this Treaty will immediately consult in regard to the joint measures which must be adopted for the purpose of restoring and preserving international peace and security." (N.N. Rodionov et. al., eds., *Organizatsiia Varshavskogo dogovora, 1955-1975: dokumenty i materialy* [The Warsaw Treaty Organization, 1955-70: documents and materials] (Moscow: Politizdat, 1975), p. 7.

Article Seven of the 1970 Soviet-Romanian treaty specifically limits the function of the WTO to defense of state borders and to observing the requirements of the 1955 Warsaw Treaty concerning consultation over the aid each member state shall decide to give to another member state subjected to armed attack. Article Seven states: "The High Contracting Parties declare that one of the main preconditions of the guaranteeing of European security is the immutability of the state borders in Europe which were established after the Second World War. The Parties express their firm resolve in accordance with the Warsaw Treaty of Friendship, Cooperation and Mutual Aid of May 14, 1955, to take jointly with other member states of the Treaty all necessary measures for the prohibition of aggression on the part of any forces of imperialism, militarism and revanchism and for the securing of the inviolability of the borders of the member states for the Warsaw Pact and for the securing of the rebuff of aggression."

In its bilateral treaties with the loyal members of the WTO, the Soviet Union obtained pledges to respond to an armed attack on one of the signatories with military aid from the other signatory. Article Eight of the Soviet-Romanian treaty avoids making a commitment to send military forces to the other state without first determining whether such aid is necessary. This article does not indicate which party shall make the determination. Article Eight reads: "In the event that one of the High Contracting Parties is subjected to an armed attack by any state or group of states, then the other Party for the realization of its inalienable right to individual or collective self-defense, in accordance with article 51 of the United Nations Charter, will immediately render the first Party all-round aid with all means which it has at its disposal, including military, which are necessary for the repulsion of armed attack.'' The last phase leaves open the question of who will decide what aid is necessary for the repulsion of armed attack. This phrase is in clear contrast to the strict obligations of the other bilateral treaties which unconditionally require the dispatch of military aid in the event of an armed attack on either contracting Party.

53. A typical circular definition of these terms appears in an article by the late WTO Commander, Marshal I.I. Iakubovskii, ''XXV S''ezd KPSS i ukreplenie boevogo sodruzhestvo armii stran Varshavskogo dogovora'' [The 25th Congress of the CPSU and the strengthening of the combat confederation of the armed forces of the Warsaw Pact countries] in *Voenno-istoricheskii zhurnal* 8 (1976); 4: ''The Warsaw Pact is based on the Marxist principle of proletarian internationalism and of a close union of the countries of the victorious proletariat. This concept was worked out in an all-round manner and developed by the great Lenin. . . . The Leninist ideas of the military defense of the gains of socialism and of the international character of such defense determine the basic propositions of the policy of the Marxist-Leninist parties of the socialist confederation in the area of the organization of national defense systems and they comprise the theoretical basis of the combat confederation of the peoples and armed forces of socialism. The combat confederation of the armed forces of the socialist countries is one of the manifestations of proletarian internationalism expressing its readiness to defend and protect jointly with arms in hand the interests of socialism and peace.''

54. See the discussion on the origins of military conflict in the modern world in *Marxism-Leninism on War and the Army* (Moscow: Progress Publishers, 1972) chapters 1, 2, 4; S.A. Tiushkevich et. al., eds., *Voina i armiia* [War and armed forces] (Moscow: Voenizdat, 1977), chapters 2, 4, 6; S.A. Tiushkevich, *Filosofia i voennaia teoriia* [Philosophy and military theory] (Moscow: Nauka, 1975), chapters 1, 2: A.S. Milovodov, *The Philosophical Heritage of V.I. Lenin and the Problems of Contemporary War* (Washington, D.C.: Government Printing Office, no date), chapters 1, 2, 4. V.I. Nechipurenko, *V.I. Lenin o zashchite sotsialisticheskogo otechestva* [V.I. Lenin on the defense of the socialist fatherland] (Moscow: Izdatel'stvo moskovskogo universiteta, 1973), Chapter 3.

55. Maj. Gen. V.F. Samoilenko, ''Voennoe sodrudruzhestvo stran sotsialsizma'' [The military confederation of the countries of socialism] in Tiushkevich, et. al., eds., *Voina i armiia,* p. 366.

56. A.A. Epishev, *Ideologicheskaia bor'ba po voennym voprosam* [Ideological struggle in military questions] (Moscow: Voenizdat, 1974), p. 91.

57. *SVE,* Vol. 7, p. 563.

58. Ibid., p. 564.

59. See Iakubovskii, *Boevoe sodruzhestvo,* chapters 4, 5.

60. See Footnote No. 52. See also Robin A. Remington's comprehensive account of the policies of the WTO Political Consultative Committee, *The Warsaw Pact* (Cambridge, Mass.: MIT Press, 1972); see also the text of PCC Communiques in Rodionov, et. al., eds., *Organizatsiia.*

61. Col. A.A. Timorin, *''Sotsialno-politicheskaia priroda i naznachenie sot-*

sotsialisticheskikh armii" [The socio-political nature and function of socialist armed forces] in Tiushkevich, ed., *Voina i armiia,* pp. 352-53.

62. Iakubovskii, *Boevoe sodruzhestvo,* p. 30.

63. Epishev, *Ideologicheskaia bor'ba,* pp. 71-72.

64. See Footnote No. 52.

65. Iakubovskii, *Boevoe sodruzhestvo,* p. 133.

66. *Marxism-Leninism on War and the Army,* pp. 195-210; Samoilenko in Tiushkevich, ed., *Voina i armiia,* pp. 362-71; Nechipurenko, *V.I. Lenin,* pp. 147-48; See also Col. N. Cherniak, "V.I. Lenin on Proletarian Internationalism and Its Role in the Defense of the Achievements of Socialism," *Voennaia Mysl* 2 (Feb. 1969) in CIA FBIS FPD 0060/60 18 June 1969 "Selected Translations from *Voennaia Mysl'*," p. 19. "The organizers of the revolt in Hungary tried to implant fascism in the country. They made fierce attacks on the Warsaw Pact, announced the unilateral withdrawal of Hungary from the Pact and thus tried to isolate Hungary from the fraternal countries and deprive it of the ᵢecessary military, economic and political support.... Fulfilling their internationalist duty, the Soviet Armed Forces gave the Hungarian people timely assistance in routing the black reaction. At the time it was not necessary to use the armed forces of the other participants of the Warsaw pact, although the fraternal allied armies were ready to give aid and in case of necessity it would have been given." See also Maj. Gen. N. Kirayev and Col. A. Bezhentsev, "The Ideological Foundation of the Military Unity of the Socialist Countries," *Voennaia Mysl'* 5 (May 1969) in CIA FBIS FPD 0116/60, Dec. 18, 1968, "Selected Translations from *Voennaia Mysl'*," p. 35. "When a real threat to socialism developed in Czechoslovakia the allied nations, true to Lenin's ideas and the principles of internationalism, acted in full accord with their duty and their treaty obligations. They lent urgent assistance to their ally, including armed force. The soldiers of the allied armies entered Czechoslovak territory as class brothers of the Czechoslovak workers, peasants, and intellectuals, refraining from interfering in the internal affairs of this sovereign state."

67. Epishev, *Ideologicheskaia bor'ba,* p. 104.

68. Ibid., p. 110.

69. M.S. Kirichenko, *Nadezhnyi strazh mira* [Reliable guard of the peace] (Minsk: Belarus, 1975), pp. 71-74. Kirichenko discusses and rejects each of these propositions.

70. Iakubovskii, *Boevoe sodruzhestvo,* p. 247. This theme appears throughout the military-political literature. For example see Maj. Gen. N. Kirayev and Col. A. Bezhentsev, "The Ideological Foundation of the Military Unity of the Socialist Countries," *Voennaia Mysl'* 5 (May 1969) in CIA FBIS FPD 0116/60, Dec. 18, 1969, pp. 29-30.

71. Iakubovskii, *Boevoe sodruzhestvo,* p. 248.

72. Grechko, "Boevoe sodruzhestvo" *Kommunist* 15 (1972); 38.

73. Iakubovskii, *Boevoe sodruzhestvo,* pp. 119-20. See also pp. 138-39: "Marxist-Leninists categorically reject the position of those who assert that each socialist country should rely only on its own forces in the organization of its defense.... The Maoist preaching of 'reliance on one's own forces' is a theory which has the objective of breaking the unity and solidarity of the socialist countries."

74. See Footnote No. 52.

75. General Dobri Dzhurov, "Na strazhe mirnogo truda naroda" [On guard of the peaceful labor of the people] *Krasnaia Zvezda,* Sept. 22, 1974, p. 3.

76. Kirichenko, *Na strazhe mira*, p. 75. See also N. Cherniak, "V.I. Lenin on Proletarian Internationalism" in CIA FBIS FPD 0060/69, Selected Translations from *Voennaia Mysl'*, 18 June, 1969, p. 19-20: "The neutralism of a bourgeois country under the present international circumstances signifies a struggle for national independence and a struggle against the policy of aggressive imperialist blocs. The 'neutrality' of a socialist country leads to directly opposite results under the conditions of the existence of two world systems. It signifies a break away from the world system of socialism and the national interests of its people and the threat of absorption of that country by imperialist predators." In the publicly available journal, *Kommunist vooruzhennyk sil* 12 (1969): 21, this same author in an article entitled "Bourgeois Nationalism — The Poisonous Weapon of Reaction" specifically criticizes the "Yugoslav revisionists" for "abstract preaching of 'neutralism.'"

Notes to Chapter Seven

1. In its discussion of the functions of the Soviet Main Political Administration, the *Soviet Military Encyclopedia,* Vol. 2 (Moscow: *Voenizdat,* 1977), p. 56, notes: "One of the responsibilities of the Soviet MPA is the strengthening of the fraternal cooperation of the Soviet armed forces with the armed forces of the other socialist countries." Fulfillment of this responsibility would not rule out a WTO agency to preside over the joint activities of the political administrations of the alliance.

2. Ibid. See also A.A. Epishev, *Partiino-politicheskaia rabota v vooruzhennykh silakh SSSR, 1918-1973* [Party-political work in the armed forces of the USSR, 1918-1973] (Moscow: Voenizdat, 1974), p. 93 and ff; See also Michael J. Deane, *Political Control of the Soviet Armed Forces* (New York: Crane and Russak, 1977), pp. 281 and ff.

3. See Col. Gen. P.I. Efimov et. al. eds., *Boevoi soiuz bratskikh armii* [The combat union of the fraternal armed forces] (Moscow: Voenizdat, 1974) for outlines of the political administrations of the following armies: Bulgaria (p. 51); Hungary (p. 78); East Germany (p. 115); and Czechoslovakia (p. 225). For Poland see A. Dmitriev, "Narodnoe voiska pol'skoe" [The Polish People's Army], *Kommunist vooruzhennykh sil (KVS)* 14, (1970). In this article Dmitriev observes, "The structure and functions of the political organs and party organizations is basically analogous to the structure and functions of the political organs and party organizations of the Soviet Armed Forces." Col. A. Verbitskii, "Bolgarskaia narodnaia armiia [The Bulgarian People's Army], *KVS* 11 (1970): ff; notes: "The political organs and party organizations in the Bulgarian armed forces have basically the same structure and functions and fulfill the same tasks of the political organs and party organizations of the Soviet Armed Forces."

4. See A. V. Antosiac et. al. eds., *Zarozhdenie narodnikh armii stran-uchastnits Varshavskogo dogovora, 1941-49* [The birth of the peoples' armies of the member states of the Warsaw Pact, 1941-1949] (Moscow: Nauka, 1975).

5. S.M. Shtemenko, "Bratstvo rozhdennoe v boiu" [Brotherhood Born in Battle] *Za rubeshom* [Abroad] 19 (1976): 7.

6. See Epishev, *Partiino-politicheskaia rabota,* p. 357. Article by V.V. Semin in S.K. Il' in et al. eds., *Partiino-politcheskaia rabota v Sovetskikh vooruzhennykh silakh* [Party-Political Work in the Soviet Armed Forces] (Moscow: Voenizdat, 1974), p. 593.

7. See the discussion on the Czechoslovak MPA further on in this chapter.

8. Colonel Jan Khmelik, "Voploshchaia idei oktiabria" [Carrying out the ideas of October] *Krasnaia Zvezda* (October 6, 1977): 7.

9. Epishev, *Partiino-politicheskaia rabota,* p. 357.

10. This quotation is taken from the following passage: "The political organs do a great deal for the strengthening of contacts among the fraternal armed forces and the development of their all-round cooperation. At meetings of the representatives of the main political administrations, the political administrations of branches of the armed services, of military districts and of force groups and of political workers of formations and units and at conferences and seminars a broad exchange of experience is organized on various problems of the guaranteeing of the high quality of the combat training of troops, of Marxist-Leninist training of officers, of the political studies of soldiers and non-commissioned officers, of the organization of socialist competition and on other forms of the teaching and training of the soldiers of the socialist confederation." A.A. Epishev, *Ideologicheskaia bor'ba po voennym voprosam* [Ideological Struggle in Military Questions] (Moscow: Voenizdat, 1974), p. 110.

11. "We should mention also such an important form of collaboration as the interworking of the political organs of the allied armed forces. This has the goal of exchanging experience in party-political work among the troops, resolution of common tasks and assistance in such important matters as internationalist education of soldiers and familiarization with the foremost experience of fraternal armies. For this purpose there is an exchange of visits of delegations of political workers of the fraternal armies, *meetings of the chiefs of the main political administrations* (my emphasis), exchange of military-political and specialized literature, movie films, photo exhibits and visual aids....In recent years a form of contact among political organs such as the exchange of military lecturers has recommended itself highly." Col. D. Diev, Lt. Col. K. Spirov, "Combat Collaboration of the Armies of the Warsaw Pact States," *Voennaia Mysl',* 2, (1968) in CIA FBIS FPD 0049/69, *Selected Translations From Voennaia Mysl', April 25, 1969, p. 65.*

12. *I.I. Iakubovskii, ed., Boevoe sodruzhestvo bratskikh narodov i armii* [The combat confederation of the fraternal peoples and armed forces] (Moscow: Voenizdat, 1975, p. 289.

13. "The principal forms of the structural activity of the United Command are...meetings of the generals and officers of the main political administrations (September 1970, April 1972)..." M.S. Kirichenko, *Nadezhnyi strazh mira* [Reliable guard of the peace] (Minsk: Belarus, 1975), pp. 112-13.

14. Iakubovskii, *Boevoe sodruzhestvo,* p. 292.

15. Col. A. Verbitskii, "V dukhe proletarskogo, sotsialisticheskogo internatsionalizma" [In the spirit of proletarian and socialist internationalism] *KVS*

17, 1977, p. 80. See also B. Bochkov, "Sfera bratskogo sotrudnichestva — ideologicheskaia rabota" [Ideological work is a sphere of fraternal cooperation] *KVS* 6 (1977); 14.

16. Col. Gen. P.I. Efimov, et. al. eds., *Boevoi soiuz,* p. 28.

17. I.I. Iakubovskii, "XXV S" ezd KPSS i ukreplenie boevogo sotrudnichestva armii stran Varshavskogo dogovora" [The 25th Congress of the CPSU and the strengthening of the combat confederation of the armed forces of the countries of the Warsaw Pact] *Voenno-istoricheskii zhurnal* [Military-Historical Journal] 8 (1976); 12.

18. Col. V. Semin, "Partiino-politicheskaia rabota v armiakh stran Varshavskogo dogovora" [Party-political work in the armed forces of the Warsaw Pact Countries] in *Partiino-politicheskaia rabota* eds. S.K. Il'in et. al., p. 599.

19. Efimov, *Boevoi soiuz,* p. 29.

20. A.G. Ovchinnikov et. al. eds., *Krasnoznamennyi Belorusskii voennyi okrug* [The red banner Belorussian Military District] (Minsk: Belarus', 1973), p. 505.

21. N.T. Panferov, et. al. eds., *Odesskii krasnoznamennyi* [The Red Banner Odessa Military District] (Kishinev; "Kartiia Moldoveniaske', 1975), p. 283.

22. Iakubovskii, *Boevoi sodruzhestvo,* p. 165; Efimov, *Boevoe soiuz,* p. 29.

23. A.I. Prokhvatilov, *V.I. Lenin i sovetskaia voennaia pechat'* [V.I. Lenin and the Soviet military press] (Leningrad: Izdatel' stvo Leningradskogo universiteta, 1976), p. 83: "Friendly relations have developed and great experience has been acquired in the joint creative work of the newspapers of the Soviet armed forces and the armed forces of the socialist countries." Prokhvatilov cites as a "characteristic example" of such work, the joint publication of the same texts under the logos of the military newspapers of different armed forces, such as the August 19, 1969, issue of *Volksarmee* and *Sovetskaia Armiia,* the newspapers of the GDR defense ministry and the Group of Soviet Forces in Germany.

24. Epishev, *Ideologicheskaia bor'ba,* p. 11. Marshal Iakubovskii arrived at the same conclusion. In his signed article, Marshal I.I. Iakubovskii, *Sovetskaia voennaia entsiklopediia* [Soviet Military Encyclopedia] 1 (Moscow: Voenizdat, 1976) p. 527; he states: "Close ties among the political organs of the fraternal armed forces play a great role in the strengthening of the combat confederation of the armed forces of the socialist confederation." See also Iakubovskii, *Boevoe sodruzhestvo,* p. 166: "Close-knit contacts among the political organs of the allied armed forces is an important means of strengthening brotherhood and friendship among them. They permit the exchange of experience of ideological work and of the education of personnel in the spirit of high revolutionary vigilance and of proletarian socialist solidarity."

25. See the biography of Epishev in *Sovetskaia voennaia entsiklopediia, (SVE),* Vol. 3, p. 312.

26. Ibid.

27. Roman Kolkowicz, *The Soviet Military and the Communist Party* (Princeton: Princeton University Press, 1967), pp. 166-70 and pp. 262-64.

28. See *Krasnaia Zvezda,* Oct. 10, 1962, for coverage of the exercises in Poland; see the October 20 issue for coverage of the exercises in Romania.

29. See Footnotes 11 and 45.

30. See Golikov's biography in *Sovetskaia voennaia entsiklopediia, (SVE)*, Vol. 2, pp. 585-86. During World War II Golikov headed a Soviet military mission to the United States and Britain; held commanding posts in the battles of Moscow, Voronezh, Briansk, and Stalingrad; served as the head of the cadre administration of the Defense Ministry; and as the head of the agency responsible for the repatriation of Soviet citizens captured by the Nazis. From 1950 to 1956 he served as the head of a department of an army group in the USSR, and from 1956 to 1958 as the commandant of the Academy of Armored Troops. In 1958, he became Chief of the MPA; following his removal from his post he became Chief of the Group of General Inspectors of the Soviet Defense Ministry.

31. See the article on the Military Institute in *SVE*, Vol. 2, p. 267.

32. Ibid.

33. See Antosiac et. al. eds., *Zarozhdenie narodnikh armii*, passim. Some of these formations were created as early as 1941.

34. *SVE*, Vol. 2, p. 267.

35. See chapter 8 of this study.

36. Kolkowicz, *The Soviet Military,* passim.

37. Timothy J. Colton, *Commissars, Commanders and Civilian Authority: The Structure of Soviet Military Politics* (Cambridge, Mass.: Harvard University Press, 1979).

38. Dale R. Herspring, *East German Civil-Military Relations: The Impact of Technology, 1949-72* (New York: Praeger, 1973); also Herspring and Ivan Volgyes, eds., *Civil-Military Relations in Communist Systems* (Boulder, Colorado: Westview Press, 1978).

39. Alex Alexiev, *Party-Military Relations in Eastern Europe: The Case of Romania* (Los Angeles: Center for International and Strategic Studies, University of California, 1979).

40. In my view Alexiev's evidence and even some of his own conclusions contradict his assertion that the Kolkowicz thesis is valid in the case of Romania. Although Alexiev states that the structural antagonism between political and professional officers determines the nature of party-military relations in East Europe, he ends by seeming to say that the Soviet factor is the really critical element in East European party-military relations. See pp. 3-4 and pp. 32-33 from Alexiev's study.

41. These three themes appear throughout the discussion of political work in the section below in the text on bilateral Soviet-East European relations and also in the military-political axioms discussed in chapter 6. A passage from a joint Soviet-Polish study specifically, albeit briefly, identifies these three themes: "The personnel of the Polish armed forces are educated by the Polish United Workers' Party in a spirit of devotion to the homeland, to proletarian internationalism and of class hatred for the imperialists. P.A. Zhilin and E. Jadziac, eds., *Bratstvo po oruzhiiu* [Brotherhood in arms] (Moscow: Voenizdat, 1975), p. 249. Dale Herspring, *East German Civil-Military Relations,* p. 168, notes the same three themes in a particular program of education for East German officers.

42. Epishev, *Ideologicheskaia bor'ba,* p. 75.

43. The Soviet literature which falls under this classification is very large. In

"Marxist-Leninist teaching on war and armed forces," *Soviet Military En-cyclopedia* Vol. 5, pp. 153-54, makes clear in its discussion that this body of literature deals not only with the Soviet army but with the armed forces of all other socialist armed forces. For instance, the following passages from page 154: "The Marxist-Leninist teaching on war and armed forces makes clear the necessity of constant support of the defensive might of the USSR and of the other countries of socialism, of the combat readiness of their armed forces on a level which guarantees a decisive and full destruction of the imperialist aggressors.... The propositions of the Marxist-Leninist teaching on war and armed forces lies at the basis of the contents of the military doctrine of a socialist state.... This teaching instills in soldiers belief in the invincibility of the armed forces of the countries of socialism and in their capability to carry out their historical mission to the end. ... The teaching on war and armed forces...is the reliable instrument of the Communist and workers' parties and the governments of the socialist countries of the socialist confederation and of the international Communist, workers and national liberation movement in the struggle for peace and international security, for the freedom and independence of peoples."

44. For an examination of these factors on the WTO see Dale R. Herspring, Ivan Volgyes, "Political Reliability in the Eastern European Warsaw Pact Armies," *Armed Forces and Society* (Winter 1980).

45. See Rear Adm. F. Chernyshev and Col. V. Koniukhovskii, "The Army of Friendship of Peoples and of Proletarian Internationalism," *Voennaia Mysl'* 11 (1967) in CIA FBIS FPD 0157/68, *Selected Translations from Voennaia Mysl,* Nov. 18, 1968, pp. 86-88. "The Soviet Armed Forces are called upon to defend the interests and security not only of our homeland, but also of the entire socialist community...in the interests of the strengthening of the security of the European socialist countries on the basis of the appropriate agreements, a number of Soviet army units and formations are stationed on the territory of several friendly countries. Carrying out their noble mission outside the country, the Soviet troops are actually implementing the principles of proletarian internationalism.... The composition of our armed forces was and continues to be multinational. Our country's multinational nature is practically expressed in the units and formations of the army and navy. This stems from the specific peculiarities of their recruitment.... Internationalist indoctrination acquires special significance for the troops who are beyond the boundaries of the homeland and for the border districts and fleets. Considerable work is being carried out among the Soviet troops stationed temporarily on the territory of the GDR, Poland, and Hungary to explain the basic principles of military organization in the fraternal socialist countries and the successes achieved by the workers of these countries in the construction of socialism are graphically demonstrated. The troops familiarize themselves with the traditions of the German, Polish and Hungarian peoples, and with the life and combat experience of their armies." See also Gen. K.M. Kalashnik, "A Half Century of Dedicated Service to the Party and the People," *Voennaia Mysl'* 5 (1969), in CIA FBIS FPD 0116/69 Dec. 18, 1969; *Selected Translations from Voennaia Mysl'*, p. 12: "Our nation's army is an army of the friendship of peoples. It carries high the banner of proletarian internationalism, *closely bound by the ties of friendship with the armies of our brother socialist nations* [my emphasis]. Our wise party, guided by Lenin's definition of internationalism, has successfully resolved *the most difficult problem in the process of building Soviet society — the nationalities problem* [my emphasis]. In our coun-

try, which contains more than 100 different nationalities and ethnic groups, it has been resolved in full conformity with Marxist-Leninist teaching on internationalism and friendship among peoples."

46. See Col. N. Cherniak, "V.I. Lenin on Proletarian Internationalism and Its Role in the Defense of the Achievements of Socialism," *Voennaia Mysl'* 2 (February 1969) in CIA FBIS, FPD 0060/69 June 18, 1969, *Selected Translations from Voennaia Mysl',* pp. 14-15.

47. "National Formations in the Armed Forces of the USSR," *Soviet Military Encyclopedia,* Vol. 5, pp. 552-53.

48. Ibid.

49. Ibid.

50. V.I. Nechipurenko, *V.I. Lenin o zashchite sotsialisticheskogo otechestva* [V.I. Lenin on the defense of the socialist fatherland] (Moscow: Izdatelstvo Moskovskogo universiteta, 1973), p. 127.

51. Ibid., pp. 131-32.

52. A.V. Antosiac, et. al. eds., *Zarozhdenie narodnikh armii stranuchastnits Varshavskogo dogovora* [The birth of the peoples armies of the member states of the Warsaw Pact] (Moscow: Nauka, 1975, 1975), p. 61.

53. Ibid., p. 117.

54. Ibid., p. 107.

55. Ibid., p. 178.

56. Ibid., p. 181.

57. Ibid., p. 179.

58. Ibid., passim. The chapters on the national armies of each of the WTO members discuss in some detail the role of Communist military officers in achieving control over national defense ministries; these chapters also discuss the roles of national defense ministries in the consolidation of power by the East European Communist parties.

59. Admiral V. Verner, "Natsional'noi narodnoi armii GDR - 20 Let." [The national people's army is 20 years old] *Kommunist vooruzhennykh sil* 4 (1976): 87.

60. Col. D. Diev, Lt. Col. K. Spirov, "Combat Collaboration of the Armies of the Warsaw Pact States," *Voennaia Mysl'* 2 (1968) CIA FBIS FPD 0049/69, *Selected Translations from Voennaia Mysl,* April 25, 1969, pp. 59-60. See also the article by A. Staroverov, "Vooruzhennye sily sotsialisticheskikh gosudarstv i ikh boevoe sodruzhestvo" [The armed forces of the socialist states and their combat confederation], *Kommunist vooruzhennyk sil* 17 (1970): 62.

61. Col. V. Nagornyk, Lt. Col. A. Pimenov, "Polki-pobratimy [Brother Regiments], *Krasnaia Zvezda,* Sept. 24, 1977, p. 3.

62. A.A. Epishev and Velko Palin, eds., *Naveki vmeste* [Forever Together] [Moscow: Voenizdat, 1969), pp. 302-4.

63. Efimov, *Boevoi soiuz,* p. 62.

64. "An enrichment of new forms and methods of training soldiers has been promoted by mutual visits of the delegations of leading political workers led by the Chief of the Main Political Administration of the Soviet Army and Navy General of the Army A.A. Epishev and the Chief of the Main Political

Administration of the Bulgarian People's Army, General K. Kosev. The political organs of the BPA maintain ties with the political organs of the other fraternal armies" (Col. A. Verbitskii, "V dukhe proletarskogo sotsialisticheskogo internatsionalizma" [In the spirit of proletarian socialist internationalism], *Kommunist vooruzhennyk sil* 17 (1977): 80.

65. Epishev and Palin, eds., *Naveki vmeste,* pp. 302-4.

66. Ibid., p. 301.

67. Ibid., p. 305.

68. Lt. Gen. M. Sobolev, Maj. Gen. S. Il'in, "V obstanovke druzhby i serdechnosti" [In a situation of friendship and sincerity], *Krasnaia Zvezda,* Dec. 8, 1973.

69. Ibid.

70. Efimov, *Boevoi soiuz,* p. 53.

71. Col. Filiu Khristov, et. al. eds., *B''lgarskata komunisticheska partiia i narodnata armiia* [The Bulgarian Communist Party and the Peoples Army] (Sofia: Voennoizdatel'stvo, 1976), p. 376.

72. Ivan Volgyes, "The Military as an Agency of Political Socialization: The Case of Hungary," in *Civil-Military Relations in Communist Systems,* eds. Volgyes and Herspring, pp. 159-61.

73. "V stroiu odnom—k edinoi tsel' " [In one order for a common goal] *Kommunist vooruzhennykh sil* 13 (1976): 90-91.

74. Maj. Gen. Balakirev and Col. O. Gromov, "Pod znakom boevogo sodruzhestva" [Under the sign of the combat confederation] *Krasnaia Zvezda,* Sept. 28, 1974, p. 4.

75. Ibid.

76. Efimov, *Boevoi soiuz,* p. 95.

77. Col. Gen. B.P. Ivanov, "Bratstvo voinov" [The brotherhood of soldiers] *Izvestiia,* Feb. 19, 1975, p. 4.

78. Efinov, *Boevoi soiuz,* p. 81.

79. Ibid.

80. "According to the Regulations of the party and the decision of the Central Committee of the Hungarian Socialist Workers' Party the party organs of the Hungarian Peoples Army must regularly inform local party organs about the political life of units and sub-units, about their moral-political situation, and also interact with them in the carrying out of common tasks. While maintaining constant, close contacts with the local party organs, the party organs and organizations of the Hungarian People's Army actively cooperate with them in the conduct of many important general-state measures and campaigns. The party organs and organizations of the Hungarian People's Army, for example, take a most active role in the preparation and conduct of elections for the National Assembly and the local organs of power and the Hungarian Socialist Workers' Party. Many of the military personnel of the Hungarian People's Army — the outstanding individuals in combat and political training and the activists of social work — are members of election commissions, and run as candidates and are elected to the organs of state power of the country" (Ibid., p. 82).

81. See E.F. Ivanovskii et. al., eds., *Na boevom postu: kniga o voinakh*

Gruppy sovetskikh voisk v Germanii [At the battle station: a book about the group of Soviet forces in Germany] (Moscow: Voenizdat, 1975), pp. 268-318.

82. Quoted in ibid., pp. 273-74.

83. Quoted in ibid., p. 274.

84. Efimov, *Boevoi soiuz,* pp. 124-25.

85. Ibid.,

86. Ibid., p. 126.

87. See Col. A. Khorev, "Iz putevogo bloknota: Krepnut novye traditsii" [From a travel notebook: new traditions are strengthening] *Krasnaia Zvezda,* Nov. 15, 1977, p. 3.

88. Ivanovskii, *Na boevom postu,* pp. 276-83.

89. Ibid., p. 282.

90. Efimov, *Boevoi soiuz,* p. 126; and Ivanovskii, *Na boevom postu,* pp. 288-89.

91. Khorev, "Iz putevogo bloknota".

92. Verner, "Natsional'noi narodnoi armii" *Kommunist vooruzhennykh sil,* p. 88. For similar enthusiastic pledges of loyalty to the USSR see the annual declarations of friendship by Defense Minister Hoffmann, *Krasnaia Zvezda,* over the last 20 years on March 1.

93. P.A. Zhilin, et. al., eds., *Bratstvo po oruzhiiu,* p. 359.

94. Ibid.

95. Ibid.

96. Ibid., p. 360.

97. Ovchinnikov, et. al., eds., *Krasnoznamennyi Belorusskii,* pp. 501-4.

98. Zhilin and Jadziac eds., *Bratstvo po oruzhiiu,* pp. 362-63.

99. V. Savchuk, "Slavnye stranitsy letopisi sovmestnoi bor'by" [The glorious pages of the annals of joint struggle] *Krasnaia Zvezda,* May 11, 1975.

100. Zhilin and Jadziac, eds., *Bratstvo po oruzhiiu,* pp. 364-66.

101. Ibid., p. 367.

102. Lt. Col. A. Pimenov, "Sem'ia splochennaia i krepkaia" [A united and strong family] *Krasnaia Zvezda,* May 31, 1974, p. 3.

103. Ibid.

104. Ibid.

105. Col. K. Klievskii, "Dostoino vypolnaia zavety Kostiushkovtsev," [Fulfilling in a worthy manner the behests of the followers of Koscziusko] *Krasnaia Zvezda,* Oct. 12, 1975, p. 2.

106. Quoted in Zhilin and Jadziac, eds., *Bratstvo po oruzhiiu,* p. 349.

107. Iakubovskii, *Boevoe sodruzhestvo,* pp. 292 and 293 for exercises of February 1973 and 1974.

108. Interview with General Ilie Ceausescu, March 18, 1978, Boston College, Boston, Mass. When asked why there were no WTO field exercises in Romania, General Ceausescu replied that because Romania is such a small country there was simply not enough room for Romanian and Soviet troops to maneuver together.

109. Efimov, *Boevoi soiuz,* p. 183.

110. Col. V. Semin, "Segodniia i zaftra sotsialisticheskoi Rumynii" [Today and Tomorrow in Socialist Romania] *Kommunist vooruzhennykh sil* 17 (1976): 75.

111. Ibid.

112. "In full accordance with the internationalist policy of the Romanian Communist Party our armed forces develop military cooperation with the armies of all socialist states on the basis of relations of a new type, which have been established among the peoples of our countries" (Gen. Ion Ionitse, former minister of defense, "Armiia sotsialisticheskoi Rumynii" [The Armed Forces of Socialist Romania] *Krasnaia Zvezda,* October 25, 1974, p. 3) "The Romanian army participates in various joint activities as agreed upon, in the exchanges of experience carried out in several spheres between the socialist armies, in the actions designed to lead to the improvement and modernization of the processes of instruction and education, in the specialized consultation and in symposia and conferences; it carries out exchanges of military delegations, has cultural, artistic and sports links and exchanges military publications, etc." (Col. Traian Grozea, "The Socio-Political Foundations of National Defense," in *National Defense: The Romanian View,* ed. Col. Iulian Cernat et. al. (Bucharest: Military Publishing House, 1976), pp. 71-72.

113. Alex Alexiev, *Party-Military Relations in East Europe: The Case of Romania,* (Los Angeles: Center for International and Strategic Affairs, University of California, 1979), pp. 26-27.

114. See Col. A.N. Ratnikov, Col. V.I. Zabialov, *Vooruzhennye sily Iugoslavii* [The Armed Forces of Yugoslavia] (Moscow: Voenizdat, 1971), pp. 160-62. The text mentions exchanges of various military delegations and naval ships. These delegations have included Soviet veterans of the liberation of Belgrade, journalists, lecturers, and staffs of military museums. There have also been exchanges of military textbooks and the writing of joint works by military historians. In a picture of a visting Soviet delegation, Marshal Grechko is identified in the caption. I believe that one of the faces in the delegation is that of General Epishev and another of the faces is that of Marshal Iakubovskii.

115. Col. D. Diev, "Vooruzhenny sily sotsialisticheskoi respubliki Rumynii" [The Armed Forces of the Socialist Republic of Romania] *Kommunist vooruzhennykh sil* 16 (1970: 73. Diev is the author of two books on the Romanian military, neither of which I have been able to obtain: the 1960 and 1966 editions of *Rumynskaia narodnaia armiia* [The Romanian People's Army] (Moscow: Voenizdat).

116. "Statement of the Stand of the Romanian Workers' Party...," April 1964 in *Sino-Soviet Relations, 1964-65,* ed. William E. Griffith (Cambridge: MIT Press, 1967), pp. 292-93.

117. Efimov, *Boevoi soiuz,* p. 177.

118. Iakubovskii, *Boevoe sodruzhestvo,* p. 199.

119. Efimov, *Boevoi soiuz,* p. 178.

120. See the Romanian-language text of Lt. Gen. Gheorghe Gomoiu, "The Organizational Development of Party Work Within the Army, 1948-75," in *File din istoria militara a poporului roman,* ed. Maj. Gen. Ilie Ceausescu, Vol. 4 (Bucharest: Editura Militara, 1977).

121. "Law Concerning the Organization of the National Defense of the Socialist Republic of Romania," *Scienteia,* Dec. 29, 1972, pp. 4-7 in Joint Publications Research Service 58017, Jan. 18, 1973, *Translations on East European Political, Sociological and Military Affairs,* p. 32.

122. "Speech by Nicolae Ceausescu at the Plenary Session of the CC of the RCP," in *Romania: Documents, Events,* November 1978, (Bucharest: Agerpress), p. 7.

123. Text in N.N. Rodionov et. al. eds., *Organizatsiia Varshavskogo dogovora 1955-75: dokumenty i materialy* [The Warsaw Treaty Organization, 1955-75: Documents and Materials] (Moscow: Politizdat, 1975), p. 7.

124. See articles 7 and 8 and the preamble.

125. Colonel Traian Grozea, "The Socio-Political Foundations of National Defense," in *National Defense: The Romanian View* eds. Col. Iulian Cernat et. al. (in English) (Bucharest: Military Publishing House, 1976), p. 70.

126. Col. V. Samoilenko, "Voennoe sodruzhestvo stran sotsializma" [The Military Confederation of the Socialist Countries] in *Voina i armiia* [War and Armed Forces], eds. S.A. Tiushkevich et. al. (Moscow: Voenizdat, 1977), p. 374.

127. Nicolae Ceausescu, *Report at the 10th Congress of the Romanian Communist Party* (Bucharest: Angerpress, 1969), pp. 107-8.

128. See the English-language edition, *Pages From the History of the Romanian Army* (Bucharest: Military Publishing House, 1975); see also "The Armed Struggle of the Entire People: Romanian Traditions," in *National Defense,* eds., Cernat et. al., Chapter 2; see also Ilie Ceausescu, ed., *File,* Vol. 3 and 4.

129. Cernat et. al. eds., *National Defense,* pp.47-48.

130. For an account of Romanian-Soviet differences on these issues see Alexiev, *Party-Military Relations,* pp. 15-20.

131. As the authors of the Gottwald proposals observed, in their discussion of the Czechoslovak defense system, "it is not the problems of tactical-technical organization that are primarily involved but rather political and doctrinal problems and their confrontation with reality." Quoted in Miroslav Starosta, "How the Postulate of Neutrality Arose," *Tribuna* (Czechoslovakia) 32, Aug. 20, 1969, in Radio Free Europe (RFE) *Czechoslovak Press Survey,* 2256 (Sept. 10, 1969): 4. See also the quotation from the Gottwald proposals in J. Hechko, "Scientific Hypothesis or Political Speculation," *Rude Pravo* (Prague) Jan. 8, 1979, translated and reprinted in *Pravda pobezhdaet* [The truth shall prevail] (Moscow: Politizdat, 1971, p. 290) which quotes the Gottwald proposals as saying, "The formulation of the military doctrine of a state has great reverse effect on political doctrine and strategy."

132. See Col. Milan Matous, "The So-Called Memorandum—What It Was and the Purpose It Served," *Zivot Strany,* 42, Oct. 15, 1969, RFE, *Czechoslovak Press Survey,* 2273 (Nov. 18, 1969): 7.

133. Ibid., p. 8: "Another document of the Military-Political Academy was a proposal to revise the political system in the army. In essence it was proposed that the Party should be deprived of any decisive influence upon the army's system of political organization and on its political life. The political organization was to be divided into a service organization and a small party organization." This statement is partially confirmed by the statement of Lt. Gen. Prchlik in his

press conference of July 15, 1968, in which he declared, "It stands to reason that in our preparations of congress materials we will also deal with a number of other problems, such as the structure of the party and other institutions in the army and security agencies, the system of their management, and many other problems." "Report on the Press Conference of Lt. General Vaclav Prchlik...," *Winter in Prague,* ed. Robin A. Remington, (Cambridge: MIT Press, 1969), p. 217.

134. Quoted in Starosta, "How the Postulate of Neutrality Arose," p. 3.

135. Matous, "The So-Called Memorandum," p. 4.

136. Ibid., p. 5.

137. "In one of the sections of the memorandum the position of Czechoslovakia in the Warsaw Pact was characterized as the position of a victim of processes on which we were not able to exercise influence. The authors of the memorandum put forward arguments against the participation of Czechoslovakia in the Warsaw Pact..." (Hechko, "Scientific Hypothesis...," p. 292).

138. Ibid., p. 293.

139. See the resolution adopted by the Czechoslovak Central Committee, "The Lessons of Crisis Development," in *Pravda pobezhdaet,* p. 43: "One of the political and ideological centers of the rightists [in the Czechoslovak Communist Party] was the Military-Political Academy which during the summer of 1968 actually adopted an official memorandum which demanded a review of the principles of the military policy of our party and state...and changes of Czechoslovak military doctrine on the basis of a revision of our relationship to the Warsaw Pact. The strengthening of negative phenomena in the army was in a significant degree promoted by General V. Prchlik who after June 1968 left his post as head of the Main Political Administration for the responsibility of directing a department of the Central Committee of the Czechoslovak Peoples Army for leadership of party work in the armed forces, organs of security and prosecutor's office." See also Gen. Frantisek Bedrich, chief of the Czechoslovak MPA, "The Army, The Party and Patriotism," *Tvorba,* 6 (Oct. 8, 1969) in RFE *Czechoslovak Press Survey,* 2270 (Nov. 10, 1969). In this article, General Bedrich declared, "Advantage was taken of strong anti-Soviet sentiments and the position of our army within the framework of the Warsaw Pact was attacked. At the same time an attack designed to discredit the army was launched from within the army itself.... [T]his was intended to bring about differences of opinion within the army and to weaken its ability to defend socialism, not only in this country but also within the framework of the socialist camp. The attempts to discredit the army in the eyes of others were chiefly made by attacking its internationalist position in the coalition of Warsaw Pact states.... In this respect it was the former head of the Main Political Administration, Prchlik, who in particular committed himself." See also the interview with Bedrich's successor, General Vaclav Horachek, quoted later in this chapter. See also the account of this process in an article by a Czechoslovak officer, A. Mikhiak, "Razvitiia Chekhoslovatskoi narodnoi armii" [The development of the Czechoslovak People's Army] in the Soviet journal *Voenno-istoricheskii zhurnal* 10 (1976):58 "...at the end of the 1960s the rightist-deviationist and anti-Soviet elements began an attack on the political course conducted by the Communist Party of Czechoslovakia and above all on internationalist ties of the CSSR with the Soviet Union and the countries of the socialist confederation. The objective of their attack was the policy of the party in the area of the organization and development of a

national defense system...."

140. Matous, "The So-Called memorandum," p. 6 and 10.

141. Gen. D.D. Lelishenko, "Druzhba skrepennaia krov'iu" [Friendship sealed in blood] *Krasnaia Zvezda,* May 9, 1968, p. 3.

142. Ibid., p. 6.

143. I.I. Iakubovskii, "Veliki podvig" [The great victory], in *Krasnaia Zvezda,* May 9, 1968, p. 2.

144. See the *Krasnaia Zvezda* articles of May 11, 12, 14 and 15.

145. "O prebyvanii delegatsii vooruzhennykh sil Sovetskogo Soiuza v Chekhoslovatskoi Sotsialisticheskoi Respublike" [On the visit of the delegation of the Armed Forces of the Soviet Union in the Czechoslovak Socialist Republic] *Krasnaia Zvezda,* May 23, 1968, p. 1.

146. See Chapter 4 of this study for the discussion of this and subsequent 1968 exercises in Czechoslovakia.

147. Iakubovskii, *Boevoe sodruzhestvo,* p. 286.

148. See Chapter 2 of this study for a discussion of these elections in the intraparty struggle of 1968.

149. Hechko, "Scientific Hypothesis," p. 287.

150. According to Colonel Matous, Prchlik relied upon the officers of the Gottwald Academy, especially Colonel Blizek, for drawing up unspecified documents and preparing Prchlik's speeches. "The So-Called Memorandum,"p. 10. It is likely that one of the speeches Colonel Matous had in mind was Lieutenant General Prchlik's press conference of July 15; it is also likely that the documents to which Prchlik referred in his press conference were the documents which Colonel Matous accused Colonel Blizek of drafting.

151. "Press Conference of Lt. General Prchlik" in *Winter in Prague,* ed. Remington, p. 217.

152. See the editorial in the July 23 issue of *Krasnaia Zvezda, Winter in Prague,* ed. Remington, pp. 220-23. The Soviet army newspaper waited a full week before publishing a reply to Prchlik. In this reply, *Krasnaia Zvezda* stated: "First General Prchlik assured his audience at the press conference that 'Czechoslovakia supports efforts aimed a further strengthening and improving the Warsaw Pact.' But he immediately followed this with arguments whose meaning belies this."

153. "Press Conference of Lt. General Prchlik," in *Winter in Prague,* ed. Remington, pp. 216-17.

154. Ibid., p. 117.

155. Ibid.

156. See Chapter 1 of this study.

157. Ibid., pp. 218-19.

158. Ibid., pp. 220-23.

159. See RFE, *Situation Report:* Czechoslovakia, 82, (July 26, 1968).

160. RFE, *Situation Report:* Czechoslovakia, 83 (July 30, 1968).

161. Robert Dean, "Political Consolidation of the Czechoslovak Army," Radio Free Europe Research, April 29, 1971, p. 20.

162. Ibid., p. 21.

163. See Chapter 5 of this study for an examination of the changes introduced in the WTO administration after 1969.

164. See the preamble to the 1970 treaty in Ministerstvo innostrannykh del, SSSR, *Sbornik deistvuiushchikh dogovorov* [Ministry of Foreign Affairs, USSR, *Collection of treaties in force*] vol. 27 (Moscow: Mezhdunarodyne otnoshenniia, 1973), p. 42.

165. *Pravda pobezhdaet*, p. 43.

166. XIV S"ezd Kommunisticheskoi partii Chekhoslovakii [*The 14th Congress of the Communist Party of Czechoslovakia*] (Moscow: Politizdat, 1971), p. 260.

167. "Chekhoslovatskaia narodnaia armiia" [The Czechoslovak People's Army] in *Boevoi soiuz*, eds. Efimov et. al., p. 251.

168. Dean, "Political Consolidation," p. 23 citing Col. E.C. Rubasic, "Problems of Party-Political Work in the Czechoslovak People's Army, *Zivot Strany*, Dec. 10, 1969.

169. Ibid., p. 24.

170. "The Lessons of Crisis Development," *Pravda pobezhdaet*, p. 44.

171. Efimov, *Boevoi soiuz*, p. 253.

172. Dean, "Political Consolidation," p. 26.

173. "Interview with Lt. General Vaclav Horachek by Lt. Col. Frantisek Kudrna," *Tribuna*, Nov. 15, 1972, JPRS, *Translations on Eastern Europe: Political, Sociological and Military Affairs; JPRS 58017, January 18, 1973, p. 39.*

174. *Ibid.,* pp. 38-39.

175. Maj. Josef Dobosh (CSPA), "Gotovnost' k podvigu" [Readiness for Victory], *Krasnaia Zvezda,* Oct. 10, 1970, p. 1.

176. Ibid.

177. Jan Khmelik, ed., *Obrana Lidu,* [Journal of Czechoslovak Army] "Predannost' delu sotsializma" [Devotion to the cause of socialism] *Pravda,* October 6, 1973, p. 5. See an account of a joint political exercises between a regiment of the Czechoslovak army and a unit of the Central Force Group in Maj. General M. Loshchits, "Pamiat' serdtsa," [Heart-felt memory] *Krasnaia Zvezda,* October 5, 1974, p. 3.

178. Lt. General Vaclav Horachek, "Plechom k plechu s sovetskim narodom i ero armiei," [Shoulder to shoulder with the Soviet people and its armed forces], *Kommunist vooruzhennykh sil* 9 (May, 1975): 71.

179. P.A. Zhilin and E. Gefurt, eds., *Na vechnye vremena* [For all time] (Moscow: Voenizdat, 1975), p. 307.

180. Ibid.

181. Ibid., p. 305.

182. Ibid., p. 307.

183. S.K. Il'in, *Moralyni faktor v sovremennoi voine* [*The moral-political*

factor in modern war] (Moscow: Politizdat, 1967); Il'in, et. al. eds., *Partiino-politicheskaia rabota v sovetskikh vooruzhennykh sil: uchebnoe posobie* [Party-Political Work in the Soviet Armed Forces: A Textbook] (Moscow: Voenizdat, 1974).

184. See General S. K. Il'in, "B obstanovke druzhby i serdechnosti" [In a situation of friendship and sincerity] *Krasnaia Zvezda*, Dec. 8, 1973.

185. Maj. General S. Il'in, "U chekhoslovatskikh druzei" [With our Czechoslovak friends] *Krasnaia Zvezda,* August 3, 1974, p. 3.

186. Ibid.

187. Ibid.

188. A.A. Epishev, ed., *Partiino-politichesksia rabota v vooruzhennykh silakh SSSR, 1919-1973* [Party-political work in the Armed Forces of the USSR, 1919–1973] (Moscow: Voenizdat, 1974), p. 357.

189. Col. Jan Khmelik, "Voploshchaia idei oktiabria," [Carrying out the ideas of October] *Krasnaia Zvezda,* October 6, 1977, p. 4.

Notes to Chapter 8

1. As the previous chapter on doctrine noted, a series of Soviet academies, particularly the Voroshilov, Frunze, and Lenin academies, maintain regular contacts with East European military academies to coordinate writings on military doctrine. Marshal Iakubovskii's study, *Boevoe sodruzhestvo bratskikh narodov i armii* [The combat confederation of the fraternal people's and armies] (Moscow: Voenizdat, 1975), p. 164, notes that there is a series of bilateral, Soviet-East European exchanges of textbooks, lecturers, and study programs. Occasional biographies of East European officers in the Soviet military press note that award of a degree from a Soviet military academy is often followed by a tour of duty as a faculty member at an East European military academy. See "Ozarennye oktabrem" [Men inspired by October] *Krasnaia Zvezda,* June 9, 1977, and "Tri Kovacha" [Three members of the Kovacs family], *Krasnaia Zvezda,* Feb. 5, 1977. Information, contained in the rest of this chapter indicates that several Soviet academies confer doctoral degrees, as does the General Military Academy of Romania. I have not encountered any discussion of which, if any, East European military academies confer doctoral degrees or train faculty members for lower-ranking military-educational institutions.

2. See *Sovetskaia voennaia entsiklopediia (SVE)* [The Soviet military encyclopedia] Vol. 2, p. 565 for the article on the Main and Central Administrations of the USSR Ministry of Defense.

3. E.E. Mal'stev, ed., *KPSS—Organizator zashchita sotsialisticheskogo otechestva* [The CPSU—organizer of the defense of the socialist fatherland] (Moscow: Voenizdat, 1974), p. 482.

4. Iakubovskii, ed., *Boevoe sodruzhestvo,* p. 164.

5. See previous chapter of this study for a discussion of both of these developments.

6. Iakubovskii, *Boevoe sodruzhestvo,* p. 215. His figure is for officers with either a secondary or higher education—which in effect is really a figure for

officers with secondary education.

7. V. Buravchenko, "Uvernoi postupiiu k slavnym sversheniiam" [Certain entry to the glorious heights] *Kommunist vooruzhennykh sil*, [Communist of the armed forces] 14, (1976): 79.

8. See Iakubovskii, ed., *Boevoe sodruzhestvo* for information on East Germany. See remainder of Chapter 8 for information on other WTO members.

9. In an interview on March 18, 1978, at Boston College, Boston, Mass., General Ilie Ceausescu of Romania stated that Romanian officers ceased studying in Romania in 1960. Soviet discussions of the education of WTO frequently mention that officers from Bulgaria, Hungary, East Germany, Poland, and Czechoslovakia have studied in Soviet military-educational institutions even before the formation of the WTO—see Iakubovskii, ed., *Boevoe sodruzestvo;* P.I. Efimov et. al. eds., *Boevoi soiuz bratskikh armii* [The combat union of the fraternal armed forces] (Moscow: Voenizdat, 1974), and the series of articles on the WTO armed forces in the 1970 issues of *Kommunist voouzhennykh sil. (KVS)* These discussions either omit any reference to officer education in Romania or, as Colonel Diev, "Vooruzhennyi sily sotsialisticheskoi Respubliki Rumanii [The Armed Forces of the Socialist Republic of Romania] *KVS* 16 (1970):73, outline the components of the Romanian higher military education system and use the past tense to state, "Part of the generals and officers of the Romanian military received a higher and secondary military education in the military-educational institutions of the Soviet Union." In its discussion of the officer responsibilities of the Romanian Defense Ministry, in Article 4 of the 1972 Defense Law, the law does not mention Soviet or WTO military-educational institutions, although it does give the Ministry the right to consult with "foreign" institutions. See Decree on the Organization of the Ministry of National Defense from *Buletinul Oficial al Republicii Socialiste Romania*, Nov. 21, 1972, pp. 1048-51 Decree 444 *Translations on East European Political, Sociological and Military Affairs* 1972 in Joint Publications Research Service 57812, Dec. 19, 1972.

10. A.V. Antosiac, *Zarozhdenie narodnikh armii stran-uchasnits varshavskogo dogovora, 1941-49* [The birth of the people's armies of the member states of the Warsaw Pact, 1941-49] (Moscow: Nauka, 1975), p. 229.

11. Mihai Inoan et. al. eds., *Armata Romana in primii ani ai revolutiei si constructiei socialiste* [The Romanian army in the first years after the revolution and socialist development] (Bucharest: Editura Militara, 1975), p. 153.

12. Antosiac, *Zarozhdenie,* p. 230; Inoan, *Armata Romana,* p. 154.

13. Inoan, *Armata Romana,* p. 292.

14. Ibid.

15. Ibid., pp. 292-93.

16. Antosiac, *Zarozhdenie,* p. 229.

17. "Along with the Soviet soldiers a group of officers from the Bulgarian People's Army and of the Romanian People's Army completed the course of study at the Zhukovskii Military-Air Engineering Academy" (*Krasnaia Zvezda,* July 4, 1965 "Vse sily i znanie" [All forces and knowledge] p. 1.

18. See V.G. Kukilov, *Akademiia generalnogo shtaba. . . Voroshilova* [The Voroshilov General Staff Academy] (Moscow: Voenizdat, 1976), pp. 205-7.

19. The Romanian English-language text on military doctrine, Col. Iulian

Cernat, et. al. eds., *National Defense: The Romanian View* (Bucharest: Military Publishing House, 1976), p. 173, notes that troops must be "systematically train-ed to fight in situations where their actions assume a marked independent character, relying solely on their own equipment and relatively few means of rein-forcement."

20. Constantin Antoniu, et. al. eds., *Armata Republicii Socialiste Romania* [The Armed Forces of the Socialist Republic of Romania] (Bucharest: Editura Militara, 1978), pp. 157, 178-82.

21. Ibid., pp. 184, 187-89.

22. Ibid., p. 190.

23. "Speech Made at the Festive Meeting Held in Bucharest on the Occasion of the Graduation of the 1968 Batch from the General Military Academy" in Nicolae Ceausescu, *Romania on the Way of Completing Socialist Construction,* Vol. 3 (Bucharest: Meridiane Publishing House, 1969), pp. 335-36. In the citation above, slight changes have been made in the Romanian English-language version to minimize awkward phrasing.

24. Efimov et. al. eds., *Boevoi soiuz,* for Hungary, p. 74; for the GDR, p. 109; for Poland, p. 146; for Czechoslovakia, pp. 253-54. For identification of the Bulgarian military colleges, see Iakubovskii, *Boevoe sodruzhestvo,* pp. 175-76.

25. Scotts' information in Lt. Col. Richard G. Head, "Soviet Military Education," *Air University Review* 30 (Nov.-Dec. 1978): 47.

26. The quotations in the following section suggest East European atten-dance at Soviet higher military schools; the material in Antosiac, *Zarozhdenie,* in-dicates that East European officers regularly attended Soviet higher military schools before the formation of the WTO.

27. Lieutenant Colonel of the Hungarian army, I. Bertalan, "Tri Kovacha" [Three Kovacs] *Krasnaia Zvezda,* Feb. 5, 1977, p. 3.

28. For Bulgaria, see Iakubovskii, *Boevoe sodruzhestvo,* p. 176; for Hungary and the GDR see Efimov, *Boevoi soiuz,* p. 74 and p. 109.

29. Based on one conversation with a well-informed Polish reserve officer and several conversations with Polish emigres and material below on the Voroshilov Academy.

30. Efimov, *Boevoi soiuz,* p. 140.

31. Ibid., pp. 253-54.

32. SVE, Vol. 2, pp. 172-267.

33. Efimov, *Boevoe soiuz,* pp. 48, 76, 109, 146, 254. See also the *SVE* Vol. 2 article on "Military-Educational Institutions," which says, "In a series of socialist countries (Bulgaria, Hungary, the German Democratic Republic, Poland, Romania, and Czechoslovakia) the training of command, political and engineering cadres is carried out in military academies and military schools. The education of the officer cadre of the armed forces of the socialist countries and of developing countries also takes place in the military-educational institutions of the Soviet Armed Forces." This statement avoids the question of whether Romania joins Bulgaria, Hungary, East Germany, Poland and Czechoslovakia in sending its officers to the USSR for study.

34. "The Council of Ministers of the German Democratic Republic has presented 15 Soviet military-educational institutions with state awards in recognition of their high-quality training of officers" (Efimov, *Boevoi soiuz,* p. 109).

35. *SVE,* Vol. 1 on *Boevoe sodruzhestvo,* p. 527.

36. Kulikov, ed., *Akademiia . . . voroshilova,* p. 228.

37. A.A. Epishev and Velko Palin, eds., *Naveki vmeste* [Forever together] (Moscow: Voenizdat, 1969), p. 297.

38. Ibid.

39. P.A. Zhilin and E. Jadziac, eds., *Bratstvo po oruzhiiu* [Brotherhood in arms] (Moscow: Voenizdat, 1975), p. 358.

40. Professor Colonel K. Schutsle, "Stanovlenie i razvitie Natsional'noi armii GDR" [The establishment and development of the National People's Army of the GDR] *Voenno-istoricheskii zhurnal* [*Military-Historical Journal*] 10 (1974): 116.

41. Mal'tsev, ed., *KPSS,* p. 482.

42. Iakubovskii, *Boevoe sodruzhestvo,* p. 163.

43. V. Semin, "Natsional'naia narodnaia armiia GDR" (The National People's Army of the GDR), *Kommunist vooruzhennykh sil* [*Communist of the Armed Forces*] 13 (1970): p. 76.

44. "In the Academy study generals, admirals and senior officers of all branches of the [Soviet] Armed Forces who have completed military academies and are destined for work in command, political and staff responsibilities at the operational-strategic level and also generals and senior officers of the armed forces of the socialist countries who have completed a higher military education." (*SVE,* Vol. 2, p. 172).

45. "The [Frunze] Academy . . . gives aid in the education and training of command cadres for the armies of the socialist countries." (Ibid., p. 175).

46. Mal'tsev, *KPSS,* p. 482: "The Communist and Workers' Parties and the governments of the fraternal countries highly value the generous aid of the Soviet people and its army in the training of officer cadres with an all-round education. A recognition of these services of the military-educational institutions of the Soviet army is the presentation of medals by a series of socialist countries to the Voroshilov General Staff Academy, the Frunze Military Academy, the Lenin Military-Political Academy and several others." See also *SVE,* Vol. 2, p. 248 to the effect that the Lenin Academy has been decorated for unspecified reasons by "a series of socialist countries."

47. "Along with the officers of the Soviet army personnel of the armies of the socialist countries study in the [Malinovskii] Academy." (*SVE,* Vol. 2, p. 172).

48. "The [Budennyi] Academy gives aid in the training of officer cadres for the armies of the socialist countries," (Ibid., p. 178).

49. "For services in the training of military engineers and for carrying out scientific research the [Kuibishev] Academy has been decorated with the order of the Red Banner (1944), the Order of Lenin (1968) and also with the orders of a series of socialist countries" (Ibid., p. 220).

50. "The services of the [Grechko] Academy in the training of officer cadres

for the Soviet navy and for the navies of the socialist countries have been recognized by the Order of Lenin (1944), by the Order of Ushkov First Degree (1968) and also by the orders of a series of socialist countries" (Ibid., p. 231).

51. *SVE*, vol. 2, see preceding footnote for page numbers.

52. *SVE*, vol. 2, notes that all of the first three listed academies have received decorations from "a series of socialist countries," on pp. 179, 199 and 201 respectively. For the Timoshenko and Kalinin academies, *SVE*, vol. 2, mentions a decoration from the GDR only, pp. 179 and 180 respectively.

53. Epishev and Palin, eds., *Naveki vmeste,* pp. 299-300.

54. Ibid., pp. 297-98.

55. Ibid., pp. 297-301.

56. "Once an officer has successfully completed work at an academy, he is assigned under a special *nomenklatura* or list of positions that can be filled only by officers who are graduates of military or naval academies or their equivalents" Harriet F. Scott, William F. Scott, *The Armed Forces of the USSR* (Boulder, Colorado: Westview Press, 1979) p. 352.

57. "Otkrytoe pis'mo piatomy s"ezdu Kommunisticheskoi partii Iugoslavii" [Open letter to the Fifth Congress of the Yugoslav Communist party], *Pravda,* July 23, 1948, p. 4.

58. Bela Kiraly, "Hungary's Army: Its Part in the Revolt," *East Europe* 7 June 1958, Vol. 7, No. 6, p. 9.

59. A.I. Radzievskii, et. al. ed., *Akademiia imeni M.V. Frunze* [The Frunze Military Academy] (Moscow: Voenizdat, 1973), pp. 222-26.

60. Ibid., p. 240.

61. Ibid., p. 254.

62. This information comes from either or both of the following two sources: Borys Lewytskyi and Juliuz Stroynowski, *Who's Who in the Socialist Countries* (New York: K.G. Saur Publishing Co., 1978) and the *Soviet Military Encyclopedia* (*SVE*), whose first seven volumes contain entries only for the defense ministers of Bulgaria, East Germany, Czechoslovakia, and Romania. The Czechoslovak defense minister, Martin Dzur, is a graduate of the Academy of Rear Services and Transport in Leningrad. The Romanian Defense Minister is a graduate of the General Military Academy in Buchrest. Volume 8 should contain information on the defense ministers of Hungary and Poland. The *Encyclopedia* does not have entries for WTO officers other than defense ministers. The *Who's Who* entries on military officers often lack information on educational background.

63. Lt. Col. Eng. E. Bogdanov and Lt. Col. (Czechoslovakia) J. Pikouz, "Vernost' traditisiiam" [True to traditions], *Krasnaia Zvezda,* October 5, 1975, p. 2.

64. See footnote no. 46.

65. Epishev and Palin, eds., *Naveki vemste,* p. 298; P.A. Zhilin and E. Gefurt, eds., *Na vechnye vremena* [For All Time] (Moscow: Voenzidat, 1975), p. 305: "In 1971 President Ludvik Svoboda decorated that Lenin Academy for "aid in the establishment and training of the party-political apparatus of the Czechoslovak People's Army."

66. See *Krasnaia Zvezda* issues of June 30, 1977, p. 3; July 1, 1976, p. 1; June 29, 1960, p. 1; and July 4, 1965, p. 1.

67. *SVE,* Vol. 2, p. 247.

68. *Krasnaia Zvezda,* July 5, 1970, p. 1.

69. Mal'tsev, in *SVE,* Vol. 2, pp. 247-48.

70. Ibid.

71. *SVE,* Vol. 2, pp. 172-73.

72. See Kulikov, et. al. ed., *Akademiia . . . Voroshilova,* pp. 203-11.

73. Ibid., p. 228. See also the volume's discussion of the curriculum of foreign students on p. 231: "The naming of the General Staff Academy as the highest military-educational institution of the operational-strategic profile defines the course of study and training of the generals and officers of the friendly socialist countries."

74. Ibid., p. 242.

75. Biographical information from Lewytskyj and Stroynowski, *Who's Who.*

76. *SVE,* Vol. 4, p. 252 and entry on Ion Gheorghe in *Who's Who.*

77. Kulikov, ed., *Akademiia . . . Voroshilova,* p. 242.

78. Ibid., p. 243-44.

79. Ibid., p. 244.

80. See the appropriate issues of *Krasnaia Zvezda* in the later June or early July issues of the appropriate years.

81. Col. Gen. A. Radzievskii, "Thirty Years of the Academy of the General Staff," *Voennaia Mysl'* 10, 1966 in CIA FBIS FPD 0504/67, May 20, 1967, *"Selected Translations from Voennaia Mysl':* 9.

82. Kulikov, ed., *Akademiia . . . Voroshilova,* p. 232.

83. Ibid., p. 242.

84. Ibid., p. 243.

85. Ibid., p. 229.

86. Ibid.

87. Ibid.

88. Ibid., pp. 233-34.

89. Ibid., pp. 239-41.

90. Ibid., p. 234.

91. Ibid., p. 230.

92. Ibid., p. 233.

93. Ibid., p. 237.

94. Ibid., p. 238.

95. Ibid., p. 240.

96. Ibid.

97. Ibid., pp. 230-33.

98. "The generals and officers of the armed forces of the socialist countries, just like the students of the Soviet Armed Forces, by studying in the Academy of the General Staff, successfully master a Marxist-Leninist methodological approach to the study of the many-sided manifestations of military affairs and acquire a deep all-round knowledge of the most important questions of the preparation and conduct of modern operations and of the use in them of all types of armed forces and types of troops. They also improve their practical skills in the administration of troops. As a result of their creative mastery of the studied materials and of the exchange of experience in the course of joint study, there is achieved a unity of views of the leading staff of the United Armed Forces on all questions of the theory and practice of the organization and development of national defense systems and on the combat and operational training of troops and staffs" (Ibid., p. 230).

99. Ibid., pp. 229-30.

100. *Krasnaia Zvezda,* June 30, 1979, p. 3.

101. See Kulikov, ed., *Akademiia ... Voroshilova,* pp. 264, 270, 266, 264 and 270 for listing of the award of gold medals to D.M. Dzhurov, A.G. Semerdzhiev, K.D. Kosev, M. Dzur, and V. Savchuk.

102. *Krasnaia Zvezda,* June 30, 1977, p.1.

103. Kulikov, ed., *Akademiia ... Voroshilova,* p. 243.

Notes to Chapter 9

1. A.A. Grechko, "Patrioticheskii i internatsional'nyi dolg Vooruzhennykh sil SSSR" [The patriotic and internationalist duty of the Soviet Armed Forces] *Krasnaia Zvezda,* October 6, 1961, p. 2.

2. Ibid.

3. *Sovetskaia voennaia entsiklopediia, (SVE)* [*Soviet Military Encyclopedia*] Vol. 1, (Moscow: Voenizdat, 1976) p. 525.

4. *SVE,* vol. 4, p. 518.

5. A.A. Epishev, *Ideologicheskaia bor'ba po voennym voprosam* [Ideological struggle in military questions] (Moscow: Voenizdat, 1974), pp. 71-72. The reference to "peaceful counterrevolution" is a reference to the Czechoslovak events of 1968. Soviet journalists occasionally used this term in 1968 to describe the events in that country. For example, S. Kovalev declared, "...a revolution has the objective of scrapping the socialist state apparatus and replacing it by its own. At first, however, they try to do so through peaceful means, through replacing cadres loyal to socialism by adherents of so-called liberalization," (S. Kovalev, "On 'Peaceful' and Nonpeaceful Counterrevolution," *Pravda,* p. 4). A *Pravda* editorial nine days later complained of "creeping counterrevolution."

Table 1 — Warsaw Pact Exercises, 1961–79

Name/Date	Location	Participants	Commander	Forces	Sources
1961: Oct.–Nov. **Buria**	GDR, P, CS, w. USSR	GDR, P, CS, USSR	Grecho (USSR)	Staffs, troops, GF, AF, Nav., Airborne	KZ: 10/6/61 Iak.: p. 282, 151
1962: Spring	H	H, R, USSR		Staffs, troops	VM (CIA): p. 64
Sept.	CS	CS, P, USSR			Turbiville
Oct. 1–9	P, n. GDR	GDR, P, USSR	Spychalski (P)	AF, GF, Nav.	VM (CIA): p. 6 KZ: Oct. 10, 11, 1962 Iak.: p. 282
Oct. 19	R	R, B, USSR	Salajin (R)		KZ: Oct. 19–21
1963: Sept. 9–14 **Quartet**	s. GDR	GDR, CS, P,	Hoffmann (GDR)	40,000 troops 700 tanks 8,300 arm. veh. 500 artillery 300 aircraft Sim. nuclear devices Airborne troops	Iak: p. 152, 282 KZ: passim
Fall	R	R, B, USSR	Salajin (R)		VM (CIA): p. 6
1964: June	CS	CS, GDR, USSR			Turbiville
July 7–15	CS	CS, USSR	Lomsky (CS)	Command staff	KZ: 7/17/64
Sept. 15–20	B	B, R, USSR	Dzhurov (B)	Nav. Airborne GF:?	KZ: 9/22/64 Iak.: p. 283

Table 1 — Warsaw Pact Exercises, 1961–79 (continued)

Name/Date	Location	Participants	Commander	Forces	Sources
1965: April 5–11	GDR	GDR, USSR		GF, AF, Airborne	KZ: April 9, 11, 1965
Oct. 16–22 **October Storm**	GDR	GDR, CS, P, USSR	Koshevoi (USSR)	50,000 troops 800 tanks 1,000 armored veh. 5,000 motorized veh. 400 aircraft	Iak.: p. 284, 152–53 KZ: 10/24/65 : passim
1966: July 20–27	Baltic Sea	GDR, P, USSR		Nav., AF	Iak: p. 284
Sept. 20–25 **Vltava**	CS	CS, H, GDR, USSR	Lomsky (CS)	Staff, troops 20 adm. organs	KZ: Sept. 21, 22, 25, 1966 Iak.: p. 153, 285
1967: May 27– June 5	P, n. GDR	GDR, P, USSR	Spychalski (P)	Multi-stage command-staff exercises	Iak.: p. 285 KZ: 6/7/67
June 14–19 **Maneuver**	H, CS	H, CS, USSR	Iakubovskii (USSR)	Operational staffs, all types of forces	Iak.: p. 285 KZ: 6/21/67
Summer	P	P, USSR		Irkutsk-Pinsk Div. (Belorus. Milit. Dist.) Polish soldiers	KBMD: p. 501
Aug. 20–27 **Rodopy**	B, Black Sea	B, USSR (R?)	Dzhurov (B)	GF, AF, Nav. Airborne	NV: p. 289–91 Iak.: p. 153, 285
August **Florett**	GDR	GDR, USSR			Turbiville
October **Oder**	P	P, GDR, USSR			Turbiville

Table 1 — Warsaw Pact Exercises, 1961–79 (continued)

Name/Date	Location	Participants	Commander	Forces	Sources
1968					
May 30	CS	USSR	(probably USSR)	GF, Airborne	*Le Monde:* 5/31/68
June 20–30 **Shumava**	CS, P, GDR, USSR	H, CS, GDR, P, USSR	Iakubovskii (USSR)	Operational tactical staffs, Communications, Logistics, Others, 30 adm. organs	Iak.: p. 154
July 5–19 **Sever**	No. Atlantic Norwegian Sea Barents Sea Baltic Sea	GDR, P, USSR	Gorshkov (USSR)	Command-staff, Nav. amphibious	Iak.: p. 154, 286 Turbiville
July–August **Sky Shield**	WTO states	WTO states		Anti-air	Turbiville
July 24–Aug. 9 **Neman**	USSR, P, GDR	USSR, P, GDR	Mariakhin (USSR)	Rear services	KZ: July 24, 26, 31 Aug. 9–10
Aug. 11–20	w. Ukraine, P, GDR	USSR, P, GDR	Shtemenko (USSR)	Operation staffs, Communications troops, GF	Iak.: p. 286 KZ: 8/20/68
Aug. 17–20	H	H, USSR		Communications	Turbiville AP #58, p. 14
Aug. 20–21	CS	B, H, GDR, P, USSR	Pavlovskii (USSR)	Invasion force: GF, AF, Airborne	AP #58, p. 14

Table 1 — Warsaw Pact Exercises, 1961–79 (continued)

Name/Date	Location	Participants	Commander	Forces	Sources
1969: March 1–7	GDR	GDR, USSR	Iakubovskii (USSR)	Iak.: p. 286	KZ: 3/29/69, passim
March 25–April 1	B	B, USSR R (?)	Iakubovskii (USSR)	Operational staffs, GF, Nav.; Anti-air	NOV: p. 293 / Iak.: p. 287
March 30–April 4 **Spring 69**	P, GDR, CS	P, GDR, CS, USSR	Chocha (P)	Staffs, GF, Communications	Iak.: p. 287 / KZ: 4/6/69
April 4–16 **Zenit**	P, H, CS, w. USSR	P, H, CS, USSR	Batitskii (USSR)	Anti-air, AF	Iak.: p. 158, 287
May 14–19	USSR	USSR, B, H R (?)	(probably Soviet)	GF	Iak.: p. 287 / KZ: 5/20/69 / Sov. Moldavia: 5/20/69
June 2–7	H	H, USSR			KZ: 6/8/69 / Iak.: p. 287
July 4–11	P	P, GDR, USSR	Shtemenko (USSR)	Staffs, rear services	KZ: 7/12/69 / Iak.: p. 287
July 23–Aug. 2	GDR, P, CS, USSR	P, CS, USSR	Kutakov (USSR)	AF	Iak.: p. 287 / KZ: 8/3/69
Aug. 10–15	w. CS	CS, USSR	Maiorov (USSR)	Command-staff	Iak.: p. 287 / KZ: 8/16/69

Table 1 — Warsaw Pact Exercises, 1961–79 (continued)

Name/Date	Location	Participants	Commander	Forces	Sources
1969: Sept. 21–28 **Oder-Neisse**	P, Baltic Sea	P, GDR, CS, USSR	Jaruzelski (P)	GF, AF, Anti-air, Nav., Sim. nuclear weapons	KZ: passim, Sept. 27, 28, 1969 Iak.: p. 155— Largest WTO exercise to date
Oct. 10–16	GDR, P, CS, w. USSR	GDR, P, CS, USSR		Staffs of GF of GDR, P, CS: Staff of AF of USSR	Iak.: p. 288 KZ: 10/17/69
1970: July 1–9	H	H, USSR	Iakubovski (USSR)	Operational staffs of: GF, Anti-air, AF, Nav. (?!?)	KZ: 7/10/70
July 13–17 **Zenit**	WTO states	WTO states	Batitskii (USSR)	Anti-air.	Iak.: p. 158, 289
Aug. 17–19	CS	CS, USSR	Valo (CS)	GF	KZ: 8/19/70 AGSh.: p. 243
Oct. 12–18 **Brotherhood in Arms**	GDR	B, H. GDR, P, CS, USSR, R(?)	Hoffmann (GDR)	GF, AF, Nav. of GDR, P, USSR; GDR local def. units; GDR workers militia (KZ: 10/8/70—Largest WTO exercise to date)	KZ: passim Iak.: p 155, 259

Table 1 — Warsaw Pact Exercises, 1961–79 (continued)

Name/Date	Location	Participants	Commander	Forces	Sources
1971: June 24–July 2	GDR, CS	Staff of WTO; GDR, CS, USSR	Iakubovskii (USSR)	Staff of WTO; Operational staffs of: GF, AF, Anti-air	KZ: 7/3/71 Iak.: p. 290
July 5–12	CS, P	CS, P, USSR	Dzur (CS)	AF, Anti-air, GF (?)	KZ: 7/14/7 Iak.: p. 290
July 12–21 **Visla-Elbe 71**	GDR, P	Staff of WTO; GDR, P, USSR	Shtemenko (USSR)	Staff of WTO; Staffs, Rear orgs. of GDR, P, USSR	Iak.: p. 290 KZ: 7/22/71
Aug. 2–5 **Opal-71**	H, CS	H, CS, USSR	Czinege (H)	GF	Iak.: p. 290 KZ: 8/7/71
Sept. 14–19	GDR	DGR, P, USSR	Hoffmann (GDR)	Staffs, formations	Iak.: p. 290 KZ: 9/21/71
Oct.	CS	CS, USSR			Turbiville
1972: Feb.	R	R, B, USSR			Turbiville
Feb. 28–March 4	P	Staff of WTO; P, GDR, USSR	Iakubovskii (USSR)	Staff of TWO; Staffs of GF, AF, Nav., Anti-air	Iak.: p. 291 KZ: 3/5/72
March 21–28	B	B, USSR, R(?)	Dzhurov (B)	Command staffs	Iak.: p. 291 KZ: 3/29/72
April 18–23	Black Sea	Staff of WTO; B, USSR, R(?)	Iakubovskii (USSR)	Staff of WTO; Nav. staffs, fleets	Iak.: p. 291 BKPNA: p. 363

Table 1 — Warsaw Pact Exercises, 1961–79 (continued)

Name/Date	Location	Participants	Commander	Forces	Sources
1972: Sept. 4–16 **Shield 72**	CS	Staff of WTO; CS, H, GDR, P, USSR	Dzur (CS)	GF, AF, Anti-air, Staff of WTO (Iak.: p. 156 approx. same size as **Oder-Neisse, Brotherhood in Arms**)	KZ: passim Iak.: p. 156, 291
1973: Sometime	CS, H	CS, H, USSR		Operational staff	Iak.: P. 158
Sometime	WTO states	WTO states	Batitiskii (USSR)	Anti-air	Iak.: p. 158
Feb. 12–21	R	Staff of WTO; R, B, USSR	Iakubovskii (USSR)	Map exercises: Staff of WTO; Operational staffs of: GF, AF, Nav., Anti-Air	Iak.: p. 292 KZ: 2/22/73
June 26–July 5	GDR, P	GDR, P, USSR	Iakubovskii (USSR)	Operational staffs of rear services	Iak.: p. 158, 292
Summer	Carpathian Military Dist. USSR	USSR, B, H	Abashin (USSR)	Sov.-Bulgarian Friendship Mech. Inf. Regt. (Lt. Col. L.E. Generalov) Hungarian Regiment (Col. Mikhai Gerov) Bulgarian Regiment (Col. Delcho Delchev)	KPVO: p. 188
Sept. 19–24 **Vertes**	H	H, USSR		"Units" (?)	Iak.: p. 292 KZ: 9/25/73 Turbiville

Table 1 — Warsaw Pact Exercises, 1961–79 Continued

Name/Date	Location	Participants	Commander	Forces	Sources
1974: Sometime	WTO states	WTO states	Batitskii (USSR)	Anti-air	Iak.: p. 158
Feb. 17–22	R	R, USSR		Map exercises: Operational staffs of R, USSR	Iak.: p. 293 KZ: 2/23/74
May 14–24	H, CS	H, CS, USSR		Operational staffs, Troops	Iak.: p. 158, 293 KZ: 5/24/74
June 4–14	B, R(?)	B, USSR, R(?)	Iakubovskii (USSR)	Staff exercises, Rear services	Iak.: p. 158, 293
June 17–24 **Summer 74**	w. P	P, USSR	Jaruzelski (P)	Staffs, troops	Iak.: p. 293 *Trybuna Luda:* 6/25/74
Sept. 4–13	Baltic Sea	GDR, P, USSR	Iakubovskii (USSR)	Staffs, fleets	Iak.: p. 293 KZ: 9/14/74
1976: Sept. 9–15 **Shield 76**	P	P, GDR, CS, USSR	Jaruzelski (P)	35,000 troops	U.S. State Dept. Report KZ: 9/16/76, passim
Oct. 18	H	H, USSR		18,000 troops	U.S. State Dept. Report
1977: July ?	S. Baltic Sea	GDR, P, USSR	Kulikov (USSR)	Staffs, fleets	KZ: 7/8/77
1979: Feb. 2–7 **Friendship 79**	CS	CS, USSR		26,000 troops	U.S. State Dept. Report KZ: 2/8/79
May 12–19 **Shield 79**	H	H, B, CS, USSR	Czinege (H)	Less than 25,000 troops	U.S. State Dept. Report KZ: 5/20/79

Table 1 — Warsaw Pact Exercises, 1961–79 (continued)

CODE:

B = Bulgaria
GDR = German Democratic Republic
H = Hungary
P = Poland
CS = Czechoslovakia
R = Romania

GF = Ground Forces
AF = Air Forces
Nav. = Navies
Anti-air = Anti-aircraft troops
Airborne = Airborne troops

Iak. = Iakubovskii, *Boevoe sodruzhestvo*
KZ = *Krasnaia Zvezda*
VM (CIA) = CIA FBIS FPD 0049/69 "Selected Translations from *Voennaia Mysl*' April 25, 1969
Turbiville = Graham H. Turbiville, Jr., "Soviet Bloc Maneuvers," *Military Review*, August, 1978
KBMD = *Krasnoznamennyi Belorusskii voennyi okrug* (Minsk: Belarus, 1973)
NV = *Naveki vmeste* (Moscow: Voenizdat, 1969)
AP #58 = *Adelphi Paper #58*.
AGSh = *Akademiia generalnogo shtaba* (Moscow: Voenizdat, 1976)
BKPNA = *B"lgarskata kommunisticheska partiia i narodnata armiia* (Sofia: Voennoizdatelstvo, 1976)
KPVO = *Krasnoznamennyi pricarpatskii* (L'vov: Kameniar, 1976)
U.S. State Dept. Report = U.S. State Department, *Implementation of the Helsinki Accord* (Semi-annual reports beginning December, 1976)

NOTE: If more than one source is listed, this means that each source listed must be consulted to obtain the information listed for that exercise.

NAME INDEX

Alexiev, Alex, 89, 171
Antonov, A.I., 141
Apro, Antol, 73
Arsintescu, Colonel, 89, 92
Artem'ev, A.P., 107, 108

Balakirev, Major General, 180
Ballaku, Bequir, 93
Barbirek, Frantisek, 46, 48, 53, 56
Batitskii, Marshal P.F., 139, 140
Bator, Sukhe, 176
Batov, P.I., 114, 141
Belishova, Liri, 34, 35
Berman, Jacob, 27
Bezushko, P.P., 33
Bierut, Boleslaw, 27, 71
Bilak, Vasil, 44–46, 48–49, 53, 56
Bragin, Colonel, 143
Brezhnev, Leonid, 10, 11, 12, 19, 20,
   202; and Czechoslovak crisis, 44–45,
   100, 103, 115
Bromke, Adam, 26, 70
Broz, Josip (*see* Tito, Marshal)
Brezezinski, Zbigniew, 71, 77
Bulganin, Nikolai, 28, 67

Ceausescu, Nicolae, 55–56, 83; and
   Romanian autonomy, 20, 62, 63,
   209; and Romanian defense doctrine,
   83, 90, 157, 187, 189
Cernat, Colonel, 86–87, 88, 89
Cernik, Oldrich, 43–49, 51, 56, 101–
   102, 193
Chaplevskii, General, 217
Chernig, Lt. Colonel Wolfgang, 126
Chervonenko, Stepan, 102, 103
Colton, Timothy, 171
Coman, Ion, 219
Csinege, Laoish, 219
Cyrankiewicz, Josef, 27, 28

Dean, Robert, 198, 200
Dedijer, Vladimir, 65, 66, 67, 99

Dej, Gheorghe Gheorghiu- (*see* Gheor-
   ghiu-Dej, Gheorghe
Diev, Colonel D.V., 186
Dimitrov, Georgii, 156
Dinca, Lt. General, 90
Djilas, Milovan, 6, 25
Drljevic, Col. General Savo, 66, 80
Dozet, Maj. General Dusan, 80, 81
Dubcek, Alexander, 11, 43–59, 98–104,
   115–116, 191, 193
Dudas, Josef, 33
Dusynski, General Zygmunt, 94, 157
Dzhurov, Dobri, 217, 219
Dzur, Martin, 49, 115, 155, 193, 219

Efimov, Col. General P.I., 167, 183;
   and WTO study, 179, 180, 182, 199,
   200, 212, 213
Epishev, General A.A., 148, 166, 170,
   175, 177, 178; and *Ideological Struggle,* 159–161, 173, 233–234; as Soviet
   delegate, 183, 185, 186, 190, 194, 202

Fisher-Galati, Stephen, 38, 39, 84
Floyd, David, 38

Galati, Stephen Fisher- (*see* Fisher-
   Galati, Stephen)
Gabelic, Colonel, 81, 82, 83
Gega, Liri, 34
Gero, Erno, 31–33, 72
Gheorghe, Col. General Ion, 90
Gheorghiu-Dej, Gheorghe, 15–16, 36–
   39, 62, 63, 84
Gierek, Edward, 27, 28
Golikov, General F.I., 170
Gomoiu, Maj. General Gheorghe, 185
Gomulka, Wladyslaw: and Polish auto-
   nomy, 6, 7, 17, 62, 63; and Soviet-
   Czechoslovak crisis, 99–100; and
   Soviet-Polish crisis, 20, 26–29, 60,
   68–72, 100

SUBJECT INDEX

Academy of National Economy, 13
Academy of Social Sciences, 13
"Action Program," 46–48, 95, 191
Afghanistan, 12, 173
Agencies, TWO (*see* WTO agencies)
Albania, 1, 2; autonomy, 14, 15–16, 21, 42, 227–228; C.P. of, 5, 21, 23, 37, 42, 93, 227; and Italian occupation, 15, 34, 64, 83, 92, 227–28; military doctrine of, 1, 64, 82–83, 92–94, 106, 227–228; and Soviet crisis, 23, 34–36, 58, 64, 92–94, 227–228
Albanian Party of Labor (APL), 34
Albanian People's Republic
  (*see* Albania)
All-World Congress of Supporters of Peace, 65
Angola, 12, 143
Anti-Communist movements, 1, 8, 14, 30
April Plenum, 46–48
Armenia, 107, 174
Austrian State Treaty (1955), 84, 227
Autonomy, 42; in Albania, Romania, and Yugoslavia, 1, 2, 14, 62; and nationalism, 9–11, 61–62; and "New Course," 8–9; pursuit of, 14–22
Azerbaidjan, 107, 174

Balkans, 85
Baltic Sea, 172
Bandung Conference, 30
Belorussia, 108, 148, 149, 173
Belvedere Palace, 69
Black Sea, 86, 91, 117, 172, 178
Bohemia, 41, 42, 49, 99, 115
Bolshevik revolution, 4, 173–174, 232
Borba, 25
Bratislava Declaration, 53–55, 56, 57
Brotherhood in Arms exercises, 123, 126, 128, 129, 221
Bucharest Defense Council, 90
Bucharest People's Council, 90

Budennyi Military Communications Academy in Leningrad, 212, 215
Bulgaria, 5; C.P. of, 5, 11; and national defense, 156, 228; and Soviet ties, 117–179 (*see also* Bulgaria and WTO)
Bulgaria and WTO, 1, 12, 118; joint exercises, 114, 116, 117, 118; officer education, 204–205, 213–214, 218; MPA, 117–179
Bulgarian People's Army, 178
"Buria" exercise, 110, 111

Carpathian Military District, 148
Catholic Church, 27
Central Committee for Czech Lands, 48
Central Committee of the Slovak Party, 48
Central Force Group, 119–121, 128, 132, 145, 198, 201
Central Intelligence Agency (CIA), 139 141,166,220
Charles University, 98
China (*see* People's Republic of China)
CIA, 139, 141, 166, 220
Cierna, 55, 116
Civil War of 1918–1921, 4, 173–174, 232
Combat confederation: as concept of WTO, 159, 213, 231–234
Combat Confederation of the Fraternal Peoples and Armies (Iakubovskii), 232; on joint exercises, 110, 121–125, 127, 140; on military doctrine, 154, 160–162; on officer education, 205 214; on staff and agencies, 138–141, 142, 152, 166
Cominform, 24, 25, 26, 37, 64–65
Comintern, 4, 36–37, 170
Committee of Defense Ministers (*see* Council of Defense Ministers)
Communist Information Bureau (*see* Cominform)

ABOUT THE AUTHOR

Christopher Jones currently holds a Ford Foundation Fellowship in International Security/Arms Control and Soviet/East European Area Studies. From 1978-80 he wrote a study of Soviet-East European military-political relations for the National Council for Soviet and East European Research. During 1977 he held a fellowship from the Joint Committee on Soviet Studies of the American Council of Learned Societies.

From 1975 to 1977 he was an assistant professor of political science at Marquette University, Milwaukee, Wisconsin. He took a leave of absence in 1977 to go to Boston, where he began work on this study and where his wife, Helena, entered Tufts University Medical School, from which she graduated in 1981. He has published articles in *Armed Forces and Society, Arms Control Today, Orbis, Soviet Armed Forces Review Annual, Survey,* and *World Politics*. Several of his articles have been republished in edited collections.

Mr. Jones holds an A.B. degree from Princeton Unversity and an M.A. and a Ph.D. from Harvard University.